SPEAKING WELL

McGRAW-HILL SERIES IN SPEECH

John J. O'Neill
Consulting Editor in Speech Pathology

SPEAKING WELL

THIRD EDITION

LOREN REID
UNIVERSITY OF MISSOURI, COLUMBIA

McGraw-Hill Book Company

New York   St. Louis   San Francisco
Auckland   Bogotá   Düsseldorf
Johannesburg   London   Madrid
Mexico   Montreal   New Delhi
Panama   Paris   São Paulo
Singapore   Sydney   Tokyo   Toronto

SPEAKING WELL

34567890   DODO   78321098

This book was set in Helvetica Light by University Graphics, Inc.
The editors were Donald W. Burden, Ellen B. Fuchs, and James R. Belser;
the designer was Jo Jones;
the production supervisor was Angela Kardovich.
R. R. Donnelley & Sons Company was printer and binder.

Library of Congress Cataloging in Publication Data

Reid, Loren Dudley, date
    Speaking well.

    (McGraw-Hill series in speech)
    Includes index.
    1. Public speaking. I. Title.
PN4121.R429   1977   808.5   76-41335
ISBN 0-07-051783-5

CONTENTS

Suggested Solutions to Assigned Exercises

PREFACE

In the last decade, teachers of speech communication have increasingly moved to an introductory course in which not only speech making but interpersonal communication and group discussion are studied.

We have not relaxed our interest in speaking to an audience; in fact, the growing insistence that communication courses have a vocational as well as a theoretical context has kept speech making strongly in the picture. We do, however, visualize audiences as being modest in size, growing out of business and professional careers—and the community activities—of the young men and women who study with us. The attention to interpersonal communication and small group theory springs not only from our discipline but also from the interest of students and teachers in psychology, social psychology, business management, and anthropology.

In writing *Speaking Well,* third edition, I have attempted to reflect the view that interpersonal communication, group discussion, and speech making do not have separate boundaries, but are interrelated. A notion like *self-disclosure,* an important concept in interpersonal speaking, has implications as well for group process and for speech making. Similarly the concept of *structure,* copiously developed in speech making, can be applied to group discussion and occasionally to interpersonal communication. Opportunities for short informal talks arise in connection with an interpersonal or group discussion assignment as well as with a speech-making assignment. Interesting, controversial issues brought up in group discussion may be developed later through individual speeches. Again, *variety* of assignments and procedures, one of the four qualities of good teaching and learning (see page 321), is no stranger to speech communication teachers. The net impact of this approach should help the student make the great carryover from the classroom to what we call *real life.*

In this third edition I have tried to write a text that students can read and understand on their own. Although most teachers enjoy occasional lecturing, they find that in the introductory course there is never time enough to do all the things they wish. If the textbook is understandable so that it does not have to be clarified or translated during class time, the teacher is free to use the few available discussion periods for presenting other insights or special resources that fit the needs of that particular class.

Examples are used abundantly, drawn from a wide variety of business, professional, and community contexts. I have cited new research studies, expanded the material on communication theory and interpersonal communication, doubled the amount of material on group process, and revised the treatment of nonverbal communication. I have added a chapter on interviewing because of the obvious demands of today's economic situation. I have broadened the chapter on language, which for many teachers has always been a helpful and highly teachable chapter. The chapters on organization again contain sample outlines, both short and long, to help students with their own problems of selection and arrangement. Lists of suggested topics appear at the ends of five different chapters, to help meet the perennial problem of deciding what to talk about. I consider the use of visual aids useful and specific, and have kept that chapter intact.

As chapter arrangement is important in a text, I have consulted with various teachers on this point. The basic difficulty is that all aspects of communication are significant, and although the student needs them all at once, we have to teach them one at a time. The initial section, "Getting Under Way," includes chapters on gaining confidence, adaptation, listening, language and style, and organization. These should help students with initial concerns and, of even greater significance, help them identify strengths. All of these can be applied to whatever assignments the teacher decides to use in interpersonal speaking, group discussion, and speech making. Toward the end of the book are chapters on narrative, expository, and persuasive speaking, the discussion focusing on specific problems of these specific types.

No doubt there is more in the book than any one class will be able to use. I am never able to teach everything, even in my own book. Teachers will use different chapters in different ways. Some teachers may want to use the chapter on interpersonal speaking and interviewing as outside assignments, to be read for the student's own information. Others will want to use classroom exercises supporting one or both, covering a span of several assignments. I use the chapter on gaining confidence either as the basis for a short classroom discussion or simply as a reading assignment. Though research in this area is continuing, I have limited the chapter mainly to practical suggestions. I seldom use the chapter on voice and pronunciation as a basis for a classroom exercise, though not infrequently I refer students with specific problems to sections of it; for example, students may profit from its examples of vocal variety. I use an assignment in group discussion partly as a way of introducing variety into classroom speaking performances, though others may want to use the concepts in these two chapters as the basis of a major unit in the course.

Reading through the book, the student will notice these points of view surfacing from time to time:

Vocational   Speech communication is indispensable to self-fulfillment in any vocation. The opening chapter has a strong vocational slant, with references to business, industry, education, and the community. In later chapters also, allusions to careers are frequent.

Cultural   Defined simply, *culture* is the sum total of all the things we know and do. It represents our habits, our customs, our preferences, and our ways of relating to one another. This text makes reference to many cultures that make up America as we enter our third century. Speech communication is the central, essential part of any culture. Our culture dictates what kind of talk or other behavior is meaningful and what is not.

Pragmatic   This text has strong emphasis upon what is usable here and now. The outlines are a way of showing the student how to organize thinking. The suggested topics are those that students have used in classroom exercises. The examples are nearly always actual, not invented. Many of them illustrate a principle that can be applied to a variety of situations. If they illustrate a novel way of using statistics, or a specific way of using words and phrases, or a combination of logical reasoning and emotional appeal, it is so students will be encouraged to apply this principle to other situations, and to seek out imaginative procedures of their own.

I do not share the point of view that a textbook should be descriptive and not prescriptive. I find myself both describing situations and then offering advice. Prescriptive/descriptive is a shaky dichotomy, anyway. We have been saddled with it long enough. *Prescriptive* is not necessarily bad nor *descriptive* necessarily good. A description can be limiting, and a prescription can offer choices. A broken bone can be described to perfection, but the moment comes when the patient asks, "What is the treatment? Do I lose my leg, or what?" The physician spells out alternatives and makes recommendations, but the patient makes the decision. In some ways the relation of author and reader, or teacher and student, is similar.

The pleasant part of writing a preface is thanking the people who helped. A hundred or so authors, editors, and publishers have generously given permission to cite their researches or quote from their speeches. At numerous state, regional, and national conventions I have heard papers, visited workshops, and participated in corridor shoptalk. Though I have scrupulously footnoted known sources, I have drawn freely from the public domain, and perhaps unknowingly from a domain not quite so public and if I have failed to acknowledge a source at some conspicuous point, I express my regrets in advance.

I do need to mention specifically a number of people. Ellen B. Fuchs, sponsoring editor of McGraw-Hill Book Company, has encouraged me at all points and has made helpful suggestions at various stages of the revision. She enlisted the services of critics, unknown to me, in accord with publishers' practice, who read carefully an early draft of this manuscript, and provided a number of suggestions about sources, organization of chapters, and general tone and scope. When she resigned her position, Don Burden continued as sponsoring editor.

James R. Belser, subject-area supervisor, has worked with the manuscript since it was turned in to the publisher, with the responsibility of reviewing and coordinating both editorial aspects and illustrations. I have profited by his personal interest and his sound advice at many points. I am grateful also for the assistance of Cheryl Mehalik, picture researcher, and Judi Allen and Angela Kardovich, production supervisors. I am enthusiastic about the typographical decisions that were made along the way: the choice of type faces, the generous use of white space, the arrangement of illustrations and other teaching aids. The staff of University Graphics, which took the manuscript at this point and got it ready for the printer, has worked with accuracy and competence, using computer techniques far more sophisticated and versatile than the linecasting-machine operation that I grew up with in a newspaper office.

John A. Kline, communication skills consultant, Academic Instructor and Allied Officer School, Maxwell Air Force Base, gave me the benefit of his teaching and research especially with four chapters.

John Ware of the Rand Corporation and David Potter and Keith R. Sanders of Southern Illinois University helped with the "Doctor Fox" study.

Thomas F. Daly, managing editor of *Vital Speeches of the Day,* gave permission to quote not only a number of excerpts from speeches appearing in that publication but, in one or two instances, complete speeches.

John Jamieson, editor of general publications, the H. W. Wilson Company, gave permission to quote a number of excerpts from *Representative American Speeches,* currently edited by Waldo W. Braden.

I am deeply indebted to the many publishers and scholarly associations that subscribe to a "fair use" policy, permitting authors to use short excerpts without seeking specific authorization. William Work, executive secretary of the Speech Communication Association, sent me a list of seventy journals, including all SCA publications, that have formally adopted this policy. The American Psychological Association and the American Educational Research Association routinely allow citations of 500 words or less.

Distinguished people from various walks of life have taken time from their busy schedules to write short notes indicating the importance of speech communication. Their contributions are acknowledged in the appropriate footnotes. Students and teachers alike will appreciate their comments, written from their varying points of view.

Those mentioned above are in no respect responsible for the faults of this text. An author is not always persuaded by those who read the manuscript and may discover, after the book is in print, that some readers agree with the critics. One characteristic of an introductory text is the tendency to generalize and simplify; this dismays the specialist though it makes life tolerable for the rest of us. Years ago when I was a student in a botany class at Grinnell I remember a professor firmly generalizing that a certain plant characteristic was true of all plants everywhere. Suddenly he paused—the silence gripped everyone's attention—then he continued with memorable patience and forgivable weariness, "Must I always mention the exceptions? There is, in Venezuela, a certain plant that shows this variation. . . ." I have long since forgotten the variation, and the name of the Venezuelan exception, but I recall the moment as if it just happened. I invite readers who note misinterpretations, oversimplifications, or other debatable points to call them to my attention.

Loren Reid

PART ONE

GETTING UNDER WAY

The opening chapter looks first at the increasing importance of communication, reporting recent surveys. Communication theory, basic to all types of communication, is then reviewed. Two chapters follow on interpersonal speaking: the first considers ways in which we perceive ourselves as communicators and in which we perceive others; the second discusses interviewing, a vital necessity in this day of more applicants than jobs. The next chapter discusses the problem of gaining poise and confidence, an area in which notable improvement is almost always made. Chapters on adapting to listeners and on listening are designed to increase your competence in this aspect of the communication transaction. The chapter on language offers specific suggestions showing not only how to be clear but also vivid and colorful.

1 Communicating with Others

The public speaking approach □ Other approaches □
Communication in the schools □ Communication in business and
the professions □ Communication in public life □
Communication in interpersonal situations □ Concluding note
□ Assignments and exercises

The art of speaking goes back more than two thousand years, but changes in teaching methods have altered so drastically during the last decade that you may profit by gaining perspective before beginning your current study. About the turn of the century an assistant professor named James A. Winans was preparing his syllabus for his course in *Extempore Speaking,* which he taught in the Department of English at Cornell University. He proposed to break with the traditional plan of teaching students to speak well: instead of asking them to memorize selections from Patrick Henry, Daniel Webster, and the classical orators, he decided to ask them to prepare original speeches on topics from current issues—to be spoken extempore, not written and memorized.

From that point on there was no turning back. In the next decade speech pulled away from departments of English and began to be taught in separate departments, most of which had "oratory" or "public speaking" in their titles—for example, Northwestern's "School of Oratory and Physical Education" and Wisconsin's "Department of Public Speaking." In a few years these were changed to departments of "Speech," offering only a short list of courses at first, then minors and majors, and eventually graduate programs. Especially after World War II, the field expanded rapidly.

Right now the number of Ph.D.'s in speech exceeds 5,000, and the number of M.A.'s or M.S.'s exceeds 50,000. The number of students enrolled in courses is probably more than 600,000— enough to fill every stadium in the Big Ten. No discipline can report a more rapid growth than has occurred in this field, and in closely-related disciplines such as anthropology, sociology, and psychology.

THE PUBLIC SPEAKING APPROACH   So much for the impressive growth of the field. The public speaking approach that Winans and his successors developed is oriented toward front-of-the-room performance: short talks on topics of the student's own choosing. The talks may be of different types: narrative, expository, persuasive, or others. The class also considers problems of gaining confidence, selecting and organizing ideas, adapting to listeners, and using language effectively. The phrase "thinking on your feet" is often heard, along with "Good speaking is good thinking." Attention is also given to effective use of the voice and body. At times, use is made of assignments in group discussion, in which three or four students—seated in front of the others—present an "inquiry" into a controversial topic, working toward a solution. Students often find that what they learn in class helps with oral reports or written papers in other courses, and with campus or off-campus speaking activities.

The growth of enrollments in this type of course comes partly because students do gain self-assurance, partly because they do become more effective in presenting their ideas, and partly because they do see the vocational usefulness of being able to speak effectively.

OTHER APPROACHES Many teachers employ a multipurpose approach, teaching a combination of interpersonal and small group situations along with speech-making situations. Attention is paid to communication theory to explain what goes on between sender and receiver whether two, or many, people are involved; to explore what goes on between people who are trying to explore an idea or to enhance a personal relationship. Principles of group discussion are discussed, considering not only task- or problem-oriented groups, but also how to make a group more cohesive or supportive. The major activity of the course continues to be speech making, studying the principles mentioned in the preceding section, though members of the class may give fewer speeches than formerly. Although the student gets direct exposure to different kinds of situations, certain basic principles apply to *any* situation: we are responsive to vocal tones and facial expressions whether the group consists of two or twenty or more. We are also steadily involved with problems of organizing, adapting, using language, mobilizing facts and reasons, and reacting to show awareness of needs, sentiments, and feelings.

Other disciplines are also giving attention to problems of communication. Psychology, social psychology, anthropology, psychiatry, and business management are concerned with improving communication, though they are more interested in twos and threes and small groups than in speech making. For example, many books about management contain a chapter on communication theory that could be inserted almost verbatim in a book about speech communication, although as a profession management people seem not properly concerned about speech making, despite the growing number of public appearances by business and professional men and women (see any issue of *Vital Speeches of the Day*). Of course by *speech making* we are thinking primarily of talks given to relatively small audiences—a city council, a board of directors, a business club, a community meeting—and not so much about formal addresses to mass meetings or rallies.

We now look briefly at areas in which nearly everyone is involved and in which communication is vital.

COMMUNICA-TION IN THE SCHOOLS One American in every three is associated with a school, a college, a university, a factory or military school, or other type of organized instruction. More than 2 million students attend community colleges, the fastest growing segment of the educational population. More than 6 million attend other colleges and universities. This total of about 8½ million is one-twenty-fourth of the total population. By contrast Great Britain, a nation with a little less than one-fourth the population of the United States, has a college and university enrollment of approximately 225,000, or 1 in 250, contrasted with our 1 in 30.

Only an affluent society could afford the cost of higher education for so many of its young people. All of us are the beneficiaries of countless hours of public discussion, starting even before the founding of the Republic, that led to the decision that higher education should be made available to large numbers of students.

On the campus itself are hundreds of lectures and discussions. The educational world carries on substantial dialog between students and teachers, between students and administrators, between teachers and administrators, between all of these groups and the general public.

A tenth of one's active career is spent on campus, and it is an important tenth.

COMMUNICA-TION IN BUSI-NESS AND THE PROFESSIONS

Professor of management Joe Kelly states the issue as well as anybody: "All organizations are communication systems."[1] Most books about management have this notion in one form or another: "A competent manager is nearly always a good communicator." For *manager,* substitute any business or professional person: *nurse, teacher, salesperson, politician, attorney, minister, physician.*

Once I wrote the personnel officers of a hundred corporations—insurance, farm implement, office equipment, automobile, electronics, hotel, and so on—and asked what kinds of positions they would give to newly hired graduates who had studied communication. These personnel officers mentioned sales, public relations, and employee relations, but many of them also wrote to this effect: "We would put a young man or woman who has basic skills in communication in our junior management (or executive development) course." What I am doing in these paragraphs is to give you good reasons for becoming a better communicator. (And when later you interview for a job, mention the fact that you have had this kind of experience.)

James W. Lohr of Iowa State University asked 137 alumni of the University of Iowa (86 males, 51 females) who had been graduated

[1]*Organizational Behaviour: An Existential Systems Approach,* rev. ed. (Homewood, Ill.: Irwin, 1974), p. 156.

Magnum Photos

ten to fifteen years, to indicate the most important communicative activities. The group included farmers, engineers, homemakers, managers, professionals and semiprofessionals, scientists, supervisors, and teachers. In order of importance the activities were:

1 giving information to one person
2 making decisions with one person
3 giving information to a group
4 persuading one person
5 listening to one person's requests or difficulties
6 making decisions with a group
7 persuading a group
8 listening to a group's requests or difficulties
   (and so on, to)
13 listening to radio, and
14 viewing TV for entertainment.

From the point of view of difficulty, they ranked these activities as follows, the first item on the list being most difficult:

1 persuading a group
2 making decisions with a group
3 persuading one person

4 listening to a group's requests or difficulties
5 giving information to a group
6 making decisions with one person
7 listening to one person's requests or difficulties
(and so on, to)
13 listening to radio and
14 viewing TV for entertainment.[2]

In short, these people report that persuading is more difficult than informing, that speaking is more difficult than listening, and that talking to a group is more difficult than talking to one person.

These lists give a glimpse into the careers of many different people. They do not pretend to be the final word in planning your own career. A single conversation *can change the course of a life*. A single speech *can bring recognition that otherwise would have come only after years of patient endeavor*.

A revealing study by Kathleen E. Kendall has recently been reported, entitled "Do Real People Ever Give Speeches?" She identified a group of 202 residents of Albany, New York (130 females, 72 males) as being representative of the blue collar, working class, and undertook door-to-door interviews to learn about their actual speaking experiences. "Speaking in church" was the most frequently mentioned experience; others gave driver-safety lectures, talks to Catholic youth organizations, talks to nursing aides, talks to the kitchen staff where they worked, or in their unions. "Since those with more education spoke the most frequently," she noted, "one can expect that more highly-educated persons would give speeches more often." As she concluded, "real people are giving speeches."[3]

Peter F. Drucker, management consultant, whose career is devoted to advising corporation executives about problems that confront them, and who is tremendously interested in the education of young people, wrote a famous article, "Some Truths That Every Young College Graduate Should Know." One of these outstanding truths is the importance of effective communication, both spoken and written:

> As soon as you move one step up from the bottom, your effectiveness depends on your ability to reach others through the spoken or the written word. . . .
> The larger the organization of which you are an employee, the

---

[2]"Alumni Use of Communicative Activities and Recommended Activities for the Basic Course," *Speech Teacher*, 23 (September 1974): 248–251.
[3]*Central States Speech Journal*, 25 (Fall 1974): 233–235.

more important it will be that you know how to convey your thoughts in writing or speaking. . . .

The foundations for skill in expression have to be laid early; if you do not lay these foundations during your school years, you may never have an opportunity again.[4]

Even so, as William R. Sears, a specialist in executive manpower development points out, "We don't give students anywhere near the exercise they need in public speaking. The result is they exhibit all the elements of stage fright—halting speech and no flow of ideas." The best managers, he argues, are the best communicators. The art of improving communication "is just like push-ups. You can watch the instructor do calisthenics all day long and see him get big muscles. But unless you do them yourself, you won't improve your physique."[5] A message from another discipline may be inserted here to bolster the point: kittens carried through a maze do not learn the maze as well as do kittens that have to walk the maze themselves.[6]

It is therefore evident that in the world of business and services, into which most students go, the need for effective communication has high priority. At one moment the message to be communicated takes the form of public speaking, at another the form of conference and discussion. The flow of ideas in an organization is different from what it formerly was. One used to think of a brilliant, hard-driving man at the top, barking orders at a subordinate who relayed them through the line of command. Now considerable informal talk precedes the decision.

Young men and women entering organizations are urged to do a certain amount of "systems thinking"—related to the whole organiza-

---

[4]Peter F. Drucker, "Some Truths That Every Young College Graduate Should Know," in "How to be an Employee," *Fortune* 45 (May 1952): 126. *Forbes* describes Dr. Drucker as "probably the most sought-after consultant to big business in the U.S. today. More than 50 top U.S. firms currently engage Drucker to stimulate the thought processes of their high-paid brass. . . . His book, *The Practice of Management,* is a classic and is required reading at the Harvard Business School." (February 15, 1962): 34–35. His more recent book, *Management* (New York: Harper & Row, 1974) is widely acclaimed.

I wrote Dr. Drucker, inviting him to comment further, for the benefit of readers of this text. He wrote: "Let me say that the more I see—and in my daily work I see a great many promising young executives in government, in academic life and in business—the more distressed I am by the tremendous waste of ability, effort and talent that results from the lack of skill in presenting one's ideas in speaking or in writing.

"I see far too many people with real ability who get nowhere because they can not say what they have to say, either on paper or through the spoken word. And the man who can do so, even though he may have much less ability and much less to contribute, gets the big job, gets effectiveness, gets attention every time."

[5]"Why Best Managers are Best Communicators," *Nation's Business* 57 (March 1969): 82–87. The Sears and Co. roster of clients includes executives from General Motors, General Dynamics, Hughes, and others.

[6]Edward T. Hall, *The Hidden Dimension* (Garden City: Doubleday, 1966), p. 62.

THE ABILITY TO COMMUNICATE IS IN ONE WAY HARD AND IN ANOTHER WAY EASY

One of the most insightful passages in Aristotle's works comes from the *Metaphysics.* Instead of giving the Oxford professor's scholarly but somewhat wordy translation, I put it in my own brand of American English:

> The search for truth is in one way hard and in another way easy. No one can master it wholly or miss it entirely. Each of us contributes a little to the nature of things, and, by the efforts of all, a great deal is achieved.

The ability to communicate is also in one way hard and in another way easy. No one can master it wholly or miss it entirely. One moment we see communication as a basic, primal, elemental trait of human beings and we exclaim, "Everybody can communicate." Another moment we see so many different kinds of listeners, and so many different kinds of situations, and so many possibilities for misunderstanding, that we wonder that anyone can communicate to anyone.

In the communication class each of us, teacher and student, can contribute a little to the nature of things. By the efforts of all, a considerable amount can be achieved.

---

tion—as well as "departmental thinking"—related to their corner of it. Many, however, are unable to think broadly; marketing people, who are supposed to know what will sell, are notoriously unable to communicate with research people, who know what will work; design people, who arrange and shape things, seem remote from engineers, who build them, and both from service personnel, who repair them. Hence interface specialists, also known as project planners or project managers, find a place in the organization to do the necessary coordination.

My interest in business and professional speaking leads me to read the classified advertising in the daily newspapers under headings like "executive positions available." Along with items like "exciting incentives" and "key management" are notations like "your strong points should include organizing, analyzing, and motivating people to perform at capacity" and "opportunity for enthusiastic executive with the ability to motivate others." I do not seem to find ads reading "moody type needed with established ability to keep thoughts to self and to keep other people at a distance." More and more I expect to see ads seeking young men and women who can become advocates for industry as it enters into public discussion of social and environmental problems.

COMMUNICA-TION IN PUB-LIC LIFE   As the nation faces weighty issues, its officials increasingly take to the platform and the microphone to discuss the pros and cons. Since the days of Woodrow Wilson, chief executives have made more speeches to the country than to Congress. Recent presidents, and for that matter vice presidents, have followed this trend. Members of the Cabinet and of the Congress regularly talk to their constituents, face the nation, and meet the press. A typical radio or TV newscast will invariably present the comments of many public servants in their own voices.

On the necessity of speaking out on civic affairs, a distinguished judge of the United States Court of Appeals, who was awarded an honorary degree of doctor of laws by more than twenty colleges and universities, wrote:

> The importance of public speaking to our community life cannot be overestimated. . . . Without the opportunity to speak in public, how would the high-minded public servant have a chance to meet with his constituents, to express his views to the persons whose support is so vital to his program, and finally to win authorization for worthy projects?[7]

In similar vein the Athenian statesman, Pericles, is said to have observed that "one who forms a judgment on any point but can not explain himself clearly to the people, might as well have never thought at all on the subject."[8] This statement would certainly be true of a citizen who not only wanted to vote wisely, but who also desired to be able to inform, encourage, and persuade others.

Nor are audiences happy to let a speaker depart when he has delivered his carefully prepared address; those present want to hear answers to specific questions growing out of their own specific concerns. These inquirers seek additional information or more definite evidence on points already covered or bring up matters that the speaker omitted—even some he would prefer to discuss at another time or place. More important, questions give the well-prepared

---

[7]Letter to me from Judge Florence Allen, sixth circuit, Cleveland, Ohio.
[8]Richard Whately, *Elements of Rhetoric* (Louisville: John P. Morton & Co., n.d.), p. 21.

speaker an opportunity to learn which of his ideas or attitudes are of most interest to his listeners. A speaker will be happier about his performance if he speaks well during not only the formal part of the program but also during the discussion period that follows.

COMMUNICA-TION IN INTERPER-SONAL SITU-ATIONS

In relationships with others, you have two useful servants: *what you say* and *how you say it.*

If you have an academic difficulty, your wiser friends will say: "Talk to the teacher about it." If you become estranged from a relative or an acquaintance, again your advisers will say: "Have you discussed it personally?" Rather than write a letter, or even use the telephone, we prefer a face-to-face situation to correct misunderstandings, solve problems, make arrangements, or close deals.

A prosecuting attorney who was a prominent part of the legal machinery for sending many individuals to prison, once said that he did not believe any of them had any personal animosity toward him. "So far as my personal relationship with them was concerned," he explained, "I showed them every consideration I could. I was firm but fair. I was never vindictive. They saw that I was performing the official duties I had been charged with." Both what he said and how he said it were at the service of the state, not designed to demean the individual who had fallen afoul of the law. Both by word and by manner we can improve the texture of our interpersonal relationships. "Civility is not a sign of weakness," said John F. Kennedy on his inauguration day, "and sincerity is always subject to proof."

Between gruff bluster and the other extreme of fluff and bubbles is a wide field for effective interpersonal communication. One executive suggests this procedure for motivating the secretary: "Hazel, I want you to type this letter without a flaw, because it is going to be seen by the President of the United States." After her response, he invites her judgment on the question of how long it will take her to type it. That procedure, he says, is far better motivation than: "Hazel, type this without a damned mistake."[9]

A recent survey revealed that adults spend approximately three-fourths of their waking hours in communication activity: talking, reading, listening, writing. The survey further reported that, as one would expect, approximately two-thirds of adult waking hours are spent in *oral* forms of communication: talking and listening. "Occupations which require greater contact with other people," these researchers noted, "are generally associated with greater communication activity." They commented: "McLuhan's argument that we are

---

[9]Sears, "Why Best Managers are Best Communicators," pp. 86–87.

returning to an oral-aural tribal society appears to be an understatement. Our data indicate we are there today."[10] One could also argue that we have never left it.

CONCLUDING NOTE

The purpose of this chapter has been not only to indicate that the study of speech communication is important, but to support that statement by the authority of a wide range of people. This chapter has quoted, among others, experts who visit ailing corporations, study what is making them fall apart, and make recommendations; legal minds who work with a wide variety of human problems and difficulties; and researchers who poll men and women in the everyday walks of life, recording their speaking experiences. It has also noted that teachers, not only from speech communication but from other domains, have become involved in problems of communication. Further, it has indicated that our field is growing, not diminishing; expanding its borders, not shrinking them; attracting steadily increasing numbers of students, with an increasing variety of interests and concerns.

In the chapters that follow this text will explain principles, illustrate them with relevant examples, suggest choices and alternatives, and at times offer outright advice. I hope that this text, along with your instructor, your classmates, and your own efforts, will contribute something of permanent worth to your growth and development in the field of speech communication.

ASSIGN-MENTS AND EXERCISES

1 An assignment combining interpersonal speaking with either group discussion or speaking to a group:

   a Select a partner, preferably someone you do not know. Get acquainted with him or her and ask questions about background, interests, and experience, so that later you can introduce him or her to others. Follow up promising leads with further questions. Your partner will then interview you.

   b Your pair will then join with other pairs, so that the class is now divided into three or four groups. Each person will then introduce his or her partner to the group. After your introduction, other members of the group should ask further questions of the person being introduced. In turn each member of each pair will be introduced.

   Or Make a short talk to the class, introducing your partner,

---

[10]Larry A. Samovar, Robert D. Brooks, and Richard E. Porter, "A Survey of Adult Communication Activities," *Journal of Communication,* 19 (December 1969): 303, 306.

selecting the most interesting information gleaned from your interview. After your introduction, members of the class may ask further questions of the person being introduced.

2 Make an informal talk to the class in which you introduce yourself. Tell unknown, little-known, or notorious facts about yourself that will help your classmates become acquainted with you. Draw upon such items as hometown, vocational objective, hobbies, family background, and special interests or talents.

3 Report on the communication that goes on in a business or profession with which you are familiar. Consult house organs, trade journals, or professional journals.

4 Discuss the importance of communication in connection with the alleviation of some social or economic problem: poverty, unemployment, rights of minority groups, or improvement of educational opportunity.

5 Review a recent volume of a business publication (such as *Fortune, Money, Business Week, Forbes, Nation's Business*) and discuss the kinds of communication or the problems in communication that are reported therein.

6 Consult a file of community or student newspapers, and report on the different kinds of speeches and other forms of communication that make the news. Add examples from your own observation.

7 Select a field of interest in which you plan to study in preparation for later speeches, reports, discussions, or conversations. Perhaps you would like to explain, interpret, or defend modern art, modern music, a social problem, trends in religious thinking, labor unions, investing in the stock market, our relations with a foreign country, medical practices or innovations, or national defense. This subject should preferably be one in which you now have an above-average interest and would like to extend your study.

 # Basic Communication Theory

Definitions ☐ Models, Approaches ☐ Feedback ☐ The end result ☐ Assignments and exercises

Fourteen million years ago our apelike ancestors left the shelter of the jungles of east Africa to make their way on its vast plains. These human beings had to compete for survival against thousands of lions, leopards, rhinoceroses, cape buffaloes, and other predators. A lion or leopard can run faster than a human being; the rhinoceros has a tougher hide; the buffalo is mean-tempered and, in addition, has vicious horns. As for food, smaller animals that might serve can climb trees, and others are fleet-footed.

No visitor surveying that primeval scene could have predicted that thin-skinned, defenseless, prehistoric man-creatures and woman-creatures would not only survive but multiply and ultimately possess the earth. That they did so was because they had:

A brain that could solve problems instead of reacting by instinct and could remember what worked and what didn't.

An upright posture that freed the hands. The human hand with its opposed thumb gradually became a precise instrument for making weapons, starting a fire, cooking in vessels, fashioning clothing, and storing food.

And also because:

The art of communication makes it possible to hunt in pairs or in small groups. Directions can be shouted, refined, relayed; objects can be given names, and classified as fast or slow, safe or dangerous, edible or inedible. Not only words but gestures and facial expressions can be utilized. Events can be recalled, analyzed, discussed, and lessons learned that can be used in the future.

Communication makes teamwork and group effort possible. You can teach a reasonably smart baboon to stack three boxes on top of one another and reach a stalk of bananas. But to teach three baboons to build a stack with three boxes is something else again. That is one reason why the world is full of people instead of baboons.

Somewhere along the line, communication became more than utilitarian or pragmatic. Human beings developed a sense of fun; events struck them as being strange or incongruous, and they learned to laugh at themselves and at one another. They also learned to weep when events overwhelmed them. They developed the art of personal decoration and adornment; they drew pictures; they danced and told stories; they evolved forms of worship. These traits had immense survival value. Through these forms of communication they encouraged and sustained one another.

This introductory statement should give us a perspective on the significance of communication. To say that communication is the most humanlike thing we do is a truism. Without the ability to communicate we are not human at all. If serious illness removes from a friend or relative the power to understand and to express, we feel that the personality we knew—the humanness—has also departed. Of an extremely reticent individual, we say: "She's a wonderful girl" (or "He's a great guy") "but you have to get to know her" (or him). Translated, this statement means: "If only she (or he) would communicate more freely . . ."

DEFINITIONS We may look at selected definitions of *communication.* Bernard Berelson and Gary A. Steiner offer: "Communication: The transmission of information, ideas, emotions, skills, etc., by the use of symbols—words, pictures, figures, graphs, etc. It is the *act* or process of transmission that is usually called communication."[1] Wilbur Schramm observes: "Communication is a relationship, an act of sharing, rather than something someone does to someone else."[2]

The components of these definitions may be listed:

1 **Sender** The person originating the message.
2 **Message** The verbal or nonverbal symbols being communicated.
3 **Channel** Sound waves, light waves, electronic waves; i.e., the medium—radio, TV, face-to-face. Sometimes also: the series or network of individuals through whom a message is relayed.
4 **Receiver** The person or persons listening. Note that *sending* and *receiving* may go on simultaneously; sender is also a receiver, and receiver also a sender.

Words like *source, speaker, listener* will also be used in this text. *Sender* seems appropriate when discussing communication impersonally; *speaker* seems appropriate when the image of a human being *speaking* is prominent. One may communicate with oneself, in which case an internal channel is used. We will also need to consider the *setting* in which messages are communicated. We cannot overlook both the short-term and the long-term *effects* of the message. In this text we will also note the *culture* in which the communication transaction operates.

In the last dozen years terms like the foregoing have come to live alongside, and in some instances have supplanted, terms like

---

[1]*Human Behavior* (New York: Harcourt, Brace, 1964), p. 254.
[2]Wilbur Schramm and Donald F. Roberts, eds., *The Process and Effects of Mass Communication,* 2d ed. rev. (Urbana: University of Illinois Press, 1971), p. 8.

speaker, audience, and *listener,* just as *communication* or *speech communication* is replacing *speech,* and just as *speech* has supplanted *elocution.* The newer terms and others like it—*feedback, input, noise*—grow out of our present-day involvement in electronics and its sophisticated offspring, the computer.

MODELS, APPROACHES
Today many disciplines utilize a *scheme,* or *diagram,* or *model* to illustrate a theory or process. This trend grows from a desire to visualize ideas so that we may understand them better. Imagine a mechanical exhibit showing how Mercury, Venus, the Earth, and other planets are spaced as they journey around the sun; this is an astronomical model. Another model is the blueprint of colored wires and relays that help tell how to fix the dishwasher; still another is the famous double helix representing the genetic code that determines heredity.

The definitions in the preceding section, and others suggested by your own reading, need to be put into a general category. Here we have a choice:

The circular model This model, with a centuries-old tradition behind it, reached its peak twenty or twenty-five years ago. Its principal features were:

(speaker) — (subject) — (audience) — (occasion)

It was as much of a checklist as a model; it seemed to say that the act of communication begins with the speaker and subject; the subject (the content) is transmitted to the audience; the audience interprets this content according to its own experiences; all of this takes place on and is influenced by a definite occasion. Teachers and students of this earlier day well knew, of course, that the content must be planned with an audience and an occasion in mind. They knew that the reactions of the audience would affect the speaker, leading him sometimes to alter his message, which in turn led to further reactions from the audience. They spoke of *circular response;* hence the term *circular* to describe this model.

To the questions, "Don't sending and receiving go on concurrently? Can't the audience start sending messages even before the speaker says a word?" these teachers would have answered, "Of course." After all, they were not dummies. Even with this awareness of the audience, however, the emphasis of the model was tilted toward the speaker. The subject was linked more closely to the speaker (his information and experience) than to the audience. If the teacher were himself well-versed in drama, interpretation, and litera-ture generally (which involves the interpretation of events and move-ments), he might tilt his instruction even more toward speaker-subject.

The process model   Often the term *process* is used in defining *communication*. A process model starts with this core:

(sender) — (message) — (channel) — (receiver)

But it must go further; it should suggest visually the internal transac-tion that goes on as messages are zapped back and forth. *Sender* may be thought of as "encoder-interpreter-decoder" and "receiver" as "decoder-interpreter-encoder." The term *interpreter* is necessary because sender and receiver must each assign a meaning to each symbol. What the sender means even by a term like *good* may not be the same as what the receiver means; what is *good* to one may be *not so good* to the other. An early but still helpful form of this model is:[3]

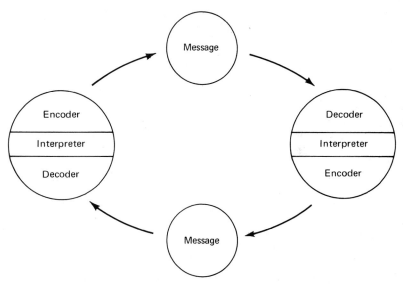

Later models have become more complex, as theorists have drawn in additional lines and arrows to demonstrate the refinements. As Schramm says, models may show more details because:

---

[3]C. E. Osgood, from Schramm and Roberts, *The Process and Effects of Mass Communica-tion*, p. 24.

[T]he receiver's social relationship to the sender, the perceived social consequences of accepting it or acting upon it, must be put together with an understanding of the symbolic and structural nature of the message, the conditions under which it is received, the abilities of the receiver, and his innate and learned responses, before we can predict with any real confidence the consequences of an act of communication.[4]

The systems approach A *systems approach* provides a framework for looking at a communication task in a detailed, orderly manner. Rather than hurriedly preparing a message on the most convenient topic, you may analyze a wide range of your available resources, capabilities, and desired outcomes. You may make a step-by-step survey of your current knowledge; note points at which further research is needed; study the characteristics of the receiver or receivers; outline and compose the message; and, after the message is presented, appraise the result.

A systems approach tends to be minute in its analysis of steps and procedures. It considers possible relationships among a group of things or parts or objects. It also recognizes that the whole is greater than the sum of the parts. It crosses disciplines. An example is the environmental system—the different kinds of life and their interdependence—in a forest or bay or prairie or along a seacoast. Drain a swamp and the supply of alligators and pelicans diminishes. Build the High Dam at Aswan and Turkish fishermen wonder what happened to the herring. It notes two kinds of systems, *closed* and *open,* and classifies communication as a *complex, open system* since human beings involved in a group interact not only with one another but with the total environment.

Systems theory was rapidly developed during World War II, when the problem was not merely to add to the supply of existing weapons but to start afresh after a detailed study of what was needed, in, for example, submarine detection or long-range bombing. Systems theory also loomed large in the development of the computer. Often the overall study of a problem reveals ways of describing relationships among individual components and processes (termed *subsystems*) that at first glance might have seemed unrelated.

The systems approach is useful for speech communication.[5] It

[4]Ibid., p. 7.

[5]See Thomas R. King, "The Systems Approach and Its Implications for Teacher Education in Speech Communication," paper presented at the Memphis Conference of Teacher Educators, 1973, later revised for Judson Newcombe and R. R. Allen, eds., *New Horizons for Teacher Education in Speech Communication* (Skokie, Ill.: National Textbook Company with the Speech Communication Association, 1974), pp. 112 ff.

is also being applied to other educational disciplines. Recently systems experts reported an investigation of the sequence of steps or skills a student must take in mastering reading (a communicative skill) and mathematics.[6]

Obviously much of the old appears in each of the newer models or approaches just described. Nowadays human knowledge seldom makes a quantum leap. We took a giant step, to be sure, when we were persuaded that the earth was round and not flat. But then came refinements: Well, the earth *is* round, but not so round as we thought. It appears to be flattened at the poles. And it goes around the sun, but not in a circle as we supposed; rather, more of an ellipse. At least a kind of ellipse. Moreover, it proceeds at varying rates of speed; its rate seems to be affected by heavenly bodies way out there that we do not know about yet. But after thousands of observations had warranted refinements here and there, the day came when Americans could land on the moon, not once but six times, and on the return splash into the Pacific within yards and seconds of the predicted place and time.

As Edward Sapir wrote, the birth of a new concept is invariably foreshadowed by a strained or extended use of old terminology. A discipline goes through three stages, as philosopher Alfred North Whitehead observed: the romantic stage, the descriptive stage, and the precision stage. Speech communication is attempting an approach to the precision stage and, like other domains in the behavioral sciences, is beginning to stake out its boundaries. A domain that has successfully used and moved away from *elocution* and *oratory* in my lifetime, however, is not likely to be happy forever with *process* or *system*. Students and teachers will, pragmatically, enjoy the juice of these conceptual oranges and blow out the seeds.

What we do like about *process* is that it contains the root meaning *proceeding:* moving progressively, flowing onwardly, continuing in activity or function. A process is dynamic; it does not hold still. As scholars we can, of course, create an instant replay at any point so that we can take a steady look at a certain feature. We speak of life processes, like digestion, or the process of government. Yet the term is too limiting to suit everybody. "Process of government" does not wholly explain the superb talents of Roosevelt or Kennedy, who worked on the inside, or Martin Luther King, who worked on the outside.

What we like about *system* is its emphasis upon taking a

---

[6]*Newsweek* 85 (Feb. 10, 1975): 44. (Copyright 1975 by *Newsweek*, Inc. All rights reserved. Reprinted by permission.) The article claims results described as "spectacular." It also noted that a total of ten American doctorates in general systems theory had been awarded. (In 1928 it could have been said that there were only ten American doctorates in speech; so much for perspective.)

detailed look at both analysis and synthesis. *System* is almost pure Greek: "to bring together, to combine." Its basic definition is: "a complex unity formed of many often-diverse parts." What we also like is that it embraces many parts and aspects. To paraphrase John Donne: "No message, or sender, or receiver, is an island, entire of itself; every message, or sender, or receiver, is a piece of the continent, a part of the main." In planning a conversation, an advocacy, a confrontation, an interview, or a speech, systems theory would remind us to consider all possibilities. Yet we do not need an expert's opinion to tell us that we are not likely to splash down precisely where we hoped.

A cultural framework This text suggests that the communications model, whether process, systems, or something else, be placed in a *cultural framework.* (*Occasion* and *setting* have also been used to describe this framework.) *Culture* means "the sum total of the ways in which human beings live. . . . It includes the relation between people in pairs and in groups . . . the realm of symbols, including speech, music, the visual arts, and the human body itself."[7] It includes "knowledge, belief, art, morals, law, custom, and other capabilities acquired by man as a member of society."[8] These definitions, formulated by well-known anthropologists, indicate the central significance of communication in the concept of culture. Admittedly the term *cultural* is not without difficulties. The word carries too much of a burden of "refinement" and "urbanity" that for this discussion we must set to one side.

Putting the communication model in a cultural framework reflects our increasing awareness that a communication transaction operates within a culture. What goes on between a boy and a girl talking about a date reflects not only the message (what they say to each other), nor the setting (chance meeting between classes), nor the occasion (homecoming festivities), but the culture to which the two belong, with its permissiveness or restraints. A different culture might require chaperon, go-between, parental consent, different language formulas, etc. Scores of articles the last year have warned American businessmen that they cannot use American directness and forthrightness when dealing with Russians, Japanese, or representatives of the Middle Eastern nations. An American lecturer scarcely needs to be told to keep the address to one hour or less. Both the speaker and the listeners follow behavior patterns that have been long established by our culture. In India a program of sitar

---

[7]Carlton S. Coon, *The Story of Man,* 2d ed. rev. (New York: Knopf, 1962), p. 5.
[8]E. B. Tyler, *Primitive Culture,* 7th ed., cited in Harry M. Johnson, *Sociology: A Systematic Introduction* (New York: Harcourt, Brace, 1960), p. 10.

music might last five hours. American culture says that two hours is about right for any musical program, including the intermission.

Cultural differences are reflected in the formality or informality with which people talk to one another and the values, choices, options, or expectations that have usefulness in influencing or persuading.

Now that we have talked about process, systems, and culture, you may find yourself borrowing something from each concept. Awareness of process may lead you to attend not only to yourself as sender, but to message, channel, and receiver. Awareness of systems adds, probably, still greater emphasis on analysis and synthesis, on careful, detailed preparation, and on consideration of all aspects of the problem. Awareness of culture leads you to investigate the customs and traditions of the situation, the options and expectations. (What is a good way to initiate a conversation with a stranger? What kinds of humor are appropriate? What questions are asked at interviews?)

Moreover: Although the communicative transaction is dynamic and ongoing, with all parties sending and receiving simultaneously, for instructional purposes we need to look at each element singly. In learning a motor skill like golf or swimming you focus separately on arm and shoulder, or on feet and legs, even though eventually you have to put it all together. Communication is even more complicated.

The Sender The human mind busy at the act of deciding what to say and what to leave out is marvelously and magically complex. The imaginative person who declared a computer that could do all that the average human mind can do would have to be as large as the Empire State Building, would require the total power of Consolidated Edison to run it, and would need the water of Niagara to keep it cool, was not far off. The process that takes place in the mind is a sorting and arranging of ideas and a selection of symbols into which to code these ideas, in large part using patterns and arrangements that have often been used before, but assembling them in new and novel combinations. If you are preparing a message of some significance—a speech, an interview, or a meaningful conversation—you may review mentally what you will say and how you will say it. You may be guided by a set of principles, such as those described in Chapter 10, or you may proceed at random. Long ago philosopher-social psychologist G. H. Mead wrote about the "inner forum" before which we privately review and discuss our ideas with ourselves.

You find yourself participating in an interview, hoping that it will result in your getting a summer job. Your mind is busily formulating answers to the questions that the interviewer asks. Suppose the

Bruce Anspach/EPA Newsphoto

question is, "Tell me about your family." Part of your mind is devising a structure ("Tell him about your father, then about your mother") and part of it is selecting and explaining details ("Talk first about his vocation, then about his personality"). Part of your mind also is carefully watching the interviewer ("Is he interested?" "Am I making an impression?"). A mumble of approval, a short follow-up question, may lead you to say more about some aspect of your family than you first planned. At one and the same time your mind is carrying on two or three trains of thought, part of your mind being concerned with "encoding," part with "interpreting," and part with "decoding."

Often you have expressed opinions about a communicator from your viewpoint as listener. You have heard an instructor say, "This morning I am going to demonstrate the solution to Problem 97," a sentence that can be described as *feedforward,* since the instructor has told you in advance what he was going to do. Perhaps you reacted with some *feedback* (more about feedback later on), telling him with an interested look what you thought of his plan; that is, you reflected, "That's good—I worked two hours on 97 last night and didn't get to first base," and you permitted your face to light up, or even nodded your head slightly. The instructor got your message and others like it, if he were perceptive, and felt momentarily encouraged. Last night while reviewing his lesson plan he had said to himself, "It won't hurt to go over 97—classes have trouble with that, and the principle is basic."

You follow his step-by-step explanation. But as you can listen faster than he talks—Ralph G. Nichols says that the listener can cruise along mentally at 400 words per minute whereas the speaker plods along at about one-fourth that rate[9]—you can indulge in random thoughts such as "he really wants us to get this," "that's the point where I made my mistake last night," "this is pretty sure to come up in the test." If the explanation becomes, for you, repetitious or needlessly detailed, your features become passive and your mind wanders to other topics, coming back when you perceive a break in his flow of words—a pause, or a transition to another topic. Perhaps the instructor read this feedback and perceived that he was explaining the point in more detail than necessary, so he broke off and turned to a fresh point in his discussion. In other words, source and receivers are carrying on an exchange of messages—the professor directing the thinking of the students, but at the same time being guided by the messages being transmitted to him. You, yourself, can detail the kinds of thinking you do, during the lecture, that you do not transmit—your mental shortcuts, digressions, interpretations, wanderings. At times you may even fake attention, giving every appearance of understanding but not really understanding.

Now let us turn to a partial report of the mental activity of a speaker giving a speech to a large group. Moments before his talk is scheduled to be given, he takes his place on the platform alongside the chairperson. Although the two engage in casual talk, the speaker's thoughts are really on the listeners out front. He observes the size of the group and tries to get at its probable mood and responsiveness. He is also thinking about his speech, and perhaps wondering which of two or three possible stories he should tell to start off with. Finally he decides that he will wait until after the chairperson's introduction, and then choose. He sees the clock, notes that the meeting is late getting under way, has a feeling that his speech may now be too long, and decides to cut an illustration that he was not too happy about anyway. He has a promising last-minute inspiration and makes a mental note to bring in a briefer example that he just thought of. As the speaker listens to the complimentary introduction, he notes that the audience is in a good mood, so he

---

[9]Ralph G. Nichols, "Listening," in Ronald F. Reid, gen. ed., *Introduction to the Field of Speech* (Chicago: Scott, Foresman, 1965), pp. 158–159.

decides that one of his prospective stories is just the thing; he tells it and it is uproariously received. That major obstacle cleared, he finds himself into his speech—five minutes gone, forty-five still ahead.

He has prepared a message with a solid structure: four main points, linked in an unescapable order, so that one naturally flows into another. When speakers forget, it is usually at a break between main points; since our speaker's points follow one another as logically as beta follows alpha, he knows he is safe. Besides, he has them listed on his note slips.

As he proceeds, he watches his listeners intently; long experience has taught him to talk *to,* not *at.* As he talks, his mind actually does several things at once. Primarily he is focusing on what he is saying—he phrases his ideas in well-monitored sentences, with decent syntax; occasionally he finds himself starting a somewhat unusual sentence pattern, but he gets out of it with banners flying and might actually comment to himself, "Well, that was close." At the same moment he is aware of pausing to let an idea sink in, perhaps simultaneously gesturing. By now he is aware of specific individuals in his audience; he has spotted friendly faces, or antagonistic faces, or passive faces, and he conjectures that this part of his speech is going only fairly well, but good stuff is coming up later on. Outwardly he is uttering 100 or 125 or 150 words a minute, but inwardly he is carrying on additional snatches of dialog with himself. Repeated experience has given him an ease and a facility that he did not have when he was back in high school, or college, making his first speeches. While part of his mind is delivering the speech, part of it is thinking back over what he has just said and part of it is looking ahead to what is coming next. New materials may be brought in— given birth by a quirk of association of ideas or through the stimuli that listeners are feeding back—and the speaker hears himself uttering words that he had not planned to utter, until that very second.

Professional speakers have commented at times upon their mental processes during speech making. William Jennings Bryan admitted, long after the famous "Cross of Gold" speech, that he felt nervous on that occasion; he added, however, the knowledge that he had a good conclusion "kept him going." Woodrow Wilson accepted an invitation to address a small group, and had planned to make a short impromptu talk, but found when he arrived that a crowd of thousands was expecting a full-fledged address. On the way to the auditorium he sorted out his ideas and arranged an outline of his remarks. The actual composition of the speech, of course, had to come while he was delivering it. Charles James Fox could speak on a wide variety of current issues from one to four hours, and never use notes. The composition went on mentally, during the delivery of the speech. But the process was not flawless; once he said, "Often in speaking, when a thing occurs to me and it is not time to bring it out, I know I shall lose it when I want it, and never fail to do it."

As long ago as Aristotle, the importance of the listener was decreed: "of the three elements in speech-making—speaker, subject, and person addressed—it is the last one, the hearer, that determines the speech's end and object." But for sheer wonder, in the act of communication, nothing is quite like what goes on inside the sender's mind. Communication is not an exact science or even an inexact science—the trajectory of ideas cannot be plotted like the trajectory of a missile. Communication grows out of the totality of an individual's experience—out of what you have been taught and what you have observed—in short, your culture. You can learn from others who have come before you, and from what you can learn for yourself.

Considering the increasing impact that good communication is sure to have, as the peoples of this planet increase in number and as their problems grow in complexity, it would appear to be something like sheer lunacy for a young man or woman not to want to prize all the communicative talent he or she has, and nourish and augment it to the fullest possible extent.

The Message   The result of the individual's planning, hoping, selecting, arranging, and amplifying, is the *message*. Long or short, it becomes something to be transmitted to the receiver. Most rhetorical theory is concerned with the preparation of messages: what to put in, what to leave out, and what symbols to use.

Here it will be sufficient to make three points. One is that the message is not received intact. It is composed of symbols, not things, and each symbol must be interpreted by each listener. If a sender says "melon" to a group of a hundred people, presumably everyone will think of something with a rind and seeds. One, however, will think of something green, another of something yellow and crinkled, another of something elliptical and striped; if each listener could lay a duplicate of the imagined melon at the feet of the speaker, there would be a hundred different sizes and shapes. Even if the sender says "honeydew melon," you can be reasonably certain that a few of the receivers will still be thinking of something green, elliptical, and striped. Fantastic as the situation is with "melon," it is much more so with "freedom," even with a hundred listeners from the same community. As has been well said, the sender tells a story or explains a process, hoping the receiver will tell a similar story or explain a similar process to himself or herself.

The second point to be made about the message is that, once it has started on its journey, it has an existence in its own right. It is then too late to change it. You can deny having said it or scream that you were misquoted, but the denial and the scream simply coexist alongside the original message, like two darts on a dart board. The denial and the scream are symbolic, like the original message, and the receiver can interpret as he or she chooses.

The purpose of making these points is to underscore the difficulty of preparing a message that will be received *something like* the communicator's original, and that is not likely to be misunderstood or misinterpreted. Napoleon's dictum, "If an order *can* be misunderstood, it *will* be misunderstood," can certainly be substantiated by every reader of this book. Also by every general.

The third point is that messages may be thought of as parts of a *series* or of a *campaign,* as well as existing singly.[10] One who is vitally concerned about, for example, pollution, may decide to give years to composing messages about improving the environment. She will take notes on what she reads; write down observations, random thoughts, and other materials; and put them in a file. One can imagine her saying to herself, "I can use that in a speech." Into a folder it goes, although she has not yet been invited to make that speech, and does not know audience or setting. In an issue of *Consumer Reports* a salesman reads a commendation of his company's product. This he reads with care: "I can use that on a prospect." You have advanced as a communicator when you realize that you may make not just a single speech on a subject, but a series of speeches; you will be able to use an argument not just on a single customer, but on a series of customers.

Actually, a campaign can go on for decades or for centuries. The frailties that Jesus, Buddha, Confucius, and every other religious leader spoke about, are still with us. The slave trade, so wicked that one would suppose it could not exist for a moment, was actively the subject of speeches for the whole century preceding 1850. Even then it was not completely stamped out, and in places still exists. Religious differences are still hotly disputed and debated. Until 1960, most Americans apparently believed that a Catholic could not be President. It was as if it had been written in the Constitution: No Catholic shall be President. In Northern Ireland, tension between Catholics and Protestants still flares up. For centuries Parliament held the belief that anybody could be a member of Parliament, provided he were a member of the Established Church. After many thousands of speeches, pamphlets, etc., Dissenters were tolerated. Then, Catholics. Then, Jews. Eventually it was decided that one could be elected even if professing no religion at all. Civil capacity only, not religious affiliation, became the hallmark. Hence one does

---

[10]See Wallace C. Fotheringham, "Instrumentality and the Persuasive Campaign," in *Perspectives on Persuasion* (Boston: Allyn and Bacon, 1966), pp. 36–41.

what one can with a single message. You cannot win every time. A listener may vote against you, yet say to himself: "Though I voted against him, I did not do so with entire confidence." In baseball a player squawks, knowing he is not likely to change the umpire's mind on that decision, but, hopefully, to affect the next one.

The Channel

The *channel* is the medium through which the message is transmitted—the space between sender and receiver. If the receiver is at one end of a room and the sender at another, the message will travel through the intervening space by means of sound waves and light waves. Hopefully the communication transaction will be carried on under favorable conditions. It is proper, however, to speak of *channel capacity;* visual or auditory interference or distractions, commonly termed *noise,* may contribute to the deterioration of the signal. The hum of ventilating blowers or air conditioners, the power mower outside the window, and latecomers or other disturbances interfere with message transmission. If the distance between receiver and sender is short, the channel may be used not only for the transmission of sound and light waves but also for other sensory data: smells, for example.

The foregoing discussion of channel assumes that sender and receiver are operating face to face. We must also apply the concept of channel to mass media such as radio and TV. We know the consequences of being on the receiving end of sound or light waves that are poorly amplified or in other ways distorted. Microphone and camera may alter the signal so that matters of voice, articulation, general poise, and confidence, may or may not be changed for the better. Practically, however, the channel is the least of our concerns, as many of the problems it poses must be solved by technical means (at least in the broadcasting situation).

Many use *channel* in another sense, as when they say, in larger organizations, "You must make your request through channels." Most speech communication teachers use *channel* in the sense in which it is explained in the preceding paragraphs, and *network* to represent the situation when messages travel through a chain of individuals.

The Receiver

The complexity of communication is such that, in discussing sender and message, we have already suggested a good deal about the *receiver.*

In the conversational or interview situation, the receiver is sometimes one person, sometimes another; audible messages with visible accompaniments flow back and forth freely. In the public speaking situation, the receiver also transmits messages—many of a subtle character—to the sender.

THE HEARER WHO IS A SPEAKER

The importance of the spoken word . . . is grounded in the fact that it does not want to remain with the speaker. It reaches out toward a hearer, it lays hold of him, it even makes the hearer into a speaker, if perhaps only a soundless one.

Martin Buber in *The Knowledge of Man*
(New York: Harper & Row), p. 112. Read
Chapter 5, "The Word That is Spoken."

We have already said that the sender, in preparing a message, has considered possible responses that receivers might make. If you are in favor of a proposal and believe your receivers to be against it, you will shape your arguments to make them more receptive to antagonistic people. For example, you might start with the less-controversial aspects of your subject. Or you might start with the strongest possible argument on their side—so that even as they perceive you are "misguided" they may also perceive that you are fair—and then answer this strong argument with the most objective evidence available.

In many other ways, receiver influences sender. You may be asked to state an opinion and suddenly realize that you have no opinion on that subject; the question has not landed on your doorstep before. Here is sender, at the insistence of receiver, about to formulate a message that otherwise might not even come into being. Receiver is thus exerting a strong influence on sender to create and produce a message. After a year in England, I am asked: "Why is the British economy in trouble?" My internal computer system swings into action. From recollection of articles in *The Economist,* editorials in the *Financial Times,* discussions with Americans who head London offices, I filter one argument concerned with unions (small craft unions wildcat and tie up a whole industry), and one with management (traditional conservative attitudes toward merchandising and cost accounting). My ideas would have lain dormant but for this external prodding.

Just as "sender" is really "sender-receiver," so "receiver" is really "receiver-sender." How does "receiver" really "send"? In a large lecture class I may tell a story; the students send back "messages" expressing their pleasure. The communication is thus a transaction. Encouraged, I tell another story, *although a moment earlier I had not intended to.* Or, I tell a story and the students send back a clear signal: "Old stuff! Not funny!" Hence I retreat to a previously prepared position. At times a teacher will embark upon an explanation so cogent that students will listen with utmost attentiveness. Again, their messages are clear: "The material is absorbing." "We are interested." "Go on!" Later on the teacher may see one student close his notebook. Others follow, and let the arms of their seats down. The spell is broken; the audience has shattered into a hundred pieces. The message is: "The bell is about to ring." Receiving this message, the responsive teacher revises the closing sentences and brings the lecture to as finished an end as possible.

A similar situation exists in small communicating groups. Along with the spoken dialog of conversation and small group discussions is an unspoken dialog. If you read the signs you can tell whether you are interesting your listener or not. One can see egos being bruised or flattered. The silent language as well as the spoken language is a part of the transaction.

Although the *receiver* can determine whether or not to listen to the message and internally agree or disagree with it or ignore it, the sender plays a highly important role. In the instance of a public address, many people will come just to hear the speaker. They will cheer him on because he is who he is. They will attend to and respect his message because he is behind it. Even if they disagree, they will see the force of the reasons that lead him to take the position he does. Though relatively few enjoy national reputations, many enjoy a state, a community, a campus, or even a classroom reputation. We must note, however, that one's effectiveness depends also upon wisdom and counsel, the expressive use of voice and action, and sensitiveness and responsiveness to the listener. Thus the transaction is completed; the circle of communication is rounded.

The Setting   The *setting* in which the message is delivered must not be overlooked. A familiar scene in the movies is that of the lovely lady preparing dinner for the young man she wishes to impress. The setting includes not only the food but also the candles and the music. If a speaker is to address an audience of fifty people, she would rather have them assemble in a room that holds forty, and bring in additional chairs, so that the meeting seems crowded and prosperous, than to have them scattered in an auditorium that holds a hundred and fifty. Imagine an average meeting room that has a capacity of fifty. You would probably have a different feeling as a member of a group of twenty, sitting at the sides and back of the room, than you would as a member of a group of the same size that bunched itself toward the front. The latter arrangement invites participation; the former discourages it. You like to have society's cultural forces working for you rather than against you. Entertainers do not elect to perform in churches; symphony orchestras do not cherish field houses.

The setting also influences interpersonal communication. The dialog in a semiprivate restaurant booth will likely differ from that conducted in a hotel lobby in full view and easy hearing of others. The mood of the environment is another of the imponderables. If a community is in mourning because of some disaster, the dialog is different from what it would have been otherwise. A banquet situation imposes one set of requirements; a memorial service imposes another.

Custom, tradition, and degree of informality also enter into the setting. Sometimes a communication is twice as effective as it might have been because of a happy adjustment of sender and receivers to the spirit and mood of the occasion.

FEEDBACK I have already mentioned *feedback* in this chapter. "The principle of feedback," says Barnlund, "is central to understanding man as both a biological and social organism." Feedback "is a requirement of all self-governing, goal-seeking systems.... An autonomous system must be able to observe and scan its own performance, compare intended and actual operation, and use this information to guide future action."[11]

Applied to communication, feedback answers the question, "How are we doing?" The situation may involve two people, a hundred, or more:

Are we understanding each other?
Are we enjoying each other's company?
Did our committee make a good decision?
Is our meeting achieving its purpose?

A asks *B* for directions to find Highway 50 going west. *B* explains which way to go and which turns to take. *A*, nodding from time to time, supplies the feedback that assures *B* that the explanation is clear. *A* may also ask a question, giving *B* a cue to restate part of the explanation. *B*, sensing that *A* is appreciative, may take extra care to help *A* understand. As *A* departs, *B* can feel certain that the directions were understood. Compare this brief transaction with the situation in which *A* dials a number and listens to a recorded statement giving time and temperature: no feedback.

The term *feedback* is currently in widespread usage. You hear it

---

[11]Dean C. Barnlund, *Interpersonal Communication: Survey and Studies* (New York: Houghton Mifflin, 1968), p. 229.

in the classroom, in committee meetings, at public discussions. The manufacturer seeks feedback from customers; the professional person seeks feedback from clients or patients. Feedback may be:

1 Verbal or nonverbal   You may *say* "Good," "go on," "I understand," "that's wrong," "I'm confused," "you've made it clear for the first time," "I understood your first two points but I missed the third." Or you may smile, nod or shake your head, frown, applaud. Or you may use verbal or nonverbal feedback simultaneously.

Alphabet scene

Investigate for yourself the prevalence of verbal and nonverbal feedback as you participate in conversations or discussions. Note the variety of facial expressions, vocal tones, and kinds of comments.

'alphabet

2 Zero or free   *Zero feedback* exists in a situation in which the receiver cannot see the sender and is not permitted to make audible responses. Experimental projects are sometimes designed to take place under these conditions. Television viewing and radio listening occur under zero feedback conditions, though polls, telephone calls, and letters are ways in which the broadcast station eventually secures feedback. Free feedback exists in a situation in which sender and receiver may readily react, as in a discussion in which participants ask questions, volunteer information, and exchange points of view.

*zero feedback.
k. talk with no
me back to partner*

As most problems begin and end with an "I," you may ask yourself whether your feedback tilts toward *zero* or *free* when you find yourself in a small group. Invent a scale of 1 to 5, 1 being minimum feedback, 5 indicating that you supply a maximum amount of verbal and nonverbal feedback, and 3 being average. (You cannot "not communicate." Even if you are silent and passive you are communicating something.) Compare and contrast yourself with others. You will likely find yourself using more feedback in some situations than others. Equally important: are you aware of the feedback that others make to your comments?

An aspect of *free feedback* is whether it is brief or lengthy. The human organism can accept only so much feedback at any one time. If you seek to praise someone, find words that specifically express what you like, rather than escaping with a brief grunt and a weak nod. At the other extreme of prolonged feedback, even praise loses its bloom if the sender begins to repeat, and even criticism loses its usefulness if the sender heaps it too bountifully and abundantly.

Expectancies loom large in communication. If you take a decided position on an issue, you expect a certain amount of feedback. You will likely set to one side both the fragmentary comments (both of agreement and disagreement) and the lengthy repetitive discourses, and be most helped by those of appropriate length.

3 **Positive or negative**   *Positive feedback* is encouraging, approving, rewarding. It says, "You're doing fine." *Negative feedback* is disagreeing, disapproving, criticizing. It says, "Hold on," "Are you sure?" or, perhaps, "You're wrong." Positive feedback is supportive. Negative feedback may go all the way from demoralizing to challenging.

Everybody needs to be appreciated. Those who show their appreciation of the achievements of others are prized members of the group. The ability to express appreciation is associated with generosity of spirit and largeness of heart. This statement is not made to suggest that you show approval of notions or actions that you do not really approve, but rather that you do not withhold your approval of those you do.

Although positive feedback generally helps a group to perform better and with less hostility than negative feedback, negative feedback can also be of the highest value. We know the folly of being surrounded by yes-men. If you make an incorrect statement, or are about to undertake a course of action that may end in disaster, you can profit by hearing the opposing evidence. The problem is to express the disagreement as related to the issue, not to the person; to indicate that your concern is with correcting an error, not in proving someone wrong. Not only words but vocal tones and facial expression are involved.

Negative feedback sometimes wrongly criticizes people for doing something they cannot help. You are not likely to be an attentive, productive member of a group discussion if you are worried or distracted by a personal problem. Nor should negative feedback relate to faults that are, in time, self-correcting. For example, as a teacher I never comment on signs of nervousness which are certain to disappear routinely with more speaking experience.

4 **Immediate or delayed**   Feedback is usually immediate, as when you react to direct questions, reflect attitudes by facial expression, or offer comment. Occasions arise, however, when you cannot say all you wish to say, or perhaps cannot express your opinion at all. At the close of the meeting you may wish to offer some feedback, but find no opportunity. A week later you may say to the proper person: "That was an excellent presentation; I approve the strong stand you took on the bond issue."

That the feedback is delayed makes it no less useful. Who among us has not received a delayed compliment, of any sort, and has not valued it? The one who tenders the compliment has had ample opportunity to reflect, so we prize it even more highly. If the compliment is a criticism, the same observation applies. Though most feedback is immediate, delayed feedback has its own worth.

5 **Intentional or nonintentional** Feedback is often spontaneous and free from specific *intent.* Sometimes, however, we specifically intend to encourage the sender by smiles, cheers, or comments, or to discourage the sender by other signals. Feedback may also be interpreted differently from what was intended if the receiver, for example, is unaware that what he feels as "interest" is being interpreted by the sender as "disinterest" or even as "disagreement."

Facial expression sometimes misleads. When *A*'s features are relaxed, he may appear to be more solemn than he really is. When *B*'s features are relaxed, she may appear to be happy when she is really neutral. *A* and *B* may therefore at times give unintentional feedback. Words or comments may be interpreted as indifference when they are meant to be tentative or noncommittal. You may be made aware that you are one of those whose feedback can be misinterpreted if people occasionally say to you, "You seem out of sorts today" (when you're not) or "Why are you so happy about that decision?" (when you're really dubious).

6 **Public, private** Most feedback is overt, observable, and public. Feedback may also be private and internal. You may carry on a dialog with yourself: reviewing, summarizing, appraising. You may feel proud of yourself for not having lost your temper, for perceiving the mood of others present, for defining an issue rather than attacking a personality, for acknowledging a compliment gracefully instead of belittling it, for taking a strong position, or for soothing ruffled tempers. You may arrive at an overall judgment about what you did, and note ways to improve.

A colleague of mine who makes scores of speeches each year invariably reflects about each performance, giving himself a grade of A, B, C, or F. On rare occasions, when he feels he has outdone himself, he records "Masterpiece."

This discussion is offered to introduce you to the importance of feedback. Further observations will be made in later chapters.[12]

---

[12]I have found these sources helpful: Barnlund, *Interpersonal Communication,* already cited; John W. Keltner, *Elements of Interpersonal Communication* (Belmont, Calif.: Wadsworth, 1973), chap. 5; C. David Mortenson, ed., *Basic Readings in Communication Theory* (New York: Harper & Row, 1973), chap. 10; "Feedback," by Theodore Clevenger, Jr. and Jack Matthews, reprinted from their *The Speech Communication Process* (Glenview, Ill.: Scott, Foresman, 1971); Gail E. Myers and Michele Tolela Myers, *The Dynamics of Human Communication* (New York: McGraw-Hill, 1973), pp. 86–90.

THE END All of the foregoing factors are considered in connection with a
RESULT desired *end result.* We are interested in the kinds of messages for
which the sender has a goal or purpose. If you seek to change the
behavior of your receivers, in what ways? Are there times that you
want to hold them in suspense, to make them laugh? Do you hope
that you will allay prejudices, change images, nourish egos, modify
beliefs, initiate action, get votes? Or if you do not succeed in
fulfilling your expectations, do you hope that next time you will
succeed, or that the next communicator will have a better chance of
success? Is part of your immediate goal the hope that receivers will
ask you questions after your formal presentation, or that, later, they
will discuss your ideas with others? Is it a part of your expectation
that newspapers or other media will carry a report of your speech, or
that years later someone will remember a part of what you said? Or
was your goal more modest: to get acquainted, to learn the ropes, to
share your ideas and experiences?

In summary, the preparation of a message is limited not simply
to a consideration of what to say and how to phrase it, but a review of
the entire communication process: the sender, the message, the
channel, the receiver; the interactions between sender and receiver
that we know as feedback; all assessed with reference to a specific
situation, with some goal or purpose, and in the framework of a
particular culture.

ASSIGN- 1 An assignment combining interpersonal speaking with group
MENTS AND discussion or speechmaking:
EXERCISES
    a Pair with a classmate and exchange experiences and obser-
vations with respect to such situations as greeting, dating,
getting acquainted, etc. Or: Explore differences in your
behavior in conversation, small group, academic lecture,
sermon, and other situations. Determine how you will each
report your observations to others, dividing the material so
your two reports will not overlap.

    b Join two or three other pairs, and report your observations to
the group. Or: Make a short talk of two or three minutes in
which you report your observations to the class.

2 Construct a model of a communication system, showing the
interactions among source, message, receiver, and other components as you visualize them. Parts I and II of Kenneth K. Sereno
and C. David Mortensen, *Foundations of Communication Theory*
(New York: Harper & Row, 1970), will be helpful. Or: Review the
model on page 19 and consider what additional arrows, areas,
verbal notations, etc., you would add.

3 An assignment combining interpersonal speaking, group discussion, and speaking to a group:

   a Select a partner. You and your partner are to discuss: "What events have given you the greatest satisfaction?" Excellence in sports or other activity? Achievements of a loved one? Travel? Winning some prize or recognition? *A* will interview *B,* asking questions that will give *B* opportunity to state his point of view; *B* will then interview *A.*

   b Your pair will then join with other pairs, so that the class is divided into three or four groups. Each member of the pair will then report the result of the interview with the other. After each report, the group will ask further questions or offer comment.

   c Each person will make an informal speech on "Two Moments to Remember: Some Second Thoughts." In the talk the speaker can review two events that seemed rewarding—comparing, contrasting, reflecting, or even changing and substituting—on the basis of his or her "second thoughts."

4 Comment on the description in this chapter of the operation of the speaker's thought processes while making a speech. Compare or contrast this description with the mental activity of a beginning speaker. Compare or contrast the speaker's thought processes with the mental activity that goes on during the performance of some other art or process.

Laima Druskis/EPA

3 Interpersonal Speaking

The perception of others ☐ The perception of self ☐ Self-disclosure ☐ Risk ☐ Trust ☐ Role ☐ Assertiveness ☐ Summary: The unfreezing process · ☐ Assignments and exercises

This chapter will describe basic concepts that apply to the problem of communication with others. Although these concepts are usually discussed in connection with interpersonal communication, they are also relevant to group discussion or to speech making.

THE PERCEPTION OF OTHERS

A *perception* is an individual's interpretation of something seen, heard, or otherwise received through the senses; perhaps also through intuitive or extrasensory cues. Your identification of a tree bearing a certain kind of leaves and nuts as an *oak* is a perception. A more highly trained observer might further identify it: *white oak, black oak,* or *red oak.* Perception grows out of experience and training and can therefore be developed and enhanced. What you perceive about a person yields data not only concerned with physique, sex, color of eyes, etc., but also with mood, disposition, approachability, alertness, etc. The other person, meanwhile, is perceiving things about you. Obviously the perceptions we have of others, the perceptions they have of us, and the perceptions we have of ourselves, are factors that enter into communication.

Some things happen before two people meet to begin a conversation. Each may already know details about the other's personality, attainments, or reputation. This advance information shapes the messages that ensue by suggesting questions to ask, topics to discuss or avoid, and also the mood and tone of the meeting. Much also happens before a speaker appears before an audience. Listeners know something of the speaker's reputation; the speaker in turn has inquired about them, to guide selection and arrangement of what is to be said.

Some things also happen when two people meet, before either says a word. Each studies the other for helpful clues: appearance of energy or vitality, attire, facial expression. Much also happens when a group assembles for a discussion, before anybody says anything. Suppose the group is a grievance committee. The initial perceptions that workers have of supervisors, and the other way around, affects the spoken messages that follow later.

Much of our perception of others comes from our attempt to *structure, classify,* or *describe* them. We are affected, for example, by *age* and *sex*. The other person is your peer; or older or younger than you are; or older or younger than you expected; or the behavior doesn't fit the age. If the other person is of your sex, you may be more at ease than if the other person is of the opposite sex. We are increasingly aware of differences in *culture*. You may find it difficult, at first, to converse with someone whose standard of living is vastly different from yours. You may have stereotyped conceptions of Indians, blacks, Chicanos, or Europeans that have strayed from reality.

Experience helps you sharpen your perceptions so that you are more poised—and more effective—in a wider variety of communicative situations.

We also perceive various qualities of temperament and personality. Recently I had separate conferences with three students for whom I had agreed to write letters of recommendation. One student talked continually; I had to wedge each of my questions into the stream of words. One was silent and reserved; I had to ask repeated questions to get the information I needed. The third supplied answers of a helpful length. I had the obvious perceptions that the first was anxious and perhaps overcompensating, the second was one of those many individuals who long ago fell into the habit of not taking a strong lead in any conversation, and the third was the most mature and best adjusted of the three. Of course one also makes judgments about the content as well as the package and each of the three was, for different reasons, a strong applicant. You have perceived in your own interpersonal communications these differences in personality.

We also perceive differences in vitality, exuberance, disposable energy. You perceive at once that the other person is worn, drawn, weary, before a word is spoken. You perceive qualities of aggressiveness or compliance—the person who usually disagrees or the person who usually agrees. After an interpersonal communication gets under way, you may become aware of religious or political affiliation, social prestige, economic status.[1]

Or you may not be sensitive enough to perceive these matters. You may be walking home with someone, after a party, and hear your companion say: "Did you notice how uptight A was?" Perhaps your companion perceived something you did not. One who perceived A's mood would interpret A's messages somewhat differently from someone who interpreted A's mood as entirely usual and normal. In fact, one who wanted to ask a substantial favor of A would conclude, "This is not the proper moment; A is distracted, anxious; I will wait until A is more relaxed." Speakers at times also have deficiencies of perception about the attitude of their listeners, failing to realize that their material is not so clear as it should be, or even that they have far exceeded the agreed-upon time limit.

To improve your ability to communicate in a wide variety of situations, you may need to begin to look for cues and clues that heretofore you have overlooked.

---

[1]For discussion of these and other notions, see Michael Argyle, "The Meeting of Personalities," in *The Psychology of Interpersonal Behavior* (Harmondsworth, England: Penguin, 1967), pp. 46–67. Argyle mentions, for example, such characteristics as rate or tempo of talking, dominance, intimacy, emotional tone. Cited in C. David Mortensen, *Basic Readings in Communication Theory* (New York: Harper & Row, 1973), pp. 243–263.

THE PERCEPTION OF SELF We need to grow not only in our perceptions of others, but in our perceptions of self. On all sides we hear about "identity," "self-image," "self-concept." If you gain a clear view of your strong points and your weak points, you can better adjust yourself to a wide variety of communication situations than if you either overestimate or underestimate your capacity and potential.

A well-known method of viewing yourself is to consider your range of interests according to the four major headings: *work, play, love, worship.* If all are equally strong in your life, you could represent them in a diagram like the following:

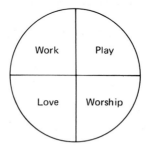

If, however, you drew a diagram to represent your own distribution of interests, it might look like this:

You spend much time at play (games, sports); almost as much at work (studies, waiting tables); your love life (friends, home and family) commands less of your time; your worship (religion, spiritual aspects) a moderate amount. In the circle below, you may apportion these as they actually are in your own life:

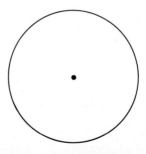

Each of these diagrams illustrates a different set of values—and a different self-concept—from the others. Each diagram also suggests the different areas from which you draw ideas for conversing or discussing. If your play-quadrant is dominant, you probably find yourself talking about sports or other forms of entertainment a good share of the time. If your work-quadrant is dominant, you probably talk frequently about your job, your studies. You may, or may not, elect to broaden your field of conversational interests as you find yourself exposed to all kinds of opinions and judgments in this course, in other courses, and in various campus activities.

Now suppose you compare and contrast *your view of yourself* with *what others may think of you.* You have certain perceptions regarding yourself; do these correspond with the perceptions of others? In this connection, the "Johari Window" provides a useful insight.[2] This model was devised by Joseph Luft and Harry Ingham, named after their first names, and pronounced "Joe-harry." They drew a window with two panes, like this:

Information
known to
others

Information
not known
to others

---

[2]Reprinted from Joseph Luft, *Group Processes: An Introduction to Group Dynamics,* by permission of Mayfield Publishing Co. (Palo Alto: 1970), p. 11. See Chapter 3, "The Johari Window: A Graphic Model of Awareness in Interpersonal Relations." The concept is further discussed in Luft's *Of Human Communication* (Palo Alto: Mayfield Publishing Co., 1969).

This diagram prods you to ask two immensely relevant questions: "What information (about me) is known to others?" and "What information (about me) is not known to others?" This approach is helpful in a variety of communication situations: "*Would my message on Subject X be more persuasive if the receiver knew A, B, and C about me—which now he does not know?*"

The Johari Window would be useful if it went no further, but its originators drew a vertical line so that the diagram looked like this:

	Information known to self	Information not known to self
Information known to others	(1) Open	(2) Blind
Information not known to others	(3) Hidden	(4) Unknown

Looking at Quadrant 1, "Open," you may conclude that there is information about you that you know, and that others know. This information would be basic to your self-concept, and basic to much of your communication.

Quadrant 2, however, suggests that you are communicating something to others without realizing it. This something may be good or bad. Perhaps you have more friends, or better friends, than you realize. After all, people do not go around making daily pronouncements of the status of their friendship, so you have to rely on subtle indications. Perhaps you have distracting mannerisms that make it more difficult for you to make a good first impression. For example, what you see in yourself as *strong, quiet reserve* may, because of facial or vocal habits, strike others as *uncertain and unsure*.

Quadrant 3, "Hidden," suggests that you should tell more about yourself than you are in the habit of telling. This kind of information may be helpful to your message.

Quadrant 4 is shaded because it represents the Great Unknown about you. This area is Undeveloped Potential, Unfulfilled Talent. Everybody, including you, would give a great deal to know what lies behind this darkened pane. Here is where a good teacher helps: "Why don't you try out for the debate team?" Or a good friend: "Why don't you run for the council?" Once Sir Winston Churchill sat down before a blank canvas, holding palette and brushes. He could not have known what talent he had, or whether he had any. Finally he summoned his courage and splashed on a daub of paint, and eventually developed a distinctive reputation as an artist. Once William Jennings Bryan left home to give a routine campaign speech. He found himself speaking with unexpected eloquence; his listeners were moved and stirred. Later he said to his young wife: "Mary, tonight I discovered I had the power of public speaking." Long ago, Barbara Jordan, later congresswoman from Texas, was unexpectedly called on when the scheduled speaker did not appear. She was amazed at the attentiveness with which she was heard.

The Johari Window can be applied to a number of communicative situations. Luft suggests its application to group discussion: what is known to the group, what is not known to the group, what is known to others, what is not known to others. Or it may be applied to the employee-supervisor relationship, or to parent and child, or to student and professor.[3] Its application to speech making deserves fuller exploration. We are always deeply concerned about what reasons, examples, appeals, etc. should go into a speech. We should also ask ourselves, "What should I tell them about me—so they will see why I chose this topic, why I am interested in it, or what special sources of information I have access to?" Or: "Is there some field of interest, which now I do not suspect, for which I might develop a real talent to talk about?" Many athletes have developed a talent for broadcasting which they did not suspect they had. Many women, thrust by a new job into a male environment, have become able to take part in the office conversation about athletics or the stock market.

Questions to start with, therefore, are: "Do I have the same view of myself that others have of me? Do I have qualities that I myself am not aware of? Can these be developed so that I can communicate

---

[3] Luft, *Group Processes*, pp. 17 ff.

more effectively?" An axiom of communication is: "No matter how much one may try, one cannot *not* communicate.[4]

If you say to yourself, "This person (or this group) will not be interested in my opinion," you may remain shy and silent. Your opinion, however, may carry more weight than you suspect. You may also note that some opinions that are expressed seem no wiser than the one you suppressed. If you are one of the quieter participants, you may be interested in learning that some evidence suggests that even people with high self-esteem contribute fewer than half of their thoughts or questions to class discussion.[5]

In the process of being educated we are exposed to various systems of appraisal and reward that help shape individual self-concept. One who receives high grades and gracious compliments will feel confident in those areas. If a man repeatedly hears that he is good-looking, he will take pride in his appearance. If a girl is told by her dates that she is an excellent dancer, she will interest herself in learning the new steps. Yet the situation must not be oversimplified. One teenager hearing the comment, "You will never be able to go to college," may placidly accept the verdict. Another may be all the more determined.

Years ago in another book I reported the case of a girl, plain-looking and listless; her classmates and I noted her first signs of improvement in the speech class. We commented encouragingly, and she gradually developed a talent that we had barely suspected was there. John W. Kinch reports an incident in which five male members of a seminar in social psychology wondered whether they would be able to alter the self-concept of the one woman in the group, who was ordinary-looking. The males conspired to treat her as if she were the best-looking woman on campus. The story proceeds:

> They drew lots to see who would be the first to date her. The loser, under the pressure of the others, asked her to go out. Although he found the situation quite unpleasant, he was a good actor . . . and got through the evening. . . . It was now the second man's turn and so it went. . . . In a matter of a few weeks the results began to show.

Before long, the story continues, the woman was taking more care with her personal appearance, even going to the beauty parlor to have her hair styled. By the time the last man in the conspiracy asked her

---

[4]Paul Watzlawick, Janet Helmick Beavin, and Don D. Jackson, *Pragmatics of Human Communication* (New York: Norton, 1967), p. 49.
[5]Thomas L. Morrison and M. Duane Thomas, "Self-Esteem and Classroom Participation," *Journal of Educational Research,* 68 (July–August 1975): 377.

for a date, he was informed that she was pretty well booked for some time in the future.[6]

Professor Kinch does not vouch for the absolute accuracy of this incident, but almost any student could attest to its plausibility. Often we do not "discover ourselves" until later in life; a situation gives us a chance to shine, and someone takes notice; and from then on our self-concept is enhanced. Such an experience shows that our self-concept is altered by association with others.

The Tennessee self-concept scale, one often used, analyzes the notion of self-concept into five basic items:[7]

1 physical self
2 moral-ethical self
3 personal self
4 family self
5 social self

Each term suggests a way of looking at yourself. William H. Fitts, who devised the scale, argues that the person who has a

> consistent, positive, and realistic self-concept will generally behave in healthy, confident, constructive, and effective ways. Such persons are more secure, confident, and self-respecting; they have less to prove to others; they are less threatened by difficult tasks and situations; they relate to and work with others more comfortably and effectively, and their perceptions of the world are less likely to be distorted.[8]

One may also think of specific dimensions of the self: vocational dimension, sports dimension, religious dimension, academic dimension, and other areas in which an objective or semiobjective appraisal may be made, as was suggested earlier in the chapter. You may find it helpful to enter into a mutual appraisal with someone who knows you. Long ago it was suggested that some people are good at knowing themselves, others at understanding their friends, and still others at judging strangers. You may perceive a woman in your class as quiet and reserved; then, as she makes helpful comments about classroom exercises, you perceive her as a friendly and alert listener whose judgments are valuable; then, when she makes a talk about her summer job as an assistant buyer in a large department

[6]"A Formalized Theory of the Self-Concept," *American Journal of Sociology,* 68 (January 1963): 481–483.

[7]William H. Fitts, *Manual: Tennessee Self-Concept Scale* (Nashville, Tenn.: Counselor Recordings and Tests, 1965).

[8]"The Self-Concept and Performance," *Research Monograph No. 5* (Nashville, Tenn.: The Dede Wallace Center, 1972), p. 4.

store, you perceive her as an experienced, professional, business-woman.

Right now our interest in self-concept is not only as a general notion about human behavior, but particularly as it applies to communication. Make a list of communication skills, such as:

transacting business over the telephone
telling a funny story
entertaining children
canvassing door-to-door
persuading a parent
asking a favor
explaining an oversight

and add others that come within your own experience. Rank each skill on a 1 to 5 scale: 1 representing a situation that you think you handle poorly; 2, worse than average; 3, average; 4, better than average; 5, a situation that you think you handle well. Your self-concept may undergo changes as you participate in communication activities both inside the classroom and elsewhere, sharing comments and criticisms with instructor and classmates.

SELF-DISCLOSURE Early in his career as a professional psychologist, Jourard developed the notion of self-disclosure and devised a questionnaire to explore the topics that people seek to learn about one another. They have to do with six content areas:

1 attitudes and opinions, such as religion, politics, racial integration, sexual morality
2 tastes and interests, such as music or reading
3 work or studies: what I find boring or pleasant
4 money
5 personality: things that make me ashamed, furious, depressed, or proud
6 body: what I like about my appearance; my illnesses or health

Jourard's point of view is that among the characteristics that indicate a healthy personality is the ability to make oneself fully known to at least one other significant human being. He also proposes that low disclosure may reflect an inability to grow as a person.[9]

---

[9]*The Transparent Self*, 2d ed., pp. 32, 213–216. Copyright 1971 by Litton Educational Pub. Co., Inc. Reprinted by permission of D. Van Nostrand Inc.

Self-disclosure is the revealing of information about yourself to someone else. When two people meet for the first time as complete strangers, neither knows anything about the other. The initial impressions that come from appearance, facial expression, movement, and gesture, may or may not encourage the relationship to develop. The first words and phrases that are exchanged may or may not be encouraging. Various levels of self-disclosure may be attained:[10]

1 **Low level**   Comments about the weather or the immediate surroundings; simple inquiries such as "Where do you live?" "How long have you been here?" "What is your field of work?"
2 **Middle level**   Ideas, events, current happenings. At this level some of your own values and judgments begin to appear.
3 **Peak level**   (This term is suggested by Maslow; see p. 373.) Intimate facts about yourself: problems, successes, shortcomings.

The low level of communication is highly important if a relationship is to get started. The casual acquaintances or strangers one meets fall into these groups:

Those who drown the effort to get a conversation started with silences, monosyllables, or derogatory comment
Those who continue a conversation in a restrained or measured manner so that the relationship does not grow
Those who supply additional details or extend their comments so that new topics are opened up

To a question like "Where do you live?" an answer like "Illinois" helps only a trifle compared with "I lived in Springfield until I was twelve, then my father got a position in Chicago with U.S. Steel, and I finished high school there." The second answer discloses additional details, and also indicates an interest in furthering the conversation.

Talk at the middle level gives each participant opportunity to self-disclose meaningful and revealing information on issues that are broader than the casual details of your own existence. The extent to which you take a position depends upon how much you are willing to disclose at this stage of the relationship. You may hold back for fear of offending the other person; or you may start moderately and strengthen your position as the discussion continues. Self-disclosure at this level occurs in good writing and good speaking. The receiver

---

[10]This classification is suggested by John Powell, *Why I Am Afraid to Tell You Who I Am* (Chicago: Argus Communications, 1969). Powell describes five levels of conversation.

wants to know how you, personally, think and feel about the topic. As you become more confident of yourself as a communicator to other people, you will probably be less hesitant to take a stand.

In connection with the peak level, we often use the term *sharing*. We share our experiences or our inner thoughts. A famous tennis player tells about her abortion, revealing her reasons and also her feelings; a prominent newscaster comments on his divorce. These facts were not generally known; the tennis player and the newscaster probably wished to share an intimate personal experience with the view of reaching others who faced similar problems. A favorite question of reporters is, "How did you feel when . . ." as in "How did you feel when you learned that your son was safe?" or "What went through your mind when you sank that sixty-nine-foot match-winning putt?" Many a speaker, when preparing a speech, has pondered a question such as "Shall I tell them about the doubts I had before I finally decided to support the Equal Rights Amendment?" "Shall I confess that, although frankly the future looks cloudy at this point, I believe this plan has the best chance of succeeding of all those now before us?"

Your present friendships probably had humble beginnings like those described under "low level." "I will tell you a little about me, and in return I hope you will tell me a little about you. If this exchange is promising, we will self-disclose further." You are not likely to begin a conversation with a complete stranger by declaring, "I am absolutely opposed to capital punishment under all circumstances." Hold your heavy artillery for a few minutes.

The teacher utilizes self-disclosure. The routine drill on French vocabulary may be interrupted for a personal narrative about an incident in Paris. The disclosure enables the students to glimpse the teacher in a personal as well as a professional framework. One of the factors appearing on most teacher-evaluation scorecards is "warmth, rapport, sharing atmosphere." These items, contrasting sharply with "mastery of subject" or "discipline and control," indicate that a certain amount of self-disclosure by the instructor has taken place.

Self-disclosure requires judgment, sensitivity, and good taste. It may offend. Suggested guidelines are:

1 **Risk**   Other persons may not react to your disclosure as you anticipated. They may not be willing to disclose in return.
2 **Extent**   Determine the extent to which you want to self-disclose. Feel your way by making small disclosures before you make extensive disclosures. Be guided at each step by the verbal and nonverbal responses that are elicited.

3   **Feedback**   Both the verbal and the nonverbal responses elicited by your self-disclosure are meaningful. You may get a green light, an orange light, a red light—or no light at all.

4   **Timing**   A direct question invites self-disclosure. An emergency excuses or justifies it. Other situations may say "This is a good time to self-disclose" or "This is not a good time."

5   **Need to know**   In special situations, certain individuals need to know more about us than we usually disclose. Physicians need to know personal, even intimate, details in order to arrive at a diagnosis. Failure to self-disclose is critical. Bankers need financial details in order to make a loan. Peace officers and tax officials may seek private or personal information. If we are less than candid, the result may be to our disadvantage.

6   **Culture**   The storehouse of past experiences may warrant, or forbid, self-disclosure. Election campaigns, courtroom trials, religious revivals, business practices, neighborhood relations, and dating practices offer clues that encourage or discourage self-disclosure.

You do not need to bare your soul to every listener you meet. Each of Jourard's six content areas may, in some situations, prove to be a bear trap. Take, for example, *work or studies;* we can be bored by individuals so wrapped up in their work that they can talk of nothing else, even though ordinarily we are interested in what others do. Better keep away from an author in the middle of writing a book. Talk about *money* (wealth, possessions, luxuries), in a way that suggests it is all-important, may offend. *Body* (for example, details of bodily functions or unusual concern about appearance) may be unwelcome talk. One who is dieting or has stopped smoking or drinking is a conversational hazard. One authority writes about the "ideal sphere" that surrounds every human being: "This sphere cannot be penetrated, unless the personality value of the individual is thereby destroyed."[11]

The most useful contribution of this section is to alert you to the concept of self-disclosure, along with guidelines. You do not want to be overly confessive or overly reticent. Some things you should not inquire into; some things you should be slow to reveal. In between is a theory and a practice with which you will feel comfortable. Most people, no doubt, can usefully reveal more than they do.

The concept of self-disclosure, moreover, applies not only to

---

[11]Paul C. Cozby, "Self-Disclosure: A Literature Review," *Psychological Bulletin,* 79 (February 1963): 88.

interpersonal but to small group and speech-making situations. In a speech you may sometimes tell listeners things about yourself that they did not know, and probably could not find out, in a way that reveals your deeper, human qualities.

RISK Some *risk* or hazard is involved in deciding to make any kind of utterance. You may ask a stranger for directions without running much risk that he will reply rudely or sarcastically, since a deeply imbedded part of human culture is the willingness to help the lost stranger. In preparing a speech, you may ponder the risk you take in relating an incident: will the listeners find it as humorous, exciting, or interesting as you believe it to be?

If you enter an argument, however, you may be accepting an even greater degree of risk. If you offer a judgment or opinion you face the possibility that it might be shot down. Although argument is person-risking, it is also person-making. One who accepts the risks implicit in an attitude of restrained partisanship both bestows "personhood" on his opponent and gains "personhood" for himself. Douglas Ehninger, who states this position in an award-winning article, continues by stating that this situation is one in which the opponent is no longer regarded as an "object" to be manipulated, but is endowed with those qualities of "freedom" and "responsibility" that change him into a "person."[12]

Another way of looking at this concept is to say that one's ego is involved. The ego functions to protect the individual and to maintain the position that he or she perceives himself or herself as holding within the social environment. One's ego has been augmented or diminished since birth by parents and by peers. It has also had to sustain itself against the assaults of those who tried to injure it. It helps us cope with frustrations, worry, and anxiety; teaches us to learn from our errors; and helps us to adjust to our listeners (but not to let them sway us too readily). We are receptive to stimuli that nourish our ego and move away from, or make other adjustment to, those that bruise it.

Although the concept of risk is a useful one, we should not overemphasize it. Many communication situations not only involve little risk but are in fact eagerly welcomed. We are pleased to be consulted or recognized. Between sender and receiver is often a feeling of sympathy and understanding. Invariably the sender's minor faults do not loom so large to the receiver as to the sender. On

---

[12]*Speech Monographs*, 37 (June 1970): 109–110.

INTRAPERSONAL AND INTERPERSONAL EXERCISES

1   Construct a list of *intrapersonal* situations that you commonly confront. For example:

   a   persuading yourself to begin a difficult task
      (Do you find yourself postponing a task more than you should? And when you finally get started on it, do you find it more stimulating than you expected?)

   b   planning a schedule for an eventful week
      (Do you frequently, or infrequently, schedule a busy week? Do any of your friends prepare schedules or "flow charts"?)

   c   preparing mentally for an important conversation or interview
      (Do you review arguments, reasons, approaches? Or when an important examination is coming up, do you anticipate possible questions, and outline answers?)

   d   (Add others.)

   Discuss one or more of these with a classmate.

2   Construct a list of *interpersonal* situations that you commonly confront, particularly those that you find awkward. For example:

   a   initiating a conversation with a stranger or with someone you know slightly

   b   extending condolences

   c   expressing your appreciation, or accepting praise

   d   asking, accepting, or refusing in a dating situation

   e   asking a favor

   Discuss one or more of these with a classmate. Work out "things to say" in each situation. For example if someone admires your jacket, don't say, "Oh, that's an old thing I have had for years." Such a statement downgrades your admirer's judgment. Respond with a statement that shows you appreciate and value your admirer's taste and discrimination. In extending condolences, it is comforting to the bereaved person to hear a comment about him or her: "I know you were very close to your father" or "You meant so much to him" or "All of you did everything you possibly could for him."

3   **a**   Join other pairs and exchange experiences. Or:

   b   Make a short talk to the class about your own experiences.

the contrary, as listeners we tend to be kindly and helpful—willing to enjoy the sender's humor, participate in his or her enthusiasm, and in general wish that she or he does well. Often a speaker speaks in our behalf, giving words to our beliefs, experiences, aspirations, and hopes. This possibility lessens the degree of risk.

TRUST   Closely related to risk is the notion of *trust;* we take chances because we have confidence in the responses of others. Historically, trust goes back to the primitive human creatures who lived at Olduvai Gorge and their ancient forebears. No cooperative endeavor, such as the vital activities of hunting and gathering, could have succeeded without trust. In the face of danger, every human being needed to feel that other members of the group would do what they said they would.

The wheels of business would come to a dead stop if human beings could no longer trust each other's promises and commitments. Millions of dollars change hands at the nation's stock, bond, and commodity markets at the nod of a head. In the social world, a girl and a guy agree to a dinner-movie date, and each makes extensive plans, fully trusting that the other will keep the agreement. If someone breaks an agreement, our culture calls for explanations, expressions of regret, appeasements, and even damages. We expect children to acquire habits of trustworthiness at an early age. If the messages of adult men and women cannot be trusted, whether they speak as private citizens or as public officials, we perceive them to have a grave flaw in their character.

In 1957 an experiment to study trust was devised by Luce and Raiffa, becoming famous as the Prisoners' Dilemma. It involves two suspects believed to have committed a major offense, though the District Attorney does not have as much evidence as he would like. He offers them these choices:

1 If one confesses and the other does not, the confessor will be treated leniently and the other will get the book thrown at him.

2 If both confess, the District Attorney will recommend something less than the maximum sentence.

3 If neither confesses, the District Attorney will book them on a minor, trumped-up charge, such as petty larceny.

As the two prisoners sit in their separate cells, each wonders which choice the other will make. Both know the DA does not have adequate evidence to convict them of a major crime; both know that he can convict them on a minor charge. If *A* has maximum trust in *B,* he will make one choice; if he has minimum trust in *B,* he will make another.[13] Psychologist Morton Deutsch, using an adaptation of the Prisoners' Dilemma and other games, has conducted research on trust since 1958, and the literature has now become extensive.

The outcome of interpersonal communication obviously depends on the opinion that each participant has of the other. Two other concepts, somewhat related to trust, may be discussed at this point. If *A* feels that she is going to succeed in a speech-making venture, or is assured by *B* and others that she is going to succeed, she is more likely to do so than if she and others believe she is certain to fail. The term *self-fulfilling prophecy* has long been used to describe this behavior. If you believe you have a good chance to accomplish a goal or solve a problem before you attempt it, you are more likely to do so than if you believe you are likely to fail. A *self-defeating prophecy*—a feeling that your preparation is inadequate, that your material is not interesting or relevant—makes success more difficult.[14] In the language of the old saying, "Never let a negative thought cross your mind."

ROLE We like not simply to describe communicative behavior, but to affix a name to it; hence *role* and *role playing.* Psychologist William James decades ago observed that we play as many different social roles as there are distinct groups of persons about whose opinion we care. Sociologist George Herbert Mead forty years ago wrote of man as a role-taking animal. You carry with you a set of behaviors to exhibit when you assume the role of son or daughter, candidate for office, worker on the job, or communicant in church. Within certain boundaries these behaviors are governed by the culture in which you operate. Some things you cannot say and still fill the role of "candidate" or "worker" or "communicant."

Remove communication from the concept of role, and very little remains. "Candidate" involves "voter" and the talk, along with the smiles, frowns, and gestures, that takes place between them. "Son" or "daughter" involves "parent," and the ideas and feelings that they exchange. Child and parent may be having an informal, merry conversation; the telephone rings and one of them takes the call; the talk becomes solemn and the person seems changed because of a new role assumed that reflects an adjustment to the individual on the

---

[13]R. D. Luce and H. Raiffa, *Games and Decisions: Introduction and Critical Survey* (New York: Wiley, 1957), p. 95.

[14]For a helpful discussion of this and related theories, see W. Peter Archibold, "Alternative Explanations for Self-Fulfilling Prophecy," *Psychological Bulletin,* 81 (January 1974): 74–84.

other end of the line. Role is often affected by areas: stewardesses relax and act more casually among themselves, in the galley, or in the rear of the plane, after their official duties have been performed. Waiters act differently in the kitchen, among the cooks and other employees, than when they are seeing customers.[15]

Some of these facets of role are suggested in the following diagram.[16]

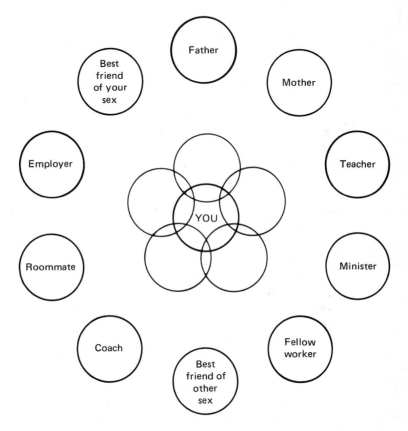

The inner circle represents the basic "You." The circles intersecting it represent a few of the different roles you are called upon to act. The outer circles represent a selection of the people who bring about a change in your role.

---

[15]See Erving Goffman, *The Presentation of Self in Every Day Life* (Garden City: Doubleday, 1959), chap. 3, "Regions and Region Behavior." See also Dean C. Barnlund, *Interpersonal Communication: Survey and Studies* (Boston: Houghton Mifflin, 1968), pp. 160–161.

[16]Adapted from Alfred R. Lindesmith and Anselm L. Strauss, *Social Psychology, 3d ed.* (New York: Holt, 1968), p. 264.

In our culture these roles allow both for agreement and disagreement. Oriental culture has much less provision for disagreement. And among the Tasadays, that pocket of isolated Stone Age people recently discovered deep in the jungles of the Philippines, so little argument or dispute goes on that there is not believed even to be a word for it.

In communication situations one is likely to reflect, "What expectations will I have to meet?" If I am a newcomer in a group of newcomers, I may not have to meet any external pressure whatever. No one knows me; hence no one will expect anything from me. I can converse with others, or not, as I like. If, however, I am known to possess a certain kind of expertise, I have a role to live up to. Perhaps I have a reputation for being well informed, and I do not want to tarnish that reputation. Besides the usual roles mentioned above, one may have a collection of more specialized roles—of athlete, of art major, of humorist, of political worker. When I plan a message, I may cast myself in one or more of my specialized roles.

You can visualize yourself in similar situations. In your differing roles, which is the *real* you? Undoubtedly it is a composite of your most usual roles, and that is why it seems proper in the diagram to represent the *you* at the center as a composite of circles.

ASSERTIVE-NESS

Assertive training, first developed as a form of behavioral therapy in the late 1940s, long lay dormant as a concept except in professional circles. In the last few years, however, it has received widespread attention because of the publication of half a dozen books aimed at lay readers. Still more recently it has appeared as a topic of study in speech communication journals and classrooms.[17]

You may recall situations in which you did not stand up for your own proper rights and concerns, or failed to give someone your support when he or she needed it, or allowed an erroneous and therefore perhaps damaging statement to go uncorrected, or an obvious prejudice to go unchallenged because you hesitated to say that you, for one, believed something different, or failed to express your appreciation for the talents or generosity or thoughtfulness of others. You may therefore say to yourself, "Perhaps if I developed more of this quality of assertiveness I would be more effective in my

---

[17]In preparing this section I have found helpful: Barbara Bate's "Assertive Speaking: An Approach to Communication Education for the Future," *Communication Education,* 25 (January 1976): 53–59; John P. Galassi, James S. DeLo, Merna D. Galassi, and Sheila Bastien's "The College Self-Expression Scale: A Measure of Assertiveness," *Behavior Therapy,* 5 (March 1974): 165–171. Both articles also include useful references.

communication." In certain situations you may reflect that you should not only have been mildly assertive, but even bold, forthright, and aggressive.

Or you may recall situations in which, on reflection, you were overly assertive or aggressive. You may decide that you talk so much that others are denied an opportunity to state their points of view. You may ask yourself, "When was the last time I commended someone for an achievement or expressed my appreciation for a courtesy?"

Assertiveness may therefore be defined as behavior in which you stand up for your own proper rights and concerns, or for those of someone else, in a way that respects the rights and concerns of others.[18] Four types of behavior may be considered:

1 **Acquiescence** When another person says something with which you disagree or which you disapprove—or does something that you do not like—you may say or do nothing. If the matter is trivial, or if little would be gained by comment or discussion, your acquiescing may be the proper response.

2 **Assertiveness (praising, commending)** If a friend wins an award or other recognition, or extends you a courtesy, or commends you for an achievement, mere acquiescence is inappropriate. You need to go further and assert yourself by expressing your appreciation in a way that will make the person who commended you pleased that he or she made the effort to do so.

3 **Assertiveness (disagreeing, disapproving)** At times each of us has a responsibility to disapprove as well as to approve. If you are a member of a group that is about to take action on the basis of wrong information or poor judgment, and you have accurate information or a better proposal, you should state your point of view even though it is counter to something already said. You may be justified in expressing your feelings of disagreement or even of dissatisfaction.

4 **Aggressiveness, intimidation** You may find yourself in a situation where niceties are overruled by stronger considerations. Faced with the threats of a burglar, rapist, or obnoxious and offensive person, you may be aggressive or intimidating because something in the situation tells you that this kind of behavior will be effective. In the event of a panic, you may be the one who needs to take charge and issue directions.[19]

---

[18]Adapted from R. E. Alberti and M. L. Emmons, *Your Perfect Right: A Guide to Assertive Behavior* (San Luis Obispo, Calif.: Impact Press, 1970), cited in Galassi et al., p. 165.

[19]This classification is adapted from Bate's *Assertive Speaking,* citing the Seattle NOW booklet, *Assert Your Self,* p. 54, and Galassi et al., p. 168.

The current advice in some circles, however, to be intimidating for its own sake—to gain a strictly personal advantage—can be misleading. Many people are perceptive enough to see through selfish maneuvers. Moreover, the fact that techniques of intimidation are being widely discussed will help people to recognize them. A syndicated columnist amusingly describes what happens when somebody who has read *Winning Through Intimidation* sits next to someone at a party who has just finished *Power: How to Get It, How to Use It.*[20]

You may want to observe interpersonal speaking in order to note varying degrees of acquiescent-assertive-aggressive behavior. Meanwhile, here are general suggestions:

1 **Variety** Different situations call for different responses. If you identify an area in which you lack experience, you may give it special attention.

Example 1: A classmate gives an interesting speech. You may say simply, "That was great," or be even more appreciative: "That's the best speech you've given yet" or "That's one of the best we've heard all term." You may add: "You have a spontaneous way of adapting to the situation."

Example 2: The person who sits behind you at the game uses offensive language. You may begin a conversation by saying, "Let's make a deal. If you'll limit yourself to three damns a half, I'll turn my transistor down nice and low. . . ."

Variety especially becomes important when we consider that each of us is involved in merchant-customer, landlord-tenant, teacher-student, parent-child, public official–citizen, majority group–minority group relationships.

2 **Habit** This point is similar to (1) but stated differently. You may have fallen into the habit of acquiescing in almost all situations, or behaving aggressively in almost all situations, when you should seek experience in making a wider variety of responses.

3 **Maturity** Perhaps the greatest single talent we can develop is maturity. In order to hold responsible positions we must convince others of our maturity. We must be able to stand up for ourselves and for others in a mature way. We can be firm and still reflect consideration for others.

Example: Two candidates are seeking office. One trait certain to be reviewed by voters is: "Which candidate will best be able to

---

[20]Gerald Nachman, "Squeak Up!" *Newsweek,* 87 (April 5, 1976): 13.

lead us?" And: "Which candidate will represent our group most effectively in persuading others to help us achieve our goals and develop our programs?" The successful candidate will likely be the one who reflects his maturity in using all the techniques we have described.

4   Kinds of situations   As a guide to help you study assertiveness, consider such situations as:

You are interrupted in a conversation or discussion.

You are in a well-formed line to get a ticket, and tickets are scarce. Someone pushes in ahead of you.

You really do not want to buy a ticket to the Boy Scout circus even though the cause is a good one and you are being approached by a friend.

You hate to ask directions.

When you leave the party, all you can think of to say to the host and hostess is, "Had a nice time."

You seldom volunteer in class even though you know the answer.

Other situations appear in the assignments at the end of this chapter.

SUMMARY: THE UNFREEZING PROCESS   Some behavioral scientists believe that the field of interpersonal communication is so complex that a student cannot be taught all he or she needs to know in order to behave competently in situations to be faced. Chris Argyris, often cited in this area, uses the helpful phrasing that "much unfreezing is usually required."[21] Even so, most teachers have found that one can be taught a great deal of what needs to be known. So as President Kennedy said on his inauguration day, "All this will not be finished in the first 100 days. . . . But let us begin."

This chapter has indicated basic ideas:

1   Perception   We need not only to look at people and hear their voices, but to *perceive* and *interpret* what our senses (or our intuition) tell us. By the same token, other people perceive our meanings, attitudes, and feelings.

2   Self-concept   We need to generate a realistic appraisal of our-

---

[21]"The nature of competence-acquisition activities and their relationship to therapy," in Warren G. Bemis et al., eds., *Interpersonal Dynamics: Essays and Readings on Human Interaction*, 3d ed. (Homewood, Ill.: Dorsey, 1973), p. 547.

selves. Something is certainly lost when we underestimate either our capabilities or our potential. We can make an inventory of ourselves, either under "love, play, work, worship," or more specific, detailed categories. Through a concept such as the Johari Window we can think of ourselves in relation to what others think of us. A categorizing system like the Tennessee Scale helps us to review physical self, moral-ethical self, personal self, family self, social self, and thus identify our strong points.

3 **Self-disclosure** Following Jourard, we can be more or less disclosing to others about our attitudes and opinions, tastes and interests, work or studies, money, personality, and body. We can open a conversation at a low level, moving into, as situations warrant, middle level or peak level.

4 **Trust** The basic attitude that we have toward people in general guides us in shaping our messages. If we trust others and believe that their motives are good, we will use different language than if we believe most people are not to be trusted. Experience in communication situations helps us to develop a realistic attitude.

5 **Role** The concept of role also helps us understand the communication process. In one situation you are sonlike or daughterlike; in another clerklike or customerlike; in still another friendlike or candidatelike. We learn to interpret messages in the context of the roles that are being played. Is the salesperson making this statement primarily to get the sale? or is he or she giving me objective facts so that I can make up my own mind?

You will observe illustrations of these concepts, and ways of applying them, not only in interpersonal speaking, but also in group discussion and in formal and informal speech-making situations.

ASSIGN-MENTS AND EXERCISES

1 Divide the class into pairs. One person will ask the questions below, the other person reacting. The second person will then ask the questions of the first person:
   a What things make you the happiest?
   b What do you consider to be your greatest strengths?
   c What person would you like to emulate?
   d In what ways do you think you have grown and developed in recent years?
   e If you could have your choice of jobs, what would you choose?

2 After completing the foregoing interview, or some equivalent, answer the following questions about your partner:
   a Could he (she) be a friend of mine?
   b Would it be difficult to meet and talk with him (her)?

   c Would he (she) fit into my circle of friends?

   d Could we ever establish a personal relationship with each other?

   e Do I think he (she) is quite handsome (pretty)?

   f Is he (she) very sexy looking?

   g Do I find him (her) very attractive physically?

   h Do I dislike the way he (she) looks?

   i Have I confidence in his (her) ability to get the job done?

   j If I wanted things done, could I probably depend on him (her)?

   k Could I get anything accomplished with him (her)?

   l Would he (she) be a poor problem solver?[22]

3 Compare and contrast the first eight items on the foregoing list (a–h) with the last four (i–l) from the point of view of communication. To what extent does skill in communication help one reach a decision on each item?

4 Note that your reactions to the items represent your *perceptions* of the other person. Select two or three items on which you are most sure of your perceptions, and describe the cues or clues you used to arrive at your conclusion.

5 Review the items on either or both of the above lists from the point of view of *risk*.

6 Discuss *trust* from the point of view of age differences, sex differences, big city versus small town differences, nationality or other cultural differences. Are we becoming more or less trusting?

7 Discuss *role* as you observe it in your family, school, or business experience.

8 Apply the concepts of *risk, trust,* and *role* to public speaking, either to your public speaking experiences or to speeches you have heard.

9 An assignment combining interpersonal speaking, group discussion, and speaking to a group:

   a As pairs, work through Exercise 1, and read Exercises 2 and 3, above.

   b Your pair will then join other pairs, so that the class is divided into three or four groups. Select a leader. The leader will then invite discussion on such questions as: "How do we know whether we would likely be friends with someone we have met only briefly?" "How do we determine whether someone we have conversed with briefly will accept responsibility to do an assigned task?" Recall *spe-*

---

[22]Adapted from, James C. McCroskey and Thomas A. McCain, "The Measurement of Interpersonal Attraction," *Speech Monographs,* 41 (August 1974): 261–266.

cific words, spoken vocal tones, or gestures that helped you arrive at your judgment.

c Each person will make an informal talk on his choice of the following:

(1) What I have learned about myself as a communicator from this exercise.

(2) Additional information about myself I would like to share.

(3) Why I think *X* (a member of the group) communicates effectively.

10 An assignment combining interpersonal speaking, group discussion, and speaking to a group:[23]

a As pairs, compile a list of situations in which people should be more, or less, assertive. The following items, taken from the College Self-Expression Scale, are typical of those used to measure different aspects of assertiveness. You may use or modify these and add others:

When you decide that you no longer wish to date someone, do you have marked difficulty telling the person of your decision?

Would you exchange a purchase you discovered to be faulty?

Are you inclined to be over-apologetic?

Do you insist that your roommate do his or her fair share of the cleaning?

If food which is not to your satisfaction is served in a restaurant, do you complain about it to the waiter?

If a friend makes what you consider to be an unreasonable request, are you able to refuse?

b After compiling your list, join with two or three other pairs. Determine the items of most interest and discuss ways of managing these situations.

c Make a short talk to the group in which you identify a situation which has been troublesome to you, and indicate how you think you would now manage it.

11 In interpersonal situations it often helps to know how others meet certain situations. Discuss with two or three others the probable usefulness of the following, or other, strategies:

a When bearing both good news and bad news, determining which to present first;

---

[23]Galassi et al., pp. 166–167.

b Selecting a time when the receiver will be in a good mood;

c When you say "no" to a request, follow with conversation on a topic in which you can show your basic interest or friendliness (i.e., turning from the topic that brought your refusal to another of current mutual interest);

d Instead of asking for more than you expect actually to receive, asking for exactly what you need and emphasizing that fact;

e Taking a memo to an interview to serve as an agenda, or to be left as a reminder;

f Showing someone a letter that you plan to send to him or her, in advance of actually mailing it, so that you can mutually agree on the points covered;

g Throwing your hat into the room before you walk in (or other nonverbal or verbal equivalent);

h Transacting business over coffee or a soda.

12 For those interested in self-concept, and in the possibility, held by some, that normal people often do not develop a coherent sense of identity, read Kenneth J. Gergen, "Multiple Identity," *Psychology Today* (May 1972).

13 For additional reading: one of the footnote references; Chapter 1, "Lower than the Angels," in Jacob Bronowski, *The Ascent of Man* (Boston: Little, Brown, 1973); selected chapters in Warren G. Bennes, et al., eds., *Interpersonal Dynamics: Essays and Readings on Human Interaction,* (Homewood, Ill.: Dorsey, 1973).

Eugene Luttenberg/EPA

Interviewing

Shortcomings of the interviewing process □ Employer
expectations versus applicant deficiencies □ Preparing for the
interview □ Information sought by employer from applicant □
Opening the interview □ Developing the interview □ Closing
the interview □ The information-seeking interview □
Appraising the interview □ Assignments and exercises

This chapter deals with one of the important kinds of interpersonal communication.

The ability to conduct an interview to gain a job, or to be promoted to a better or different job, or to secure information that will make one more efficient on the job, is indispensable. This chapter should help you improve such skills as preparing a strategy for an interview and presenting your qualifications or stating your questions so that the outcome will be favorable. Daniel P. Moynihan, who has held many positions of public responsibility including that of Ambassador to the United Nations, wrote:

> The principal measure of progress toward equality will be that of employment. It is the primary source of individual or group identity. In America what you do is what you are: to do nothing is to be nothing; to do little is to be little. The equations are implacable and blunt, and ruthlessly public.[1]

Moynihan wrote this statement with civil rights in mind, but it can readily be extended to cover the thought that most human beings primarily seek to find a spot in which they can serve others and gain a measure of fulfillment for themselves.

In our culture, the interview is not only the means of opening the door to job, position, appointment, scholarship, or award, but also, after you become established, of reporting to your associates or to your superiors information about your work and the new ideas or programs you wish to develop. If you resign, you may terminate the relationship with an interview. Even if you are dismissed, your superiors may offer you an exit interview if for no other reason than as a friendly or public relations gesture.

Your life work may or may not involve wages or salary; you may center your interests on a church, a hospital, a library, a community center, or a political party. In any event you will operate from time to time through interviews.

These paragraphs have described one type of interview: seeking employment and improving your status in your chosen field of endeavor. Another type is the interview in which you seek information. Familiar examples are: the reporter gathering facts for a news story, the physician asking questions to aid in diagnosis, and the social worker collecting data. As a student you sometimes schedule interviews to gather material for a speech, a term paper, or a project.

---

[1]Quoted in Stanley P. Herbert and Charles L. Reischel's, "Title VII and the Multiple Approaches to Eliminating Employment Discrimination," *New York University Law Review,* 46 (May 1971): 450.

This chapter will discuss both types, with particular emphasis on the first.

This text is being written during a down side of the economic cycle rather than during an up side. In many fields schools and colleges are educating more applicants than the job market will absorb. Any given position may attract ten applicants or three hundred. We have reason to believe this situation will improve, though it could continue the same or even get worse. In any economic climate, however, an employer will interview several people, if the position is important, before making a decision.

For six years I directed the placement service of a national educational association. At that time the demand for teachers was so strong that I could say to an applicant, "Throw a dart at a map of the United States; we can help you find a position close to where it lands." This light-hearted statement was often put to the test by, for example, married women who wanted to teach only in or near the community where their husbands were employed. Although this requirement sharply limited the wife's choice, more often than not, through diligent effort, she would be successful. At the height of a later boom in the mid-1960s I recall reading a classified ad by a school superintendent who sought a teacher of social studies. "Don't write a letter of application," he advertised. "Just send us your name and address on a post card. We'll get in touch with you." This freak instance and others like it were the consequence of a high birth rate and a nationwide teacher shortage. Now the situation has changed. In many fields the applicant will need to schedule not one interview but many.

In recent years a prodigious number of books and articles have been published about interviewing. More of these books discuss "how to interview applicants" than "how to interview prospective employers." A young man or woman could wish it were the other way around. Employers, however, realizing the importance of recruiting good people in today's competitive world, need interviewers who know what kind of people the company needs, and *who can recognize them when they see them.* This chapter explores ways in which you can improve your interviewing ability in the most basic types of situation you are likely to meet.

SHORTCOMINGS OF THE INTERVIEWING PROCESS

You need to know the built-in shortcomings of the interviewing process, so that you can supply information that will fill the gaps. The interview is not a perfect device for identifying the best available candidate. It cannot yield positive information about your sincerity, loyalty, motivation, energy, promptness, or industry. As one of the best of the modern experts puts it:

There are people who can appear bright and intelligent in conversation. But some of these appear very different when they have to get down to the routine of a job. The drive and keenness soon evaporate when confronted with the harsh reality of getting things done and overcoming difficulties in practice, while the brightness and intelligence do not always stand up to the demands of sustained intellectual effort.[2]

What you achieved in school, and what you will achieve for the Acme Box Corporation or the community playground, is the result of brains and motivation (the old formula is: achievement equals brains times motivation). You were graduated from high school, whereas some of your classmates were not, because you had a mixture of the two qualities. Some of your classmates who dropped out had more brains than you, but lacked motivation; others were strongly motivated, but were short on brains. In one way or another the interviewer will be looking for evidences of both. During the interview you may be able to give him at least verbal reassurance.

Another shortcoming of the interview process is that interviewers often disagree among themselves about the qualifications and the potential of applicants. Interviewers *A* and *B*, members of a medical school faculty, interview applicants *X, Y,* and *Z. A* likes *X* and *B* strongly prefers *Z.* After discussion, they decide to admit *X* to medical school and turn away *Y* and *Z.* In two years, however, *X* flunks out, whereas *Y* and *Z,* who were admitted elsewhere, eventually earn degrees. How did *A* and *B* go wrong on their decision? This instance is not an isolated one, and results in *A* and *B* and people like them giving renewed study to the interview process. Interviewers sometimes overawe applicants; and applicants sometimes fail to ask any questions.

Interviewers also often need to use supplementary sources of information: letters of application, transcripts, letters of reference, aptitude or psychological tests. One student, applying for a civil service position in Washington, reported that he and three other candidates were asked to hold an impromptu panel discussion on the topic, "What can be done to improve the quality of life in the average American town?" The interviewers selected him because he was superior in the give-and-take of discussion. A news story reports that candidates for the nation's intelligence service are asked to give an impromptu speech. (A spy often has to talk himself out of a sticky situation.)

---

[2]John Munro Fraser, *Employment Interviewing,* 4th ed. (London: Macdonald and Evans, 1966), pp. 67, 143. Mr. Fraser is a Reader in the Department of Industrial Administration at the University of Aston in Birmingham, England. His book reflects immense good sense.

The time may come when an applicant may need to submit a videotape on which he discusses his qualifications, just as applicants in some fields now submit samples or portfolios of their work.

Regardless of its shortcomings, the interview is still part of the crucial process of selecting applicants. Next to grade-point-average, the interview may be the most important determinant, for example, of who is admitted to a medical or other professional school and who is not. *Selecting individuals for important, long-term positions, without an interview, is unthinkable.* Even though past achievement is the best single predictor of future achievement, employers still want to talk to the applicant, even one with fine references and outstanding qualifications on paper, before making a decision.

EMPLOYER EXPECTATIONS VERSUS APPLICANT DEFICIENCIES

The well-known annual *Endicott Report* ranked a number of factors generally considered by college recruiters, as reported by 215 employers. The result was as follows:

1   For graduates in all fields of study, including engineering, accounting, and liberal arts, first in importance are personal qualifications such as maturity, initiative, enthusiasm, poise, appearance, and *the ability to work with people* (italics mine).
2   Grades are second in importance. This is true in all fields.
3   For most graduates specialized courses relating to a particular field of work ranks third in importance. For liberal arts graduates, however, this factor ranks fifth.
    For liberal arts graduates experience in campus activities—especially leadership and participation in extracurricular life—ranks third. For other graduates, this factor ranks fifth.
4   In all fields, the kind and amount of part-time or summer employment while in college.

Special advice to women graduates includes: take technical or business-related courses; get experience in business through summer or part-time jobs; be willing to travel or relocate. Special advice to black graduates includes the foregoing, plus the suggestion to be better prepared for interviews and to improve interviewing techniques.[3]

The following list offers complaints that interviewers have about applicants:

---

[3]*The Endicott Report, 1976, Trends in Employment of College and University Graduates in Business and Industry* (Evanston, Ill.: Northwestern University, 1975), pp. 5, 6, 11.

Has a belligerent attitude; is rude or impolite
Lacks sincerity
Is evasive concerning information about himself
Is concerned only about salary
Is unable to concentrate
Tries to use pull to get a job
Is intolerant and has strong prejudices
Has a limp-fish handshake
Is unable to express himself clearly
Shows lack of planning for career
Has not done research into history and products of the company
Wants to start in an executive position
Presents extreme appearance[4]

Harry W. Hepner, Syracuse University professor who has written widely in the field of applied psychology, tells in the fourth edition of his *Psychology Applied to Life and Work* of the principal concerns of a hundred college students and graduates with respect to interviewing. Following are six problems, with typical questions, and the number of times each problem was mentioned:

1 **Experience** (27 times)   Should I admit that I have had no experience? Is there any way in which I can compensate for the lack of experience?
2 **Telling the truth** (19 times)   Should I discuss my religious or political beliefs or my ideas about unions?
3 **Salary** (38 times)   How am I to know that I will not ask too much or too little?
4 **Reasons for choice of firm** (19 times)   Why did you choose this firm? Should I talk freely and frankly about my ability?
5 **The job itself** (15 times)   Should I try to determine my chances for advancement? Should I ask questions about the firm during the interview?
6 **Results of the interview** (48 times)   How can I judge the success of the interview? What kind of impression did I make? How soon should I go back and talk to the interviewer again? Should I have influential friends intercede in my behalf?[5]

---

[4]Charles S. Goetzinger, Jr., "An Analysis of Irritating Factors in Initial Employment Interviews of Male College Graduates," unpublished doctoral dissertation, Purdue University, 1954. Quoted in Charles J. Stewart and William B. Cash, *Interviewing: Principles and Practice* (Dubuque, Iowa: Wm. C. Brown, 1974), pp. 162–163.
[5](Englewood Cliffs, N.J.: Prentice-Hall, © 1966), p. 247. Reprinted by permission of Prentice-Hall, Inc. The list above is adapted from the original study. See also his Chapter 15, "Hiring the Employee—the Interview," pp. 301–322.

PREPARING FOR THE INTERVIEW You may start your preparation by considering the questions raised in the foregoing study. No one single answer is possible, but the following suggestions may facilitate your thinking:

1 **Experience** Make a list of the things you have done that are *similar to* the capabilities required by the job description. "Have you ever sold shoes?" Maybe you have not sold shoes, but you have had other selling experiences. Perhaps, in anticipation of that question, you have gone around and watched shoe salesmen. If you think you are a rapid learner, that capability itself is relevant.

2 **Telling the truth** You must tell the truth. In the first place, you are probably not a very good liar. In the second place, investigation will usually reveal your real beliefs. Most of all, we have a moral if not a religious obligation to be honest. The business and political world is built on individual integrity. You may do what Kennedy did: "I am a Catholic, but my being a Catholic will not interfere with my being President." Or what Lincoln did: "I am opposed to slavery, but I must put the Union first." Perhaps you feel that your religious, political, or union views will not interfere with your competence as an employee.

3 **Salary** The answer to this question depends so much on individual situations and the current economic picture. If salary is an overriding requirement, try to learn before the interview the salary contemplated. If you are asked to suggest a salary, it is usually (not always) better to be too high than too low. It is easier to retreat from a too-high figure than to move up from a too-low figure. Mr. Lowly Beginner may have to accept the first salary offered. Mr. Highan Mighty will be able to haggle. A middle-of-the-road stance is to say that you will work for "the prevailing wage."

4 **The job itself** You should come to the interview prepared to ask and answer questions about the firm and the job. Find out in advance everything you can. Reflect upon your own motives and aspirations. If I were buying a used motorcycle or car, I would certainly ask: Why are you selling this motorcycle (or car)? So: Why are you applying for this job?

5 **Hard questions** Some interviewers purposely ask hard, tension-creating questions. Why did you leave your last employer? How many interviews have you already had? What about your boyfriend (girlfriend)? Are you a good (typist, receptionist, mechanic, salesperson)? Or questions related to the occupation: How can we reduce shoplifting? Can you handle discipline problems? What interests you about our product or service? Or thoughtful questions: How much money do you expect to earn at age 30? 35? Do you prefer working with others or by yourself?

YOUR PERSONAL SYSTEMS ANALYSIS

This chapter has suggested that you make an inventory of basic things you can do—a procedure similar to a systems analysis.

If you are interested in a business or office position, your inventory might include elementary but basic items like these:

> answer a business telephone
> write a ticket or order
> keep an appointment book or schedule
> operate a hand calculator, typewriter, copying machine, or other piece of office equipment
> make change

If you are interested in a teaching, camp, or playground position—even though you have never actually had that precise experience—you might have some of these basic skills:

> tell a story or anecdote
> treat people with fairness
> avoid bitterness, sarcasm, or ridicule
> prepare a chart or other teaching aid
> make clear explanations
> listen attentively
> keep attendance, grade, or other records or scores
> show patience with beginners
> ask questions
> deal with individual differences
> learn more by reading and study

Construct a similar list for the specific position you are interested in. When the important questions, "What experience have you had" or "Why do you want this position" are asked, you will not need to answer impromptu.

What kind of boss do you prefer? Can you take instructions without feeling upset? Did you do the best scholastic work of which you are capable?[6]

---

[6]See the pamphlet, *Making the Most of Your Job Interview,* published and distributed by the New York Life Insurance Company, 51 Madison Ave., New York, N.Y. 10010. It lists sixty questions commonly asked during interviews.

6   **Results of the interview**   What you have studied and will study in this course will help you form impressions, both from verbal and nonverbal cues, of your success or lack of success. You may pick up hints that will help you in your next interview from, for example, questions that you fielded poorly, or from signs of impatience or disinterest. A comment such as "I've enjoyed our visit very much" is not so meaningful as "We certainly want to talk to you again" which in turn is not so significant as "Your qualifications are excellent; let's go down and talk to the chief of the section, Mr. Atkinson." In other words, reflect not only upon what was said and done but what was *not* said and done. You may want to inquire, "When do you expect to make a decision?" Or: "Could I send you further information (i.e., a statement from a former employer)?" If you know an influential friend who can intercede in your behalf, ask him, if you know him well enough, but only if he thinks his intercession will be welcomed.

In your planning, remember that the telephone is widely used. Many firms have WATS lines, with cheaper bulk rates. Moreover, since letters of reference, once considered entirely confidential, may now under certain circumstances be viewed by the applicants themselves, employers may place more reliance on phone calls in order to get candid appraisals. Employers can also call former employers. Since they themselves are accustomed to calls, you may often use the telephone yourself to arrange appointments or follow-up interviews.

Again, the foregoing comments are intended to be exploratory, not prescriptive. The following statements should also be helpful in your preparation:

1   **The job**   What do I know, or what can I discover, about the prospective employer, the nature of the position, the qualifications required, the salary? Can I find out the name of the interviewer? Do I know people who work there who can give me information?

2   **You yourself**   What experience have I had that directly fits the position? What experience have I had that is related to, or suggests an aptitude for the position? What experience have I had that suggests my ability to learn quickly, or that indicates my potential for growth?

   A   Prepare an *inventory* of the different kinds of experience you have had that suggest special skills, qualities of leadership, or opportunity to meet people. Experiences in camping, scouting, canvassing, membership or offices in clubs or groups, special tests or examinations, prizes. (See the extensive list of self-questions on pages 169–172, Chapter 9.)

B Recall specific books or magazines that you have read, plays or movies you have seen, special interests like art or sports; the interviewer may seek information about your avocations.

C Be prepared to answer questions about your goals, your likes and dislikes, and your strong and weak points.

The purpose of an inventory is to enable you to answer questions thoughtfully as well as promptly. You may find yourself disclosing more about yourself to the interviewer than you have to all but your closest friends. The interviewer is trying to arrive at a judgment about your potential for growth and other intangibles as well as about the posted requirements for the position.

INFORMATION SOUGHT BY EMPLOYER FROM APPLICANT

During the interview you will have an opportunity to supply information about yourself under one or more of the following six headings:

1 **Innate abilities** The interviewer will make judgments concerning your intelligence, ability to solve problems, facility with language or numbers, good sense, imagination, tact, sense of humor, sense of public relations, and energy and physical strength. If you do not fit the specific job he has in mind, he may see your aptitude for another job; some people, for example, lack the physical strength for certain types of work.

2 **Specific qualifications** Can you repair radios, TV's, bicycles? Do you have a chauffeur's license? a teaching certificate? Can you type or operate other kinds of office equipment? If you lack the specific qualifications for the job, or if it is not practicable to acquire them through on-the-job training, there is little need to talk further.

3 **Potential** For many positions, the applicant's potential is of high importance. Here is where the applicant with a brand-new diploma will want to make a favorable impression. The telephone company does not expect you to be able to use its equipment but will expect to train you; it therefore looks for aptitude or potential. An attorney may hire you for his office even though you do not know what a writ or a deed is. A school or college can give you only a certain amount of vocational skill. In the interview you should be able to suggest your potential for future growth.

4 **Motivation** The interviewer will want to be assured that you will be a contented employee, will stay with the firm, and will grow on the job. He will look for signs of interest and enthusiasm. He will inquire into your goals, drives, and career targets. He will ask you why you are applying for this specific position. He may ask why you left your last position. These questions are not easy to answer impromptu.

5 **Ability to work with others**   Most work today is teamwork. Others will be associated with you in the office, warehouse, sales force, research group, or work crew. You will likely deal with customers or with the public. Employees invariably welcome the new man or the new woman on the job and offer the most cheerful assistance in learning routines. The employer will not want to bring into this family someone with unusual problems of adjustment. Ability to communicate well appears on most lists of desirable qualities sought in an applicant. The ability to work as a member of a team is rooted deeply in human culture. Over the millennia we have learned that we must work together. Sometimes the compelling reason is love, sometimes hunger, sometimes fright; but work together we must.

6 **Appearance**   Personal appearance has for many years headed the list of desirable qualities in applicants. Our culture allows individuals a generous range of styles in dress, grooming, and neatness, but certain standards are expected of those who work in public or semipublic places. The interview is a poor time and place to experiment. You want the interviewer to concentrate fully on your outstanding qualities, not puzzle about whether your carelessness or poor taste in dress indicates that you are careless or insensitive in other things as well.

OPENING THE INTERVIEW   The experienced interviewer will do what he or she can to put you at ease. The employer is as eager to select a good employee as the applicant is to find a good position. Opening questions are likely to be casual and informal. Relax and follow the routine that is set; you need not worry about hurrying the interview along.

You may usefully collect impressions about the interviewer that will guide your responses. What the interviewer says may give you clues as to what values or qualifications are relevant. The questioning may or may not give you specific opportunity to touch on matters you want to stress; if not, you may find it necessary to introduce that information. Nonverbal as well as verbal cues help you develop your own strategy.

DEVELOPING THE INTERVIEW   You are certain to be asked specific questions about your qualifications unless these are well known to the interviewer through other sources.

When you do not have the precise qualifications for a position but are confident of your ability to meet these requirements, you should be prepared to offer equivalents. A young woman applied for a position on the assembly line of a small factory. The interviewer asked her if she had had any experience with machinery. "Yes," she said promptly, "sewing machines and washing machines." The interviewer was inclined to dismiss this information as having little relevance. "Did you ever operate a sewing machine?" she asked, earnestly. "You have to clean it, oil it, thread it, adjust the stitching, regulate the tension, and work with different kinds of material. If you had to call an expert every time something snagged you would never get any sewing done." As her statement put the matter in a new light, he hired her; in due course she easily learned to operate drill presses, lathes, and other machine tools.

Experiences you have had with games and sports are relevant to becoming a park or resort recreation director. Delivering papers or selling Girl Scout cookies are first steps in merchandising. One applicant was asked unexpectedly if he had any experience working with children. As a starter he promptly said, "I have ten young nieces and nephews, and I have been close to them." Being an officer even of a small club says something about leadership and acceptance by your peers. A young man applying for admission to a dental college described his work with scouts, his volunteer work at a local mental hospital, his summer job as a lifeguard. These experiences showed an interest in people; an asset to a dentist, or to anyone.

Suppose you are asked, "What do you consider your strong points to be?" Questions at this level often arise, and are difficult to answer. "I think of myself as taking pride in my work," you might say. Or: "More than anything else, I want to gain experience in many different aspects of newspaper publication." Or: "I think of myself as a good learner." Or any of a hundred things. This question may be followed by, "What do you consider your weak points to be?" "I need to do more reading," or, again, any of a hundred things. You might recall the four-fold life pattern on page 41 (love, religion, work, play) and what was said about self-disclosure in Chapter 3. Your reflection on your own strengths and weaknesses is useful apart from its relation to interviewing.

An English major applying for a Woodrow Wilson scholarship was asked, "What magazines do you read?" She was so flustered she could think only of *Good Housekeeping*. Later she realized she could have added others; but the interviewer had not been impressed. "What is the best book on current issues in education that you have read recently?" was asked of a candidate for a teaching position. Luckily he could suggest two or three. Many a young woman, finding herself working in an office with many men and few women, has suddenly developed an interest in sports, at least to the extent that she knows current scores, standings, and personalities and can enter into informal office conversation.

As game theory invaded the business world long ago, you may

CIVIL RIGHTS LEGISLATION AS IT AFFECTS INTERVIEWING

An applicant may wonder if he or she will need to carry into the interview a disadvantage because of race, color, religion, sex, or national origin.

In this connection, one should have in mind the basic provisions of Title VII of the Civil Rights Act of 1964. This important law, initiated by President Kennedy, was signed by President Johnson after heated debate in Congress, including more than 500 hours of filibustering. Essentially it states that an employer or an employment agency cannot discriminate against an individual with respect to compensation, terms, conditions or privileges of employment, because of race, color, religion, sex, or national origin. Exceptions may be justified in situations where religion, sex, etc., is a bona fide, reasonably necessary, occupational qualification, as for example, a school controlled by a particular religion directed toward the propagation of that religion. An individual, moreover, is not required to reveal his arrest record; he can be asked if he has been convicted of a crime.

The law does not apply to small businesses (as originally written, one with fewer than twenty-five employees) and it is rooted in the notion of interstate commerce, broadly interpreted. The principle of civil rights as stated in the law is being tested in the courts at nearly every conceivable point, so that a substantial body of court decisions is accumulating. It is, moreover, buttressed by civil rights legislation in most states. If you have a specific point in mind, you may want to seek current, expert advice. What is important is that a climate of basic fairness is being established with respect to race, color, religion, sex, and national origin, so that wider opportunities are being opened up to large segments of the population. Questions that used to be asked at interviews or printed on application forms have now become irrelevant.

The job field is also being opened up in other ways; "hire the veteran" and "hire the handicapped" campaigns are more frequent, and retirement programs that arbitrarily dismiss older people who are still fully competent are being tested in the courts.

Much ground, of course, still remains to be covered. College graduates, especially those with higher degrees, are now occasionally subjected to a subtle type of discrimination on the basis that they are "overqualified." The employer may feel that the applicant's interest in the lower-level job is temporary, and that the applicant will, instead of becoming a contented, productive employee, use the job simply as a springboard to something better. In this situation the applicant may need to show that simple fairness indicates that he or she should be considered on the basis of actual qualifications and bona fide interest in the job, not on anybody's preconceptions about what might happen in the future. The "overqualification" may lead to one's being able to contribute to the job in a beneficial way that no one can anticipate.

The opposite situation also presents a sticky problem: whether an employer can refuse to hire an individual at a low level on the ground that this individual may not be promotable to a higher level. The refusal obviously keeps the individual out of a job for which he or she is now suited and denies the opportunity to develop the skills and gain the experience that might lead to future promotion.[7]

Title IX of the Education Amendments of 1972 is another statute that broadens the rights of applicants with respect to sex. It forbids educational discrimination in admission, treatment of students once admitted, and employment. As with Title VII, institutions that receive federal support will need to comply.

What should you do if you are asked questions that affect your civil rights, under Title VII or Title IX or later amendments or state laws, or even that get into a shadowy area? You need to be governed by the situation. You may or may not want to comment, "That strikes me as a question that opens up the possibility of discrimination. Would you mind telling me whether your company has a policy that bears on that issue." Still better may be the strategy of making a brief response and then shift the discussion to areas where your case is strong and turning to the highlights of your own, positive, qualifications.

This brief discussion is written to alert you to changing developments in this rapidly enlarging field of employability.[8]

---

[7]Judith Bartnoff, "Title VII and Employment Discrimination in 'Upper Level' Jobs," *Columbia Law Review,* 73 (December 1973): 1621.

[8]Articles on various aspects of discrimination are appearing with some regularity in law review journals and in other periodicals. Consult the Education Index or other indexes, or your placement or guidance offices.

find yourself asked to suggest a solution to an imaginary situation. An incident may be described involving an angry customer, a picket line, or a shoplifter. How would you deal with it? Or: How would you increase sales, improve service, build an image, etc., in this business?

Instead of repeatedly giving monosyllabic answers to routine questions, you should call occasionally on your talent for amplification. Suppose someone asked you about your high school. Would you say: "I graduated from Roosevelt in 1973." Or: "I graduated from Roosevelt High—boy, was I glad to get out of there." Or: "I graduated from Roosevelt High in Des Moines—" and then add a sentence or two about Roosevelt's being a good school, and about your activities there.

The first answer tells the interviewer little. There are dozens of Roosevelt Highs. The second gives the wrong impression unless you can amplify your answer. The third tells something about what kind of person you are. We know that if a person is happy in one place, he gets along well with people, and will probably be happy in another place.

Suppose the interviewer said, "I see from your application blank that you were graduated from BU in 1977. Tell me about it."

(This is an *open-ended* question allowing you to take the ball and run with it, as opposed to a *closed* question like "When did you graduate from BU?" which permits only a brief answer.)

Would you reply, "There isn't much to say. I went there four years. I was a freshman my first year, a sophomore my second, a junior my third, and a senior my fourth."

Or would you say: "I had some fine teachers at BU. My major was XYZ, one of the strong departments on the campus. Some of my professors had national reputations. Besides XYZ, I was also interested in—" and then give a few clues. (An open-ended question deserves an open-ended answer. Your answer gives you opportunity to talk further about what was obviously a stimulating experience for you.)

You may be asked about your family background. Would you say, "I had two parents, a father and a mother"? Or you might say, "My father is a—" and then name his occupation. Would you like to add, "I come from a family with a strong college tradition. My father and mother both went to college, and so did my older brother"? A statement like that strikes an interesting note. So would a statement like this: "I am the first member of my family ever to go to college." That says something about your motivation, and also suggests your family wanted you to have an advantage that was denied them.

Contrast that interview with the following:

Q. What study did you like best in school?
A. History.
Q. What kind of history?
A. American history.
Q. What period in American history?
A. Civil war.
Q. Who was your favorite teacher?
A. I forget his name.

You need to use judgment in the length of your answers; you are not expected to give an essay in response to every question. But the interviewer can hardly be expected to stumble on questions that will bring out your unusual or distinctive traits unless you help.

Our culture, moreover, does not interpret favorably silence between two people meeting for the first time in a situation that normally calls for talk. A steady stream of short answers throws a burden on the interviewer, and although he or she is entirely capable of handling the situation, he or she probably will bring it to a close sooner than usual. You may be asked to amplify, clarify, summarize, or even repeat your answers. If you hear an open-ended question like "*Review for me* your previous job experience" or "*Tell me about* your home and family background" you have a clear invitation to give a full (not to be confused with rambling) response.

You may be asked, "Why do you want to work for Acme Box Corporation?" Or, "Why do you want to attend Grand College?" A candidate for lieutenant governor was once asked, on television, why he wanted to be elected to that office. "Because I would like to have the $28,000 salary," he replied. Voters quickly lost interest. When John F. Kennedy was campaigning for the Senate, he answered a similar question by saying, "Because I can do more for Massachusetts than my opponent can." An answer such as, "Well, actually I have two reasons" indicates that you have given previous thought to this kind of question.

In my own experience I have had best luck with applicants who talk about half of the time. I like to hear an applicant amplify or develop an idea; it gives me a notion about him as a person. I become restless, however, if he talks at great length. For one reason, I need to get four or five different kinds of information about him; for another, I need to tell him about the position and what is expected of the successful applicant. Most applicants, however, probably do not talk enough; they answer questions with only the bare bones of information; they do not disclose the kinds of attitudes or judgments that stimulate special questions. Of course, I have also been impressed by people who do not talk very much but who do listen well, and who give sensible responses when they do respond to a question.

CLOSING THE INTERVIEW

Often an interview is closed with the inquiry, "Do you have any questions?" To answer this question with a simple "No" is unimaginative. To say, "I don't believe so; we've covered the requirements of the job pretty well, so I think I know what will be expected of me" is better. Perhaps you can do still better: "What kind of people work for Acme Box Corporation?" Or: "Is Acme Box developing any new products?" Ask about the company's problems or achievements. Questions like these give the interviewer a chance to talk about the company's achievements and concerns and, coming from a young person, reflect thoughtfulness and maturity.

If important details like working conditions, stipend, opportunities for advancement, have not been discussed, you may ask specifically about them. You may want to inquire whether you can provide additional information: "Would you like a note from my last employer?" Naturally you will want to know when a decision will be made, and you will make sure that your address and phone number are available.

THE INFOR- MATION- SEEKING INTERVIEW

Sometimes you need to schedule interviews to get information for a discussion or a speech, a term paper, a story for the school newspaper, or a project for a course. The setting for this type of interview is different from that of the job-seeking interview: you yourself are not under the same kind of tension; the purpose is simply the dissemination of information; and the respondent is often eager to talk about the subject.

These steps in the process are significant:

1 **Topic** Formulate the topic on which you seek information: For example: "Should we increase the city library tax?" "What are the opportunities for women in the . . . profession?" "What progress is being made in treating VD?"

2 **Sources** Prepare a list of individuals who can provide specific information. On your list have people who represent different points of view. In preparing your list, consult with teachers or other residents who have a wide acquaintance. Consider also the availability of the prospective source: whether he or she has the free time, and is willing.

3 **Preliminary research** Find out what you can about the topic on your own. Extensive research will help you come to the interview with a better list of questions to ask.

4 **Make appointments** You can probably set up specific times and places by telephone.

Show up at the appointed time with your notebook and questions (ask permission to use a tape recorder if you bring one). Start with the general and lead to the specific.

Your list of questions is tentative. You will be reminded of additional questions as you proceed. You may stumble upon reasons or facts that you had been unaware of, and will want to exploit these new avenues. You may be led to change altogether the wording or the emphasis of your topic. The classic story is of the reporter who went to cover a speech. He returned to the city editor empty-handed, saying there was no story since a free-for-all fight had broken up the meeting.

Your source may mention names of other informed people; in this way you may uncover different points of view that will lead to a better-balanced speech, report, or news story. Along the way you may learn anecdotes or surprising facts that will add human interest.

Attentive listening is imperative. Show by your facial expression as well as by your words your realization that certain information has special significance: "That's unusual. . . . I didn't realize that. . . . Is this generally known? . . . That information is helpful. . . . Where can I find more on that point?" Offer the respondent time for reflecting.

Capitalize upon the distinctive advantage of the interview format: the opportunity to ask follow-up questions, to explore lines of thought you had not previously anticipated, to seek amplification or clarification, to get up-to-the-minute data, to see the problem from an experienced point of view.

APPRAISING
HE INTERVIEW   After an interview of any kind, appraise what you have accomplished. Were there questions that you could have asked or answered more effectively? Did you overlook an important question, or an experience that would have strengthened your case? Did the other person seem interested? In the case of a job-seeking interview, did you talk only to one person, or were you invited also to talk to someone higher up the line? In the case of an information-seeking interview, did you gain helpful information, new insights, or valid reasons or arguments? Settle in your own mind things you learned that will help you do better next time.

COMMENT   This chapter offers little advice about attire, grooming, hair or beard styles. Standards vary widely depending upon the age and sex of the applicant and the requirements of the situation. The informal attire and casual grooming of the classroom may not be suitable, in our culture, for an important interview. On the campuses job-hunting time brings an epidemic of hair cutting and beard trimming; jeans are set aside for whatever is prevalent in the business or profession into which entrance is desired. Moreover, styles change year by year.

Principles of good communication discussed throughout this book apply to interviewing as well as to other situations. Both verbal and nonverbal stimuli are interpreted by interviewer and interviewee. Both participants indulge in a certain amount of role playing. Specific instances are useful to support a claim. Amplification, repetition, and clarification are called upon. Self-disclosure, self-concept, and image are illustrated. Strategy is evolved. Like many other interpersonal situations, interviewing is in one way hard and in another way easy; no one can master it entirely or miss it wholly. Your good features may be so translucent that they stand out (despite a little bungling on your part) in any kind of interview situation, but on the whole it is better to make as good a case for your desire for a job, or for information, as you can.

**ASSIGN-
MENTS AND
EXERCISES**

1   Each member of the class, or of a small group, should make a list of work experiences. Make a parallel list of work experiences that each member might seek. Select three or four students to conduct interviews for specific positions selected from these lists with students interested in being interviewed for those positions. Examples: secretary, junior sales manager, talent or beauty search, highway construction, playground director, scholarship, admission to a professional school, corporation employee. Prepare an oral or written appraisal of each interview.

2   Make a similar arrangement to conduct information-seeking interviews.

3   Share with the class an *unusual* interview situation you have experienced. The following are examples:[9]

   a   An engineering student wishes to receive credit for his experience as a self-employed electrical contractor. He is interviewed by an engineering professor. The interview consists of a set of 15 questions taken from standard lists. In addition to the oral trade test, the assessor asks questions that require the candidate to relate his work experience to his course in electrical engineering.

---

[9]Joan Knapp and Amiel Sharon, *A Compendium of Assessment Techniques* (Princeton: Educational Testing Service, 1975), pp. 37–41.

b A student has contracted for a cross-cultural learning experience in which she works on a kibbutz in Israel. Her learning experience is supervised and directed by an interdisciplinary committee at the institution in which she is enrolled. Upon her return to the United States, she is interviewed by a faculty panel, the members of which represent the following subject areas: international relations, economics, Hebrew, anthropology, and social psychology. Each participant on the panel asks a sequence of open-ended questions that require the student to relate her experience to that particular discipline. After her interview, the panel evaluates her responses.

c A student requests credit for his prior experience as a radar technician in the Air Force. The assessor interviews the student and asks questions concerning his job duties and what he thinks he learned while working as a technician. Scale items are used to assess his attitudes toward his supervisors and co-workers. Open-ended questions are used to obtain information concerning his satisfaction with the job and what learning outcomes were achieved that would transfer to his present career choice or course of study. The interviewer records the student's responses, then compares this information with references, anecdotal reports, and ratings obtained from the student's supervisor in the service to arrive at an overall rating for the student's experience.

d A candidate has spent the previous seven years running a household and rearing two children. Prior to marriage, she attended a liberal arts college for two years. During her marriage, she has organized and directed children's play groups with other mothers. In addition, she has spent considerable time as a member of a baby-sitting pool and therefore has had experience in taking care of children other than her own. For assessment, she is required to participate in a group interview with three other women with similar backgrounds. In the interview the women must develop a list of skills or dimensions relevant to their home management and child-rearing experiences in order to rate themselves individually on these dimensions. The interviewer will act as a facilitator by asking appropriate questions to keep the discussion focused on the skills inventory and by probing the individuals when more information is needed.

Members of the class may be able to suggest similar interview experiences: after a religious mission; after an unusual educational experience like Head Start or a debate or theater clinic; after an overseas or other unusual work or travel experience; after a trip to outer space. Note that these, like some of those cited above, are basically a *debriefing* by interview.

4 Read and report on selected articles from *Psychology Today,* 1 (March 1968). For example, see Mary Harrington Hall, "A Conversation with Peter F. Drucker on the Psychology of Managing Management," pp. 21ff. This includes wise advice about how to find a place in the world, how to review your potential, and possible likes and dislikes. On page 63 of this issue is a reprint of "How to Be an Employee," an excerpt from which appears in Chapter 1 of this text. See also Edgar H. Schein, "The First Job Dilemma," pp. 28ff.

For additional reading, consult the following:

Fraser, John Munro, *Employment Interviewing* 4th ed. (London: Macdonald and Evans, 1966).

Gorden, Raymond L., *Interviewing: Strategy, Techniques, and Tactics* (Homewood, Ill.: Dorsey, 1969).

Hepner, Harry W., *Psychology Applied to Life and Work,* 4th ed. (Englewood Cliffs, N.J.: Prentice-Hall, 1966).

Lopez, Felix M., Jr., *Personnel Interviewing: Theory and Practice* (New York: McGraw-Hill, 1965).

Peskin, Dean B., *Human Behavior and Employment Interviewing* (no city: American Management Association, 1971).

Stewart, Charles J. and William B. Cash, *Interviewing: Principles and Practice* (Dubuque, Ia.: Wm. C. Brown, 1974).

5 Gaining Confidence

Nature and extent of speech tension ☐ Ways of gaining added
confidence ☐ The cultural background of communication ☐
Assignments and exercises

Although students of speech communication and their teachers spend hours on problems growing out of *message, channel, and receiver,* they consider the *sender* to have a special importance in the total process. What can be done, not only to give the sender the fullest information about ways of communicating, but also to heighten such personal attributes as self-confidence and poise? Formal and informal surveys are often made by teachers, asking students to list the important contributions of the speech communication course. The results confirm the general impression that an important value is to increase the student's self-confidence and to decrease the apprehension often connected with experiences in communicating. The term *stage fright* is still commonly used to describe this kind of concern, although terms like *speech anxiety, speech tension,* or *communication tension* are found in the literature and are more descriptive and more accurate.

NATURE AND EX-TENT OF SPEECH TENSION Two observations may usefully be made about the nature and extent of the problem: *frequency* and *symptoms.*

Frequency Researchers have made surveys of the frequency of speech tension to learn how often it occurs and have reported that about 70 to 85 percent of college students indicate that they worry about nervousness in communicating. Most of these describe their tension as *moderate* or *mild;* comparatively few as *severe.* These sentences are written primarily to assure you that speech anxieties are fairly commonplace. They are, in fact, as a group, among the most-frequently experienced fears of human beings: not entirely an unexpected statement, since communication is so basic to human existence. A recent survey involving 2,543 male and female adults asked respondents to pick items from a list representing situations in which they had some degree of fear. The results were:

Speaking before a group	40.6%
Height	32.0
Insects and bugs	22.1
Financial problems	22.0
Deep water	21.5
Sickness	18.8
Death	18.7
Flying	18.3
Loneliness	13.6
Dogs	11.2
Driving or riding in a car	8.8
Darkness	7.9
Elevators	7.6
Escalators	4.8

More women than men indicated that "speaking before a group" was one of their anxieties. Income and education were also relevant as the report states:

> There is little difference by age, but people in the $15,000 plus income group seem somewhat less concerned about public speaking. The more education a person has, the less likely he is to fear addressing a group. People living in the southern part of the United States seem to have the greatest fear while those in the northeast seem less concerned.[1]

This information may be especially helpful to those who feel that their problems are more unusual, or more severe, than those of others. A little self-disclosure among you and your classmates will indicate, however, that nearly everyone reports a certain amount of anxiety and tension.

A fair question to ask at this point is whether an individual with speech tension, whether moderate, mild, or severe, is likely to be able to learn to reduce anxiety. The variety of experiences made available in speech communication classes has led to good results. Edward R. Robinson, who made a careful analysis of a number of surveys and experimental investigations, concluded: "Almost without exception studies which have tested specific methods for the development of confidence have shown that repeated performances will increase confidence."[2] To cite two instances: Louis Lerea reported that a small class participating in an experiment at Northern Illinois University indicated extreme nervousness during the first speaking performance and practically no nervousness during the final speech.[3] Using a novel test administered before and after a speech course, Paul D. Brandes concluded that the beginning course reduced the anxiety of students toward situations where stage fright was involved.[4]

Speech communication teachers agree that if a coast-to-coast survey were conducted to determine whether speech-course experiences reduce the anxieties and tensions of students in the course, using rigid controls, the outcome would confirm the sources cited above. Another question is whether confidence gained in one situation will carry over to another. The answer is in the affirmative, although it is supported more by the accumulated experience of

---

[1] The survey was conducted by R. H. Bruskin Associates, 303 George Street, New Brunswick, N.J. 08903. Reported in *Spectra,* 9 (December 1973): 4.

[2] Edward R. Robinson, "What Can the Speech Teacher Do about Students' Stage Fright," *Speech Teacher,* 8 (January 1959): 10–11.

[3] Louis Lerea, "The Verbal Behavior of Stage Fright," *Speech Monographs,* 23 (August 1956): 233.

[4] Paul D. Brandes, "A Semantic Reaction to the Measurement of Stage Fright," *Journal of Communication,* 17 (June 1967): 142–146.

teachers and students than by experimental research. One researcher, Stanley F. Paulson, reported an experiment in which students in one class spoke to the members of a different class. Their scores as recorded on a standardized test indicated no decrease in confidence.[5] No one can claim that individuals perform equally well in a variety of situations; this condition prevails whether the game is communication or tennis. Repeated experience, however, helps an individual perform effectively under many different circumstances.

Symptoms   What was said in a previous chapter about *self-concept, self-esteem,* and *self-image* is related to speech anxiety. A woman who underestimates her competence as a communicator will likely feel more anxiety than she should. A man who underestimates his effectiveness with others is standing in his own light. Kim Giffin describes an introspective pattern of "low self-image, low trust of others, high speech anxiety, high motivation to avoid failure, low motivation to achieve success" that combine to make communication more difficult.[6] Gerald M. Phillips and Nancy J. Metzger note that reticence occurs from not knowing what is expected, adding: "The individual who does not have the ability to perceive or interpret the cues of others cannot use the cues of others as guides to his own behavior."[7] Speech anxiety has long been described as a conflict between two basic aspects of behavior that human beings display when confronted with a threatening situation: fight or flight; or, in other words, the desire to perform and the eagerness to flee.

Surveys reveal, however, that much inner fear and anxiety *is never suspected by listeners, even trained listeners.* A University of Southern California experimenter asked sixty-one speech communication teachers and graduate students to check observable degrees of anxiety in beginning speakers. When he compared the reports of these trained listeners with reports that the students themselves made about their anxiety, he found that receivers underestimated the fears of a speaker more frequently than they overestimated them.[8] In other words, you are likely to appear more at ease than you yourself realize.

Obviously certain symptoms of speech tension are associated with that part of the nervous system traditionally believed not to be under conscious control. To calm a pounding heart or to regulate excessive perspiration seems beyond us, except through the pro-

---

[5]"Changes in Confidence During a Period of Speech Training," *Speech Monographs* 18 (November 1951): 260–265.
[6]"Social Alienation by Communication Denial," *Quarterly Journal of Speech* 56 (December 1970): 355.
[7]"The Reticent Syndrome," *Speech Monographs,* 40 (August 1973): 225.
[8]Robinson, "What Can the Speech Teacher Do. . .," pp. 9–10.

cesses of adaptation and habituation. Scientists have been experimenting, however, with procedures generally grouped under the heading of "biofeedback," with the result that subjects have achieved success in controlling brain-wave activity, rate of heartbeat, blood pressure, and other bodily functions. Experiments have also attempted to discover how information is stored and processed, and to learn more about human moods, drives, and tensions. What a subject does in a typical experiment is to observe an appropriate signal—waves recorded on an electroencephalograph, flashing red or green lights, high- or low-pitched beeps. One signal indicates, for example, that your heart is beating rapidly; you then do "something" internally—you may not know what it is—and the signal changes, indicating that your heart rate has slowed. With practice you gain proficiency in slowing heart rate.

This kind of situation is not entirely new; trained actors can produce tears at will, though they may not know exactly how they do it, and yogis and mystics are able to control visceral organs. And as everyone knows, a person learning a muscular skill, like typing or water-skiing, will learn to make countless adjustments in nervous and muscular systems, as a result of the feedback he or she gets from successes and failures. Later he or she may not be able to describe precisely what was done to improve the skill.

Biofeedback procedures are in a preliminary stage, and are mentioned here chiefly to inform you that investigations into the world of involuntary visceral activity are beginning to throw new light on these bodily systems. The situation may not be so mysterious as we have supposed. A person seeking to function as a communicator also needs to learn to control certain involuntary systems (rapid heart rate, trembling of hands or knees), and this is done by adjusting to various kinds and degrees of feedback. The feedback available may not be so precise as flashing lights or EEG waves, but it is nevertheless effective, and in the future we may be able to come up with still more refined approaches to the problem of speech tension.[9]

Another technique receiving attention from teachers of speech communication is *systematic desensitization.* If you have such fear of a situation that you avoid it, even though you want to be involved in it, you may be interested in this technique. If, for example, you had a fear of height, the second item on the list given at the beginning of the chapter, and wanted to paint a three-story house, you would start

---

[9]For popularized accounts of biofeedback, see Barnard Law Collier, "Brain Power: The Case for Biofeedback Training," *Saturday Review,* 54 (April 10, 1971): 10ff.; "Probing the Brain," *Newsweek,* 77 (June 21, 1971): 60–67. The October 1970, issue of *Psychology Today* also has nontechnical articles about biofeedback.

at lower levels and work up, gradually accustoming yourself (i.e., becoming less sensitive) to the higher levels. You would place the ladder carefully, assuring yourself that it could not possibly slip, and so, gradually, you would accustom yourself to working at the top of the ladder, and thus would be able to get the job done.

The fear of speaking is more subtle. The theory assumes that speech tension is a learned muscle reaction, and that its alleviation calls for muscular (and mental) relaxation, followed by mentally visualizing a graded series of increasingly difficult communication situations. An easy situation would be to imagine that you are in your room, writing an outline for your speech; an intermediate situation would be to imagine that you are in class, listening to others speaking, but your turn isn't due for a week; a difficult situation would be to imagine that you are in class, you hear the instructor call your name, you walk to the front of the room and begin your talk.[10]

If, during one of the intermediate steps, you find yourself becoming tense, you do further muscle relaxing, and start over. Something loosely approximating systematic desensitization may occur when a group is participating in a classroom exercise: the first person has to break the ice, but those who follow have opportunity not only to imagine but actually to see what is going on and thus gain reassurance.

Gordon L. Paul and Donald T. Shannon identified a group of fifty college students who feared public speaking, worked with the group for six weeks, and observed notable improvement. An advantage is that the technique is one that individuals learn and can use themselves after the formal session is over.[11]

The desensitization procedure has been studied in connection with *insight procedures,* in which the individual either receives advice from a teacher or reasons with himself. This method is also helpful. People often talk out their problems internally or with another person. In fact a characteristic of American culture is the strongly entrenched belief that human beings do improve, as opposed to a fatalistic culture that bids us to be happy with our lot, since it is fixed and unalterable.

---

[10]See James C. McCroskey, David C. Ralph, and James E. Barrick, "The Effect of Systematic Desensitization on Speech Anxiety," *Speech Teacher,* 19 (January 1970): 32–36; McCroskey, "The Implementation of a Large-Scale Program of Systematic Desensitization for Communication Apprehension," *Speech Teacher,* 21 (November 1972): 255–264. Copies of this article plus a cassette may be purchased from the Speech Communication Association, 5205 Leesburg Pike, Falls Church, Va. 22041.

[11]"Treatment of Anxiety Through Systematic Desensitization in Therapy Groups," *Journal of Abnormal Psychology,* 71 (April 1966): 124–135; a description of their procedure appears on pp. 127–129. See also Arthur J. Frankel and Paul H. Glasser, "Behavioral Approach to Group Work," *Social Work,* 19 (March 1974): 163–175. These authors also cite other useful studies. See further Paul, *Insight vs. Desensitization in Psychotherapy: An Experiment in Anxiety Reduction* (Stanford: Stanford University Press, 1966).

WAYS OF GAINING ADDED CONFIDENCE

What we have discussed so far is the negative part of the emotional basis of communication: the problems wrapped up in anxiety, tension, and worry. Your teacher will help you manage these problems: teachers not only want you to master your worries but also want to help you cross over to the positive side so that you will reflect self-assurance and poise. The important suggestion is: get actual experience in a wide variety of communicative situations. More specifically, the following practices are reported as ways of gaining added confidence.

Prepare Thoroughly

Whether the situation that you plan to confront is interpersonal, small group, or speech making, give it advance thought.

If an impending conversation or interview is worrisome, seek specific information about the other person. If you learn that *Mr. A* is silent as the grave on every subject except Oriental philosophy, be prepared to ask a leading question on that topic if you want to start him talking. If you know that *Mr. B* likes to talk about sports, perhaps his interest will coincide with yours. If you seek information, or a job, from *Ms. C,* learn something about her, or her field of expertise, or the company for which she works.

When you are asked to speak to a group, select a topic with which you feel intellectually at home and on which you have the advantage of study or experience. In this way you can draw upon your storehouse of ideas. Later, as you become familiar with the requirements of speaking, you can and should go further afield.

Solid preparation will give a feeling of assurance as nothing else can. What you lack as a speaker can be more than made up by the subject.

Though you should prepare with care, you can avoid some tension by refusing to take yourself too seriously. Advice like this should be dispensed cautiously, since one always wishes to do well, yet the simple fact remains that the world will not cave in if you stumble a little. Learning theory advises us to set a modest standard at first, not an unattainable one; that we should try to do our best, not somebody else's best; that we work better with some pressure rather than with no pressure or with tremendous pressure; that as we improve we can raise our goal. Constant fretters may welcome this advice from Frank Lloyd Wright: "You can't keep pulling yourself up by the roots to see if you are still growing."

"Prepare thoroughly" is a simply worded statement that involves sophisticated principles. It is no small matter to be able to analyze listeners and to make preliminary decisions about their interests, moods, experiences, and values; to learn what is relevant to a message, and therefore likely to hold attention, and what is not; to be able to arrange ideas in an order that helps the listener to comprehend more readily; to have them firmly enough in mind so that you can proceed with confidence rather than with lingering worry or doubt.

Having prepared thoroughly, act confidently. Why say, "I haven't prepared as carefully as I should have" when it is closer to the truth to say "I have given considerable thought to what I want to tell you today"? Is it better to say, "I don't claim to be an expert on this subject" than to disclose your competence: "For the last three summers I have been an assistant to the state highway engineer"? Even if you cough, stutter, stumble, forget, or repeat, accept the incident for what it is, an extremely minor matter, one that probably can be ignored altogether or handled in an offhand way. The suggestions apply to interpersonal communication as well as to formal speaking. People may be perceived to be less interesting as conversationalists, interviewers, or discussants, if they belittle their own information or competence or show concern for trivialities.

Study the Theory of Communication

Communication can never be an exact science but it does follow useful principles. It was not invented by Sir Winston Churchill over there or Daniel Webster over here; twenty-five centuries of speech making have gone into the development of the Greco-Roman-Anglican tradition. These twenty-five centuries have taught people much about communicating: how to partition and develop ideas; how to adapt to listeners; how to use example, illustration, and other forms of argument and appeal; how to use voice and gesture; how to employ words and phrases; and how to conclude. A lawyer ignorant of law is only a little worse off than a communicator who relies upon hunches, guesses, instinct, or inspiration instead of upon a grasp of principle. Almost any situation you will ever face has already been faced thousands of times. The theory of communication has evolved from those thousands of experiences.

Though principles of good communication remain fairly constant, people of different generations evolve different ways of applying those principles, so that it is entirely correct to say that yesterday's approach may be ineffective today. We are creatures of our culture, and our methods of sending and receiving are responsive to a culture that is continually changing. We note this readily in dress, hairstyle, and grooming: we feel most comfortable if we conform to the general level of attire that we see all around us, although many of us evolve our own variations. Styles of communication also change. We use highly informal (compared with yesterday) methods of asking and accepting dates, of expressing our appreciation, of supporting or criticizing one another. In the field of speech making, different individuals devise their own variations on the principles of communication. Robert M. La Follette, Mike Mansfield, and Thomas Eagleton represent different generations of statesmen; their speeches represent different speaking styles. Somewhere on a campus are the senators of tomorrow, and even though they will face the familiar problems of foreign affairs and domestic disturbances, they will use the style, manner, and language of their own day, adapted to their own experience and personality.

This is why new textbooks in communication (and in writing) continually appear: principles change little, but applications change greatly. Each textbook includes a little of what Emerson called "the conventional, the local, the perishable" and the examples, the incidents, the personalities that must be continually changed in order to make the book meaningful to the current generation of readers.

Organize   It is as hard to carry ideas in your mind without a plan as it is to carry an armful of groceries without a basket. Even an experienced speaker would get rattled if he tried to proceed without organization. Let us say that, early in the year, you want to tell us that the school team is certain to have a good season. Instead of merely rambling along, prepare a little outline. Talk first about the team's *offense,* offering examples; talk second about the team's *defense,* with other examples. Such a plan has a steadying effect.

Does *organization* seem too formidable a principle to apply to situations where the number of your listeners will be small? Suppose you need to appear before a college dean, loan official, or committee to apply for an undergraduate or graduate school scholarship. Is "rhetorical strategy" out of place here? Why not anticipate the questions you will be asked and organize your prospective answers? To a question like "Why do you want to study at Southern State University?" (a highly probable question), you can reply: "Well, I have three reasons," and then state them.

Use Visual Aids   In more formal situations such as group discussion or speech making, you can increase your self-assurance by using a visual aid. A visual device is effective and imaginative for its own sake (see Chapter 18), and also helps to keep a tense and worried communicator on track. A chart on which the principal ideas are displayed keeps you from losing your way. Handouts help the listener follow your chain of reasoning. An actual object that may be displayed and manipulated adds interest. A diagram drawn on a blackboard adds to clarity and understanding. By giving you work for your hands, or by encouraging you to move around as you walk over to the chart or hold up an object for a better view, you dissipate some of your tension. Since visual aids give a listener something to look at, they may help you feel less exposed. Many subjects are vastly improved by the use of a visual aid, so this suggestion should not only help you feel more comfortable in the communicative situation, but should also help you make a more effective presentation of your message.

Rehearse   Judge Harold R. Medina, who had a distinguished career as circuit judge of the United States Court of Appeals, wrote the following on the importance of training, practice, and rehearsal:

> I think such capacity as I developed for public speaking is wholly the result of experience. . . .
> I would practice . . . arguments in appellate courts for hours on end in my office or in my apartment or in my library building down at Westhampton so that I could proceed without notes and with considerable flexibility.

Give your talk aloud several times. Become accustomed to hearing yourself. While rehearsing, time yourself; you may have too much material. If so, chop some of it out, and that will make your task simpler. Don't be shy about discussing your talk with a friend. As you rehearse, don't try to memorize; follow your planned train of thought, but feel free to change the wording. Be prepared to show your enthusiasm, sincerity, fairness, conviction, interest in others. These help lead you through the neutral zone, and place you squarely on the positive side. Self-assurance in itself will generate a certain amount of momentum. A deep breath before speaking may quiet the fluttering. Yawning, or stretching, may help overcome part of the nervousness (these techniques are also part of the desensitization program). Professional actors have reported that these and similar procedures help counteract the physical strain and tension.

Reassure Yourself   Believe in yourself; be a self-fulfilling prophet. Franklin D. Roosevelt said, less than twenty-four hours after Pearl Harbor, "With the unbounding determination of our people—we will gain the inevitable triumph." Winston Churchill repeatedly declared: "Victory—victory—victory." What if either of them had mumbled, hesitantly: "My God, boys, we'll never make it!" In her bid for the Democratic presidential nomination, Shirley Chisholm, the first black congresswoman, declared:

> First and foremost, it is essential that you believe in yourself and your ability to handle the job you are seeking. If you don't, it is difficult to persuade others to support you. . . . Over and over in the campaign, I was asked, "But why are you running, Mrs. Chisholm?" Over and over I

would reply, "Because I think I can do the job." "Because I think I am better than the rest of the candidates in the field."[12]

Harry S. Truman was overawed, after a successful campaign, that he had actually become a United States Senator. But, he said afterward, jokingly, he felt better after he saw who else was in the Senate. (The opposition may not be so formidable as we think.) In his famous 1948 campaign to be reelected to the presidency, he said repeatedly, "We are going to win, and don't you forget it." He continually reassured himself and his listeners despite the fact that the polls were against him right to the finish.

Take a Speech Communication Course This step you have taken, or may take, to enroll in a speech communication course, is *the best way possible* to learn to manage tension. In *no other situation* will you be exposed so frequently to the two factors the beginner most needs: (1) actual experience and (2) perceptive and sympathetic suggestions for improvement. A young painter shut himself in his studio and laboriously worked out his own methods. One day he came forth jubilant, and imparted his discovery to his teacher. "My dear boy," answered the master, "I could have shown you that in five minutes, and saved you two years of time."

In a speech communication class, you have an opportunity to make communications at a simple, nonthreatening level, before proceeding to a more complex level of difficulty. You are likely to start by presenting a brief message about yourself, or about some other member of the group. You will have an opportunity to see who else is in the class, and to learn that their expectations and feelings are similar to yours. You may find yourself as a member of a group of three or four—perhaps gathered in a corner of the room or sitting around a table in front of the room—sharing the responsibility of presenting the message. You are not likely to be called upon to make a long, formal report on an *assigned subject* in the opening days of the course—perhaps not during the closing days, either. The assigned tasks are designed to be those well within the capabilities of those in the room.

Considerable laboratory experimentation is emerging to sup-

---

[12]Waldo W. Braden, ed., *Representative American Speeches: 1972–1973* (New York: Wilson, 1973), pp. 80–81.

In his editorial comment, Dr. Braden wrote: "Shirley Chisholm is a most effective speaker. She . . . uses excellent language, and is direct and persuasive. Schooled in rugged political speaking in New York City, she is able to build rapport and to meet an audience on its own ground. She is equally effective before women's groups, black groups, street rallies, college assemblies, the National Democratic Convention, or the House of Representatives. She is adept in extemporaneous and impromptu situations and knows how to cope with the questions of reporters. She is among the best women speakers on the American scene today" (p. 79).

port established practice in speech communication classes for helping students gain self-assurance. Laboratory rats subjected to a sharp stimulus, such as a loud sound, react by noticeable and measurable startle responses, characterized not only by overt motor activity but also by increased electrical activity in the brain, reduction of blood flow to the extremities, and other phenomena. Subsequent exposures to the sound, however, provoke less-marked responses; the rats become *habituated* to the stimuli. The ability to habituate has been traced to activity of pituitary-adrenal hormones. It is no large leap to the conclusion that speakers become accustomed to problems connected with facing audiences; experience lessens the startle effect.

Experimenters are also demonstrating that in many different kinds of situations adults perform their best *when exposed to optimum levels of stress*. Students have observed themselves, for example, working at high levels of efficiency when under the stress of a deadline or of a crowded schedule. Speakers also report a similar experience with audiences: at times the stimulus of the audience leads them to perform at a higher level of accomplishment than they anticipated. This result, again, may be a function of the activity of the pituitary-adrenal system. Additional experimentation in this field may lead to an even better understanding of the process by which one human being, communicating to others, is able to make the stresses in the system operate to his advantage.[13] As the social psychologists phrase it, "the presence of others increases the individual's level of motivation."

THE CULTURAL BACKGROUND OF COMMUNICATION

Over the years you have absorbed a body of information about the way people in your cultural setting react in certain kinds of communicative situations. You have observed receivers and senders in school situations, family situations, and neighborhood situations. You may have had experience with "customers" or "patients." If you have been exposed to parties, weddings, illness, funerals, or other events, you have learned a little about how people communicate in those circumstances. These experiences will help you proceed more confidently.

Our culture also has expectations and customs in connection with speaking to an audience. Knowing them will also help give you confidence. For example, Americans have specific expectations about hours of beginning and concluding and about time limits. As

---

[13]Two names attached to these lines of thought are those of Hans Sayle and Seymour Levine. See the article by the latter, "Stress and Behavior," in *Scientific American,* 224 (January 1971): 26–31, and the bibliography on p. 122.

other customs of speech making may not be so familiar, the following suggestions are offered as a checklist.

When you are invited to make a speech, be sure about the day, the place, and the time limits. Often you need to ask the program chairperson about the length of the speech, the occasion, and the audience, so you will know what is anticipated. Information like this will shape your preparation and add to your assurance. If you can be one of the early arrivals at the place where you are to speak, you will have a chance to sense mood and atmosphere and perhaps pick up information you can work into your talk.

You may or may not be formally introduced. In either event, don't be in too great a hurry to start the flow of wisdom. Deliberateness accompanies experience. I recall seeing Satchel Paige go in as relief pitcher. He did not trot to the mound like a colt but walked with measured steps. Arriving there he took another moment to survey the infield and shift the position of the outfielders. Then he gave the batter and the catcher his full attention. Finally the mighty cannon that is his right arm exploded. The game had been fully resumed. I see no real difference between him and Sir Winston Churchill, taking command of the House of Commons, or, for that matter, between either of them and thousands of competent young communicators.

A deeply rooted part of our culture calls for the speaker to be poised and deliberate. Tradition accords him this respect, dating back to American frontier days when the speaker was the bearer of news from the outside. We are not basically a heckling people, nor are we a yelling, shouting, spear-shaking, shield-thumping people. In fact the unruly audience that insults a speaker or attempts to break up the meeting promptly makes the headlines. You are entirely in order to take a moment to collect yourself before you begin your prepared remarks.

If you have been introduced in a complimentary way, you may open with a few comments of your own about the introduction. You may also say a few words about a speech that has just preceded, or an event that has just taken place in the classroom or auditorium; this practice shows adaptability to the situation.

Occasionally a speaker will say "Thank you" at the conclusion of the speech. President Truman has said, especially when talking to audiences of young people, "Thank you; you couldn't have been nicer to me." Other presidents have used complimentary closings such as "Thank you and good evening." Probably most speakers quite properly do not thank the audience at all; they finish their speeches, give their audiences a smile and a slight nod, and take their seats. If, however, you feel the audience has been unusually attentive, say so, in a short sentence of your own phrasing.

The foregoing are the *usual* customs, the *usual* formulas. They are stated here to acquaint you with what is conventional and traditional. They are not inflexible rules. Although they make good sense for most situations, you will meet situations where you will want to act differently.

Your instructor's suggestions should help make sure that the general principles here discussed are executed to the best advantage, with due regard to individual variations and adaptations that fit your own style and personality.

CONCLUDING NOTE The suggestions given in this chapter about studying the principles of effective speaking and about organizing, rehearsing, and generally doing the things that generate confidence, should help you get under way. Experience should cultivate the positive emotional attitudes of a good speaker: enthusiasm, sincerity, and conviction.

ASSIGN- MENTS AND EXERCISES

1 An assignment combining interpersonal speaking with group discussion or speech making:

  a Make a list of eight or ten of the types of communicative situations that you face most frequently. List them in order, starting with those "least fearful" and ending with those "most fearful."

  b Make a list of other kinds of situations that you face most frequently. For a starter, consult the list on page 86 of this chapter. List them in order, starting with those "least fearful."

  c Compare your list with that of a classmate. Discuss ways that you have used to manage these situations more effectively.

  d Join three or four other pairs, and compare and contrast your lists. Exchange suggestions about managing these situations.

  e Each group will select a member to present the findings of the group to the whole class; *or:*
  Each member of the class will report briefly to the whole class.

2 Make a survey of your friends and acquaintances on the general subject of educational experiences that decrease, or increase, speech tension. To what extent have they experienced speech tension? To what extent have they, or have they not, been able to decrease it?

3 The following tests, devised by James C. McCroskey, using materials from previous tests plus other items written by him and his graduate students, may help you inventory your own feelings with respect to a variety of communicative situations.

This instrument is composed of 20 statements concerning feelings about communicating with other people.

Indicate the degree to which the statements apply to you by marking whether you (1) strongly agree, (2) agree, (3) are undecided, (4) disagree, or (5) strongly disagree with each statement. Work quickly, just record your first impression.

1. While participating in a conversation with a new acquaintance I feel very nervous.
2. I have no fear of facing an audience.
3. I look forward to expressing my opinion at meetings.
4. I look forward to an opportunity to speak in public.
5. I find the prospect of speaking mildly pleasant.
6. When communicating, my posture feels strained and unnatural.
7. I am tense and nervous while participating in group discussions.
8. Although I talk fluently with friends I am at a loss for words on the platform.
9. My hands tremble when I try to handle objects on the platform.
10. I always avoid speaking in public if possible.
11. I feel that I am more fluent when talking to people than most other people are.
12. I am fearful and tense all the while I am speaking before a group of people.
13. My thoughts become confused and jumbled when I speak before an audience.
14. Although I am nervous just before getting up, I soon forget my fears and enjoy the experience.
15. Conversing with people who hold positions of authority causes me to be fearful and tense.
16. I dislike to use my body and voice expressively.
17. I feel relaxed and comfortable while speaking.
18. I feel self-conscious when I am called upon to answer a question or give an opinion in class.
19. I face the prospect of making a speech with complete confidence.
20. I would enjoy presenting a speech on a local television show.

The test is scored in the usual 1-to-5 manner; 1 indicating least apprehension, 5 indicating most. The lower the score, therefore, the less the apprehension; 20 is the lowest possible score, 100 the highest. The theoretical neutral position is 60; a score of more than 60 suggests more than average apprehension. The items are worded so that a "strongly agree" response may be scored either 1 or 5, an "agree" response either 2 or 4, and so on. Thus a "strongly agree" response to item 1 scores 5, "agree" scores 4, "undecided" scores 3, "disagree" scores 2, "strongly disagree" scores 1. On the other hand a "strongly agree" response to item 2 scores 1, "agree" scores 2, "undecided" scores 3, "disagree" scores 4, and "strongly disagree" scores 5.

4 The following test consists entirely of items taken from the public speaking situation:

This instrument is composed of 34 statements concerning feelings about communicating with other people.

Indicate the degree to which the statements apply to you by marking whether you (1) strongly agree, (2) agree, (3) are undecided, (4) disagree, or (5) strongly disagree with each statement. Work quickly, just record your first impression.

1. While preparing for giving a speech I feel tense and nervous.
2. I feel tense when I see the words "speech" and "public speech" on a course outline when studying.
3. My thoughts become confused and jumbled when I am giving a speech.
4. Right after giving a speech I feel that I have had a pleasant experience.
5. I get anxious when I think about a speech coming up.
6. I have no fear of giving a speech.
7. Although I am nervous just before starting a speech, I soon settle down after starting and feel calm and comfortable.
8. I look forward to giving a speech.
9. When the instructor announces a speaking assignment in class I can feel myself getting tense.
10. My hands tremble when I am giving a speech.
11. I feel relaxed while giving a speech.
12. I enjoy preparing for a speech.
13. I am in constant fear of forgetting what I prepared to say.
14. I get anxious if someone asks me something about my topic that I do not know.
15. I face the prospect of giving a speech with confidence.
16. I feel that I am in complete possession of myself while giving a speech.
17. My mind is clear when giving a speech.
18. I do not dread giving a speech.
19. I perspire just before starting a speech.
20. My heart beats very fast just as I start a speech.
21. I experience considerable anxiety while sitting in the room just before my speech starts.
22. Certain parts of my body feel very tense and rigid while giving a speech.
23. Realizing that only a little time remains in a speech makes me very tense and anxious.
24. While giving a speech I know I can control my feelings of tension and stress.
25. I breathe faster just before starting a speech.

26. I feel comfortable and relaxed in the hour or so just before giving a speech.
27. I do poorly on speeches because I am anxious.
28. I feel anxious when the teacher announces the date of a speaking assignment.
29. When I make a mistake while giving a speech, I find it hard to concentrate on the parts that follow.
30. During an important speech I experience a feeling of helplessness building up inside me.
31. I have trouble falling asleep the night before a speech.
32. My heart beats very fast while I present a speech.
33. I feel anxious while waiting to give my speech.
34. While giving a speech I get so nervous I forget facts I really know.

This test may be scored like the test above. The theoretical neutral position is 102; however, according to Dr. McCroskey, 945 students at Michigan State University had a mean score of 114.62. Those interested should study the complete report in *Speech Monographs,* 37 (November 1970): 269–277. We have found these tests useful at the University of Missouri both in class study and in identifying students who might wish to volunteer for special desensitization sessions.

6 Adapting to Listeners

What adaptation is ☐ Analyzing listeners ☐ The "sleeper effect" ☐ Application to interpersonal communication ☐ Application to group discussion and speech making ☐ The audience and you ☐ Listeners and your subject ☐ Assignments and exercises

Rhetoric, says Donald C. Bryant in a famous quotation, is the function of adjusting ideas to people and people to ideas. In the second chapter of this book the communicative process was described as a continuing dialog between source and receiver, each reacting to and interpreting the visible and audible symbols transmitted by the other. The message is created with a probable receiver or receivers in mind. As this receiver will interpret the message in the light of his or her own experiences, the sender develops a sensitivity to all phases of the communicative transaction that serves as a guide in deciding what to put into the message and what to leave out.

We follow this principle many ways in interpersonal communication. We hesitate to bring up a sticky problem unless we believe the receiver is "in a good mood." We telephone a busy man at his office rather than "bother him at home." We start a technical explanation, but the feedback indicates our language is too technical, so we shift to simpler concepts. In a small group discussion we discover that Member B is "touchy" about religion, or that Member C, who suddenly lost a dear relative, is saddened by references to death and funerals.

In speech making, knowledge about audiences has a high priority. When John F. Kennedy was campaigning for the presidential nomination, he realized an important goal was the winning of the West Virginia presidential primary. Both he and Hubert Humphrey canvassed the state vigorously. Senator Kennedy and his advisers asked themselves: What are the basic concerns of West Virginia voters? The economic depression in the state loomed large, and Kennedy repeatedly stressed his interest in developing the state's resources in order to improve the standard of living. Repeated surveys, however, also showed that this state, 95 percent Protestant, was reluctant to support a Catholic candidate. Kennedy made the strategic decision to meet the religious issue head on. Here is an example of a politician making an audience analysis and adjusting his speech making accordingly. He explained his position candidly, developing arguments that he used in his campaign in other states. He won the West Virginia primary and, after that, the nomination of his party for the presidency.[1]

As most speakers do not have the service of a polling organization available, they must base their rhetorical plans on conjecture and limited information. Even so, educated guesses are better than no guesses at all. And if you are sensitive to the moods and feelings of those around you, if you can read the signs and signals that show

---

[1]Theodore C. Sorensen, *Kennedy* (New York: Harper, 1965), pp. 138–147; Theodore H. White, *The Making of the President, 1960* (New York: Atheneum, 1961), pp. 97–109.

your listeners are attentive or not, you can, if you are sufficiently experienced, tune in more sharply to them. Here you have an advantage over poll-takers, who have to close their books before election day. A familiar example from speech making is that of the speaker who writes a manuscript and then finds that the reading of it took more time than he expected. The listeners show signs of restlessness—a kind of message that can be transmitted with the greatest of ease, since it is the least sophisticated and most readily recognizable of audience signals. If, however, the speaker does not fully perceive what is going on, he grimly reads his manuscript through to the end. One of greater sensitivity (and know-how) would skip some paragraphs and paraphrase others, and so reach a conclusion more speedily.

The alternative to audience analysis is to deal in generalities and platitudes that fit one situation about as well as another. Mark Twain, who liked to use exactly the right word spoken in exactly the right tone, wearied of heavy-handed speakers, and to satirize them, devised a "Patent Adjustable Speech," good for any sort of gathering—wedding breakfast, theological discourse, political blowout, inquest, or funeral. A typical sentence might be, "Agriculture, sir [or matrimony, or religion, or politics] is after all, the palladium of our economic liberties."[2] This sort of fraudulent adaptability is a far distance from the genuine concern for listeners that competent speakers try to develop.

WHAT ADAPTATION IS

When you as a sender adapt to receivers, you do not need to sacrifice principles or beliefs. As these may be a matter of record, you would not fool anyone. You are expected to maintain your principles and beliefs, and if the situation is such that you cannot win converts, you can at least make your own position reasonable and understandable.

Although adaptation is often thought of as merely perceiving whether listeners are hostile or friendly, it has other aspects. If your subject is technical, and your listeners are laymen, you should use layman's language. One who can do this can be serviceable both to society and to his profession. A campus is filled with intellectually curious people, students and faculty, who would like to hear the visiting expert in genetics, mathematics, or the French Revolution, provided he or she will add to their store of general information; but they do not want to be clobbered by materials they do not under-

---

[2]Paul Fatout, *Mark Twain on the Lecture Circuit* (Bloomington: Indiana University Press, 1960), p. 239. Copyright © 1969 by Indiana University Press.

stand. Hence an expert should plan one kind of message for a seminar of colleagues, another for the general campus.

Imagine that you are a professional person who usually addresses general audiences, but you are invited to address a homogeneous audience such as the state bar association or the county medical society. In one instance you will comb your resources for examples having to do with lawyers, in the other with physicians. You are not trying to be a lawyer or a physician, but you use these examples because of their high interest to the people in front of you.

Sometimes an audience is composed of widely differing people. If you returned to the school from which you were graduated, and were invited to address an assembly of junior high students, senior high students, and faculty, you would see that a problem would be to choose a topic that could be made interesting to this varied age group. You would probably incorporate illustrations and examples, since this kind of material has general interest and appeal. Most audiences do not present this range of ages, but even a classroom audience has individuals with a challenging variety of backgrounds in education, vocation, religion, activities, and the like. All these factors you weigh and appraise as you choose a subject, gather materials, and in other ways plan your message.

ANALYZING LISTENERS   In addition to the usual consideration of age, sex, race, religion, and nationality, you like to know the following things about the listener or listeners: marital status; trade, business, or profession; political party; educational background; attitudes, prejudices, or biases; values; expectations of one as a speaker; mood.

From this pool of items, you may select those relevant to the given situation. In any community on a given night, groups like the following may be assembling: parents of young children, the League of Women Voters, the Junior Chamber of Commerce, a labor union, or a church guild. Any of these groups might be interested in hearing a young man who has just completed military service. To each of them he might talk on the topic, "The American Image Overseas," but each speech would have subtle differences. Listeners in the groups with which he was most successful would probably feel, "This talk was designed especially for us." Yet basically the talks could be identical: all his listeners are American, justly proud of their country and understandably interested in the experiences and observations of one of their young men overseas.

At times the *mood* is the prime consideration. Is it one of worry, apprehension? Suppose the community has lost its principal industry, or the industry has been shut down by a long strike. Is the community worried, alarmed? Suppose it is about to gain a new industry. Are the citizens divided between the advantages of the payroll and the damage to the environment? Perhaps the campus or the church is split down the middle. Mood is a powerful shaper of messages. Sometimes your questions ask about demographic matters: age, sex, marital status, and other things that can be tabulated. Other questions inquire into beliefs or motivations. Listeners seek recognition; they can be challenged to undertake something difficult; they can be successfully urged to build, to maintain, to preserve; and they respond to notions of rivalry, competition, and contest. Different appeals work at different times. A congregation that feels itself too poor to remodel its old church enthusiastically builds a new one that costs three times as much. In its discussions those who talked about cost and economy were overridden by those who discussed the need of more room for the children and young people, who showed that the church, like the community, was growing rapidly, and who described the satisfactions that other congregations felt after building their new churches. Dimes and dollars ride one set of values, man's outreaching spirit rides another.

Leon Festinger's theory of cognitive dissonance is of value to communicators in their attempts to analyze prospective listeners and to frame messages that will influence behavior. Festinger's theory starts with the notion that a human being needs to have a consistent system of beliefs and attitudes; if presented with alternatives, one tends to select the choice least disturbing to one's current beliefs. If each alternative has both positive and negative aspects, one tends to increase the attractiveness of the chosen alternatives, decrease the attractiveness of the rejected alternative, or both. Even so, after the decision has been made, certain feelings of inconsistency persist. Early in the development of his theory, however, Festinger replaced *inconsistency* with a term that had less of a logical connotation, *dissonance,* and *consistency* with a more neutral term, *consonance.* He also revived the term *cognition,* by which he meant "any knowledge, opinion, or belief about the environment, about oneself, or about one's behavior." He saw the individual as attempting "to establish internal harmony, consistency, or congruity among his opinions, attitudes, knowledge, and values": in other words, to be in a state of cognitive consonance.[3] His point of view has generated more than 300 studies.

Other investigators have pondered the general notion of bal-

---

[3]Leon Festinger, *A Theory of Cognitive Dissonance* (Stanford, Calif.: Stanford University Press, 1957). See among others pp. 2–3, 29, 36, 157, and 260–261.

ance or consistency. A classic experiment by Osgood and Tannenbaum is that of individuals who go through the process of purchasing a new car, considering various makes. When these individuals, after having made their purchases, are offered literature describing these different makes, they are likely to select materials describing the car they actually bought. In this way they increase their internal calm by reviewing the attractiveness of their choice.

A point at which these theories affect one's analysis of an audience is this: A listener who strongly believes X hears a competing view, Y, advocated by a highly credible source, A, and is thrown into a state of cognitive dissonance. He must somehow reconcile his strong belief in X with his high regard for A. His easiest choice is to change his attitude toward A: "A is not so well-informed as I thought." Another is to try to harmonize views X and Y, or to minimize the importance of X or the strength of his belief in X. Hardest, most difficult, most agonizing of all is to utter those three little words: "I was wrong." In this last instance Festinger describes the situation as divorcing oneself psychologically (p. 29), and in general tending to forget the things one disagrees with (p. 157).

As you review this facet of audience behavior, you will ponder both your own credibility with prospective listeners and also the likelihood of listeners agreeing or disagreeing with you. If you feel your topic may arouse dissonance or imbalance, you will consider ways of enhancing your own credibility and decreasing the amount of disagreement, by perhaps bringing in new evidence that listeners could not have been expected to know about. This gives them an easy out. Or you might say, as one student did, "I want to present today some of the arguments in favor of liberalizing the abortion laws. I know that many of you have strong *personal* and *religious* views against abortion; in fact I share these myself. I hope, however, that for the time being you will set these to one side, and listen to some of the *societal* reasons for making abortions more available." Lincoln also used this approach in his famous letter to Horace Greeley, explaining that what he did about slavery he did because it would help save the Union, and what he forbore, he forbore because it would not help save the Union. "I have here stated my purpose according to my view of *official* duty; and I intend no modification of my oft-expressed *personal* wish that all men everywhere could be free." The excerpt appears in greater length in Chapter 17.

Consistency (balance, congruity) theory explains a large category of communication problems, but does not pretend to account for all the complexities of persuasion. Most of us may question the judgment of a person who disagrees with us; most of us do like to be reassured that we made a good decision. Yet exceptions exist. One social psychologist has predicted that "consistency theory" may be replaced by "complexity theory." Under the former, he says, the individual

> has a penchant for stability . . . avoidance of the new, the unpredictable. Complexity theory's romantic organism works on a quite different economy. It has . . . an exploratory drive, a need curiosity. It takes pleasure in the unexpected, at least in intermediate levels of unpredictability. It wants to experience everything; it shows alternate behavior; it finds novelty rewarding.[4]

You may find yourself in a persuasive situation where you will want to push the strangeness, the newness, the novelty of your proposal to the fullest, urging your listeners "to be first," "to do something different."

Another concept by which to view listeners is the open-closed system of beliefs-disbeliefs advanced by Milton Rokeach. Everyone has a system of beliefs that he accepts and a series of systems that he rejects. One who accepts Freud may reject Adler or Jung. "The Catholic, the Unitarian, the Baptist, and the Jew," says Rokeach, "each accepts one set of beliefs and rejects *several* others." You have probably already observed that when discussing ethical or religious topics with your friends you may meet head-on a system of beliefs that your arguments cannot penetrate.

Rokeach and his associates argue further: "We cannot think of a single person who is not driven by both rational and rationalizing forces." This statement being true, they continue, the question of one's belief or disbelief system is not a conflict between the intellectual and the emotional. Rather, they affirm, "belief-disbelief systems serve two powerful and conflicting sets of motives at the same time. There is a need to know and to understand, and also a need to ward off threatening aspects of reality."[5] *Open systems* result when external pressures and irrational internal drives are pushed aside, and, accordingly, information received from the outside is discriminated, assessed, and acted upon according to the objective requirements of the situation. *Closed systems* result when the need to ward off threat becomes stronger, the cognitive need to know becomes weaker, and information is appraised somewhat arbitrarily. The

---

[4]William J. McGuire, "The Current Status of Cognitive Consistency Theories," in Shel Feldman, ed., *Cognitive Consistency* (New York: Academic, 1966), pp. 1–46. McGuire reviews a vast field of consistency studies, an area to which he himself has contributed.

[5]Milton Rokeach, "The Organization of Belief-Disbelief Systems," and Rokeach and Frank Restle, "A Fundamental Distinction Between Open and Closed Systems," in Rokeach, *The Open and Closed Mind: Investigations Into the Nature of Belief Systems and Personality Systems* (New York: Basic Books, 1960), pp. 31–53 and 54–70.

closed mind is more resistant to change than the open mind. No one, however, has a system that is entirely open or entirely closed.

The usefulness of this concept may be applied to the attitude of possible listeners, both in interpersonal and in more formal situations. Principal characteristics of *open systems* include: communication of ideas within and between belief and disbelief systems; the situation one is in at a particular moment is friendly; authority is not absolute, and people need not be accepted or rejected according to their agreement or disagreement with authority. Principal characteristics of *closed systems* are the opposite of these: isolation of parts within and between belief systems; the situation one is in at a particular moment is a threatening one; authority is absolute, and people should be accepted or rejected according to their agreement or disagreement with such authority.

Following this concept, one would visualize listeners as believing or disbelieving; and as operating in open or closed systems. If you felt you and your listeners were in a relatively open system, you would feel more free to discuss the novel features of a proposal; the extent to which it broke from custom or tradition; the threats or dangers, if any, and the ways in which they could be handled; and the risks as well as the advantages. If you felt your listeners were in a relatively closed system, you would, in all candor and honesty, have to use the same reasoning, but you would show regard for their sensitivities.

In further illustration, imagine yourself presenting proposals for an ecumenical center for Episcopalians, Methodists, and Baptists. You present the proposals to each group in turn. The core of your argument is the same with each group. The proposals do not change as you go from one group to another. Each proposal has a specific origin in religious dogma or custom. Speaking on proposal A to group A, your manner and words would say, "You will like this proposal—it suits your current belief and practice." Speaking on proposal A to group B, your manner and words would say, "Now this proposal represents a change from what you are accustomed to." The disadvantages of this change, however, which you probably could not successfully minimize, would be offset, you would point out, by certain advantages.

In their review of research in behavioral science, Bernard Berelson and Gary A. Steiner offer this conclusion:

> People tend to see and hear communications that are favorable or congenial to their predispositions; they are more likely to see and hear congenial communications than neutral or hostile ones. And the more interested they are in the subject, the more likely is such selective attention.

> This holds for personal conversation . . . : people are more likely to talk about controversial matters with like-minded people than with those who do not share their views. . . .
>
> [These predispositions include] sex role, educational status, interest and involvement, ethnic status, political attitude, and, indeed, any way of characterizing people that matters to them.[6]

One may also ask, in connection with persuading either a single individual or a group: What is the extent or degree of *ego-involvement* of that individual or that group? Is the issue one with which listeners are deeply identified and committed? Carolyn W. Sherif, Muzafer Sherif, and Roger E. Nebergall, the proposers of this concept, argue that if listeners are strongly ego-involved in a position, they are highly unlikely to alter their basic notions. In fact, these authors point out, a change in the position of such an individual "amounts to changing a part of himself." They continue:

> The frame of reference for studying attitude change, therefore, includes the individual's stand and his degree of involvement in it. . . . It includes the communication itself, its form, and the order of arguments. It includes the communicator and the source, both of which affect the extent to which the position presented in communication anchors the individual's subsequent appraisals of the issue. Thus, a source and speaker with high standing or prestige in the person's eyes, in effect, enhances the anchoring function of the advocated position.[7]

THE "SLEEPER EFFECT"
An interesting phenomenon in connection with speech communication is the *sleeper effect*. In ordinary terminology, a *sleeper* is a person, product, or device that achieves unexpected success: a book, a movie, a manufactured article. In speech communication the sleeper effect describes an idea that lingers in memory longer than expected, or that grows in importance with the passing of time; a phrase that catches on. At the time of its utterance the person who launched it might not have seemed impressive nor the situation remarkable. Yet the words persisted.

You may search your own memory for examples: a teacher who might not have been one of your favorites at the time, but whose teaching has increasingly seemed meaningful; a bit of advice, casually offered, that stuck with you.

---

[6]*Human Behavior: An Inventory of Scientific Findings* (New York: Harcourt, Brace, 1964), pp. 529–530.

[7]*Attitude and Attitude Change: The Social Judgment-Involvement Approach* (Philadelphia: Saunders, 1965), pp. 242–243.

The greatest sleeper in the history of American public speaking is the Gettysburg Address. At the time the audience was not impressed and, in fact, many newspapers ridiculed it. Now it is the one speech that nearly every American knows about.

The sleeper effect is difficult to establish experimentally, as an idea once heard may be reinforced from other sources with the passing of time—sources that cannot be experimentally controlled. Yet the sleeper effect is worth mentioning because an idea you express may persist because of the intrinsic worth of what you said.

APPLICATION TO INTER- PERSONAL COMMUNICA- TION

How can the concepts previously discussed be applied to interpersonal communication? You find yourself at a social gathering, your aim being simply to meet and mingle with other guests and have a pleasant experience. Or you seek a conversation at which you can achieve a specific purpose: to ask a favor, to remove a misunderstanding, to achieve a business or professional aim.

In any event, you will find it helpful to know as much as possible about the other person. At the purely social event, you may be able to gather helpful snatches of information. For the other type of event, you can make fuller inquiry. Nationality, religion, politics, values, vocation, achievements, all enter into your "audience analysis." Interests and hobbies are also good conversation starters. On an autumn Saturday evening people are likely to talk about the Saturday afternoon game. Someone else may be turned on by tennis or duck hunting. Someone else is up on popular music, new books, new movies. These topics lead to a fair amount of self-disclosure. They give cues also to needs and values. You are in an especially good position if you and the other person share similar interests. If you both soon weary of the football talk, no matter; you will turn to something more satisfying to both, and the football will have served as a bridge to a better topic.

If two people seem to get along well, they will become pleased with themselves and with each other and perhaps take up meatier issues. If their opinions vary, they will nevertheless have some regard for each other (i.e., less dissonance); the disagreement is "an honest difference of opinion," and respected as such. Note also that there are ways of stating differences without invading the other's personal integrity. Listen to the experienced politicians on TV—the people who live at the center of controversy—and note how adroitly they express their differences and disagreements. One strategy is to refrain from attacking the other person's argument but, instead, strengthen your own.

In discussing serious matters, you may have this question in the back of your mind: "Is this other person one who is receptive to new ideas?" (Open mind or closed?) "If I present him with a new idea, should I emphasize its novelty or otherwise? Or should I do both: indicate the new and novel features, but also point out that these features have proved successful in other localities?" Does he have a system of beliefs that focusses on economy, low taxes, bureaucracy, so that he would oppose a plan involving expense? If so, is he in a position of authority where he has high esteem and self-actualization needs—and might want to make a contribution that would stand as a marker to his career?

Interpersonal communication goes better if each participant talks a comfortable percentage of the time. It is fine for the other person to talk 70 percent of the time if you are comfortable with the remaining 30 percent. Otherwise you might find yourselves interrupting one another.

Every communicative transaction has two sides, talking and listening, so it is helpful to excel at both. J, applying for a professorial appointment, learned that all members of the interviewing committee approved him except K, the Dean of the College of Engineering. J, knowing that Dean K was a consultant for the Tennessee Valley Authority, opened the conversation with a reference to TVA, a topic which the Dean liked to discuss. After several minutes of exposition interrupted only by further questions by J, K said: "Well, this has been a pleasant conversation; I hope you get the appointment." J was successful—and to this day K probably thinks of J as being an excellent, perhaps even a brilliant, conversationalist.

The gist of this brief section is to indicate that interpersonal communication can be planned ahead as well as managed impromptu, and that theory often supplies a handle to a perplexing situation.

APPLICATION TO GROUP DISCUSSION AND SPEECH MAKING

Much of what has just been said applies to the talk that goes on in small groups as well as to interpersonal communication. In preparing for the type of group discussion that goes on in front of an audience, and for speech making, you may do one or more of the following:

1 **Make a mental analysis of your possible listeners** As already said, you may reflect not only about the obvious matters of age, size of the group, sex, and academic or other vocations, but also about their basic needs as human beings, their systems of beliefs, the openness or closedness of their approach to new proposals. Topics involving strictly male interests would be difficult to adapt to females, and vice versa. Problems about child-

rearing would be difficult to adapt to a group of single people years away from matrimony.

2 **Prepare a questionnaire**   Inquire into experiences, information, and attitudes. Combine specific questions with open-ended requests for comments. Comments often supply quotable materials.

3 **Gather information of specific interest**   If your audience is to be all grocers, all insurance brokers, or all nurses, read trade publications, house organs, and professional journals and saturate yourself with the problems of your future listeners.

4 **Secure details about the occasion**   as follows:

When is the speech to be given?   Is there anything special about this particular date? Is it a holiday or anniversary?

Where is the speech to be given?   How small or how large is the room? Are the acoustics favorable? Is a microphone provided? Are conditions suitable for the use of visual aids? Is there a speaker's table? a lectern? a reading light?

Are there special features?   Is it founders' day or ladies night? Will well-known guests be present? Is special dress required?

How is your speech to fit in?   Are you the principal speaker? Are you one of several speakers? Do you follow a seven-course dinner or a long program of musical or other events? How much time is allotted for your speech? Does the meeting adjourn at a fixed hour? You will be able to judge from this information whether you may have to cut out part of your speech at the last minute to compensate for another part of the program that ran too long.

An important way in which a speaker must adapt himself to the situation (and to the audience as well) is to respect the *time limit* set for the speech. (This book has pointed out previously that time limits, and a high degree of punctuality, are features of American culture.) By custom or arrangement speeches are expected to be of a certain length. If sermon time is customarily twenty minutes, a half-hour sermon may seem long and forty minutes uncommonly so. If a businessmen's club has traditionally scheduled thirty-minute addresses, members may become restless if the speech grows longer (and would perhaps be surprised and disappointed if the speech were only ten).

The length of speeches may be fixed in part because of a previously scheduled time for adjournment: one church service must end on time in order to make way for the next; a businessmen's club adjourns at 1:15 because members must go back to work. Other

Diana Henry/EPA

situations, however, are open-ended, with no set time of adjournment. Suppose the local chamber of commerce is having an evening banquet followed by speeches. Although a century ago such a function might have run into the early morning hours, this generation prefers to stop at 10 p.m. or so—earlier if listeners have to drive long distances home. Your program chairperson should give each speaker a time allotment; even so, each speaker should, that evening, note whether events are moving on schedule. For if the dinner is delayed and the presiding officer is long-winded, you may sense that although earlier in the evening the audience might have listened happily to your thirty-minute speech, realistically you must now conclude that you will be more effective with a more compact version of it.

THE AUDIENCE AND YOU
A good question to ask yourself is: *What do I know that will be useful to this audience?* Are there topics of interest to listeners about which I may be better informed than they are? People like baseball, and you have been an umpire. People are interested in safe driving, and

you have administered driver's tests. People know about the Salvation Army or the Red Cross, and you have worked with them. People enjoy popular music, and you are a life-long fan.

A related question is: Do I have a reputation that will lead listeners to expect me to talk on certain topics? Will I appear in a specific role? (People might be disappointed to hear an entirely serious talk by Bob Hope. But if he entertains them first, they might listen to a thoughtful message.) You would rather hear a sportswriter talk about his experiences in that field than discuss a topic like "The Future of the Panama Canal" that he understands only at second hand. You would be willing to hear a prominent automobile executive talk about "Success in Life," but you would anticipate with special pleasure his including firsthand experiences with the manufacture of automobiles. Your own role may be a more modest one, yet you may be able to capitalize upon it. Or maybe your role needs some bolstering: you come from a rival firm; you have received bad publicity recently; your former speeches have been soundly criticized for their faulty information; in the past you have been humorous, but today you want to be serious; you are a defeated candidate, or an erring prophet. In these situations get yourself on firm ground, not by apologizing, but by showing your tact and friendliness, or by poking fun at yourself, or by candidly confessing your faults (not to be confused with apologizing for them). Perhaps the *title* of your speech can help with the problem of adaptation.

Still another important question to ask is, "How can I make this subject useful to this audience?" To remind your listeners that your information will have practical value later on, when they are married, when they have children, when they are established in their careers, is of course helpful. Still better is to remind them that your information has value now. We remember better the facts that we will speedily put to use.

LISTENERS AND YOUR SUBJECT   You need also to anticipate the possible attitude of your listeners toward your subject.

Will they be friendly?   If your topic is not controversial, your listeners will give you a hearing provided you select materials with care and judgment. Perhaps you can use humor, suspense, novelty in a way that will make attention gaining and attention holding relatively simple. If your topic is persuasive, and provides listeners with a quick, easy decision, you should get a favorable response.

Will they be indifferent or neutral?   Although your topic is important, is it one that your listeners have perhaps neglected? Is it more significant than at the outset they will realize? Have they heard so many discussions of the same topic that they may ignore another? If your answer to these questions is *yes,* you will see that you need to use material that will seek to get the listener off his dead-center position.

Will they be hostile, antagonistic, prejudiced? Is your position unpopular? Will you run into a "closed system" of beliefs? If your answer is *yes,* you will need to use a disarming approach in order to get a hearing. You need to support your views rather than attack those of the other person. Remembering Rokeach's observations, you will want to avoid being threatening, and also to recall that people are moved by feeling as well as by reasoning. Remembering dissonance theory, you may be able to show that your viewpoint is not so different from that of the other person as he thinks.

Actually, hostile listeners may be more rare than one supposes. You are more inclined to attend meetings that favor your own interests and attitudes than you are to attend meetings that are opposed to your views. This principle has been surveyed in connection with such widely varying topics as political campaign issues, bond purchasing, donating blood, the relationship between smoking and cancer, and the United Nations. Behavioral scientists argue that persuasion is more likely to reinforce or modify a listener's position than it is to convert him to the other side; they therefore speak of *selective exposure,* or the tendency to choose communications that one favors, and *selective retention,* or the tendency to remember ideas in harmony with one's own. For example, a much advertised documentary film stressing such highly important civic activities as donating blood and buying bonds was attended mainly by individuals *already prominent* in community affairs. Another investigator reported that articles dealing with the possible relationship between smoking and cancer were read by 60 percent of male *nonsmokers,* but only 32 percent of male *smokers.* Still another reported that twice as many Republicans as Democrats viewed a Republican-sponsored TV program. The speaker to a Rotary or Kiwanis club, a Junior Chamber of Commerce, or a congregation, will, however, pretty much have to deal with his audience as he finds it.[8]

COMMENT   This chapter emphasizes the importance of studying the *receiver* of the message, in both formal and informal situations. You are naturally concerned with yourself: the impression *you* will make, the anxieties *you* have. These concerns are important, but should not lead you to overlook the other person or persons.

---

[8]See Joseph R. Klapper, *The Effects of Mass Communication* (Glencoe, Ill.: Free Press, 1960), pp. 19–22. The studies reported deal with various forms of mass communication, but the conclusions are worthy of consideration in connection with speech making.

At times your contribution may make a difference even if you are unable to perceive any. The person who argues stoutly against you may, later on, accept a part of your reasoning. You may not have persuaded this person, but later he or she may be more readily persuaded by someone else. Once an elegant Englishwoman found herself the dinner companion of Gladstone, and at a later event the dinner companion of Disraeli. Gladstone impressed her as being the most brilliant man she had ever met. Disraeli left her with the impression that she was the most delightful conversationalist he had ever met.

You may, moreover, have a larger group of listeners than those physically present. Something you say may be relayed to people not there. Lincoln's statement, "You can fool some of the people all of the time . . . but you cannot fool all of the people all of the time" was originally uttered to a single listener, who told others, and eventually this bit of wisdom got in print. Something you say casually could be remembered by someone else forever. Your own memory may supply other examples.

ASSIGN-MENTS AND EXERCISES

1 From your own experience, supply examples of:
 a people whose lives seem motivated by one or more basic needs
 b a situation you have experienced where Festinger's theory of cognitive dissonance seemed to operate
 c an outline of your own belief-disbelief system, one or more systems that you regard as "closed," one or more that you regard as "open"
 d a personal example of "selective exposure," i.e., a meeting you attended because you expected to hear views in harmony with your own
 e a personal example of "selective retention," i.e., the tendency to remember ideas in harmony with your own
2 Suppose you are supplied with complete information about a listener or listeners. Give examples showing how this information might lead you, as a communicator, to:
 a change your subject
 b alter your choice of examples
 c determine the amount of preliminary or background information to present
 d use technical terms
 e be conciliatory or forceful
 f use more or fewer transitions, repetitions, restatements, summaries
 g use visual aids
3 Suggest topics from your own experience where knowledge

about the *age* of the audience would be especially relevant. Consider also: sex, marital status, vocation, nationality, race, religious faith, educational background, and membership in a specific organization.

4 From your knowledge of some other member of the class, suggest a topic that a local audience would like and expect to hear him discuss.

5 Report an experience you have had in studying a particular group to which you were to speak.

6 Prepare a questionnaire to distribute to members of the class designed to yield specific information to help you prepare speeches on the topics you are likely to deliver: political affiliation, church preference, academic interests, possible vocation, athletic or avocational interests, and the like, as appropriate.

7 To what extent can a speaker create an audience for his speech? What methods or media are available? (For his first public lecture, Mark Twain composed humorous copy for a poster. At the bottom was the line, "Doors Open at Seven. The Trouble Will Begin at Eight.")

 Listening
Well

Good listeners and poor listeners □ Kinds of listening □
Assignments and exercises

Epictetus once wrote, "There is an art of hearing as well as of speaking. . . . To make a statue needs skill; to view a statue aright needs skill also. . . . One who proposes to hear philosophers speak needs a considerable training in hearing. Is that not so? Then tell me, on what subject are you able to hear me?"

Throughout this book references have been made to the *listener*. Messages are organized partly to add to the speaker's comfort and assurance but primarily to aid the comprehension of the *listener*. The examples we select and the words with which we clothe ideas are aimed at the *listener*. All in all, speech communication requires us to be thoughtful about the ultimate consumer of messages—the *listener*.

How much of our day is spent in listening? From 40 to 50 percent, say the experts; you can adjust this figure to your own situation. Do we listen well? Most people do not, say the experts; in a few weeks' time 75 percent or more of a given lecture has slipped away. Does the ability to listen vary? Yes, widely, say the experts; some retain much more than others. Some students have a listening efficiency of only 10 percent; others as high as 70 percent. What about conversing with the foreign-born people in our midst? Here the situation becomes more complex. What about daydreaming? Much occurs even when people are supposed to be attentive.

GOOD LISTENERS AND POOR LISTENERS In an experiment that has become a classic, freshmen on the University of Minnesota campus listened to lectures on a variety of subjects. After each lecture, the students took an objective test over the material.[1] The 100 best and the 100 poorest listeners were selected and were given tests, followed by a personal interview. Investigators then formulated differences between good and poor listeners; a few of these differences follow:

1 **Poor listeners usually decided, after hearing a few sentences, that the material would be dull.** Good listeners were more patient and more willing to assume that the material would have a future, if not a present, usefulness; they therefore listened more attentively.

2 **Poor listeners often found immediate fault with personality or delivery.** A poor listener easily forgets that senders come in all

[1]See Ralph G. Nichols and Leonard A. Stevens, "Listening to People," in *Harvard Business Review,* 35 (September–October 1957): 85–92. And see also, by the same authors, chap. 9, "Six Bad Habits," and chap. 10, "Pencil and Paper Listening," in *Are You Listening?* (New York: McGraw-Hill, 1957). See also Nichols, "Listening," in Ronald F. Reid, ed., *Introduction to the Field of Speech* (Chicago: Scott, Foresman, 1965). Used by permission. The material in this section is based largely on these sources.

sizes, shapes, lengths, breadths, and talents. They have a variety of voices and postures, and they gesture in different ways. Some are more fluent than others—some have mannerisms that distract. The poor listener was inclined to assume that if personality or delivery were displeasing, the ideas would not be worthwhile. The good listener refrained from making snap judgments until he had listened to the *ideas*. As for the lecturer's appearance, the good listener should practice the courtesy implied in the comment about Lincoln: "He is homely, but on him it looks good."

3 **The poor listener listened best when the speaker's message was carefully outlined.**   Often she was lost if the lecture were not clearly organized. The good listener had several systems of taking notes; if the lecture did not follow a methodical plan, she caught its gist with another system of outlining.

4 **The poor listener listened mainly for facts.**   His long exposure to objective tests had probably made him sensitive to dates, names, formulas, and other specific items. The good listener not only caught the facts, but was also more likely to seize upon *interpretations, generalizations, implications, applications, and trends.*

5 **The poor listener had had less experience in difficult listening than had the good listener.**   The poor listener preferred television and radio programs that were easy to follow, like westerns, instead of more difficult programs like interviews with thoughtful persons. The good listener could draw upon a wider background of listening experience, and therefore, when the teacher's exposition became more complex, the good listener gave even closer attention to the discussion and tried to follow it.

Among the anonymous people on this planet, students who participate in classroom experiments deserve a special tribute. The 282 psychology students at the University of Southern California, the 1,162 social psychology students at Syracuse University, the 295 students of speech at Michigan State (the exact numbers are fictitious)—along with thousands of others—have made a generous, largely unrecognized, contribution to education. Add to that list the 100 good listeners and the 100 poor listeners from Minnesota (who not only listened to lectures, but participated in interviews) who also deserve our praise. Now they are men and women in their forties, established in their communities, their sons and daughters in high school or college, all of whom, hopefully, listen as well as or better than their parents.

After that light-hearted diversion, we return to the problem. Listening is so important a communication skill, and one so easily neglected, that we need to know what researchers have learned about it.

KINDS OF LISTENING   Improvement begins with discovery and analysis. The following discussion of the kinds of listening may help you with your inventory of strong and weak points.

Empathic Listening   Charles M. Kelly calls attention to the importance of *empathic* listening.[2] The mental set of the empathic listener is to understand the sender, to explore the sender's point of view, and to share in the spirit of that point of view. In general, the listener supports the sender as a person (*empathy* contains the root meaning "suffering," so in a sense the receiver "suffers" with the sender).

If in a private conversation you are talking with your girl friend about your difficulty with botany, you are fortunate if she by her words and manner shows that she is listening attentively, with sympathy and understanding. When you have stated your difficulty, she may ask a question that probes a little deeper into some aspect of your problem. She helps you get it out in the open. Before long you may find that you understand your own difficulty better, and may even see a solution to it. Admirers of Carl Rogers and his school of nondirective counselling will perceive that she is not overwhelming you with advice, at least not at the outset, but is giving you full opportunity to talk your problem out at your own pace. If you evolve alternative solutions, she will help you explore them.

What you hope does not happen is that as soon as you pause for air, she starts talking about *her* problem with chemistry. This diversion breaks the transaction. Instead of listening to you, she was mentally reviewing her worries about chemistry. Instead of a genuine communication, there were two people broadcasting alternately on different wavelengths. It is as if you went to a physician, to tell him about your headache; as soon as you paused, he started to talk about *his* headache. If afterward he gave you some pills, you could not be sure whose headache he was treating. Give botany the full treatment, *then* chemistry.

A good listener builds our self-esteem, enhances our self-concept, buoys our ego. Good listening gives us the red carpet, the seat down front, the souvenir program, the free popcorn. At a dance the wise girl gives her full attention to her partner. She does not continually look over his shoulder to catch the glance of other boys. Even in a large class private sendings and receivings go on between lecturer and students. Here and there students will signal signs of their interest—a slight nod, a smile, an intent look—the lecturer manages to say, in subtle fashion, "I read you loud and clear." Individual conversations after class also help the learning process on both

---

[2] "Empathic Listening" by Charles M. Kelly, in Robert S. Cathcart and Larry A. Samovar, eds., *Small Group Communication: A Reader* (Dubuque: Wm. C. Brown Co., 1970), pp. 251–259.

sides of the desk. Who knows but that as a result of these two-way transactions, during and after the hour, the teacher instructs more effectively and the students learn more.

The best teachers, like the best students, are good listeners. Were it not for the dialog that continually goes on, teaching and learning would wither on the vine.

The business world is also concerned with improving the ability of its people to listen. Top management does not listen to middle management, it is alleged, and middle management does not listen to the lower echelons. Sales people are much too casual with customers. The editor of *Administrative Management* argues that many organizations make a botch of their internal communications because their administrators think that communication is only "show and tell." Management should create "the right type of framework so people feel they are contributing." This dialog may not convince everyone to like a policy, but at least the charge cannot be made, "They wouldn't even listen."[3]

Discriminative Listening   Larry L. Barker has analyzed *discriminative* listening, describing these characteristics, among others:[4]

The retentive listener seeks to understand and to remember. At the moment of listening, the listener perceives the information as being useful, something to recall later.

The reflective listener not only retains the information, but mentally evaluates it.

The reactive listener supplies verbal or nonverbal feedback to the sender. He may nod and smile, or the opposite, ask questions or make comments showing approval or disapproval.

The mind of the discriminative listener is busily churning away, not so much sympathizing with the sender as concentrating on the message, perhaps reflecting, "That's a new idea; I'll remember that," "I wonder where that information came from," "I must ask the sender to go more deeply into that point," or other comment. As in other types of listening, the discriminative listener is mentally alert, fully engaged at the task of comprehension.

Critical Listening   Critical listening introduces a certain wariness into the situation. The evidence, the reasoning, and the conclusions, must meet certain standards of judgment. If the standards are met, fine; if not, then the conclusions need to be discounted. Note the following:

---

[3]Reprinted from *Administrative Management*, 29 (September 1968): 21. © Geyer-McAllister Publications, Inc.
[4]*Listening Behavior* (Englewood Cliffs, N.J.: Prentice-Hall, 1971), pp. 12–13.

Sweeping generalizations   Conclusions should follow from the evidence offered. Assertions without proof can mislead. In 1848 Daniel Webster stoutly declared that California and New Mexico "are not worth a dollar." But before the year was out, the great gold rush had begun.

Predictions   When a message offers to foretell the future, whether it concerns the stock market, an election, or other event in the future, the listener should remind himself that a prediction is only a prediction, and that prophets can be mistaken. The usual tests of reasoning can be applied to help determine whether the prediction is reasonably sound.

Even when the prediction is based on facts, the strong possibility exists that someone else might have interpreted the same facts differently. All economists, for example, have access to the main facts about unemployment, income, capital expenditures, carloadings, and the various indexes; but at a given moment one economist may feel that the country is headed for further recession, a second that it has hit the bottom of the recession, and a third that it is beginning to head upward out of the recession.

Polls, surveys   Polls and surveys are useful, and this book recommends them, but they are not conclusive evidence, and the listener must still use his best judgment.

Expert opinion   Nearly always good, but sometimes experts get set in their ways, and others have to come along with a fresh outlook. The testimony of experts testifying outside the field of their specialty is demonstrably specious.

For example, American visitors overseas who offer observations on the basis of brief tours should remember that Americans are widely traveled, and among your listeners will be some who have also been there. Adlai Stevenson once remarked that whenever he spoke about his travels, he was sure to discover, during the question period, that Eleanor Roosevelt and Marco Polo had been sitting in the front row. Once an American went to Paris. "When did you arrive?" asked a friend. "Yesterday." "When are you leaving?" "Tomorrow." "Why are you here?" "To gather material for a speech." "What's the subject of your speech?" "Paris: Yesterday, Today, and Tomorrow."

Everybody's doing it   At times we are urged to do what everybody's doing. But the majority is sometimes right, sometimes wrong. Anatole France wrote: "If 50 million people say a foolish thing, it is still a foolish thing."

Social psychologists have long established that individuals have a strong desire to conform to the opinions and judgments of those about them. The message that suggests without much evi-

dence that "most good students" support a point of view is employing a subtle persuasive factor; the listener should be on guard.

Propagandistic devices Opinion is not fact; assertion is not evidence. Repeating a lie does not make it true. Making the lie a bigger lie does not make it true. Calling names is not logical argument. Testimonials of actresses, socialites, do not make the product better. The *plain folks* appeal is also used to convince listeners that the speaker and his ideas are good because they come from "just plain folks." It also comes in forms such as "I'm no orator," or "I'm not a big city lawyer," or "I'm a country boy."

Definition Terms may be undefined or defined loosely. One speaker quoted a medical authority to the effect that "tobacco in any form is not harmful when used sensibly by a reasonable man." This statement seemed wise until one listener inquired, "How do you define 'sensibly'? Who is a 'reasonable man'?" Although the speaker made a spirited defense of the medical man's statement, most listeners decided that the advice was too general to be truly helpful.

On the positive side, look for the exact, accurate statement; the willingness to consider both sides, even though the speaker favors one side; the perceptive limitation of the subject that shows the speaker is not biting off more than she can chew; the evidence that has internal consistency; the speaker's basic sincerity and integrity; and the quality of ideas, sympathy, considerateness, understanding, and range of information.

The subject   The quotation from Epictetus on the first page of this chapter raised the pertinent question: "On what subject are you able to hear me?" A good listener will get some things out of a speech that the speaker did not put into it.

The critique   Listen to be able to answer the question: "How could this topic have been presented more effectively?" The 24-year-old Thomas Erskine once listened to the barristers in an English courtroom, thinking to himself that he perceived ways of presenting the evidence more effectively; in the years to follow he became perhaps the greatest of all English courtroom pleaders. The 20-year-old William Pitt once discussed arguments heard in the House of Commons with a friend, Charles James Fox: "But surely, Mr. Fox, his argument might be met thus." The 20-year-old Henry Clay attended a debate, listening attentively, and afterward he heard the chairman call for the vote; Clay quietly observed that the topic was not exhausted; the chairman invited him to present his views, and thus Kentucky began to become aware of the eloquence of a famous future senator. Listen therefore not merely to pass judgment on what the speaker said or did but also to answer questions like: "How would I have handled this topic?" or "What suggestions can I give for presenting this topic more effectively?" Under this heading you can review choice of topic and ways in which it was limited and adapted to the audience; organization; reasons, evidence, and examples; factors of delivery such as voice, articulation, body action; the total impact that the message appears to make upon the listeners.

Appreciative Listening   *Appreciative* is used by Barker in the sense of the expert who is able to identify the skill of another expert in the same area; in the field of communication, the expert—you, for example—notes that the sender is using principles of arrangement, selection, language, body action, etc., in an effective way. After reading only this far in this book, you may find yourself thinking, "That's a good example of self-disclosure," "That speaker has a good self-concept," "This lecture is generating a lot of feedback," or "The speaker is perceiving us as a closed audience." As a participant in classroom exercises, you will increasingly value the appreciative listener, who can say not only "That was a good speech" or "Your group put on an interesting discussion," but also, "Your explanation was clear," "Your analogy was striking," "Your conclusion combined a summary and an appeal in a persuasive way," etc.

Note further how the sender leads into the central idea: the statement and development; the variety of materials (sometimes statistics, sometimes examples and illustrations); transitions; internal summaries; recapitulations; enumeration of main points. After the message is complete, can you say with confidence—and to the sender's complete satisfaction—what the central idea was? Like this:

> Betty said that the liberal arts college has a fault that few would suspect: the tendency to graduate students whose training has been overspecialized. She showed that this tendency is the result of two powerful pressures. One, students wish to take more courses in a field they like rather than to open a new field of study. The other is the likelihood of professors to encourage a student to strengthen his major continually rather than to advise him to broaden and diversify.

In other words, appreciative listeners come in various degrees of expertness. One listener will perceive, simply, "That's excellently organized, Betty," and another will offer the detailed analysis stated just above. Betty is deeply grateful to both.

IMPROVING LISTENING ABILITY You may have a head start in one or more ways in the problem of improving your ability to listen. Research tends to support these findings:[5]

Mental state Listeners who are free from momentary worries tend to be better than those who have worries or feelings of insecurity.

Fatigue A strong relationship exists between listener fatigue and listening ability; the greater the fatigue, the less the ability to listen effectively.

Scholarship A moderate relationship exists between scholastic aptitude (grade point average, rank in class) and listening.

Vocabulary Most evidence suggests a relationship between vocabulary size and listening comprehension. Research also indicates that effective listening skills help strengthen a listener's vocabulary.

Reading comprehension Listening and reading are interrelated communication skills.

Perceptions of the speaker The more visible the speaker is, the higher his credibility, the more he is liked, the better his voice and action, the more the listener will attend to him.

Teachers of speech communication have so little doubt that the ability to listen can be improved notably that they have almost stopped researching the issue. An early study that set up situations

---

[5]Ibid., pp. 46–49, 51.

in which a number of groups could be taught listening skills reported that some groups averaged a 25 percent gain in listening proficiency, with other groups attaining a 40 percent gain.[6] You may, however, have to accept a large share of the responsibility for your own improvement, because in most classroom and real-life situations you are likely to receive much more feedback about your speaking than about your listening.

The following suggestions should open up new avenues of improvement:[7]

1 **Interestingness** You may find yourself in situations in which the material seems dull. Especially if you are likely to have to recall this material later, wrest from it everything you can. *Interest grows with knowledge.* The more you learn about something, the more likely you will become interested in it.

2 **Attitude** Ralph G. Nichols stresses the importance of developing a proper attitude toward the sender. He urges the listener to keep an objective frame of mind and to avoid anger or other upsetting emotions. Meet the other person more than halfway—hear him out—you will still have the right to criticize him, disapprove of him, or vote for his opponent. A key word is *desire.* Create a desire to listen. The material may be dull, as suggested just above; or it may be controversial—in the latter situation, try to get the opposing viewpoint. This text has already commented on *selective exposure* (seeking communications that favor rather than oppose your point of view) and *selective retention* (tending to remember the facts with which you agree and to forget those with which you disagree). If in general you would rather talk than listen, sometimes change your approach.

3 **Personality and delivery** Something about the sender's personality (aggressiveness, timidity) or his delivery (poor voice, indistinct articulation) may repel you; in that event, focus on the quality and worth of the ideas. Lincoln, because of his long arms and legs, was often called a "baboon"; but those who called him that were deaf to some of the greatest eloquence ever uttered in the English language. Fortunately, we normally adjust to wide variations of personality and delivery in other people. Ask yourself what the delivery adds to or subtracts from the message you are hearing. Does voice suggest interest, enthusiasm, convic-

---

[6]Ralph G. Nichols and Thomas R. Lewis, *Listening and Speaking* (Dubuque: Wm. C. Brown Co., 1954), pp. 5–6.
[7]Most helpful in this connection are Carl H. Weaver, *Human Listening: Processes and Behavior* (Indianapolis: Bobbs-Merrill, 1972), Chapter 4, "What the Listener Can Do to Improve"; Dominick A. Barbara, *How to Make People Listen to You* (Springfield, Ill.: Charles C Thomas, 1971), Chapter 7, "How Not to Be an Indifferent or Lethargic Listener."

LISTENING AND NOTE TAKING

Since students spend a fair amount of time taking notes in connection with listening to lectures (and in preparing speeches, reports, and themes), researchers have turned their attention to the overall efficiency of the note-taking process. This chapter has already commented that a well-organized lecture lends itself to better note taking. Viewing note taking as an adjunct to better listening, we can make these observations:[8]

Selecting As a listener, you can not write everything down; you therefore go through a selecting process, determining what is relevant and what is irrelevant to the main purpose of the lecture as you conceive it. This process shows good thinking.

Reinforcing You are particularly attentive to materials that seem to have more than usual importance: statements of principles; numbered sequences such as *first, second, third;* dates, names, formulas; information that you see immediate use for on an upcoming test or elsewhere; vocal cues by the lecturer indicating his or her own feeling that the material is significant.

Initiating You react to ideas that prompt you to initiate an action by supplying you with a reason, time, or place.

It is approximately twice as likely that lecture material written down in your notes will be recalled than if it is not written down.[9]

[8]Suggested by the analysis of Francis J. Di Vesta and G. Susan Gray, "Listening and Note Taking," *Journal of Educational Psychology,* 63 (February 1972): 13.
[9]"Memory for a Lecture: Effects of Notes, Lecture Rate, and Information Density," *Journal of Educational Psychology,* 67 (June 1975): 444.

tion? Does facial expression reflect seriousness, sincerity, strength, gentleness; in short, does it help make the words more communicative? Does gesture help to emphasize ideas? You would not be wise to imitate someone else exactly, but you may ask yourself this question: "Would my presentation be better if I could disclose more of my enthusiasm, sincerity, conviction, and earnestness?" One reward of your discriminating listening may be to encourage you to work on nonverbal features during your next classroom or interpersonal communication.

4 Inner distractions We have already mentioned that being mentally at ease encourages listening. At times, however, we are eaten alive by family problems, grades, boyfriend-girlfriend concerns, and find it difficult to listen normally. Perhaps we can say, inwardly, "This lecture (interview) (conversation) is also a part of my life and, despite my own problems, I must give it my attention." At other times the inner distractions are of our own creation, taking the form of daydreaming or fantasizing.

5 **Foreign accent**   When talking or listening to a person who speaks with a foreign accent, one faces special problems. If she is talking, you may need to supply omitted words, or mentally correct grammatical irregularities or mispronunciations. If you are talking, you cannot always tell whether she is understanding you or not. Her smiling and head nodding can be deceptive. One usually finds oneself gesturing vigorously when giving directions to a foreign-born person. When receiving directions from a foreigner, one is well advised to maintain a puzzled expression until the light actually breaks through. European shopkeepers often write down the price because a tourist may misunderstand spoken words.

6 **Recognizing gaps in your background**   You may have a tough, competent thinking apparatus for social science or mathematics but find it difficult to follow a discussion of modern poetry. To help you get started on poetry, you may need to react by asking more questions than others. Your questions may prompt the other person to take a fresh grip on the topic. Clarifying technical terms, using summaries and transitions, introducing humor for mental relief, employing examples to stimulate the imagination— all of these should help the listener unfamiliar with a certain kind of material. David Lloyd George, British prime minister, liked to tell the story of the shipbuilder who said that when he listened to an ordinary sermon he could design a new ship from keel to topmast but complained that when he listened to the eloquent preacher, George Whitefield, he could not think of a single plank.

7 **Draw the other person out**   We discussed this suggestion in connection with empathic listening. If he or she pauses, instead of starting to talk yourself, ask "one more question." Listen for names, places, personal details, out of which you can formulate questions ("Oh, you spent the summer in Germany. Where in Germany?") that will give you a chance to learn something, or focus the conversation on a topic where you both will have a special interest. Reticent people on a first date, for example, need to help each other out.

Evidence is accumulating that individuals listen better if they are told what the message is to be about. Thus if you are anticipating a message, comparing what you hear with what you expected may cause you to listen more carefully to see whether or not your anticipations are fulfilled. A specifically stated idea ("I want to discuss two advantages that the Latin-American common market will have for that region") should help the listener get ready to listen, to interpret and infer.[10] A message that follows a perceived plan of organization—time order, space order, comparison and contrast, or other plan—should stimulate the listener's anticipation of what is to follow. Putting sentences in meaningful order and indicating relationships by transitions aids comprehension. In fact, listeners tend to appraise a message, at least in part, on the basis of its structure.[11]

I. A. Richards has suggested the term *feedforward* to describe a procedure in which the communicator reveals part of the structure in such a way that the whole plan is likely to be anticipated; he thus paves the way for what is to follow.[12]

COMMENT To be called "a good listener" is a fine compliment. It may be a higher compliment, in some contexts, than to be called "a good speaker"; who knows? It is certainly a skill that most people can attain. Applied to a captain of industry or a public official, to be called a good listener shows understanding and approachability—perhaps warmth and concern as well. Applied to others, it shows those qualities often at an even more intimate level.

Wendell Johnson, who went to the University of Iowa as a young man with a stutter, received perceptive help and counsel and became a speech pathologist, an authority on the management of stuttering. From there he moved on to write about problems of communication and, above that, of living, and concluded:

> We are a noisy lot; and of what gets said among us, far more goes unheard and unheeded than seems possible. We have yet to learn on a grand scale how to use the wonders of speaking and listening in our own best interests and for the good of all. . . . It is the finest art still to be mastered by man.[13]

---

[10]See Charles T. Brown, "Studies in Listening Comprehension," *Speech Monographs,* 26 (November 1959): 288–294. "Listener anticipation of the purpose of a message is an important factor in his comprehension. . . . Students at all levels of listening ability were equally aided by the statements of purpose" (p. 291).

[11]Ernest Thompson, "Some Effects of Message Structure on Listeners' Comprehension," *Speech Monographs,* 34 (March 1967): 51–57. The ability of the listener himself to organize material is also noted by this researcher.

[12]See Paul W. Keller, "Major Findings in Listening in the Past Ten Years," *Journal of Communication,* 10 (March 1960): 29–38, and Isabella H. Toussaint, "A Classified Summary of Listening—1950–59," *Journal of Communication,* 10 (September 1960): 125–134.

[13]"The Fateful Process of Mr. A Talking to Mr. B," *Harvard Business Review* (January–February 1953): 56.

Why not leave this chapter on listening with that thought . . . the finest art that we can master.

1 Discuss the place of good listening in:
   a Social conversation
   b Interviewing an applicant for a position
   c A physician's consultation with a patient
   d A lawyer's consultation with a client
   e A teacher's conference with a student
   f A supervisor's conference with an employee who has a grievance
2 Keep a diary for a week of your listening experiences. Note among the people with whom you come in contact those who listen well and those who listen poorly. Note situations in which you appear to be listening well and those in which you are turned off. At the end of the week set down your overall conclusions. Can you correlate good listening with age, sex, intelligence, and status?
3 Hand in a Listening Report of approximately . . . pages on a significant speaker. Consider his or her choice of subject, choice of material, organization, language, method of presentation, delivery, and general effectiveness. What would you consider his or her strong points as a speaker? Assuming that your advice was sought about possible ways of improvement, what would you urge him or her to consider first?
4 Make a similar report on a TV speaker. In your critique, in addition to the suggestions under "3" above, keep in mind that the opening part of a TV speech is of special importance to help make sure that the viewer does not change stations. Comment also on the use of visual aids, if any, and on such features of delivery as facial expression.

Wide World Photos

8 Improving Language and Style

Language and other disciplines ☐ Expressive, communicative functions of language ☐ Desirable qualities of language ☐ Tools for improving language ☐ A recapitulation ☐ Assignments and exercises

The significance of language is shown in the following description (some liberty has been taken with the arrangement of lines):

The fundamental fact of human existence
is man with man.

Something takes place
between one being and another
the like of which
can be found nowhere in nature.

Language
is only a sign and a means for it.[1]

More formally, *language* is the system of symbols—visible and audible—with which the members of a considerable group communicate with one another. Through custom and tradition the selecting and combining of these symbols follow patterns which become confirmed by usage.

Style refers to the distinctive or individual manner in which a given person uses language. Well-known examples of people who developed a distinctive style are Churchill, Roosevelt, and King, plus any number of statesmen, commentators, and other men and women who have achieved prominence as communicators.

Style is therefore the individual's variation of the system. Still keeping within the bounds of "the formal code," each individual can impose patterns of word selection, arrangement, and the like which stamp the utterance as his or her own. "Don't ask what your country can do for you" is an ordinary, everyday, arrangement. "*Ask not* what your country can do for you" imposes a degree of *style*. What Kennedy did was to reverse the usual order, changing "Don't ask" to the more impressive "Ask not." Even so, "ask not" lies within the system of permissible variations. The language system known as English is highly sensitive to word order: "For you don't ask what your country can do," though a simple rearrangement, requires an extra instant for decoding, and sounds strange or foreign to the ear. Examples in this chapter should suggest ways of improving your own style.

LANGUAGE AND OTHER DISCIPLINES

Language is so basic to communication that some scholars are predicting that it will become the most active area of future research in this broad area.[2] Linguists, anthropologists, social psychologists,

---

[1] Martin Buber, *Between Man and Man,* trans. Ronald Gregor (London: Kegan Paul, 1947), p. 203.

[2] William J. McGuire, University of San Diego, thinks research in language may prove to be the most active area in social psychology, perhaps through the efforts of Chomsky and his

and speech communication researchers are all concerned. Here are provocative lines of thought:

1 **Anthropological** To establish a base-line, contrast the language competence of human beings with other primates. One researcher after much observation established a total of twenty-two sounds for the gorilla (but to attain that number the researcher had to include chest-beating).[3] Another researcher contrasted the communication of gibbons and humans:

> Among the most competent of vocalists are the gibbons, whose vocabulary has been shown to possess at least nine sets of sounds with specific meanings. Sound number one: "Keep away from my wife!" Sound number two: "Let's go get some fruit!"[4]

During the long era in which human language was developing, the ability to transmit and to interpret signals had immense survival value. The human being who could not quickly interpret the danger signal, who was confused about the signals for direction, who could not distinguish between *right* and *left,* who misunderstood the plan of the hunt, who showed up at the wrong rendezvous, did not live long enough to leave any descendants. Our heritage equips us to understand language. We need to increase our competence in handling today's complex signals. We can achieve only a limited amount with chest-beating.

2 **Genetic** At one time, linguists thought that children learned to speak the language of their parents by a routine, mechanical, add-on process. Using such simple methods as imitation, selection, and repetition, a child in relatively few years, they argued, mastered the grammatical and syntactical peculiarities of English or whatever language he was exposed to. It became obvious, of course, that a child did not simply learn one sentence, then another, then another. One scholar estimated that there are at least 10^{20} sentences twenty words long, and that it would take about a thousand times the age of the earth just to listen to them, much less to learn them. Obviously a more sophisticated theory was necessary to explain the child's achievement in learning language. The notion was advanced that children are genetically endowed with a capability to learn a language; instead of learning one sentence after another, they have the ability to figure out such basic principles as word order, use of

disciples. See "The Nature of Attitudes and Attitude Change" in Gardner Lindzey and Elliot Aronson, eds., *Handbook of Social Psychology,* 2d ed., 3 (Cambridge, Mass.: Addison-Wesley, 1969), p. 141.

[3]Irven DeVore, ed., *Primate Behavior* (New York: Holt, 1965), p. 558.
[4]Carleton S. Coon, *The Story of Man,* 2d ed. rev. (New York: Knopf, 1962), p. 18.

modifiers, and tense structures, so that they are able to understand and to use sentences they have never heard. This ability continues throughout life. The discovery of the basic, underlying structure of a language is the most complex of the processes involved in learning a language, yet nearly every child masters it to some degree at an early age.[5]

What has been said above suggests that all of us have sophisticated equipment for improving ourselves in the use of language. It is related to our ability to make inferences, see relationships, and create generalizations. If you feel you have reached a plateau in your development, it may be that you need a livelier environment to bring more of this exquisite machinery into play. The examples in this chapter, by illustrating some of the refinements of language structure, may help you achieve greater competence.

3 **Intercultural** Franz Boas, pioneer anthropologist, encouraged students like Margaret Mead and Ruth Benedict to undertake detailed observations of the languages and behavior of isolated societies. Since then a massive literature has accumulated about the different ways in which languages have developed. Each language or dialect is found to be "elegant" or "sophisticated" for its own society, with its own formalized system. Vocabulary, for example, develops in response to need. Eskimos have many different words for *snow,* as the kinds and varieties of snow are closely related to their existence. We have many different words for *soil (loam, clay, silt),* since we are utterly dependent upon the produce of the earth. Arabs are said to have 6,000 names connected with *camel*—classes, breeds, etc. English has words describing different kinds of meals—*breakfast, luncheon, tea,* etc.—but Solomon Islanders find that a single word is sufficient.

Observations like these assist us to see that our own language has built-in features that reflect deeply seated cultural attitudes. In recent years we have been made aware, for example, of the sex bias built into English. Eleanor Roosevelt and her American and English colleagues on the United Nations Commission on Human Rights discovered that fact when they proposed, as a basic human right, "All men are created free and equal." At that time, *men* distinctly meant *male and female.* Other delegates, who spoke other languages, would not accept that interpretation. Eventually *human beings* was substituted for

[5]George A. Miller, "Some Preliminaries to Psycholinguistics," *American Psychologist,* 20 (1965): 15–20; Roger Brown and Ursula Bellugi, "Three Processes in the Child's Acquisition of Syntax," in Eric H. Lenneberg, ed., *New Directions in the Study of Language* (Cambridge, Mass.: Massachusetts Institute of Technology Press, 1964), p. 151.

men. Nor did all members of the Commission like *created.* This word had a religious connotation, which in turn led to debate and altercation. "All human beings are born free and equal" seemed to bridge these various gaps between languages.

Today, Americans would be less ready to accept "All men" than was Eleanor Roosevelt three decades ago. We are now more aware of the basic sex bias. We like *chairperson* better than *chairman.* Our language is defective (as we now view the situation) in that it has no single pronoun meaning both *he* and *she;* to say *"he or she"* is awkward, and the form *s/he* is clumsy to pronounce. Right now, we are happy with a single word *you* to designate both the person with whom we are intimately acquainted, and the person who is a total stranger. Other languages have a form for *you* to represent the other person who is a sweetheart, a member of the family, or a close friend, and another form for *you* to represent the casual acquaintance, stranger, or even enemy.

At times words literally do fail us. Many mystical or religious experiences can hardly be put into words. Often scientific concepts are vastly complex. In these instances we do what we can with simple analogy, or try to "believe" without really "understanding." We do what we can to bridge the gaps between cultures, or between disciplines. But this kind of reflection also adds to one's interest in language.

4 **Pedagogical** The art of using language more effectively is highly teachable. Thousands of people have successfully increased their vocabularies or heightened their sensitivity to grammar, syntax, and rhetoric. Thousands of others learn a second language, and attain a degree of proficiency in it. We need to do still more research on the problem of improving our basic language skills. Although this research would likely support much of what we are already doing through observation and experience, ultimately it would lead to insights that would suggest other methods.

EXPRESSIVE, COMMUNICATIVE FUNCTIONS OF LANGUAGE

We are easily made aware of the fact that we use language to express ourselves inwardly and to communicate to others. These have been called the *expressive* and *communicative* functions of language. As Georges Gusdorf says:

> On the one hand we have the expressive function of language: I speak in order to make myself understood, in order to emerge into reality, in order to add myself to nature. On the other hand, we have the communicative function: I speak in order to reach out to others. . . .
>
> Communication therefore has a creative power . . . one gives by receiving or receives by giving. . . .

> Nothing is completely true for us as long as we cannot announce it to the world and to ourselves . . . The lover cannot prevent himself from proclaiming his happiness, the convert his faith, or the unfortunate his despair.[6]

At times I talk to myself, to make myself understood, in order to clarify my thinking, to project my hopes into the future, to explore my concerns (expressive function). At other times I want to inform or persuade others (communicative function).

DESIRABLE QUALITIES OF LANGUAGE   We now turn to desirable goals for ourselves. For effective communication, sender and receiver should attach the same, or at least similar, meanings to the words that are spoken and heard. For centuries those who have studied the art of communication—those who have prepared and pored over and heard and recollected in tranquillity thousands of messages—have agreed that communicators should achieve two qualities of language:

> *Clarity*   Using words that receivers understand. Arranging words in groups, according to the standards required by that culture, so that the receiver can easily grasp the meaning.
> *Vividness*   Using words, or word groups, that are striking or forceful so that receivers will be more likely not only to understand but also to remember.

These qualities are illustrated in the speeches of Abraham Lincoln, one of the most proficient users of language in American political history. Early in life Lincoln became interested in speaking, possibly because he saw that good speech making would help him enter politics, possibly because he was encouraged from the outset to develop his latent talent. The text of one of his first public speeches has been reported as follows:

> Gentlemen and fellow citizens: I presume you all know who I am. I am humble Abraham Lincoln. I have been solicited by many friends to become a candidate for the legislature. My politics are short and sweet, like the old woman's dance. I am in favor of a national bank. I am in favor of the internal improvements system and a high protective tariff. These are my sentiments and political principles. If elected, I shall be thankful; if not, it will be all the same.[7]

---

[6]Georges Gusdorf, *Speaking*, trans. Paul T. Brockelman (Evanston, Ill.: Northwestern University Press, 1965), pp. 50, 67, 72.
[7]Carl Sandburg, *Abraham Lincoln: The Prairie Years* (New York: Harcourt, Brace, 1926), vol. 1, pp. 160–161.

This style is mediocre, and may not fairly represent Lincoln's ability to express himself even at that youthful age. At any rate, early in life Lincoln became impressed with the clear reasoning of Euclid's geometry: the geometrician began with a well-defined problem to prove, and then demonstrated the solution step by step. Lincoln sought to strive for this same clarity; his idea was that a speech should be a demonstration, the speaker's main idea being supported by lucidly stated reasons.

When Lincoln was elected President, however, and began to prepare his inaugural address, he realized that *clarity* alone was not enough. Citizens of a troubled nation need to be reached through their hearts and souls as well as through their reason. Perhaps he got the impetus from reading speeches by his great hero Henry Clay, and by Andrew Jackson and Daniel Webster, all of which he reviewed before he undertook to write his speech. A first draft of his inaugural reads as follows:

> The mystic chords which, proceeding from so many battlefields and so many patriot graves, pass through all the hearts and all the hearths in this broad continent of ours, will yet harmonize in their ancient music when breathed upon by the guardian angel of the nation.

Language like "mystic chords" and "the guardian angel of the nation" may well have been inspired by Webster, who knew more literature than many a professor.

Because the times were so critical that Lincoln wanted his inaugural address to strike exactly the right note, he showed this draft to his secretary of state, William H. Seward. Seward thought Lincoln's composition should have more *vividness*. This is the *second imperative quality of the effective spoken word* mentioned at the outset of this chapter. Lincoln responded to the thought of making his manuscript more vivid by rewriting the paragraph as follows:

> The mystic chords of memory, stretching from every battlefield, and patriot grave, to every living heart and hearthstone, all over this broad land, will yet swell the chorus of the Union, when again touched, as surely they will be, by the better angels of our nature.[8]

This final version is an improvement upon its predecessor; the speaker is earnestly trying for a striking, lively, colorful quality.

When Carl Sandburg speaks about Lincoln, the result is an

---

[8]This incident is based upon Earl W. Wiley's "Abraham Lincoln: His Emergence as the Voice of the People," in W. Norwood Brigance, ed., *History and Criticism of American Public Address* (New York: McGraw-Hill, 1943), vol. 2, pp. 866–868.

example of one genius with words discussing the art of another:

> His words at Gettysburg were sacred, yet strange with a color of the familiar:
> We cannot consecrate—we cannot hallow—this ground. The brave men, living and dead, who struggled here, have consecrated it, far beyond our poor power to add or detract.
> He could have said "the brave Union men." Did he have a purpose in omitting the word "Union"? Was he keeping himself and his utterance clear of the passion that would not be good to look back on when the time came for peace and reconciliation? Did he mean to leave an implication that there were brave Union men and brave Confederate men, living and dead, who had struggled there? We do not know, of a certainty. Was he thinking of the Kentucky father whose two sons died in battle, one in Union blue, the other in Confederate gray, the father inscribing on the stone over their double grave, "God knows which was right"? We do not know.[9]

Clarity   But let us leave presidential eminence and come down to the everyday level in search of usable suggestions: ways to raise your own achievement from *average* to *good,* or higher.

Numbers   Expressions like *a few, several, a whole lot,* or *millions* lead away from Euclidian clarity to a vague and fuzzy picture for the mind's eye. Often these terms show simply that the speaker has not taken the trouble to get exact information.

Suppose you want to say that there were *a whole lot* of automobile accidents in your home county. Why not get the precise figure? To say that last year eighty-seven accidents were recorded by the sheriff's office is accurate, and therefore more convincing. Instead of saying that old age pensions have greatly increased, why not say: "In the last decade, old age pensions have *doubled.*" Maybe you can draw directly on your own observation; to say "I know personally six students who went to the student clinic because of the strain of final examinations" is more convincing than to say "several students."

Nearly always a figure has to be interpreted before it is wholly meaningful. To say that your home county had "eighty-seven automobile accidents" seems to be about as specific as one can get, but you can add to the impact of the idea by continuing, "This is a 15 percent increase over last year," and the further interpretation, "and

---

[9]Delivered to a joint session of the United States Congress, Washington, D. C., February 12, 1959. Mr. Sandburg wrote the author: "You are welcome to quote from my Joint Session speech of February 12, 1959." He added: "I had a good elocution teacher in college."

THIRTY-DOLLAR SPEAKER'S LIBRARY

If you visualize your career as one requiring effective language, you will find the following books essential. The list under each heading is designed to be helpful, not exhaustive. Browse among the titles available at any good bookstore.

A college-level dictionary:
    The American Heritage Dictionary ($8.95)
    The Random House College Dictionary ($8.95)
    Webster's New Collegiate Dictionary ($9.95)

A thesaurus:
    Titles vary: *Roget's Thesaurus in Dictionary Form, The New American Roget's College Thesaurus in Dictionary Form,* etc. You will probably prefer the "dictionary form" style to Roget's original style, but most bookstores handle both sorts, so look for yourself. In paperback these range in price from 95¢ to $1.25.

A book of synonyms:
    Webster's New Dictionary of Synonyms ($8.95) or *Merriam-Webster Pocket Dictionary of Synonyms,* abridged, paperback ($2.45)

A style book:
    Margaret Nicholson, *A Dictionary of American-English,* based on *Fowler's Modern English Usage* ($1.50)

A fact book:
    Information Please Almanac ($2.95)
    World Almanac ($2.95)

Prices subject to change. A fact book such as one of the almanacs suggested is a gold mine of information that will provide specific data on a wide variety of topics.

    If your interest is historical, you will want to know about *Webster's Biographical Dictionary* ($15.00). If your interest is geographical, you will find *Webster's Geographical Dictionary* ($9.50) helpful, and also an atlas; there are dozens of titles, but an inexpensive paperback is *Van Nostrand Atlas of the World* ($1.50).

my home county has the best record (poor as it is) in the state" (or has "one of the best records") (or is "one of the ten best counties"). Skin diving is one of our most popular sports, you were about to say. Not specific enough; a million skin divers bought three times as much gear in 1976 as in 1974. In interpersonal communication as well as in public address, the exact statement makes itself felt in a way that the vague estimate does not.

"The ability of nuclear power to help solve ... [the energy] problem is easily demonstrated," said William R. Gould, Southern California Edison executive. "A single nuclear plant can save 10 million barrels of oil a year. . . ." He went on to say that with modest expansion nuclear plants could save the equivalent of 300 million barrels of oil a year.[10] Theodore G. Klumpp, consultant to the President's Council on Physical Fitness, observed: "There are some 50 million adult Americans who do not engage in physical activity for the purpose of exercise. That's equivalent to the entire population of France. . . ."[11]

The following is a novel interpretation of statistical material. The speaker is describing what this country must do to "equal" the Soviet Union:

> In order to enjoy the glories of the present Soviet system, we would have to abandon three-fifths of our steel capacity, two-thirds of our petroleum capacity, 95 percent of our electric-motor outputs, destroy two of every three of our hydroelectric plants, and get along on a tenth of our present volume of natural gas.
>
> We would have to rip up 14 out of every 15 miles of our paved highways and 2 out of every 3 miles of our main-line railway tracks. We'd sink eight out of every nine ocean-going ships, scrap nineteen out of every twenty cars and trucks, and shrink our civilian air fleet to a shadow of its present size.
>
> We would have to cut our living standard by three-fourths, destroy 40 million TV sets, nine out of every ten telephones, and seven out of every ten houses; and we would have to put about 60 million of our people back on the farm.[12]

Anything described in numbers can often be made more striking by restating the idea in other language. To say that Hawaii has an

---

[10]*Vital Speeches of the Day*, 41 (December 15, 1974): 133.

[11]Ibid., 135.

[12]The speaker is Bryce N. Harlow, addressing the Southwest Electric Conference, Chandler, Ariz., March 29, 1960. Mr. Harlow, an executive of Procter & Gamble and an adviser of various presidents, wrote the following about his speech training: "I had some formal work in speech at the University of Oklahoma as well as practical application of public speaking there in connection with numerous campus organizations. Later, in various governmental positions, both in the Congress and in the Executive Branch, as well as in private business in Oklahoma City, I have had numerous occasions to speak publicly on many matters."

Text of the speech supplied by Mr. Harlow and reprinted with his permission.

area of 6,435 square miles conveys a certain amount of information to most people. But to add that it is larger than Connecticut (5,009 square miles) conveys more meaning. To say that in area it is midway between Delaware (2,057) and Maryland (10,577) suggests that the islands constitute quite a respectable body of land (certainly large enough to be welcomed into the Union as the fiftieth state). An audience is probably surprised to learn that nearly 4 million babies are born in the United States each year, but perhaps more amazed to learn that one baby is born every eight seconds. If you have spent ten minutes reading this chapter to this point, 75 babies have been born since you started.

Specific words   The car dealer who wanted to hire a driver put an ad in the paper: "Owner wants car driven to California. Will pay all expenses." Puzzled that he got no responses, he restudied the ad and changed one word: "Owner wants Cadillac driven to California. . . ." Next day, according to a not-too-well authenticated source, he got twenty-six replies, and in three days more than sixty.

Instead of "a western state," say "Idaho," or whatever state is intended. Instead of "a comedian," "Bob Hope." Instead of "a quarterback," name a specific person known to your listeners. The employment of this principle calls for research. The specific name will help at least some listeners to identify with that bit of material. "Pine" or "white pine" is better than "tree" or even "evergreen." "Interstate 70" calls up a better image than "federal highway." "The fish were contaminated by methyl mercury" says more than "the fish were contaminated by pollution." Generalized expressions like "absolutely," "positively," "it happens all the time," "repeatedly," etc., will turn some listeners off, as in the following:

Teachers all give their exams at the same time.
Students don't read books (or are not interested in intellectual activity) (or have no serious goals).

It is more believable to say that "examinations tend to be bunched," or that "many students need to clarify their educational goals." A listener hearing "absolutely," "positively," etc., may embarrass the speaker in the question period by citing contrary instances.

Emotional implications of words   Words have connotative as well as denotative meanings. Denotative meaning is direct, specific, and literal; a connotative meaning is one suggested apart from the thing it explicitly names. The denotative meaning of *flag* is "a usually rectangular piece of fabric of distinctive design that is used as a symbol or signalling device." Its connotative meanings embrace those sentiments aroused by *the* flag: patriotism, loyalty, devotion, sacrifice, unity, and the like.

In the early days of air travel, the airlines had the idea of having young women as stewardesses aboard each aircraft. The presence of these charming girls helped to dispel feelings of fear and anxiety; patrons saw the hostesses and concluded, "if it is safe for them, it is safe for us." To counter the tension at the time of takeoff—admittedly a hazardous part of the flight—the hostesses calmly did routine duties such as greeting each passenger, helping with cabin luggage, and checking the manifest. Eventually a sign flashed, "Fasten seat belts."

Note that in all the communication, verbal and nonverbal, the smiles, gestures, and words are designed to create attitudes of confidence and relaxation on the part of the passengers. The stewardess did not greet the passenger, "Hi, sucker." She did not say, "Did you read about that crash at Toronto this morning?" When the sign appeared, it did not read, "Fasten safety belts." *Safety* leaves a different impression in the mind from the more neutral *seat*. Connotations are different. And of course it did not say, "Fasten *crash* belts." On a racetrack, however, *crash helmet* is more acceptable than *head gear*. Here the connotations of danger in "crash helmet" add to the excitement.

People are becoming increasingly sophisticated in the use of words. We are now accustomed to *social security,* which can be accepted with dignity, whereas *old-age handout* would not likely gain public support. A *city dump* is a *sanitary fill*. An *old person* is a *senior citizen. Janitor* became *custodian* and still later, in some places, *sanitation engineer. Poor farm* or *poor house* became *county home* or *home for the retired.* These and other status symbols are coming into the foreground. One hotel proposes to call its kitchen a *food preparation laboratory.* The term *domestic engineer* is suggested as a substitute for *housewife: sanitarian* for *busboy;* and *animal control warden* for *dog catcher.* Hair dye is a *tint* or *rinse.* Enemy troops are not called upon to *surrender* but instead to *come on over.* The new terms survive partly because more acceptable emotional connotations can be attached to them, but also because the denotations are more exact. The sanitary fill of today is in fact an improvement over the city dump of yesterday; a tint is more delicate and aesthetic than the dye of former years, and a senior citizen is just that—typically one who continues to pursue a good many civic, vocational, and avocational interests. One who is aware of meanings attached to words takes his knowledge into consideration in adapting his message to his listeners.

Jargon The corporation president who declared: "Major negative perturbations in the overall economy have had their inescapable effect on operational results," was really saying, "It is not our fault that we lost 40 million dollars." Another who boasted that a competitor offered minimal competition because of "the higher competence level of our executive echelon" was declaring, when translated, "Our brass is better than their brass." The military expression "effective ordnance delivery" is in fact stating, "target demolished." The military often gets its full share of criticism: a "deliberate unprovoked act of aggression" is the other side starting a war; a "pre-emptive air strike" is our side starting a war.[13] Would you be interested in knowing that atherosclerosis appears most often in connection with severe hypothyroidism, xanthochromotosis, and other lipoid metabolic disorders?

Every specialty quickly develops its own jargon; communication specialists are not immune. Lay listeners do not seek or require jargon; it is often forced upon them. If you as a specialist are preparing a message for a nonspecialist audience, you may go over what you plan to say with a layman, and seek his reactions to the language you are about to use.

Technical or unusual words   One should develop an understanding of kinds of terms that are familiar to listeners and of kinds that are unfamiliar. People like to be exposed to new ideas or new concepts if these can be made clear. If you introduce an unfamiliar word into your speech, casually explain it, and then go ahead and use it. You might say, "Engine number 3 was on fire (that's the first one on your right)." "My hometown is Poplar, ten miles south of Springfield."

The decision whether or not to use technical terms depends upon the type of audience being addressed. A student told of being in a Chicago physician's office when the physician halted the examination to answer the phone. The student could tell from overhearing one end of the conversation that the caller was a Cleveland physician inquiring about a patient who had received emergency treatment in the Chicago office. The Chicago physician explained in technical terms exactly what the symptoms were and precisely what treatment had been indicated. When he hung up, he explained in lay terms to the student what had happened: a fresh attack of an old heart condition. The student was impressed by the physician's mastery of the two communication situations: technical language for the patient's regular physician, lay language for the student; each of the two listeners received the precise information to satisfy his question.

Much higher education consists of enlarging technical as well as nontechnical vocabularies. We are introduced to different

---

[13]See these and other examples in *Newsweek,* 71 (May 6, 1968): 104ff. Copyright 1968 by *Newsweek, Inc.* All rights reserved. Reprinted by permission.

fields—humanities, social studies, sciences—and learn enough of their vocabularies to be able to communicate effectively. More than that, we learn the reasoning that goes into each term or concept. In later years the problem in communication is often to move easily from technical terms to lay terms, or vice versa, as we meet different categories of listeners. Communicators who do not develop this sensitivity are certain not to be as clear or authoritative as they would like. If you use technical terms in your communication with nontechnical listeners, you are requiring them to translate while they listen, and they may not be able to. In computer language, their minds have not been "programmed" to process such mixed data.

Enumeration; transition Language achieves clarity when it follows order, plan, and method. The discussion in this text about speech organization has already suggested the following principles, but they are reviewed here.

The formal statement of the *central idea* prepares the listener for what is to come. It has the force of a *preview,* and thus prepares the listener for the speaker's reasoning as it unfolds. If you say, "I would like to offer some thoughts about how serious pollution is, who causes it, and what can be done about it," you indicate the direction you plan to take. At times you may set forth what you are *not* going to discuss, thus:

> I would like to discuss the general problem of substitutes for steel. I am not going to talk about the ways in which the plastics industry is encroaching upon the steel market, and I am not going to say anything about concrete or copper, though these materials are important. My purpose today is to comment on three markets where aluminum is today displacing steel.

You may use the device of *enumerating* or numbering your points: this feature adds to clarity. Often you also wish to make a clear *transition* between one point and the next. Suppose the central idea is: "If you would like to achieve social success, make three personal rules for yourself." Suppose, further, the three rules are stated as follows:

1 Don't join an organization just for the sake of belonging.
2 Develop to the fullest your resources as an individual.
3 Make an effort to reach out to other people whom you admire and respect.

After discussing point 1, and showing the folly of belonging to groups just to trade on the reputation of the group and of getting into the social whirl just to be a part of the whirl, you may introduce a transition between points 1 and 2 as follows:

> So you see that if you join various organizations just for the sake of belonging, you may defeat your own purpose. A second rule to follow, if you want to achieve success in your social life, is: Develop to the fullest your resources as an individual.

These two sentences (a) review point 1, (b) remind the listener of the central idea, and (c) introduce point 2. A good transition sentence will fill each of these three functions.

When you finish point 2, you may say:

> If you want to achieve social success in the finest sense of the term, you will find it still is not enough to develop your resources as an individual. Important though this step is, you must do one further thing: you must reach out to other people whom you admire and respect.

Etymological derivations   Occasionally in defining a term it is worthwhile to look up the root meaning of the term in an unabridged dictionary. One who has *enthusiasm* is "inspired by the gods." *Missouri* means "big canoe"; the people who lived in the area graced by two mighty rivers built big canoes. *Angkor Wat* means "the great capital." In the word *science* is the meaning "to know"; in *conciliate* is the term "council," as if to win over at a council; to *educate* is *to draw out.* At a dedication occasion you may remind your listeners that *dedicate* carries the meaning, "set apart for sacred purposes." Dr. Lowell Russell Ditzen, director of the National Presbyterian Center, made this point:

> Discipline comes from the Latin word "discipulus" which has its rootage in the idea "to learn." The word is related to "disciple." A disciplined person is a learning person. He has subjected his life to a purpose, a principle, or a teacher, and so he becomes committed to a definite order and regime.[14]

After hearing that explanation, listeners would have a finer concept of "discipline" than if they thought of it as merely suggesting the following of rules and regulations.

Sometimes when your inventive fires are burning only feebly you may be able to get an inspiration by looking into the origin of some term you plan to use. What you learn may enable you to give an idea

---

[14]"The Right Ticket but the Wrong Train," *Congressional Record,* 115, 13 (June 24, 1969): 17141-17142. The speech appears in the Appendix.

INCIDENT IN NEPAL

On a trip around the world, we stopped in Nepal, a tiny country surrounded by the Himalayan and other mountain ranges. The most famous peak is Everest, nearly six miles high.

Nepal is about as far from the United States as it is possible to be and still stay on the planet. When it is Thursday here, it is Friday there. Going to Nepal is also a backward leap in time. Travel is mainly by cart or on foot. Fields and herds, not machines, are the chief interest of the people. So not only in miles, but in years, it is a remote world.

After our guide, a slender law student who spoke English, had shown us the temples and had taken us to the principal towns, we raised the question of seeing Mount Everest. By driving twenty miles to a gap in the mountains, he explained, we could have a good view. If we wanted to run the risk of fog, we could plan to arrive at the gap early in the morning, and see Everest by sunrise, "all sparkly," he went on, enthusiastically. Of course, he warned, if the fog were thick, we could not see it at all. We decided to take that risk.

Long before dawn he came to our hotel with his driver, in an ancient Chevy—I remember that the steering wheel seemed secured to the steering column by heavy wire, an intriguing situation for mountain driving. We arrived at the tiny mountain village near the gap, driving the last few miles in light to medium fog. Arriving at the village we parked near a small tavern, where a few of the villagers were having an early morning cup of tea. While waiting hopefully for the fog to lift, we got out of the car and inspected the nearby schoolhouse, a small building with a few desks bolted to the floor. We saw a woman going to the village well, carrying two buckets suspended from a bar across her shoulders. A young man trudged up the trail, dragging three lengths of reinforcing steel. We indeed felt we were as far from our own world as it was possible to be.

We discussed many things. I asked the guide if the people of Nepal had heard much about President Kennedy, who had been assassinated four years before. "Yes," he replied, "we loved President Kennedy." "For what reasons?" I pursued. He grew thoughtful. "He was sincere," he said. "He was a man of peace." "Did you ever read any of his speeches?" I continued, my occupational bias revealing itself. "Yes," he said, and, after a pause: " 'Ask not what your country can do for you. Ask what you can do for your country.' "

As the fog never lifted, we never saw Everest. But for us the moment was still a sparkly one. What clearly had happened was that an American president had put a thought into such appealing language that it had travelled halfway around the world, had penetrated another culture, and had become prized by a young man for whom English was not even the native tongue. We climbed into the Chevy and went on to the colorful city of Bhadgaon, visiting the temple square with its carved statues and its clusters of saffron-robed Buddhist monks. Memorable though this city was, I kept recalling the young president who was one of the eloquent voices of his time, to whom words like *grace* and *style* were repeatedly applied, and who concerned himself both with ideas and with the words in which they were expressed. History will appraise and reappraise his administration, but his talent for informal and formal speaking was noted by people in many walks of life and in many countries.

a humorous turn, an informative turn, or even an inspirational turn, as the foregoing examples suggest.

Vividness   Various methods make ideas vivid and memorable. These include the use of epigrammatic phrases, repetition, parallelism, question, figurative language, and unusual words.

Epigrammatic phrases   At times a speaker succeeds in compressing much into few words; the result is a phrase or *epigram* that becomes famous. Theodore Roosevelt's "big stick"; Woodrow Wilson's "make the world safe for democracy"; Franklin D. Roosevelt's "We have nothing to fear but fear itself"; John F. Kennedy's "Ask not what your country can do for you; ask what you can do for your country"; Stokely Carmichael's "black power"; Martin Luther King's "I have a dream . . .''; Harry Truman's "If you can't stand the heat, stay out of the kitchen" and "The buck stops here," are well known. Sometimes an epigram can be rephrased with novel effect; Danny Kaye once described the oboe as "an ill wind that nobody blows good." Another has spoken of "the leisure of the theory class." "No part of the packaging business is an island, a land unto itself," says another. "When packaging restrictions are passed, send not to know for whom the bell tolls—it tolls for thee."

The history of public speaking is filled with similar examples. Edmund Burke, whose speech on "Conciliation with the Colonies" was once required reading in most American high schools, earnestly asserted: "I do not know the method of drawing up an indictment against a whole people." This eloquence is recalled whenever demagogues attempt to belittle national or racial groups. Eloquent but less well known is this statement by Charles James Fox: "To propose negotiation is not to sue for peace." You may at times be able to put an idea into a short, striking statement.

Repetition The advertising experts know that the *repetition* of a slogan has a powerful effect. A good slogan, they say, may be used a year and a half—or longer—before it loses its force. Beginning speakers, too, can use this method, as when one asked, "Is it, then, so smart to drink and drive?" and then repeated it, alternating it with vivid examples showing that it was not smart to drink and drive. Ministers use repetition with compelling impact.

Senator Thomas Eagleton used repetition when he addressed the 1972 Democratic convention:

> . . . America has been *stalled* for four years . . .
> *Stalled* economically . . . with millions and millions of Americans idled by needless unemployment.
> *Stalled* in the desperate fight to save our beleaguered cities . . .
> *Stalled* in providing adequate funding for our schools . . .
> *Stalled* in its deeply felt need to find a new direction for its citizens . . .[15]

Brooks McCormick, president of International Harvester, listed eight statements that he was *dead certain* about. Among them:

> . . . we are *dead certain* that no nation can solve such problems as these [oil, currency] for itself—in isolation from the rest of the world. . . . we are *dead certain* that we must work with greater imagination and dedication than ever before to create a more favorable climate for world trade. . . .[16]

Parallelism *Parallelism* is repetition with a variation; some of the words of the phrase or sentence may be repeated, but other words are altered. This method is popular today with scores of competent speakers.

Whenever you hear parallelism you know that the speaker has given thought to phrasing his ideas; parallelism is not usually improvised on the spur of the moment.

---

[15]*Vital Speeches of the Day*, 38 (August 15, 1972): 642.
[16]Ibid., 41 (June 15, 1975): 538.

Sir Winston Churchill was an acknowledged master of English style. When preparing his speeches, he walked up and down the room, mumbling words to himself as if trying them for sound before finally dictating them to his secretary. In the course of one of his memorable speeches he paid great tribute to the airmen of the Royal Air Force who saved the nation during the Battle of Britain. Looking back at the speech itself, and at the volume of *Memoirs* in which he describes the events of that fall, one can recreate the bare statistics underlying the fight of some 600 British airmen, flying Hurricanes and Spitfires, against 1200 single- and twin-engine bombers sent against them. Churchill could have composed something like this:

All of us owe a great deal to these few airmen.

or:

Our brave boys never gave up, even when confronted by tremendous odds.

What he actually declared was:

Never in the field of human conflict was so much owed by so many to so few.

"Never" at the head of the sentence gives it dramatic emphasis; "in the field of human conflict" departs from the trite "in all history"; and the parallelism of

was so much
owed by so many
to so few

is striking indeed. Two months earlier Churchill had declared:

We shall not flag or fail.
We shall go on to the end.
We shall fight in France and on the seas and oceans.
We shall fight with growing confidence and growing strength in the air.
We shall defend our island whatever the cost may be.
We shall fight on beaches, landing grounds, in streets and in the hills.
We shall never surrender. . . .

Parallelism is not the exclusive property of genius; speakers who make no claim to be professionals can employ it. A union official could say: "Under this regulation your card could be lifted, your money could be taken out of your pocket, and your accumulated pension could be wiped away." Listeners seem to notice a series of three or more statements. Two statements are insufficient to develop the effect. A student who had spent many summers as a salesman on a used-car lot wanted to warn his listeners about unscrupulous practices of some dealers. "Stay away from the lot filled with gaudy banners; stay away from the lot with the suspicious come-ons," he concluded, and sat down. If he had added one or two additional "stay aways"—and he was sufficiently informed to do so—he would have intensified the force of his ending.

The work of the Peace Corps volunteer was once described in these parallel statements, a negative series followed by a positive series:

> He does *not* try to change their religion.
> He does *not* seek to make a profit. . . .
> He does *not* interfere in their political or military affairs.
> He works within *their* system for *them.*
> He helps to fill *their* needs as *they* see them.[17]

Similar advice, cast in similar parallel form, could be offered to teachers and others who work in the inner cities. The rhetorical force of such a series of concise statements is felt at once.

Question   The speaker may state his ideas as *questions* addressed to the listeners. The president of the Standard Oil Company of California, speaking on oil problems growing out of the Middle East, asked his audience:

> Why should these oil resources, thousands of miles from America and its western allies, particularly concern us? Why should America, the world's largest oil producer, be disturbed by the loss of access to any oil beyond its own continent?

Later in his talk he developed the structure of his speech again with questions:

> How serious then is the situation in the Middle East today? How much cause do we and our allies have for alarm?[18]

Figurative language   When you use words in a *figurative* sense— and here you will recall your previous exposure in English classes to *simile, metaphor,* and the like—you may achieve a striking effect.

Figurative language occurs in Eisenhower's statement: "In the final choice, a soldier's pack is not so heavy a burden as a prisoner's chains." Roosevelt said, in a famous fireside chat: "When you see a rattlesnake poised to strike, you do not wait until he has struck before

---

[17]Sargent Shriver, Jr., in *Vital Speeches of the Day,* 28 (April 15, 1962): 409.
[18]T. S. Petersen, speaking to the Executives' Club of Chicago. Text supplied through the courtesy of the speaker.

you crush him. These Nazi submarines . . . are the rattlesnakes of the Atlantic." Martin Luther King's famous "I Have a Dream" speech, delivered in Washington on the centennial of the Emancipation Proclamation to an estimated quarter of a million people, contains this striking metaphor: "With this faith, we will be able to hew out of the mountain of despair a stone of hope." Once Lincoln delivered a speech that hecklers sharply criticized; he replied, "There are some fleas a dog can't reach."

Classroom speakers use figurative language; the experts hold no patent on the process. One student argued: "If during your years at school you discover a shortcoming, *don't sweep it under the rug.* Hold this shortcoming up in full view, and examine it. Ask yourself what you can do about it. Maybe an activity will help, or a special course." Another student, intrigued by the discussion in newspapers about the labor union practice of featherbedding (*made* work—i.e., unnecessary or useless work), discussed featherbedding in fraternities and in classrooms. Other useful expressions like *hard sell, soft sell, hold the line, breakthrough, fallout, brainwashing, bone-tired, eyeballing disaster, thin edge of safety, domino theory,* and *military-industrial complex* are also used in a figurative sense. A professor urging a group of teachers to use clear, vivid language in their lectures to beginning classes, declared: "Don't put the fodder too high for the calves."

The unusual word   As you rehearse your speeches, pause to reflect upon a word you are using and ask yourself whether a better term can be substituted. Instead of *"serious* problem" you might like better, *"grave* problem"; one speaker said, *"distressing* problem"; still another, *"bottomless* problem." Describing a friend, the late Justice Learned Hand spoke of his *"indeflectible* loyalty." Of his own career, perhaps recalling the routine work that often comes to the bench, he said that he had spent much of his life "shoveling smoke." Justice Oliver Wendell Holmes once argued, "Strike the *jugular* and let the rest go." Sir Winston Churchill, advocating a conference of heads of state, did not use a trite phrase like "top people"; instead, he called for "a meeting at the *summit,"* and in the years since no one has been able to improve this way of putting it.

Imaginative attention to language speeds growth both as a speaker and as a writer.

Call for attention   The use of a phrase like "now get this" has been shown to emphasize the idea that follows.[19] This phrase seems to

---

[19]Ray Ehrensberger, "An Experimental Study of the Relative Effectiveness of Certain Forms of Emphasis in Public Speaking," *Speech Monographs,* 12 (1945): 94–111.

point a long finger at the words that follow, and makes them stick in the mind. We all learn that when the professor says, "Now, this is important," we should start underscoring our notes. This is an old principle. Aristotle stated that these "calls for attention" may come at any part of the speech, although it was a little ridiculous to put them at the beginning when interest was strong anyway. "Choose therefore any point in the speech where such an appeal is needed," he counseled, "and then say, 'Now I beg you to note this point—it concerns you quite as much as myself.' " The "Now get this," or "Now this is important," or "Now I beg you to note this point" are all verbal colons that emphasize the longer statement to follow.

Improper language   If you doubt the propriety of a word or expression, *don't use it.* Indecent, profane language *has no place in public speaking*. A few speakers experiment with four-letter words for their shock effect, but the repeated use of such language, barren of possibility of imagination or variety, quickly reaches a point where it has no useful effect, shock or otherwise, at all. The words or their equivalents have been in the language for centuries, and it is no accident that they have not appeared on any significant public occasion. A certain amount of dignity on the part of American public speakers is a well-established feature of our culture.

When the Irish orator, Henry Grattan, was attacked in the Irish Parliament by another member, Grattan replied: "There was scarce a word he uttered that was not a violation of the privileges of the House; but I did not call him to order . . . the limited talents of some men render it impossible for them to be severe without being unparliamentary. But before I sit down, I shall show him how to be severe and parliamentary at the same time." The assault, with its personal and professional charges, has been forgotten; the reply has an eminent place in the history of Irish public address. When one hears obscenities from a public platform, one can recall Grattan's blunt assertion—"the limited talents of some men render it impossible for them to be severe without being unparliamentary."

TOOLS FOR IMPROVING LANGUAGE   The well-known sources that follow may be consulted.

Dictionaries   When he was a young man, the British orator, William Pitt, after whom Pittsburgh is named, read Bailey's *Dictionary* through three times from A to Z in order to increase his vocabulary. It was said of him at the height of his oratorical career that he never lacked for a suitable word. You may not care to repeat his arduous exercise, but you should own a good dictionary of collegiate grade, and use it to look up meaning, pronunciation, spelling, usage, and origin.

Wordbooks   Roget's *Thesaurus,* available in many inexpensive paperback editions, lists under appropriate headings words of similar meaning. instead of saying "A good argument is . . ." you might prefer one of these (see Roget, under *reasoning*): *just* argument, *sound* argument, *valid* argument, *cogent* argument, *logical* argument, *forcible* argument, *persuasive* argument. Instead of *agreeing* (see Roget, under *consent*) you may *admit, allow, concede, grant, yield, give in to, comply with, acquiesce, accede, accept.* Suppose you are inclined to overwork *great.* Would you prefer *eminent, famous,. celebrated* or *large, bulky, ample, huge, mighty?* One of these may be more accurate for your purpose than *great,* although *great* may, on review of possibilities, be the exact word you wish.

Crabb, Webster, and other dictionaries of synonyms supply definitions and examples. As an illustration, *Webster's Dictionary of Synonyns* defines *aggressive, militant, assertive, self-assertive,* and *pushing,* and shows the differences among them (*aggressive* often suggests self-seeking, *militant* usually implies extreme devotion to some cause, movement, or institution, etc.).

Books of Quotations   At times a speaker wishes to use an apt quotation about *duty, patriotism, woman, success, teachers,* or any of a thousand other themes or topics. This quotation might suggest a title, a central idea, an opening comment, a concluding remark, or an illuminating phrase somewhere in the middle of the discourse. Therefore, as a part of your preparation ask yourself: "Could I effectively use a quotation in this speech?" Among well-known books of quotations are:

John Bartlett, ed., *Familiar Quotations,* 14th ed. (Boston: Little, Brown, 1968).
Clifton Fadiman and Charles van Doren, eds., *The American Treasury* (New York: Harper, 1955).
Rudolf F. Flesch, ed., *The Book of Unusual Quotations* (New York: Harper, 1957).
Henry L. Mencken, ed., *A New Dictionary of Quotations on Historical Principles* (New York: Knopf, 1942).
Oxford Dictionary of Quotations, 2d ed. (London: Oxford University Press, 1955).
Burton E. Stevenson, ed., *The Home Book of Quotations,* 8th ed. (New York: Dodd, Mead, 1956).

As each editor reflects his own taste in selecting his few thousand quotations from countless available items, each collection has its own contribution to make to the speaker. Perhaps the freshest and most unusual quotations are found in the Fadiman, Flesch, and Mencken volumes.

A RECAPITU- LATION
As this is the last chapter of the section "Getting Under Way," the longest section in the book, it is appropriate to review progress to date.

Several ways of self-improvement have been presented. For example:

1 What we are doing *is* important. Communication *is* worth our effort. Men and women who have attained positions of responsibility reassure us. (Chapter 1.)

2 The communication process involves not just one person— you—even though your own interests and concerns naturally loom large. Consider also receiver, message, channel. Communication theory is at your service to guide you in determining what to say and how to say it. (Chapter 2.)

3 Opportunities for improving communicative skill lie everywhere, in a variety of interpersonal situations, including interviewing. Classroom insights and performances help you identify problems in communication, and also solutions. Your self-concept (as a communicator) may gradually be enhanced, or your freedom in self-disclosing. (Chapters 3 and 4.)

4 Gaining confidence is invariably a basic reason for studying speech communication. Classroom exercises should help you feel more at home with the group. You will have observed that a certain amount of speech tension seems to be a normal, human situation; moreover, that you can live with it; moreover again, that it might key you up to do better than you expected. You probably have also observed that much tension is never suspected by the listener (you may *feel* tense, but *look* calm, poised, earnest). (Chapter 5.)

5 Studying the interests and concerns of the other person in the receiving situation—and improving your own competence as a listener—helps directly and indirectly to make you a better communicator to others. (Chapters 6 and 7.)

6 Once you get a feel for specific language, specific evidence, a specific purpose, your competence as a communicator improves remarkably. "A little boy" is more specific than *person*. "A kid wearing jeans" is even more specific. "A kid wearing yellow jeans with the price tag showing" (Erma Bombeck) is clear and vivid. In an interview you are asked to state your interest. "Research and development," you reply. This generality doesn't

satisfy the interviewer. "*What kind* of research? *What kind* of development?" Using language is the one thing that human beings are best at; don't let your own development hit a plateau. (Chapter 8.)

Here are six headings; if you have improved only 5 percent in each category, your achievement is worth noting. Or: Look around the class, and see if you can identify specific ways in which others have improved.

Still other ways of improving are discussed in subsequent chapters: selecting a topic, gathering materials, organization, use of body and voice, and special types such as group discussion and narrative, informative, and persuasive speaking.

ASSIGN- **1** Recall striking phrases from your knowledge of great speeches,
MENTS AND   or from speeches you have heard in and out of class. Contrast
EXERCISES   these phrases with more ordinary ways of expressing the same
idea. Starters:

"an iron curtain"
"give me liberty or give me death"
"I have but one lamp by which my feet are guided, and that is the lamp of experience"
"make the world safe for democracy"
"the power to tax is the power to destroy"
"nothing to offer but blood, toil, tears, and sweat"
"quarantine the aggressor nations"
"liberty and union, now and forever, one and inseparable"
"you shall not crucify mankind upon a cross of gold"
"speak softly, and carry a big stick"
"the only thing we have to fear is fear itself"
"ask not what your country can do for you—ask what you can do for your country"
"black power"

2 Consider the famous sentence, "These are the times that try men's souls," by Thomas Paine. Do you like any of these versions better:
a Times like these try men's souls.
b How trying it is to live in these times!
c These are trying times for men's souls.
d Soulwise, these are trying times.
3 Comment on: "The line between the fancy and the plain, between the atrocious and the felicitous, is sometimes alarm-

ingly fine. The opening phrase of the Gettysburg address is close to the line, at least by our standards today, and Mr. Lincoln, knowingly or unknowingly, was flirting with disaster when he wrote 'Four score and seven years ago.' The President could have got into his sentence with plain 'Eighty-seven,' a saving of two words and less of a strain on the listeners' powers of multiplication. But Lincoln's ear must have told him to go ahead with four score and seven. By doing so, he achieved cadence while skirting the edge of fanciness. Suppose he had blundered over the line and written, 'In the year of our lord seventeen hundred and seventy-six.' His speech would have sustained a heavy blow. Or suppose he had settled for 'Eighty-seven.' In that case he would have got into his introductory sentence too quickly; the timing would have been bad." Questions 2 and 3 are taken from a most excellent treatment of style: William Strunk, Jr., and E. B. White, *The Elements of Style* (New York: Macmillan, 1959), pp. 53, 63.

4 Interpret and thereby make more striking each of the following statistics:

a Trade with Russia should total $5 billion annually.

b For every ten people who entered teaching last year, only eight planned a second year, and only five planned to make it a continuous, lifetime career.

c Seventy percent of the age 16 group in America is in school; in England and France only 10 percent is in school. About 35 percent of American college-age students attends college in America; about 5 or 6 percent of college-age students in Europe attends college in Europe.

d America's yearly advertising bill is in excess of $12 billion.

e In the first twenty years that the United States was a member of the United Nations, it cost us slightly over $100 million a year.

f To get a fatal dose of fluoride, a 150-pound man would need to drink 75 to 100 gallons of water a day.

g Eighteen million Americans have stopped smoking since the cancer campaign began.

h The United States computer industry increased its exports 1,400 percent in the first decade of the space age.

i We spend $85 billion each year on health care.

j The world's population is currently about 4 billion. The annual increase is 70 million.

k Every 13 seconds a burglar is "ripping off" someone's property.

l The average American will consume as much energy in the next week as most people in the world will consume in an entire year.

m Three hundred and sixty-five of the nation's private colleges and universities may be ready to close their doors by 1981 unless immediate aid is forthcoming.

n The average family's bill for the funeral of a relative is $1,200. This expenditure is the third largest that a family ever makes.

5 Consult Roget's *Thesaurus* and compile a list of words having meanings similar to each word given below:

Example: *conventional* (ordinary, common, habitual, usual, strict, rigid, uncompromising).

bad man	*loud* (adj.)
change (n.)	*love* (n.)
cold	*mistake*
commentator	*move slowly* (v.)
concealed	*persevere*
courage	*plan* (n.)
courtesy	*poor* (adj.)
cunning (n.)	*prayer*
dilemma	*question* (n.)
easygoing	*restoration*
energetic	*severe* (adj.)
exciting	*shorten*
frighten	*supposition*
humorist	*willing*
innocent (adj.)	*work hard*

6 Discuss *usage,* with respect to the following examples:

a Each of the speakers used *(his, her, their)* own notes.

b *(This, these)* data *(is, are)* out of date.

c Between you and *(I, me)* . . .

d At the debate tournament, prizes were awarded to Joseph and *(me, myself)*.

e The *(consensus)* *(consensus of opinion)* of the group is . . .

f The *(policeman, policeman's)* arresting me was embarrassing.

g This book is stimulating, *(like, as)* a book should be.

h The reason is *(that, because)* the whole line participated in every play.

i None of us *(is, are)* perfect.

j To make a good talk, it helps *(to inquire diligently, to diligently inquire)* among experts.

k You *(can hardly, can't hardly)* imagine *(it, its)* being done better.

l I will *accept* your brother. I will *except* your brother. (Explain the difference in meaning.)

m *(Most, almost)* everybody has trouble with English.

n *(Over, more than)* 500 people were present.

o He lives *(further, farther)* from school than you do.

7 Make a speech of . . . minutes about a striking quotation, preferably one that has influenced you. This may be a quotation often heard in your home; perhaps it is a favorite of your father, your mother, a teacher, an acquaintance. Use illustration and example to impress your listeners with its significance.

Use these quotations primarily as an exercise in improving your own use of *language*. These speeches will give you an opportunity to be *stimulating, inspirational, appreciative, reflective*. They therefore call for attention to *words*.

Suggested quotations:

The race is not alone to the swift.
A long dispute means that both parties are wrong.
A rolling stone gathers no moss.
Don't swap horses in the middle of a stream.
None so blind as those who will not see.
No answer is also an answer.
Necessity is the mother of invention.
A barber learns to shave by shaving fools.
A bird in the hand is worth two in the bush.
You can't steal second with one foot on first.
A burnt child dreads the fire.
A drowning man will catch at a straw.
A good beginning is half the battle.
A light purse makes a heavy heart.
A miss is as good as a mile.
All is not gold that glistens.
We do what we must, and call it by the best names.
Any stick is good to beat a dog.
An open door may tempt a saint.
Every man, deep down, is a fisherman.
Birds of a feather flock together.
Brevity is the soul of wit.
Don't burn your house to scare the mice.
Do not keep a dog and bark yourself.
Every horse thinks his own load heaviest.
Inside every freshman is a senior struggling to get out.
Friends are a second existence.
When one is up to his neck in alligators, it is difficult to realize that the original purpose was just to drain the swamp.
Success has ruined many a man.
To teach is to learn twice.

8 Make a speech of . . . minutes about a famous man or woman. This talk may prove inspirational in nature, particularly if you provide specific examples of the qualities you admire.

9 As a variation, make a speech of . . . minutes in which you pretend that you *are* the person you wish to talk about. (Example: Assume that you are President Grant, defending your administration. Or you are Frank Sinatra, reminiscing about some of the colorful incidents of your career.)

The list of names below suggests persons to talk about in connection with assignments 8 and 9:

LAWYERS

Rufus Choate	Lord Mansfield
Clarence Darrow	Thurgood Marshall
Thomas Erskine	Daniel Webster
Abraham Lincoln	

NOVELISTS

Saul Bellow	Sir Walter Scott
Charles Dickens	Aleksandr I. Solzhenitsyn
Feodor Dostoevski	Leo Tolstoy
William Faulkner	Mark Twain
Ernest Hemingway	Kurt Vonnegut, Jr.
Hermann Hesse	Robert Penn Warren
John Dos Passos	

POETS AND PLAYWRIGHTS

Maxwell Anderson	Eugene O'Neill
Robert Bolt	Harold Pinter
Robert Frost	Edwin Arlington Robinson
Vachel Lindsay	Carl Sandburg
Amy Lowell	William Shakespeare
Arthur Miller	George Bernard Shaw
Ogden Nash	Tennessee Williams

PREACHERS, SPIRITUAL LEADERS

Thomas à Becket	Martin Luther
Buddha	Martin Luther King, Jr.
John Calvin	Mohammed
Confucius	Norman Vincent Peale
Harry Emerson Fosdick	Savonarola
Billy Graham	John Wesley
Jesus	Ulrich Zwingli

SCIENTISTS, INVENTORS

Marie and Pierre Curie
Thomas A. Edison
Albert Einstein
Enrico Fermi
Sir Alexander Fleming
Robert Fulton

Charles Goodyear
Samuel F. B. Morse
Isaac Newton
Louis Pasteur
Jonas E. Salk
Gottfried Wilhelm von
 Leibnitz

SPEAKERS

Susan B. Anthony
William J. Bryan
Edmund Burke
Stokely Carmichael
Shirley Chisholm
Sir Winston Churchill
Henry Clay
Benjamin Disraeli
Frederick Douglass
Charles James Fox
J. William Fulbright
William Ewart Gladstone

Patrick Henry
Barbara Jordan
John F. Kennedy
Abraham Lincoln
David Lloyd George
Golda Meir
William Pitt
Eleanor Roosevelt
Franklin D. Roosevelt
Theodore Roosevelt
Margaret Chase Smith
Woodrow Wilson

SPORTS: PLAYERS, COACHES

Henry Aaron
Arthur Ashe
Eddie Arcaro
Yogi Berra
Roy Campanella
Wilt Chamberlain
Jimmy Connors
Nadia Comineci
Dizzy Dean
Chris Evert
Don Faurot
Lou Gehrig
Harold Grange

Tom Harmon
Kip Keino
Billie Jean King
Rod Laver
Connie Mack
Willie Mays
Satchel Paige
Knute Rockne
Bill Russell
Babe Ruth
Alonzo A. Stagg
Bud Wilkinson
Ted Williams

The list is endless, so your own favorite may not be here. For records and statistics, consult the latest *World Almanac*. The list of categories is far from exhausted. There are business leaders and industrialists like Armour, Carnegie, du Pont, and Rockefeller; editors like Greeley, White, and Pulitzer; musicians like Landowska and Rachmaninoff; physicians, nurses, and surgeons like the Mayo brothers, Carrell, Nightingale, and Schweitzer; social workers and humanists like Jane Addams and Father Flanagan; teachers like

Montessori, Hopkins, Dewey, and Pestalozzi. For a checklist of more than 2,000 additional names, consult the current issue of *World Almanac* under "Noted Personalities."

10 Short talks:

    a Describe, *ironically,* the registration process; a physical examination; studying in the library.

    b Use *exaggeration* to describe the damage done by an old car out of control.

    c Use *understatement* to describe a boxing or wrestling match, a battle or maneuver, a stormy fraternity or sorority or residence hall session, your living quarters.

    d Use *burlesque* to describe the accomplishments of a football or basketball team.

    e Use *sarcasm* to describe the courtesy of men (or women) on the campus.

    f Use *dialog* to relate a recent interview you had with a cop, adviser, date, employer, officer, customer, tradesman, or professional man.

11 Read, for class discussion, "A Guided Tour of Gobbledegook," by Leonard R. N. Ashley, in the Appendix. He gives specific instances of (a) advertising ballyhoo, (b) unclear or confusing phrases, (c) elaborate names and titles, and (d) jargon as used by educators and others. Add examples of your own. If you are a reader of *The National Observer* you know that each issue has a "faint fanfare," often for someone who used English in a ludicrous way.

PART TWO
GATHERING AND ORGANIZING INFORMATION

This second section is designed to help with short speeches primarily, and with other kinds of communication incidentally. Choosing topics, organizing the body of the talk into major points, and developing the often-neglected beginning and ending of a message, are other ways of helping you communicate effectively. A feature of this section, as of others, is the list of suggested topics that should guide you in reviewing your own resources.

9 Selecting a Topic; Gathering Materials

The purpose of this chapter is to help you systematically to select an overall purpose, a specific topic, and sources of material. You may apply these suggestions to various situations: interpersonal (for example, an interview); group discussion (for example, a panel or symposium); and speech to an audience.

Given an assignment for one of these situations, one student may have at hand sufficient resources of material, whereas another may feel the need of study and research. Out of various possibilities, one must make a decision about a suitable topic or topics. In this situation you may:

1　**Wait for an inspiration.**　Not dependable. Creativity often follows vigorous reflecting. Sir Winston Churchill stated it in these words: "Effort generates creative force."

2　**Worry, fret.**　Not productive. This procedure leads you away from good ideas instead of toward them.

3　**Review your resources.**　Good; time-tried and speaker-tested. Get paper and start thinking with a pencil in your hand. Write down ideas. Some will be good, some indifferent, some bad; never mind. A good idea often comes by way of a poor one. To uncover a new idea, begin to explore. The pages that follow will help you with that exploration.

GOAL, PURPOSE　A good way of planning is to begin with a general purpose and then narrow it.

Historically, messages are classified according to whether their purpose is to (1) entertain, (2) inform, (3) persuade, (4) stimulate or impress. The classification has a pedagogical usefulness because it enables you to consider certain basic notions that belong with each type. The categories may be freely mixed, however; your goal may be to give your listeners useful, timely information, but you see opportunities for doing so in an entertaining way.

When you have determined your overall purpose, your next step is to be as specific about it as possible. If your purpose is to explain, then the next step is to answer the question, explain what? How a teaching machine works? How to improve study habits? How to survive when lost in the woods? How to build a dune buggy?

If you plan to be entertaining, you need to be specific. What incident do you wish to narrate—what do you wish to be entertaining about? Your trials during registration? The time you were lost in the Kaibab Forest? An incident that happened at boot camp or at the state fair, during the Easter holidays, on Inauguration Day? An occasion when you were embarrassed, frightened, or injured? Again, determining your basic purpose helps you develop your specific theme. You can tell about being lost in a forest simply to be entertaining, or you can use that incident as a reason to persuade young men and women to learn survival techniques. Your embarrassing incident might precede a discussion of the point that as one goes from high school to adulthood one becomes less self-conscious and learns to handle oneself with poise, even in awkward situations.

Perhaps your thinking will proceed like this, as you move from the broad concept of goal or purpose to a more specific topic: "I want to inform. As I am a physical education major, I want to inform about health or hygiene. I believe I will talk about posture, since that topic is fresh in my mind and since it is significant. I could talk about the psychological value of good posture. I could give my listeners reasons why people should improve their posture—but that is persuasive, and I want this talk to be expository. I believe I will demonstrate simple exercises that help to improve posture. We learned twenty, but that many would be burdensome—I'll pick just three, and explain and demonstrate them."

Or this: "We're supposed to talk about a great speaker who has aroused our interest. I could talk about Frederick Douglass—I've read his *Autobiography*—I saw the traveling Smithsonian exhibit. I might tell about several of his experiences—of course there are so many. Better limit my talk to how he learned to read and write—he was always proud of this achievement." Now the goal is getting specific. Again: "I am excited by the research coming out of biological laboratories. We now know more about the basic nature of heredity than ever before. I want to explain the nature of DNA and comment on its significance." A self-directive like this helps one to prepare and present a message that is clear-cut.

With a clear goal in mind, you will have made your topic more specific; you will better be able to know what materials to use and what to leave out. Those decisions help you plan how to begin the talk, how to develop it, and how to close it.

If you have difficulty moving from a general purpose to a specific topic, you should review the following possible sources.

YOUR OWN STOREHOUSE Subjects for speaking experiences are close at hand. In fact if they are not close at hand they probably are not anywhere. Personal experience should not be undervalued. As British philosopher Alfred North Whitehead wrote: "First-hand knowledge is the ultimate basis of intellectual life."

Mark Twain won fame as a writer because of *The Adventures of Huckleberry Finn,* in which he drew upon his boyhood in Missouri, and the first half of *Life on the Mississippi,* in which he narrated his experiences as a riverboat pilot. He is not well known for his *Joan of Arc,* largely because he really knew little about Joan. Though he read and traveled widely, the details of this last-named book are not so striking as are those in the other two.

The pamphlet, *Common Sense,* a rousing call to independence, was written by Thomas Paine, who had had many experiences in England as a tax collector and corset maker. His life was so miserable that he came to the colonies to start a new one. Arriving on this side of the Atlantic, he became involved in the struggle for independence. He saw, more clearly than most colonists, the nature of the struggle in which they were engaged. He understood the faults of the British monarchy because he had been a victim of the hardships it created. Out of his personal experiences and reflections he drew ideas for stirring pamphlets.

Your own experiences fall in two general categories: those connected with school and those connected with summer vacations and other nonschool periods. You play different roles; you are a person of many dimensions. Not only your school life but your home life, your work life, your travel life, your avocational life, even your dream and fantasy life, may suggest an interesting topic.

Vocations, Employment   Many men and women have had their education interrupted by work in business or industry. If you have never labored for a living, skip this paragraph; otherwise: Have you worked in an ice-cream plant, in a launderette, in a grocery store, in a restaurant, in a post office, on a newspaper, on a dairy farm, or on a chinchilla ranch? Have you delivered papers, sat babies, washed dishes, slung hash, mowed yards, given golf lessons, detasseled corn, worked on playgrounds or at summer camps, tended store, hopped cars, or worked on a chain-saw gang? Have you ever recycled glass or paper, worked in a mental health center, worked with diabetics? This list is only a beginning. Your listeners have not had your experiences. Moreover, as Justice Oliver Wendell Holmes wisely observed, "every calling is great when greatly pursued."

Some who read this book will be already established in a business or profession. They will naturally turn to aspects of their life careers that are suitable to present to listeners. In an evening extension class, one young man, a tailor, commented on the jackets worn by the various members, noting style features and, to everyone's entertainment, the probable date of purchase. He enabled them to look at styles in a way they never had before.

Avocations, Hobbies   Do you like to fish or tie flies? Do you work with wood or metal tools? Do you collect stamps? Are you an expert barbecuer, a sky diver, a hang glider, or a master with shish kebabs? Do you know about stereo, cable TV, C.B. lingo, baseball, or Zen? Do you fly a plane or drive a hot rod or water ski? Do you judge horses, sheep, cattle, poultry, or carrier pigeons? Are you interested in karate, judo, yoga, or mysticism? Are you a China watcher? Are you an expert beauty parlor operator or home-permanent giver or makeup artist?

A student who was compelled to spend months convalescing in a hospital spent much of that time reading novels. Ordinarily he would discuss technical subjects like "The Future of Supersonic Transport" or political subjects like "England's New Pacifist Movement." On one occasion, however, he delighted his listeners with information from what had become an avocation: he revealed his deep interest in and sensitivity to literary style, supported by his quoting brief passages from his favorite novelist.

Other Experiences

Have you had a tour of duty in the armed forces? Have you gone to summer training camps? Have you worked with VISTA or the Peace Corps? Are Sunday school and church a part of your background? Have you attended a corporation training school or an officers' training school? Have you known the great or near great? Have you mingled with the mighty, or with plain and ordinary, though uncommonly fine, people? Have you administered first aid to broken legs and sprained ankles at ski resorts, provided refreshments to donors at a blood bank, handled dice at a casino, lived in a ghetto, driven a taxi, helped fight a forest fire, or hustled sandbags to control a flood? Have you, a woman, done something that men usually do, or have you, a man, worked at a job for which women are usually hired? Have you marched in a demonstration, participated in a rock festival, organized an environmental cleanup, defused explosives, won a sky-diving prize, experimented with drugs, worked with the K-9 corps, exposed yourself to sensitivity training, or followed the golf or tennis circuit?

Have you visited Florida, California, Lake Louise, Quebec, or the Gaspé Peninsula? Have you driven to Key West, hiked into lower California, flown to the Bahamas, or bicycled to Alaska? Have you had a week in Washington, New York, San Francisco, New Orleans, Philadelphia, Denver, or Salt Lake City? Have you spent time in Hawaii, Okinawa, Viet Nam, or Japan? Do you have opinions about the English, the French, Germans, Italians, Spaniards, Brazilians, Puerto Ricans, Arabs, or Chicanos?

People are not likely to know about many aspects of your background; if you do not self-disclose, they may never find out.

Opinions, Judgments

What goes on in the discussion sessions in your home, residence hall, shop, company, or office? Any opinions about rules and regulations, the World Series, jumbo planes, careers, standards of morals and living, small town or small college versus large? Are you concerned about petrodollars, conduct of teenagers, upward spiral of inflation, overseas competition to our manufacturers, deterioration in quality of prepared foods, educating the masses, abortion, the population explosion, women's rights, air or water pollution, mass media, or hijackers? Personal judgments, backed by evidence, carry high credibility.

The Real Business of Living

In your daily work, your own background, and your own life-style, you may locate a fine topic. Perhaps you can discuss the problems that come to one who lives in a small town or a large city. Or the pleasures and burdens that accompany working one's way through school. Or what it's like to be shy; or to be an only child; or to be the youngest, the oldest, the in-between; or to be adopted; or to be a member of a minority group; or to be one in a family of twelve; or to have poorer schooling than one's associates; or to come from a different region or country. Or what it's like to have too few dates or too many with the wrong persons; or to combine marriage with education; or to compete in business or in a profession under unfair competition. Reflecting upon these experiences *may also lead you into a discussion of the social or economic issues of which they are a part.*

The Sex Approach

Occasionally the fact that the communicator is a member of one sex or the other makes possible a different approach to a topic. Although the great majority of topics is as appropriate to one sex as the other, men and women would certainly approach differently subjects such as marriage, parenthood, alimony, or professional football. Listeners appreciate certain kinds of messages because the communicator *is* a man, or *is* a woman. To get a better feeling for the kind of subject that women might use, flip the pages of women's magazines. "Problems that women have with husbands" suggests "problems that women have with courses," or "problems that women have with careers." In business and industry, women repeatedly declare that they are unfairly treated in matters of salary and promotion. Legislation revising abortion laws is an issue of grave concern to all. Some freely advocate abortion, others defend the right to live. A man may elect to state the male point of view; a woman may elect to state the female point of view. The two sexes will continue to view "equal rights" differently. A member of one sex may offer reasons why a traditional domain of the other should be invaded. Problems arise when both the husband and the wife have important, distinctive careers.

ADDITIONAL SOURCES

When you need to go beyond personal experiences, you may consult other sources.

Current Newspapers, Magazines, and Books

A book or article may suggest a subject to you. Reading about the pollution of our streams and waterways may start you on an investigation of purifying industrial wastes. Reading about a strike may start you thinking about improving relations between management and workers. Browse among magazines to gain a better idea of specialties and points of view. *Current History* follows the events of the day with articles on problems growing out of Latin America, the Far East, national defense, and the like; at times an issue focuses on a single topic like the government's role in education, or nationalism in Africa. *Changing Times* presents the viewpoint of the consumer-taxpayer. Fluoridation is a hot issue in some communities; capital gains arouses interest toward the end of the tax year; radial tires are becoming as much a required accessory as four-way emergency signals.

The news columns and editorial features of your school or community newspaper, or of the daily or Sunday paper that serves your region, may start you thinking. In all cases give credit to your source; be fair to yourself and honest with your listeners by stating what you have borrowed; and bring your own thinking and reflecting into the discussion.

Information is valuable for its own sake, and those who communicate must amass huge quantities of it if they are to be effective. Even in casual conversations about sports, the person who knows a few things must give way before the person who knows many things. On the larger scale, however, people acquire information not only for its own sake but also for the glimpses it gives of solutions to the bigger issues—political, social, and economic—on which they are to render judgment or to give advice. Frequently what starts as a search for a topic reveals so much material that you decide to alter or modify your point of view, or change it altogether; or you may encounter a topic that you like even better than what you originally had in mind.

The Calendar

Some calendars give not only the usual holidays, but other anniversaries: on September 29 Balboa discovered the Pacific, on March 3 the inventor of the telephone was born, on April 2 the United States Mint was established, on April 26 Confederate Memorial Day is observed, on May 8 V-E Day is commemorated, on June 14 Flag Day is noted, and on July 28 World War I began. Every day of the year is the anniversary of some event. Mary E. Hazeltine's *Anniversaries and Holidays* has 196 pages of information about dates,[1]

---

[1] Mary E. Hazeltine, *Anniversaries and Holidays* (Chicago: American Library Association, 1944).

George William Douglas's *American Book of Days* contains a select list of events for each date, with a helpful paragraph to assist a speaker in research about each date.[2] This source on occasion may suggest an anniversary that should be researched further.

Carl Sandburg opened an address on the one hundredth anniversary of the inaugural of Abraham Lincoln, delivered on the East Front of the United States Capitol on March 4, 1961—with these impressive words:

> Here one hundred years ago to the day were 10,000 people who hung on the words of the speaker of the day. Beyond this immediate audience were 30 million people in 34 States who wanted to know what he was saying. Over in the countries of Europe were more millions of

---

[2]George William Douglas, *The American Book of Days* (New York: H. W. Wilson, 1948). Among numerous other books in this category is Robert L. Collison, comp., *Dictionary of Dates* (New York: Greenwood Press, 1969).

people wondering whether the American Union of States would hold together or be shattered into fragments.[3]

And so this speaker continued, gathering strength from the fact that he spoke "one hundred years to the day" after Lincoln's speech, recreating hopes and events that made up the other March 4, in 1861. The nation's bicentennial suggested hundreds of topics for discussions and speeches.

The Classroom   Has something happened in the class that will serve as a springboard for additional discussion? Do you want to say more about an idea that provoked a lively debate? If the class had a discussion about tax reform, or the abolition of grades, and you, too, have ideas on this subject, develop them further. Perhaps your classmates have shown an interest in art, music, standards of morality, building a vocabulary, or an essay or speech that was assigned. Maybe someone said he did not appreciate poetry or did not approve of federal aid to schools, whereas you hold another point of view and want to explore your beliefs at greater length.

Observation   Put yourself in the position of one seeking new material. Observation is an excellent way of making yourself an authority. If you want to discuss prison reform, do as one student did: visit a prison; see what goes on. If you are inquiring into ecological problems of the community, take a look around. If, as one man did, you wonder whether the campus is intellectually stimulating, find the answer by observing talk sessions, checking attendance at recitals and lectures, and looking over the shoulders of readers in the periodical room. If you feel that the efficiency of the American laboring man is underrated, visit a shop, factory, or construction job, and note layouts, handling of materials, use of power tools, and other modern methods.

Interviewing   One student wanted to talk about cancer. As a relative had died after a long illness, the student had this experience in her memory. She visited the cancer hospital nearby and arranged an interview with the chief surgeon. As she told him she was planning a talk on the prevention of cancer, he took an interest in her project. He conducted her through the wards to talk to patients, and showed her before-and-after pictures of operations. He gave her a chart to display to her classmates. After her interview she felt so full of ideas that she could have talked an hour, but she combined in a ten-minute speech the highlights of her visit and her previous experiences. She

---

[3]Text supplied by Carl Sandburg, and quoted with permission.

spoke with the conviction of an expert; in a small way she had made herself one.

Another kind of interview is the opinion poll. Suppose you think certain procedures or regulations on your campus should be altered. To test the practicality of your idea you ask twenty-five of your colleagues a series of pertinent questions. Some replies may be shallow, but others will be provocative; and when you have finished your poll you can be assured that you have felt the pulse of a part of the campus. Or perhaps you believe your school should have more low-rent apartments for married students, or a different student government. A young man who believed that students should not be allowed to have automobiles at school discovered, after conducting a poll, so many difficulties that he needed to revise his original proposals. "What struck me at first as a simple problem," he said, "proved to be highly complex."

The strong appeal of the findings of polls lies in the way interviewees phrase their answers. Newspapers, magazines, and radio and TV stations use the interview technique not only because they want to announce that 54 percent favored the question and 46 percent were opposed to it, but also because they want to quote samples of the wide range of replies. You may find yourself quoting the responses of a few of your interviewees because of striking wordings of their answers to your questions, as pointed out in Chapter 4, "Interviewing."

Speeches and Speech Making
Since you and your classmates share a common interest in speaking, you may consider a topic dealing with a speech of historic significance. For example, you could recreate the circumstances under which Patrick Henry delivered his "liberty or death" speech; Lincoln's first or second inaugural addresses, or the Gettysburg address; Wilson's declaration of war against Germany; King's "I Have a Dream" speech; a recent, notable presidential message. For material, search out larger, comprehensive biographies, and where feasible, consult bound volumes or microfilms of newspaper files. Or you might find it stimulating to read widely about some important aspect of communication; investigate what speech texts and scholarly journals say about organization, audience adaptation, stage fright, listening, and speech making in business.

ON USING THE LIBRARY
As noted above, the search for topics leads to the search for supporting materials. We particularly like to find information that our listeners do not already know. Anthropologist Margaret Mead has commented on the risk of speaking in ignorance of what is already known. Like any investigator, each of us "has to stumble, in his race toward new truth, over discoveries already made but not taken into

account."[4] Through wide reading you collect relevant evidence, pertinent examples and illustrations; you combine these materials and your own ideas into a significant plan, clothing them in words or phrases that are striking, and dedicating them to a moral or a purpose that has a special meaning. Rules and conventions, of course, govern what can be borrowed, and what credits and acknowledgments must be made.

What you borrow should be woven in and around your own experiences. Barbara Tuchman, in writing *The Guns of August,* could not only consult library sources but she could also travel the breadth and length of Europe and visit historic scenes. Shakespeare could read Plutarch's *Lives* and Holinshed's *Chronicles* but he also knew firsthand a thousand facets of Elizabethan England. Thus we read *books* but we try to keep from being *bookish.* We therefore need to form a partnership with librarians and to spend hours in libraries.

Despite the best efforts of librarians, a library is not always an easy place in which to work. Even when you compile a list of books, you may find that some of them are out on loan, and still others in a remote part of the building. This fact could be true even of the colossal Library of Congress in Washington, so it is likely true of the modest collection of many schools. Collections are rearranged; just when you learn that the *Dictionary of National Biography* sits next to the *Encyclopedia Britannica,* it is transported to a safe refuge behind the reference librarian's counter. At times the aims of the librarian seem to run counter to yours; you like to cart the books away and keep your borrowings out of circulation for a month or two; the librarian sometimes appears to like them tidily arranged on the shelves, the DA's next to the DB's. But it is amazing how helpful librarians invariably are to those who show enough interest to ask questions.

Once you locate the item you want, you may be required to fill out a call slip in order to take the book out of the library, or, in some libraries, have a friendly computer do this for you. As procedures differ from institution to institution this chapter will not attempt any generalizations. Eventually you will get either the book or some interesting information as to why it is not available.

One or two aspects of the art of using the card catalog need to be called to your attention. Suppose you find a dozen different cards about *solar heating*—which ones should you try first? From the *title* you can make a shrewd guess as to whether the treatment will be simple or technical. From the *number of pages* you can judge the comprehensiveness of the treatment. From the *copyright date* you

---

[4]*The Small Conference: An Innovation in Communication* (Paris: Mouton & Co., 1968), p. 12.

A SUGGESTION FOR THOSE WHO WANT TO BE WELL INFORMED

If you want to become better informed in the realm of controversial ideas, either for your own satisfaction or to help shape the course of events, you will be interested in seeing the result of two surveys[5] that report on the periodicals most commonly read by active, informed people.

Two investigators compiled a list of the country's most distinguished intellectuals—people like Noam Chomsky, Norman Mailer, Daniel Patrick Moynihan, and others. From nominations made by this group they compiled a list of forty-two influential journals. Those most frequently read by the intellectuals were:

> *The New York Review of Books*
> *The New York Times Book Review Section*
> *Commentary*
> *Harper's*
> *Partisan Review*
> *The New Republic*

The greater the prestige of the intellectual, "the more of the top journals he was likely to read."

Two other investigators polled college faculties to indicate which of twenty-five general periodicals were most widely read. Those at the top of the list were:

> *Time*
> *Newsweek*
> *New York Times*
> *Science*
> *Saturday Review*
> *New Yorker*
> *U.S. News & World Report*
> *Wall Street Journal*
> *New York Review of Books*

The survey noted some differences between professors who were politically active, in that they gave money to cam-

[5](The survey of intellectuals is by Julie Hover and Charles Kadushin, "The Influential Journals: A Very Private Club," *Change,* 4 (March 1972): 38–47. Summarized by permission. The survey of professors is by Everett Carll Ladd, Jr., and Seymour Martin Lipset, "The General Periodicals Professors Read," *The Chronicle of Higher Education,* 9 (January 19, 1976): 14.)

paigns, worked for candidates, ran for office, served on government boards, and the like, and politically inactive professors who avoided these activities, noting that: "The more faculty members try to influence the course of events in the university and in society, the more they read of journals of social, political, economic, and cultural commentary." It also stated: "If one wishes to shape the world, one must know the world."

A characteristic of active people, whether academic or not, is that they comment frequently about matters outside their nominal specialties. They are men and women who not only pursue a specialty but have cultivated, thoughtfully, areas of social, economic, or political importance. Often this habit of thinking and speaking begins in high school or college days.

None of us endorses the notion of people writing and talking about topics they know little about. Most of us deeply respect a person who knows a specialty, whether that specialty is plumbing, fixing a car, singing, or cooking. On the other hand, you yourself have been surprised and delighted when someone showed a mastery of an area outside of his or her specialty. You may have discovered that others have been more impressed by your knowing something you were not expected to know than by your competence in a field in which you were recognized as an expert.

can tell the age of the book. A notation like "Fourth Edition" followed by a recent date indicates that the book has received continued approval by the readers for whom it was designed.

Like any professional person, I have necessarily spent a great deal of time in libraries. I started with the world's tiniest, the seventh grade collection in a small northwestern Missouri town. Eventually I moved to the world's largest, in Washington, London, and Paris—vast buildings with holdings in eight figures. On a few occasions I have spent months on end in libraries six days a week. Thinking of tricks of the trade, if I were to reveal two, they would be the following.

The first has to do with the card catalog. If you look up a title and it is not in the card catalog, you should not abandon the search, but you should say to yourself, "There is a fair chance that it *is* in the card catalog." (For large libraries, I put the odds at 80 percent.) Suppose you are looking for "Manheim." Should you have written it "Mannheim"? Are the first name and initials correct? Are you at the right *place* in the catalog? Sometimes you can get lost in a subclassification and miss the mainstream of Manheims altogether. Are you in the right *catalog?* Some libraries have one catalog for authors, another for subjects. If your library has changed its system, it may have one catalog for Dewey numbers and another for Library of Congress and the two not interlinked by cross references. The Bibliotheque Nationale of Paris has had about five changes of system, so if you are looking for an old book, you may have to barrel through all five. If your item is a periodical, or a government document, you need to know the name of the issuing agency.

A second trick has to do with call numbers. If the number is "HM/291/.H157/1965" and you copy it *921,* you will make a trip to the second-floor stacks for nothing, unless you just want to see what the librarian is showing in the 921s this season. If that number was preceded by "Jour." and you missed it, you are in the wrong *building.* In these instances you may conclude that the book is *out,* whereas actually it is *in,* but you are following a wrong set of clues. Before you abandon your search, review your procedure.

If you make a mistake, you are in good company. (I can still hear the stackroom attendant growl: "Your ticket shows *Star* when it should show *Evening Star.* We gotta dozen *Stars.*")

Startling changes in information storage and retrieval are ahead for all of us. A patient visits a physician, who prepares a list of symptoms and punches them into a retrieval system. Soon a printout appears listing possible ailments, with percentages showing the likelihood of a given ailment. Some day we will be able to use a system like this to help with reports and speeches. We will not have to remain in ignorance of what is already known.

Think how far we have already come. A century ago the typical landgrant university had a library of only a few thousand volumes, a collection that could be housed on one floor. The library was open only at stated intervals: Friday afternoon, for example, from 2:00 to 5:00. You could not take out a book unless you left a deposit.

Although this section has candidly pointed out difficulties of finding exactly the book you need at the instant you need it, the author also can report that many a student has gone to the library with only a vague notion of what he or she wanted to talk about, and after a session of study has discovered rewarding materials. Few things in this world are more exciting than intellectual adventure, and if you make a beginning along this line while you are still in school, you may, to quote the brilliant psychologist, William James, wake up some morning to find yourself one of the world's anointed.

TESTS OF AN APPROPRIATE SUBJECT After selecting a likely subject, predict its probable success, just as, if you were going to build a drive-in, you would want to know how much traffic was in that locality. Test your proposed subject by asking questions such as the following.

Is This the Best Subject I Can Think Of? That is not an easy question to answer, but you can say "Yes" more wisely if you have considered a number of subjects. As a rule your chosen subject will be better if it comes after a survey of many possibilities. A straw-clutching effect characterizes the search for a suitable topic. You may become discouraged as you reject one possibility after another. You may read a long list of suggestions, saying, "These are not for me"; then, hope almost dead, an idea comes that possesses a faint possibility of success, and you clutch grimly at this wisp, this filament, this straw, and try to build it into something substantial. So the advice is worth repeating: search until you uncover a topic of, for you and your listeners, genuine merit.

Is This Subject Close to My Heart? Has a part of your thinking and feeling gone into your subject? If your community was shocked by the disaster that followed a flood, if you personally saw the suffering that resulted, if you were moved by the way the Red Cross transported supplies of clothing and drugs, if you were on your feet forty-eight hours helping avert disease, you might do something eloquent with phases of this experience. If your big sister arrived home from college with her diploma; if she were in your thoughts as she arranged one interview after another; if you recall the day she came home after landing a teaching position; if you helped her assemble her wardrobe; if you sometimes, late at night, brought her coffee as she sat up writing lesson plans; if you caught a little of her wondering and apprehension as she boarded the bus to go to her new position; if you read her letters that first week, you might arouse enthusiasm for "The First Day of School—Teacher's Kid Sister's View." You might also do well with "A City Manager Plan for Roseburg" or "A New Cure for Mental Illness" if you read so much on the subject, and talked to so many authorities, that, despite your lack of firsthand experience, that subject, too, grew close to your heart.

Will My Listeners Become Interested? Will my subject appeal to my listeners because it is timely, vital, curious, or of human interest? If you decide that your subject is too technical, perhaps you can say to yourself, "If I use clear language, and simplify my presentation wherever practicable, I can hold the interest of my listeners even with this specialized subject." Or you may decide, "People may have the opinion that this subject is not a vital one—so I will begin with an example that shows its importance." Or you may have to say, "It is not interesting, and I can't think of any way to make it come to life, so I will seek another subject."

Whatever you know about your listeners will be of service here. Information about age, sex, domicile, marital status, religion, occupation and other demographic factors is useful, and not hard to come by. Information about their attitudes, opinions, beliefs, values, and aspirations is difficult but not impossible to collect, and you may have to rely on your own observations, but what you can discover may help shape your speech materials. The profit motive, for example, would not appeal to some groups as much as the service motive.

The time, the occasion, the season, the opportunities for preparation, the time allotment, the other subjects to be discussed may each be relevant. If your subject seems worthy after this analysis, you may proceed with greater confidence.

**ASSIGN-
MENTS AND
EXERCISES**

1 Read your favorite daily newspaper for a week and construct a list of subjects. Include on your list only subjects that might have interest for the members of your class.

2 Explain the difference between a subject explanatory or informative in nature, and one that is persuasive. List five informative subjects (you may use or adapt subjects in the foregoing chapter) and show how you would revise them to make them persuasive.

3 Consult a dozen recent issues of the periodical, *Vital Speeches.* List topics that seem vital. What people are making these significant speeches, and what positions do they hold? Develop your study by reading a recent volume of *Representative American Speeches,* edited by Waldo W. Braden, published by the H. W. Wilson Company. For speeches on literary, social, and historical topics, consult the British Broadcasting Corporation's publication, *The Listener.* Often texts of speeches on provocative topics appear in *Saturday Review* and *U.S. News and World Report.*

4 Visit the reference room of your library and become acquainted with important works. Inspect indexes to periodicals, dictionaries, encyclopedias, books of quotations, wordbooks, and special references. Look at: *Readers' Guide to Periodical Literature, Education Index, Industrial Arts Index, Poole's Index, Funk and Wagnall's New Standard Dictionary, Webster's New International Dictionary, New English Dictionary, Encyclopedia Britannica, Encyclopedia Americana, World Almanac, Who's Who in America, Statistical Abstract.* Broaden your acquaintance with each work.

5 Select a recent volume of the *Readers' Guide to Periodical Literature.* Locate ten different subjects in this volume, and record a specific article about each subject, giving the author, publication, date, volume, and page. Look for subjects with which you have some previous experience or about which you have a strong curiosity.

6 Inspect one of the encyclopedia yearbooks *(Collier's, Britannica).* Familiarize yourself with the range and scope of its mate-

rial. Locate ten different articles that suggest topics for speeches in which you have an interest.

7 Familiarize yourself with a standard (unabridged) dictionary by looking up the answers to the following:

Define *bibliography, camouflage, knave, laissez-faire,* and *orthography.*

What and where is the Colosseum?

What does "A.B." stand for?

Who was Samuel Langhorne Clemens, and when did he die?

What is a lute? Study the picture and compare with a violin.

What are compounds formed with *hollow?* (i.e., *hollow-*chested).

Name five members of the Hall of Fame.

When will Halley's great comet be seen again on this planet?

8 What reference works index each of the following publications: *Scribner's Magazine, Journal of the American Concrete Institute,* and the *Canadian Historical Review?*

10 Organizing Messages

The notion of organizing or structuring is central to communication, whether one is reflecting, talking to a single listener, or making a speech to an audience. This chapter will discuss organization as applied to intrapersonal and interpersonal situations, and then discuss principles of organization as applied to shorter speeches.

ORGANIZING IN INTRAPERSONAL COMMUNICATION

Organizing is useful in the conversations we carry on with ourselves in planning ahead. A woman who before important examinations devises a schedule indicating when she will review each subject and how long she will spend at it, shows maturity over one who tackles this problem haphazardly. A man about to be married will list the matters to be accomplished, including purchases, invitations, blood tests, buying the license, overhauling the getaway car, etc. Bride and groom both are more likely to get to the church on time if both have put tasks and activities in logical sequence. In countless intrapersonal situations people make basic organizational decisions involving selection and omission, sequence and order, emphasis and deemphasis—all these decisions being imbedded in a situation involving time and place and other people concerned. It is difficult to imagine a twelve-year-old making a list of errands to run or subjects to study. A talent for organization seems to await a reasonable amount of aging and sophistication.

I have a friend who carefully organizes his thoughts before making important decisions. He aids his thinking by making lists; advantages listed along with disadvantages, reasons for lined up against reasons against, short-term factors arrayed alongside long-term factors. Although he is one who can decide quickly and act quickly, he uses the slower, more thoughtful method when time allows. After this kind of preparation, he has a better notion of how to present his ideas effectively when he confronts his listener or listeners.

ORGANIZING IN INTERPERSONAL COMMUNICATION

Considering for a moment the many kinds of dialog in which you may participate—selling to a customer, advising a patient or client, seeking information or a job—you often find yourself in a situation bound by time limits and therefore demanding efficient transmission of ideas. The ability to structure messages helps you adapt to the listener, the available time, and other aspects of the situation.

In connection with interviewing, we have already discussed the importance of preparing a plan before you meet the interviewer. This plan will consist largely of possible answers to questions, if you are seeking a job, and of possible questions to ask, if you are seeking information. You are prepared to adapt to the interviewing situation as it develops, changing your plan as desirable, but your preparation makes it less likely that you will leave the interview without having accomplished most of what you wished. If, for example, you find yourself being interviewed in a barren cubicle, by someone who seems to be asking only routine questions, your preparation will allow you to bring in ideas that otherwise you might have overlooked.

Suppose you have agreed to serve as a chairperson of a committee in connection with a student activity, and need to assign duties to each member. If the committee is to plan a party for your residence hall, you want one of the members to take charge of decorations. If you put yourself in the shoes of the receiver of such a message, you would want it to be reasonably complete: what duties, what resources. You could, of course, as receiver, drag the information out of the sender bit by bit, since you would not commit yourself until you realized what was involved. As sender of the message, therefore, give thought to its framing: the material to be included that will arouse interest, the details that can await the first response and initial inquiry; in other words, what comes first, what comes second, etc.

In interpersonal communication, the originator of a message gets more help from the receiver than does the speaker in a face-to-face audience situation. At the library you ask the woman at the information desk for advice in locating a book. If you do not fully identify your book, she will ask you questions that perfect your original message. Under her questioning you supply additional information so that finally she can tell you where the book is. If, however, you know the author but not the exact title, she can consult references that supply the missing information. Obviously the more completely you can frame your original message, the more promptly she can tell you how to locate the book. Your ability to organize is valuable in interpersonal as well as in large group situations.

A similar situation arises in asking a woman for a date. She can of course make a reaction to a roving question such as, "Are you doing anything Friday evening?" but she would be more comfortable if she could respond after hearing a fuller statement of the proposed plans for the evening's entertainment. Such as: "I can get two tickets for such and such at the University theatre . . ." an attraction which you consider after a review of possibilities, as one that she would particularly enjoy. Or you might, at the outset, suggest two or three possibilities.

Physicians tell their patients, "Make a list of the questions you want to ask. In that way we will be sure to cover all of the matters that are worrying you." Such a simple structuring makes it reasonably certain that, after the consultation, when you are back home, you will not suddenly remember something that you especially wished to ask about. A student seeking a scholarship or a loan may fortify himself with a short list of reasons. This procedure avoids rambling and makes for useful talk. Various kinds of communicative situations call for different kinds of organizational patterns: time order, classification, division, and list of topics. Given two topics to present, one more complex than the other, you may decide which to discuss first. If you are the bearer of good news and bad news, you may give thought whether to begin with the good, in order to make the opening of the interview more pleasant, or to end with the good, so that the closing can be more relaxed. Given a list of six topics, you may shorten it to three. In making these decisions you may be guided by the mood and tone of the total situation.

ORGANIZING IN SPEECH MAKING

That a speech should have form or structure including a beginning and an ending is ancient wisdom handed down through twenty-five centuries of speaking experience.

Corax (fifth century B.C.) taught his clients, when preparing them to take their cases into the courtroom, to arrange their materials under five headings. (1) The *introduction* should be designed to command the attention and interest of the listener; in this situation, the judge. (2) The *narration* should inform him what the case was about. An example might be that the client had been illegally dispossessed of his estates, and sought to repossess them. (3) The *argument* consisted of the reasons supporting the client's case, and (4) the *subsidiary remarks* answered possible objections. (In that day it was believed to be good strategy, as it still is, to take note of, rather than to ignore, opposing viewpoints.) (5) The *conclusion* was not only summary but appeal. Corax's term actually was *peroration,* a term still used today to describe a formal, somewhat eloquent, ending.

Corax showed the civilized world how to organize a message. Rhetoric thus had its birth, so far as written records of the Western world are concerned, in a court of law, helping people recover homes that had been wrested from them by aggressors. Corax lived in Syracuse, Sicily, the birthplace two centuries later of another great man, Archimedes, who among other contributions formulated the laws of the lever. Although Archimedes formulated principles of physical energy, Corax worked a greater magic with words; organization is a principle that in a wide variety of situations can mobilize scattered notions into a message that is easier to communicate, easier to receive, and easier to remember.

Plato (late fifth and early fourth centuries B.C.) said that a message should have a beginning, a middle, and an end; it should be put together like "a living creature," he declared in a famous analogy, having head, body, and foot, all organized in suitable fashion. He was a great seeker after truth, but he realized that "the man who knows the actual truth of things," unless he possesses also the art of speaking, "is not thereby a whit the nearer to a mastery of persuasion."

Aristotle (fourth century B.C.) asserted that, ideally, a speaker has only two functions: he must (1) state his case and (2) prove it. He quickly added, however, that since hearers are not ideal, the speaker should open with an introduction, to help attract their attention and arouse their interest, and end with a conclusion, to remind them of what has been said and to appeal for action. Aristotle and his students realized that the effectiveness of a speech depends upon its reception by listeners, and that listeners need special help and encouragement. The plan of organization then becomes (1) *introduction,* (2) *statement of the case,* (3) *proof,* and (4) *conclusion.*

Cicero (first century B.C.) and *Quintilian* (first century A.D.) developed the classical Roman seven-part type of structure, consisting of (1) an *exordium* or introduction, (2) a *narration* or factual background, (3) a *statement* or central idea, (4) a *partition* or listing of main points, (5) *proof,* (6) *refutation,* and (7) *peroration* or conclusion. If a speaker stated his central idea, then enumerated the main points he proposed to establish, and then discussed them one by one, his procedure would recall a part of the structure advocated by speakers and pleaders of classical Rome. Both believed in the most thorough preparation, advising continual reading and study.

Cicero had many communicative talents. When he began the practice of law he was surprised to discover that most lawyers made only superficial preparation for the courtroom. They were not well versed in the law itself, much less in its history or philosophy. Often they were vague about the details of the case. Cicero's extensive background and careful preparation, plus his willingness to break with custom and to defy the establishment, earned him a lucrative practice. During his distinguished career, he delivered eloquent speeches before the Roman senate. At one point he visited the island of Rhodes, to study rhetoric and oratory at its famous school. He was as interested in writing well as in speaking well. He developed a flexible, lively style, very different from the stiff, formal prose current in his day. His *Orations* are read in high schools and colleges today, because they exemplify excellently written Latin. He wrote important works about the art of oratory; in fact he is the only great speaker that ever lived who wrote systematically about the art of speaking.[1]

---

[1]"Systematically" means that he covered the subject completely, considering both composition and delivery. Of those who attained high distinction in speaking only Cicero has written at length about his theory and practice. Gladstone, Wilson, Beveridge, and Churchill have written essays about certain aspects of oratory but their contributions are small.

Quintilian is a name well known to education majors and to teachers. Oratory was a popular subject in Rome since young men knew they must study the art in order to succeed as lawyers or statesmen. Quintilian not only offered expert instruction in oratory but developed educational methods that still have a modern look. He saw the importance of beginning instruction in speaking at an early age, pursuing a curriculum of graduated difficulty, intermingling work periods and play periods, and relating classroom assignments to practical experience. He wanted his students to become technically excellent in speaking and, more than that, to become men of character.

Modern authorities recommend a simple type of structure, closer to that advocated by Greek rhetoricians (Plato, Aristotle) than by the Romans. Most favor a three-part structure: (1) *introduction,* (2) *body,* and (3) *conclusion.* Somewhere in the message may also appear a short statement of the *central idea.*

Teachers of speech communication have in past years conducted experiments to ascertain the advantages or disadvantages of organizing speeches. In some situations the importance of organization may be overrated: listeners, if motivated, will do a certain amount of rearranging if the speaker neglects to do so. In most situations the speaker is well-advised to organize his materials. Support for this advice is found in two recent studies. Arlee Johnson designed an experiment in which 105 Purdue University students listened to organized and unorganized versions of the same speech. The original, organized version contained an introduction, central idea, supporting points, transitions, and conclusion. In the unorganized version the materials were disarranged, just enough editing being added to make a smooth flow from one idea to another. "The group which received the organized version had a significantly higher level of comprehension," Johnson concluded, "than the group which received the disorganized version."[2]

In another experiment involving students enrolled in more than thirty sections of a basic speech course, John E. Baird, Jr. concluded that well-organized expository speeches produced significantly more comprehension than did poorly organized speeches, and that the inclusion of a preview or review also produced significantly more comprehension than did the same speeches with summaries omitted.[3]

---

[2]Arlee Johnson, "Preliminary Investigation of the Relationship Between Message Organization and Listener Comprehension," *Central States Speech Journal,* 21 (Summer 1970): 104–107.

[3]John E. Baird, Jr., "Effect of Speech Summaries upon Audience Comprehension of Expository Speeches of Varying Quality and Complexity," *Central States Speech Journal,* 25 (Summer 1974): 119–127.

PRINCIPAL PARTS OF A MESSAGE

When structuring a message, you may begin by taking an overall view: *introduction, body,* and *conclusion.*

Introduction

The introduction is the opening part of the message; its function is to arouse interest in what is to follow. The introduction to a short message often consists of a single sentence that will help gain attention, followed by a statement of the central idea of the speech. For example:

1 "More than a fourth of the young people in the nation's capital are addicted to drugs. I was so impressed by this statistic that I undertook an informal survey of drug usage in this community, and have come up with two major findings."
2 "Last night's fire in the Berkeley apartment is the fourth major blaze we have had in this community this year. We should each take steps to organize a fire drill in our residence halls so that we know what to do when an emergency arises."
3 "Like nearly everyone else in the room, I contribute my full share to noise pollution in the dorms. There are two distinct varieties of noise pollution for which you and I must accept responsibility."

The central idea in the foregoing illustrations is stated somewhat informally. Other examples are:

I want to draw your attention to two new developments in air transport.

I'd like to tell you about a speech that made a deep impression on me.

My thoughts on the present crime wave fall into two areas.

It occurred to me that there are two ways of discouraging the passing of bad checks.

I want to point out three things to look for when you inspect the safety practices of a plant.

I thought of a couple of reasons why we should support the Red Cross in its current drive for funds.

In the following example, the central idea (subject sentence) is more formally stated:

Suppose . . . I ask you a few questions mainly relating to science and technology in modern perspective.

First question: Are science and technology a blessing or a curse in today's world?. . . .

Second question: Are science and technology the greatest forms of knowledge and power in the world today?. . . .

Third question: In view of the foregoing, are science and technology overemphasized in the world today?[4]

Whether the message is to be long or short, the natural starting point in preparing it is to contrive a clearly stated central idea. Here is the beginning of accurate thinking. Once a famous stonecutter was asked how to carve an elephant. "Just get a block of stone, a chisel, and a mallet," he replied, "and carve away everything that is not elephant." So the speaker gets a good central idea in mind, and then chisels away everything that does not support it. Determining the central idea is the beginning of good thinking about the subject.

The introduction, through which you make your first impression, is discussed further in the following chapter.

Body   The *body* is the principal part of the message, the part in which the theme stated in the central idea is developed.

The main points should be mutually exclusive, each supporting the central idea. "What kind of a President do we have in the White House?" asked one speaker at the opening of his talk. "Let's examine his performance from three points of view: business, foreign policy, and leadership." A critical listener may reflect: Are these three points mutually exclusive? Further reflection may ask the question, Doesn't this speaker actually have only two points of view: first, the President's handling of business problems, and second, his handling of problems of foreign policy? Moreover, does "business" parallel "foreign"? Doesn't the speaker really want to talk about the President's handling of *business* problems (1) at home and (2) overseas? As the speech in general was directed to listeners interested in business problems, the clearer organization would have given his ideas more impact for them. The "leadership" point is difficult to work in as a bona fide third point. Here is one solution: "What kind of leadership is the President giving to the solution of business problems? Let's examine his performance from two points of view: business at home and business overseas." In preparing a message, the communicator engages in a dialog like this with himself as he reflects upon the proper wording of his main points.

The main points should follow a considered order. The arrangement may be self-determining, like a time-order plan or a space-order plan. Or the speaker may open with the least controversial argument and close with the most controversial argument.[5]

---

[4]The Rev. Theodore M. Hesburgh, president, University of Notre Dame, at Massachusetts Institute of Technology commencement, *Vital Speeches of the Day*, 28 (August 1, 1962): 631–632.
[5]To read further about different methods of development, turn to pages 316–323 in Chapter 17 and pages 356–362 in Chapter 19.

Looking again at the speech discussed above, the speaker would consider the question: Would my listeners have any preference as to whether I discussed "business at home and business overseas," or, reversing the order, "business overseas and business at home"? The answer to that question is whether it is better to lead off with your stronger material, or conclude with it; whether it is preferable to get the most rapt attention possible earlier in the speech, or to end your talk on the highest possible plane of interest.

The *conclusion* is the summary, restatement, appeal, or application with which the message ends. The conclusion to a short message may consist of a single sentence or two. (1) Summary: "Remember then these two reasons for supporting the American Red Cross: In the event of a disaster in your own community, the Red Cross is the organization best prepared to give emergency aid. In the event of a disaster somewhere else in the world, perhaps one in which you would like to give personal assistance but are unable to, the Red Cross can act in your behalf and move in and help." (2) Restatement: "Let me end as I began: We should organize a fire drill in our residence halls so that when an emergency arises we will know exactly what to do." Other ways of concluding may be found in the following chapter.

We often meet situations in which we are specifically required to keep our remarks brief. Judge Florence E. Allen has written that early in life she was trained to state her points briefly and with emphasis and then sit down. As a young woman she participated actively in the women's suffrage movement. Of this experience she writes:

> On countless occasions I was given five, four, three, or only one minute to speak on behalf of women's suffrage before some important meeting. I did just that and no more. As a result I have had the honor of speaking at highly important bodies, such as the International Bar Association at the Hague. I was asked to speak at the plenary session of that great meeting representing the women, but limited to three minutes. I timed my speech again and again and put it through on schedule.[6]

SHORT SPEECH: EXAMPLES   *Example 1*   The following short speech is built around a single illustration. The speaker, aroused by assassinations and shootings, has convinced himself that gun control legislation should be more strict and offers, as a single bit of proof, the effectiveness of strict laws in Great Britain.

---

[6]Letter to me.

Gun Controls: A Lesson from the British

Whenever I read about the assassination of a public figure in this country, I am reminded again that we must have even more strict gun controls. I suggest that we look at the situation in another great English-speaking country, Great Britain, and adopt the main features of the plan used there.

The British have been licensing guns for a little more than a century. All firearms must be registered with the police, who will not grant a license until after full investigation. No one with a criminal record can own a gun. In effect, licenses go mainly to the supervised members of Britain's gun clubs and to a few others who can actually demonstrate a need for a gun. Only about one in every fifty Britons owns a gun, and only about one in one thousand British criminals.

With fewer guns in circulation, Britain today enjoys one of the lowest incidences of violent crime. Of half a million criminals arrested in a three-year period, fewer than two hundred were carrying guns. Of 5,000 robberies investigated, fewer than 400 involved the use of guns. Murders involving firearms are relatively infrequent. The assassination of public figures, alarming in the United States, is practically unknown in Great Britain.

I cannot argue that more strict gun control legislation will put an end to violent crime. I can, however, fairly argue from the British experience that, over a period of years, violent crime in the United States could be substantially reduced, and I urge us to adopt the principal features of the British plan.

The outline:

(Title) GUN CONTROLS: A LESSON FROM THE BRITISH

Introduction
Opening statement: Assassination of public figures argues for more strict gun controls.
Central idea: We should adopt the main features of the gun-control plan used in Great Britain.

Body
1 Only a relatively few people are allowed to own guns.
  A Only about one in every fifty Britons owns a gun.
  B Only about one in every one thousand criminals owns a gun.
    1 Of half a million criminals arrested in a three-year period, fewer than two hundred were carrying guns.
    2 Of 5,000 robberies investigated, fewer than 400 involved the use of guns.

Conclusion

Adopting the gun-control plan used in Great Britain should bring about a distinct reduction in the number of violent crimes in the United States.

Note that the foregoing outline consists of complete sentences. You can test your reasoning better with complete sentences than with fragments. This type of outline is different from the notes that the speaker takes to the platform. *Speaker's notes* might look like the following:

1-in-50 Britons

1-in-1,000 criminals

Half-a-million—200

5,000 robberies—400

The *outline* is a special way of setting down ideas, first to help organize thinking, and second to hand in so that the instructor can see whether the thinking is clear. Its complete sentences and its system of lettering and numbering help him to see what the speaker's purpose is.

Speaker's notes are something to take to the speaker's stand. As you designed them for your own use, you can put them in whatever form you choose.

As you progress through the course, your outlines will get longer and more detailed because you will gradually talk on subjects of increasing significance, packed with information and reasoning. Your notes will become briefer because your memory becomes more sure; you will be less likely to get rattled. Ideally you should soon find yourself making excellently organized speeches of modest length with minimum notes or none whatever.

The *central idea* sums up the message in a single sentence. Teachers of writing sometimes frown upon a candid labeling of points ("There are three varieties of pollution . . ."), but communicators in all sorts of formal and informal oral situations have found this frank labeling of points to be of advantage to the listener. (The listener, unlike the reader, cannot go back and reread; he has to get the point accurately as the speaker utters it.) So long as listening differs from reading in this regard, listeners will generally commend those who announce, "there are two reasons," "this problem has two facets," "so much for the first question; let us turn to the second."

In a short message of any kind the conclusion is necessarily brief; here it is a simple restatement of the central idea. One could add an appeal or exhortation to the listener if he thought the situation appropriate.

Example 2　Even a short message can be impressive and memorable. In the closing days of August, 1864, three-hundred-day regiments of Ohio militia were about to be mustered out. President Abraham Lincoln made short talks to each: the 148th, the 164th, and the 166th. The talk to the 166th was the briefest and most appealing.

Speech to the 166th Ohio Regiment
Abraham Lincoln

Soldiers: I suppose you are going home to see your families and friends. For the services you have done in this great struggle in which we are engaged I present you sincere thanks for myself and the country.

I almost always feel inclined, when I happen to say anything to soldiers, to impress upon them in a few brief remarks the importance of success in this contest.

It is not merely for today, but for all time to come that we should perpetuate for our children's children that great and free government which we have enjoyed all our lives. I beg you to remember this, not merely for my sake, but for yours. I happen temporarily to occupy this big White House. I am a living witness that any one of your children may look to come here as my father's child has. It is in order that each one of you may have through this free government which we have enjoyed, an open field and a fair chance for your industry, enterprise, and intelligence; that you may all have equal privileges in the race of life, with all its desirable human aspirations.

It is for this the struggle should be maintained, that we may not lose our birthright—not only for one, but for two or three years. The nation is worth fighting for, to secure such an inestimable jewel.[7]

Many interesting features may be identified in this short address, which took about three minutes to deliver. The first two sentences constitute the introduction; here the listeners are upper-

---

[7]The text originally appeared in the *New York Herald and Tribune* for August 23, 1864, and is reprinted in *The Collected Works of Abraham Lincoln* (New Brunswick, N. J.; Rutgers University Press, 1953), vol. 7, p. 512.

most in the speaker's thoughts, as is seen by the use of *you* and *your*. The central idea is stated in the second paragraph; here the speaker tells his listeners that he wants to impress upon them "the importance of success in this contest."

The opening part of the body of the speech reminds listeners, most of them young men, of their children's children, with a promise that any one of them may someday occupy the White House; the remaining part impresses them with the advantages of a free government to each one personally. The concluding sentence recalls the speaker's purpose, again reminding the listeners that the struggle has to be maintained.

You are not Lincoln, but you, like all earnest students, have a streak of Lincoln in you. Can you, or can you not, imagine yourself taking leave of a club, organization, or residence hall group that has entrusted you with an official responsibility? If so, can you, or can you not, imagine that if you uttered a few lines about what the group had meant to you and to each other, those who listened would have a deeper appreciation of your stewardship? Can you imagine yourself, after having said this, adding a few words particularly directed to those who were remaining to carry on the goals of the group? If so, what you have learned from Lincoln's example is to try to do for your group what he tried to do for the 166th Ohio.

Other Types of Design Here are other ways of subdividing a *central idea* into *two supporting statements:*

List of topics As just stated, a central idea may be subdivided into a series of supporting reasons. When the purpose is to explain, the supporting statements are better termed *topics* than *reasons:*

(Title) A TRIBUTE TO LINCOLN

Introduction
Opening statement: Lincoln's appeal for Americans is shown by the fact that more books have been written about him than about any other American.
Central idea: Abraham Lincoln had two outstanding traits of personality.

Body
  I He was witty.
      A He used humor in courtroom and campaign speeches.
         1 He said his talk would be short like an old lady's dance.
         2 He won a jury by joking about the city lawyer's fancy shirt.

    B He used humor in conversation and in conference.
       1 Once he read a humorous essay of Artemus Ward's to his cabinet.
       2 On another occasion he told the story of the little steamboat with the big whistle.
II He was humble.
    A He was easily approached by all kinds of people.
       1 Mothers of soldiers asked him to protect their sons.
       2 Job hunters took their pleas to him personally.
       3 Old friends were as welcome after he was President as before.
    B He did not claim to know it all.
       1 In 1855 he wrote that the slave problem "is too mighty for me. May God, in his mercy, superintend the solution."
       2 In 1860 he said: "I do not think I am fit for the Presidency."
       3 He gratefully accepted Seward's help with his speeches.

Conclusion
These two qualities of wit and humility are as valued in these days as they were a hundred years ago.

Time Order Certain processes, methods, procedures, or historical movements can best be explained in chronological sequence. *Time order* thus becomes the basis of the exposition.

    The young woman who explained the mouth-to-mouth system of artificial respiration used time order in her development. First she explained the preliminary steps: getting the body out of the water and getting it in the proper position, with mouth open, tongue and jaw forward. Second, she explained the mouth-to-mouth breathing process. Third, she explained how to care for the patient once he started breathing again. In the course of her exposition she mentioned "don'ts" as well as "dos." Time order is also a logical plan for discussing topics like "How to Fight Forest Fires," "How to Sell Encyclopedias," or "The Origin of the Democratic Party."

    The following partial outline illustrates the time-order development of the Common Market:

DEVELOPMENT OF THE COMMON MARKET

Introduction
Opening statement: Current problems with the European Economic Community, or the Common Market as it is better known, make it helpful to understand its background.

Central idea: The Common Market was originally planned to develop in three phases.

Body

I Phase one was a customs union in which the nations agreed to reduce duties.

II Phase two was an economic union, in which laborers and goods were allowed to move freely across national borders.

III Phase three will be a political union, in which the nations will send representatives to a common parliament and use a common currency.

Space Order A topic can be developed by areas or regions: east side, north side, west side, south side; inside the city, outside the city; the approach to the state capitol, the capitol itself; or as in the following partly outlined plan for a talk on "An Ideal Classroom Building":

I The ground floor should contain special facilities for tutorial sessions and informal study.

II The first and second floors should have well-equipped classrooms.

III The third floor should contain departmental collections with open-shelf reading rooms.

On a lecture tour, Adlai E. Stevenson discussed his trip to Africa, explaining the political situation in various African countries. He discussed them country by country: Union of South Africa, Rhodesia, the Belgian Congo, and Liberia. As he spoke, he unfolded the space-order plan of his address; starting with the southern tip of Africa, he proceeded up the center and continued toward the west. He had previously explained that he would not discuss the countries on the northern coast.

The student who discussed the construction of the St. Lawrence Seaway followed space order by starting with the mouth of the river and moving west, giving special mention to the Welland and Sault Saint Marie canals, where difficult engineering problems were encountered.

Comparison and Contrast In an address, "The United States in World Trade: Competition or Isolation," B. K. Wickstrum, president of General Time, urged that the United States should develop world trade with less advanced nations:

If the world's population of 3¼ billion were compressed to 1,000 people, only 60 would be Americans. These 60 would receive half of the total income of the world and own 15 times as many goods as the other 940 combined. The Americans would use 12 times as much electricity, 22 times as much coal, and 50 times as much general equipment as the remaining 940 persons would use. Except for 200 others among the 1,000, all the rest would be ignorant, poor, hungry, and sick. Half of them would not be able to read and write. . . . The 60 Americans would have a life expectancy of 70 years, while the rest would average less than 40.[8]

The contrast would be of prime interest to the group of internationally oriented American executives who heard it.

After a visit to Africa, the Undersecretary of State wanted to describe contrasts he had seen. What follows illustrates the Congo proverb, "Let him speak who has seen with his eyes":

In West Africa we saw the sun set on an uninhabited rain forest beach just as it might have ten centuries ago. But only a few miles away, in Dakar, we saw a spectacular urban renewal project housing 60,000.

In Zambia, we saw men pulling wooden carts to market. But only a few miles away, we saw giant cargo planes unloading barrels of oil and taking on tons of copper ingots, all within 12 minutes.

In Ghana, we saw a village woman in a red loincloth cooking over an open fire. But only a few yards away, we saw energy pouring out of the giant orange penstocks of the Volta River Dam.

We have seen, in short, the old Africa and the new.[9]

The student who explained that Alcoholics Anonymous was like a church developed his idea in an absorbing way. The sinner has broken a moral law; the alcoholic a physiological law. Neither can help himself; each seeks a counselor. Each needs continued encouragement. Quintilian rightly said: "A comparison has almost the effect of an example." He might have added: "An example has almost the effect of a lecture or a sermon."

Often a difficult topic can be made clearer by comparing or contrasting it with something familiar. The British or German system of education can be compared and contrasted with the American system. Marriage or funeral customs of another culture are made understandable by comparison with familiar customs. Sometimes the comparison is *figurative*, as when Roosevelt compared aggres-

---

[8]*Vital Speeches of the Day*, 33 (June 15, 1967): 535–538. The source of the statistics is given as *Foreign Commerce Weekly*.

[9]Nicholas deB. Katzenbach, *Vital Speeches of the Day*, 33 (August 1, 1967): 622.

sion with disease, and declared that we should quarantine the aggressor nations. At other times the comparison is *literal,* as when two systems of education, two methods of taxation, or two literary or nationalistic movements are compared.

Other Methods These ways of subdividing a central idea are those often, but not exclusively, used in shorter speeches. You may want to look ahead to Chapter 17 for suggestions about *classification and division, definition, analysis,* and others; or to Chapter 19 for ways of developing by *deduction, induction, counter suggestion, change of position,* and others.

ARRANGE-MENT The *arrangement* of ideas in the speech may be significant. Should you put your strongest materials at the beginning of the message, or at the end? Does it make a difference whether idea A precedes idea B, or the other way around?

Greek and Roman rhetoricians saw the practicality of this issue, which has also received attention from modern experimenters. At Yale University a group of thirty-five students in introductory psychology was divided into two. A speaker, introduced as a professor of psychology, appeared before one group and discussed the grading problem. He began by talking about the increasing number of high grades; he speculated on the probability of eventual lowering of grades, with the effect on parents and potential employers; and he introduced a vague statement to the effect that the present situation had provoked confusion. He then talked about grading on the curve and presented it as an efficient system which would discriminate better among students and solve the present difficulties.

To complete the experiment, the same speaker appeared before the other group and used the same material, except that he described the system of curve grading first and the "need for the change" second. Later, questionnaires were administered to both groups and the results studied; they showed that the group which was aroused first and then presented with a solution was significantly more favorable to the idea of curve grading than the group which heard the *explanation* of curve grading first and the *need* for it second.[10]

Psychologists have given much attention to this matter of arrangement. The plan of using the *strongest argument first* is put

---

[10]See the complete study by Arthur R. Cohen in *The Order of Presentation in Persuasion* in vol. 1 of *Yale Studies in Attitude and Communication,* ed. Carl L. Hovland (New Haven: Yale University Press, 1957), pp. 79–97 and 130–136. Hovland summarizes a series of experiments in the same volume, pp. 129–157.

under the heading of *primacy.* The plan of *closing with the strongest argument* is put under the heading of *recency.* The advantage of primacy lies in the persuasive effect of the first impression; the advantage of recency lies in the effectiveness of the last impression. The extensive research in this field is difficult to generalize, but perhaps it is partly true to say that not so much is claimed for the advantages of primacy as once was. Both primacy and recency are strategic positions that must be studied in connection with subject, listener, and situation.[11]

To summarize:
Given three arguments labeled *strong, stronger,* and *strongest,* should the order be:

1 strongest argument   *(primacy)*
2 strong argument
3 stronger argument

or:

1 stronger argument   *(recency)*
2 strong argument
3 strongest argument

The worst order would probably be

1 strongest argument
2 stronger argument
3 strong argument

because this arrangement shows that the reasoning is becoming progressively weaker, and puts the relatively weakest argument in the strategic last place.

This book strongly recommends the *recency* arrangement—best argument last—unless the nature of the message, the listeners, or the situation specifically suggests another order. If, for example,

---

[11]Admittedly the problem of order is difficult; the circumstances of each particular situation are overriding considerations. See Ralph L. Rosnow. "Whatever Happened to the 'Law of Primacy'?" *Journal of Communication,* 16 (March 1966): 10–27 and Norman Miller and Donald T. Campbell, "Recency and Primacy in Persuasion as a Function of the Timing of Speeches and Measurements," *Journal of Abnormal and Social Psychology,* 58 (July 1959): 1–9. Wayne N. Thompson reviews and criticizes relevant studies in *Quantitative Research in Public Address and Communication,* previously cited, pp. 68–71.

An even more recent study, by Anthony J. Clark, *"An Exploratory Study of Order Effect in Persuasive Communication,"* in *Southern Speech Communication Journal,* 39 (Summer 1974): 322–332, involving various kinds of arrangements, reported that "no general law of primacy or recency was demonstrated."

you suspected some listeners would have to leave early, or might become restless because of the next event on the program, you might decide to begin with your best material. Journalists and broadcasters usually open with their best material—the journalist because the last paragraphs might be lopped off for space reasons, and the broadcaster because the listener whose attention is not captured early may turn the dial. Debaters and lawyers, however, whose efforts are subjected to the expert scrutiny of judges, very much like to have not only a strong finish to each speech but also the last speech in the debate. Louis Nizer, famous lawyer and author, cites his experience:

> The plaintiff has a decided advantage in summing up last. He can analyze the argument just heard by the jury and point out the facts it omitted and the omissions in proof it assumed existed. . . .
>
> When I am required to sum up first, I endeavor to prepare the jury so that it will not yield to the blandishments of my adversary. I remind the jury that he will have the last word and that I will not be permitted to reply. I tell them . . . I must rely on their discriminating judgment to reject any false arguments.[12]

After determining the best logical or psychological order for arranging arguments, you may give thought to the *conclusion* of your message. Kinds and types of conclusions are discussed in the next chapter. In this connection it is interesting to note that two experimenters found that twice as many listeners changed opinions when the conclusion contained specific recommendations than when it contained indirect or vague recommendations.[13] Researchers also agree that arguments presented at the beginning or at the end of a message will be remembered better than arguments presented in the middle.[14]

A CASE STUDY IN ORGANIZING   The foregoing discussion suggests that one prepares a message by searching for a central idea, and then for supporting materials that logically develop it.

Let us examine this process by taking a specific case for study. Suppose you have been impressed by the thought that in your own day you have been exposed to three major social upheavals: the

---

[12]*My Life in Court*, pp. 432, 434, quoted in Philip Zimbardo and Ebbe B. Ebbesen, *Influencing Attitudes and Changing Behavior* (Reading, Mass.: Addison-Wesley, 1969), p. 13.

[13]Carl L. Hovland and Wallace Mandell, "An Experimental Comparison of Conclusion-Drawing by the Communicator and by the Audience," *Journal of Abnormal and Social Psychology,* 47 (July 1952): 588.

[14]Marvin Karlins and Herbert I. Abelson, *Persuasion: How Opinions and Attitudes are Changed* (New York: Springer, 1970), pp. 30–32.

change in status of women and of blacks, and the extension of rights of citizenship to 18-year-olds. So profound have these changes been that even now we are not fully aware of all the implications. Suppose you have decided to explore the present status of women's rights and have collected examples of discrimination. You list at random the statements you have accumulated, each statement being written on a separate note card:

In the business and industrial world, about 9 percent of the men earn more than $10,000 a year; only 1 percent of the women earn more than that figure.

Dr. Patricia Etham, a university dean of women, says: "Two important things have to be done to eradicate these inequities. First, women have to change their low image of themselves. . . . Secondly, employers have to be made to see that if a woman can produce the same quantity and quality of work on a given job, then she should be paid the same salary as any man who is delivering the same kind of work on that type of job." In the teaching field, typically female, only 19 percent of college-level faculties are made up of women, although thirty years ago it was 30 percent.

Only seventeen women are members of the House of Representatives.

Average starting salaries offered by major firms in all fields were higher for men than for women.

Only two women are governors of states.

"Feminist groups" are proliferating. The conservatives go in for leaflets and lawsuits. The radicals burn their bras and denounce beauty contests, use of photos of women in advertising, and even marriage.

Only 1 percent of engineers, 3 percent of lawyers, 7 percent of physicians, and 9 percent of scientists are women.

Only twenty-two women are mayors of cities with more than 10,000 inhabitants.

Only 318 women are members of state legislatures.

Women are demanding birth-control centers and relaxed abortion laws; admission of more women to universities like Yale and Princeton; more day-care centers for children, and even centers to provide twenty-four-hour care; and more female executives in business.

August 26, anniversary of the Nineteenth Amendment, should be a national day of protest.

Mirra Komarovsky, sociologist, points out that as families become smaller, women will have their second and last child by thirty. "With a life expectancy of seventy-four, they'll have a lot before them."

The Harvard School of Business Administration undertook a study of women's gains in industrial management but abandoned it because it found no progress worth mentioning.

Women hold less than 2 percent of the top civil service posts in the federal government.

No woman has served in the Cabinet since 1955.

Some predict that the political awakening of women could be even more shattering than the political awakening of blacks.

Now that your ideas are in front of you, your next step is to review them critically. You soon see that many of them support a statement such as "Career opportunities for women are so minimal that the charge of discrimination can be fairly raised." You see further that you have material supporting this point under the subheadings of *business, politics,* and *the professions.* For example, under *politics* you have these notes:

No woman has served in the Cabinet since 1955.

Only seventeen women are members of the House of Representatives.

Women hold less than 2 percent of the top civil service posts in the federal government.

and so on. You may also group your statements supporting *business* and *the professions.* As you study your notes, still other major and supporting points occur to you. Once these are arranged in outline form, you can readily detect areas where you need to do additional research. When the body of your outline is completed, you may give thought to ways of beginning and ending. A striking or humorous personal experience, for example, might serve as the beginning; a summary followed by an appeal might serve as the conclusion.

The complete outline follows:

EQUAL RIGHTS FOR WOMEN: THE 52 PERCENT MINORITY

Introduction

Opening statements: In recent years we have been exposed to an increasing amount of material about equal rights for women.

Aside from the arguments of the bra burners and girdle shunners, the debate for women's rights is attracting the attention of thoughtful educators, statesmen, and journalists.

Katherine Peden, former national president of the Business and Professional Women's Federation, says: "Not only are women more powerful in the United States today but they are going to be an even more explosive and greater source of strength in the future" [*U.S. News and World Report,* 70 (January 11, 1971): 30].

Central idea: Because the status of women in family life is changing so markedly, and career opportunities are developing so slowly, we should lend our support to the movement toward equal rights for women.

Body
  I The status of women in family life is changing markedly.
    A Marked changes are taking place in the family.
      1 Although the marriage rate is increasing, the birth rate is decreasing.
      2 What was once a universally admired goal, to have a large family, may, with the threat of overpopulation, be generally disapproved.
      3 The pattern of the nuclear family is less rigid than ever.
        a Men and women are entering into various informal and communal arrangements, without benefit of legal sanction.
        b Trial marriages are more usual than formerly.
        c Liberalized abortion laws and the pill tend to encourage nonconventional relationships.
        d Professor Urie Bronfenbrenner, in a report issued by the White House Conference on Children, said: "Not only are women discriminated against in the so-called man's world, but they have now been deprived of prestige in their role as women. It used to be that a mother would get recognition in her neighborhood for the fact that she had brought up her children well. Now the mother still has the responsibility for her children, but not enough support or recognition" [*Time,* 96 (December 28, 1970): 37].
    B The conventional ideas of career versus marriage are undergoing modification.
      1 With the released time from childbearing, women seek a career in addition to marriage.
      2 New studies show that many men actually want women to combine careers with families [*Time,* 94 (November 21, 1969): 56].
      3 Mrs. Addie L. Wyatt, union official, declared that 90 percent of American women work at some time during their lives and that they work for the same reasons men do [*Christian Century,* 87 (March 11, 1970): 305].

II   Career opportunities for women are so minimal that the charge of discrimination can be fairly raised.

  A   Women are discriminated against in business.

    1   The ratio of male to female corporate chief executives stands at a blatantly sexist 600 to 1 [*Dun's Review,* 105 (January 1975): 47].

    2   The Harvard School of Business Administration undertook a survey of women's gains in industrial management but abandoned it because it found no progress worth mentioning.

    3   The National Organization for Women (NOW) at its 1970 Midwest Job Conference declared that "justice for the human needs of women, as well as for the needs of society, is best served by encouraging all persons, regardless of sex, to consider and train for any occupation" [*Christian Century,* 87 (March 11, 1970): 304].

  B   Women are discriminated against in politics.

    1   No woman has served in the Cabinet since 1955.

    2   Only seventeen women are members of the House of Representatives.

    3   Women hold less than 2 percent of the top civil service posts in the federal government.

    4   Only 318 women are members of state legislatures.

    5   Representative Shirley Chisholm, first black woman ever elected to Congress, says she has been more discriminated against as a woman than as a Negro [*Time,* 94 (November 21, 1969): 53].

  C   Women are discriminated against in the professions.

    1   Only 1 percent of engineers, 3 percent of lawyers, 7 percent of physicians, and 9 percent of scientists are women [*Statistical Abstracts* (1970): 227–228].

    2   Only 30 percent of college faculties are women *(idem).*

    3   Women Ph.D.'s, once 15 percent, are now down to 12 percent [*Time,* 94 (November 21, 1969): 54].

    4   In the professions generally, the figure for women has dropped from 45 percent to 37 percent.

    5   In 1970–1972, formal charges of sex discrimination were filed against more than 360 colleges and universities.

Conclusion

Since the changing condition of women in the family makes it more desirable, and makes them more eager, to have careers, and since discrimination against women exists in business, in politics, and in the professions, we should lend our support to the movement for equal rights for women.

As we examine the many facets of American life in order to bring about equal opportunity for all, we should give a share of our effort toward achieving better conditions for women.

Comment: A simple test to apply to the statements on a persuasive outline is to determine whether the supporting statements actually demonstrate the validity of the main statements. Is, for example, "**II**" above adequately supported by "**A**", "**B**," and "**C**"? In turn is "**C**" adequately supported by "1," "2," "3," "4," and "5"? Social problems are highly debatable.

Study the outline with the following questions in mind:

1 Locate statements that need further proof. (For example, **I, A,** 1: Statistics of this sort often change from year to year in a dynamic society like ours.)

2 Besides statistics, what other types of supporting material are used?

3 What overall plan of development is used?

4 Which statements would be of greatest interest to a college-age audience? What other arguments can you suggest that would be of interest to a college-age audience?

5 Which statements would be of greatest interest to an audience of business and professional women? What other arguments can you suggest that would be of interest to this audience?

6 Are there local authorities, better known to your listeners, who have made statements on this topic?

7 Can you supply a specific instance or example that would make a more interesting introduction than the one suggested?

Questions like these illustrate the kind of self-interrogation that one goes through in preparing a persuasive message.

THE VALUE OF ORGANIZATION

Organization, one of the oldest of the communication arts, is also one of the most valuable. Most people have some capacity for organization; a few have it to an unusual degree. Moreover, organization is highly teachable and learnable if one will lay his or her mind fairly alongside the problem.

When preparing a message, you often start with a general notion and steadily move to a specific purpose. You start by observing as you read, interview, or reflect, "This is an example (instance, statistic) that I can probably use." Once you come to further, similar materials, your observation is confirmed: "Here are the beginnings of a point that I can support." This support takes the form of a simple list of items. As some items are more usable than others, you make a selection of the best, and thus begin to select. You give thought to the order, and begin to arrange. As major and minor points emerge, the process of selection and arrangement is sharpened. Finally you evolve an overall strategy, which among other purposes helps you decide the content of introduction and conclusion.

In this chapter I have occasionally noted that organization applies to interpersonal as well as to group speaking. Thousands of students have learned that organization also applies to *written* communication. The concept of organization is *fundamental* (from a Latin root meaning *bottom,* hence having to do with the foundation, i.e., elemental, basic), and should help you with themes, essays, and even poetry and fiction, as well as with important conversations and interviews, oral reports, group discussion, and, of course, public speaking.

Organization not only aids clear thinking, but it simplifies your preparation, since you can spend your time on the ideas you select and ignore those you reject. It also improves your fluency in delivery, as you are more certain of the order of your ideas. Finally, it increases the comprehension of your listeners, as it makes it easier for them to understand what you are trying to say to them.

ASSIGN-MENTS AND EXERCISES

1 Make a short talk or report upon the topic, "Two Principles to Follow When . . ."
  a initiating a conversation with a stranger
  b extending condolences
  c extending congratulations
  d closing a sale
  e some other interpersonal situation of your own choosing

2 Make a one-point talk or report (length to be assigned). Your goal may be to inform, entertain, persuade, impress, or stimulate.

Write the topic you choose in the form of a central idea. Use a complete sentence, thus: "The compact car should have its engine in the rear." "Featherbedding in work agreements should be deplored." "Camera fans should save their money for a zoom lens." "Railroads are doomed, unless . . ." "The automobile industry should further develop the Wankel engine."

Develop your central idea by a single well-chosen example, illustration, reason, testimony from an authority, selected group of statistics.

Plan a conclusion. A simple summary or restatement of your central idea will serve.

Last of all: plan an introduction, a single sentence that will catch attention.

Hand in an outline in the form recommended by your instructor.

3 Make a talk or report with two supporting ideas (length to be assigned). Follow the suggestions given under **2** above. Your central idea will be developed by two supporting points. Select and word them so that they represent a natural division of the central idea.

Hand in an outline in the form recommended by your instructor.

Sample topics:

a Two major crises in my life and how I met them.

b Two suggestions for getting along with the boss.

c Two steps in selling a dress (or other object).

d Two rules to follow in choosing a college.

e A definition of patriotism (Americanism) (loyalty) (etc.). Give two characteristics.

f How to improve yourself in some sport (How to improve your tennis serve) (How to catch more fish in less time) (etc.). Give two things to do.

g How to recover from a cold (or other ailment). Give two things to do.

h How to ask for a date. Give two steps.

i How to do comparison shopping. Give two suggestions.

j A definition of a good teacher. Give two characteristics.

k How to choose a musical instrument. Give two rules.

l How to direct a marching band. Give two things to do.

m How to cook (select one of your favorite dishes). Give two steps.

n How to make a budget. Give two rules.

o My favorite athlete. Give two characteristics.

p How to paint a portrait (or something else). Give two steps.

q How to profit from this semester. Give two suggestions.

r How to have a good time at a party when you are practically a stranger. Give two suggestions.

s My outstanding personal qualities. State two.

t The importance of persistence. Give two examples.

u Medical discoveries. Give two examples.

v The tragedy of fast (or drunken) driving. Give two examples.

w How to succeed in school without really trying. Give two suggestions.

x How to be a lady (or a gentleman). Give two suggestions.

y The importance to a citizen of speaking well. Give two reasons.

4 Read and report on "How to Use Your Time Wisely: Interview with Alan Lakein, an Authority on Time Management," *U.S. News &*

World Report, 80 (January 19, 1976), 45–47. He discusses the importance of making a schedule for the day, compiling lists, setting priorities, etc. Think of his suggestions as applying to preparing a speech as well as to selecting and arranging the day's activities.

11 Beginning and Ending

The introduction ☐ The conclusion ☐ Applications to interpersonal communication ☐ Assignments and exercises

In many kinds of interpersonal communications the opening statements and the closing statements are important. We are aware of the need to make a good first impression or a good last impression. Anyone attempting longer talks also needs to give thought to the beginning and the ending. Listeners are, in fact, often visibly responsive to a good introduction or a good conclusion.

THE INTRODUCTION   Unless the mood and tone of the situation were right, or unless you were hard-pressed for time, you would probably disapprove the notion of beginning a talk with a blunt statement of the central idea:

> I want to give you three reasons why you should contribute to the Community Chest.

Abrupt language such as this may put the listener on the defensive. Nearly always you want to pave the way through an informal introduction.

The purposes of an introduction may be briefly listed:

1 **To get on common ground with the listener** You may refer to a common background, a common heritage, your own interest in the listener's community, profession, or reputation.
2 **To remove a prejudice** You may feel a need to counter misinformation or alleviate misunderstanding before proceeding with the body of your message.
3 **To establish credibility** You may want to open with material that helps establish your competence to speak on this topic.
4 **To arouse interest** Actually all introductions attempt to capture the listener's attention, but at times you need to make a special effort to do so by using striking declarative or narrative materials.
5 **To state your purpose or central idea** Examples of formal and informal statements of the central idea were given in the preceding chapter. The introduction is the usual place for such a statement unless you have a specific reason for deferring it until later in the speech.

Actually, many speeches have two introductions, the first consisting of *preliminary remarks,* or informal comment, and the second the *introduction* proper. Quite likely the use of what is here casually labeled "preliminary remarks" may be an important technique that distinguishes the experienced speaker from the beginner. Through them he or she may comment on some feature of the occasion or a statement by the chairman or a previous speaker. As spontaneity is an essential ingredient of humor, these remarks give opportunity to make a spontaneous adaptation to the occasion.

Many kinds of introductions have been observed, but the following have often proved successful.

Illustration   Often an introduction may effectively lead off with informal and disarming words like "the other day," or "last week," or:

> As I was coming across the campus on my way to class, I met a young woman, a good friend of mine, and noticed tears streaming down her face.

Or:

> Yesterday when I pulled the mail out of my box at the dormitory I found a long envelope with this ominous inscription in the upper-left-hand corner: "Office of the Dean of Students."
>
> I ripped it open and unfolded the letter inside. It began: "My dear Mr. Harrison: It has just come to my attention . . ."

Opening with a pertinent illustration that can lead into your central idea helps you gain attention from the first.

Thoughtful Americans have speculated about what would happen to the country in the event of a disabling illness to the President. In a talk on "Presidential Inability: The Constitutional Problem," George Cochran Doub, Baltimore attorney, began as follows:

> On March 4, 1881, James A. Garfield, who as a boy drove the mule team of a canal boat on the Ohio Canal, became President of the United States. Only four months later, Garfield drove in his carriage from the White House down Pennsylvania Avenue to the Baltimore and Potomac Railroad depot on Sixth Street intending to take a train to New England. As he walked through the station arm-in-arm with Secretary of State James G. Blaine, an assassin stepped forward with a cocked revolver and fired two shots at Garfield striking him in the arm and side. . . .

Here is a masterful introduction, its concrete detail showing that it was taken from the pages of history, immediately inviting attention to what could have been a forbiddingly dry legal discussion. Interest in the topic, however, does not have to be forcibly whipped up; the facts are there, awaiting the researcher. Mr. Doub continued:

> When the lunatic, Charles J. Guiteau, was seized and dragged through the crowd, he cried, "Arthur is President of the United States now."
>
> Garfield lay in a coma for 80 days completely unable to perform the duties of President. During that period, he performed only one official act—the signing of an extradition paper. . . . Only routine business was handled by Department heads.
>
> Yet, nothing was done. There was criticism that Secretary of State

Blaine was attempting to usurp the President's duties and there were insistent demands that Vice President Chester A. Arthur act. After 60 days, a Cabinet meeting was held in which it was unanimously voted that Vice President Arthur should assume the powers of the presidential office. But would he become President and thus preclude Garfield from returning to office? Opinions were divided.[1]

Vernon E. Jordan, Jr., executive director of the National Urban League, opened a speech with this incident:

Two decades ago a black man in Topeka, Kansas, tried to enroll his daughter in an all-white school just five blocks from their home. He was rebuffed and his little girl was placed on a bus which travelled past that all-white school to another school, an all-black one, more than a mile away. Oliver Brown, the girl's father, sued but the lower courts said that Jim Crow schools were legal. The case made its way up to the Supreme Court, and in 1954, the historic *Brown* decision was delivered by a unanimous Court.

"We conclude," the Court ruled, "that in the field of public education the doctrine of 'separate but equal' has no place."

The *Brown* decision ushered in an era of profound social change. . . .[2]

Striking Statement   The interest of listeners may perhaps be aroused by striking, declarative sentences like these:

Every year we have about a million acres of farmland go out of production.

One-third of the people in this town are in one way or another reached by the services of the Community Chest.

There are so many cars in California that at any given moment everyone in the state could ride in the front seat.

It is no longer true that a straight line is the shortest distance between two points.

Last week, in the lives of each of you, opportunity knocked not once but five separate, distinct times.

Just as the politics of agriculture has dominated Congress for the last fifty years, I predict that the politics of education will dominate Congress for the next fifty years.

Roughly every second student living on campus now sleeps in a government-owned bed.

---

[1] Mr. Doub gave this talk as Assistant Attorney General of the United States to the Maine Bar Association, Rockland. The text was supplied for this book. An earlier version of the address, given to the Federal Bar Association in Denver, appears in *Vital Speeches*, 25 (September 1, 1959). In the address the speaker goes on to narrate a similar crisis in the Wilson administration, and proposes a constitutional amendment to meet future emergencies.

[2] *Vital Speeches of the Day*, 36 (April 15, 1972): 435.

Each new suburban home requires a public investment of $10,-000 for facilities.

In addition to what you yourself pay for tuition and living expenses, this state spends $1,900 on your education and on that of every other student.

In your lifetime, the United States will become a nation of 400 million people.

The striking statement may take the form of a question, or, as in the following example, a series of questions. A United States congressman, with interests in education, foreign affairs, and publishing, opened an address to other congressmen, on the topic "America's Greatest Invention," as follows:

> Have you ever considered this question: What was America's greatest invention? Was it Alexander Graham Bell's telephone? . . .
> Was it the Wright Brothers' airplane, which gave man wings, for good or ill? . . .
> Was it atomic energy, which ushered in an age that is only now beginning to unfold?
> Each has a claim to greatness. Each is uniquely American. Each has contributed immensely to progress. Which would you choose?
> My choice may surprise you. It is none of these. My choice is nothing more tangible than a manuscript, and yet it has become the most vital force for freedom and progress history has known. It is uniquely an American invention. It is the federal union plan for government as embodied in the United States Constitution.[3]

The introduction, like the title, withheld the answer to the question posed in "America's Greatest Invention" until the claims of several inventions had been stated.

Personal Reference   Chapter 3 discussed self-disclosure as a way of enhancing an interpersonal relationship. Principles of self-disclosure also apply to speech making. Relating a personal experience may bring you closer to your listeners, as may a brief statement of highly personal reasons why you selected your topic. Stating that one session you were a Senate page may explain your choice of a political topic. Mentioning that you nursed a favorite aunt through a long illness with arthritis will help explain your concern about that ailment. Stating that you visit a mental hospital each week with a group of YWCA workers gives you some authority to discuss the problems of the mentally ill. Without such a statement the listener may feel that you are merely summarizing a magazine article.

---

[3]Paul Findley, *Vital Speeches of the Day*, 29 (October 15, 1962): 26.

Surprisingly enough, perhaps from a sense of false modesty or because of a failure to appreciate to the full the natural curiosity of listeners, speakers sometimes omit a highly important detail. Thus a colonel told a story about a general's unusual skill at presiding over staff conferences; only accidentally, during a questioning period, did the colonel reveal that the general was George Patton, by far the most colorful military personality of World War II. The speaker gained greater authority when the listeners discovered he had been on Patton's staff.

If you have a striking personal reason for choosing a topic, you may reveal it in the introduction. A speaker from out of town will often open with a reference to the place he is visiting: "I well remember my stay in Cincinnati five years ago," or "Our company operates a division office right here on State Street," or "My parents both came from northwest Kentucky." This kind of statement helps the speaker identify with listeners: obviously they are basically the same kind of folks. An experienced speaker makes every effort to establish this identification, just as any two people, on first meeting, will attempt to find common acquaintances and common backgrounds.

The foregoing paragraphs illustrate only a few of the ways of beginning a speech. The best ones, as suggested above, are those that bind the source closer to the receiver. The "preliminary remarks" referred to previously serve this purpose, even if the speaker does nothing more than comment on the remarks of the chairman, or on those of a preceding speaker, or on some other feature of the situation. Instances, incidents, examples, humorous stories, striking statements, quotations, analogies, comparisons and contrasts, proverbs, anecdotes, questions and answers, and other devices are useful ways of beginning. So you can possibly find a way of avoiding "Fellow classmates: School spirit around here is dead." This opening might be better.

> Fellow classmates: I am here today to solicit contributions for a funeral. Before I tell you whom or what I want to bury, I want to describe the kind of funeral services that I think would be appropriate.
>
> On the mourners' bench I want to seat Coach McJohnson. He has done more sobbing recently than anyone else I know. Behind him, clothed in black and gold, I want to group the entire football squad.
>
> I have a good place for all of you, too. As you are good friends of the deceased, in fact have been constantly in the company of the deceased, I want you as honorary pallbearers. . . .

THE CONCLUSION   Experienced speakers counsel, and experiments confirm, that it is not advisable to make point one, point two, point three, and then abruptly stop. Listeners want to hear a final appraisal, recommendation, or application. Aesthetic and psychological considerations alike demand that your message have completeness, wholeness. Moreover, the last impression is a powerful one.

You may summarize; you may make an emotional appeal; you may apply or interpret your message; or you may offer a quotation, or an illustration that restates or applies or uplifts your message.

Summary   The summary is so useful a device that many speeches contain one. The speaker should make it as clear as possible; he may use "first, second, . . . finally," etc., as well as connectives like *therefore, in addition, moreover,* and *consequently.* More to the point, the evidence is overwhelming that *repetition* is the best single rhetorical device to increase the listener's retention of what he has heard, and the summary is a good place to use one of the repetitions.

Consider these examples:

> Let me repeat the four significant events in the life of Moses: the incident of the burning bush; the adventures in the wilderness; the reception of the ten commandments; and the arrival at the promised land.

Or:

> If, therefore, you wish to improve your academic standing, you must first of all make specific preparation for each day's assignment, and, more important, you must look for opportunities to show that you are developing a mastery of your materials. The habit of preparing carefully each day's assignment will, in itself, bring you to the teacher's attention, but the special opportunities you will have of writing term papers, making reports, and participating in projects and the like, let you show what you really can do.

Appeal   One criticism of the summary is that it is routine, mechanical. If the message is short and the main points have been exceptionally clear, the listeners may feel they are hearing more of the same thing. Otherwise the advantages of a summary are overriding, so the solution is to offer a summary and follow it with an *appeal.* An appeal involves emotional materials, so here you may recall Maslow's higher levels of needs or Rokeach's values: achievement, freedom, prestige, recognition, self-realization, and the like. In the example above, the ending is somewhat perfunctory and unimaginative; but if the speaker continues by *appealing* to the student to adopt the scholarly life, to recall that the college years offer one of the great chances of a lifetime to do serious thinking, his or her message should prove more effective.

A variation is to end with a summary plus a *reemphasis.* Summarizing three attitudes of the British toward American military forces in England, one speaker repeated that the British are fearful of war; they feel America is primarily interested in its own self-preservation; they are resentful of American prosperity. But, the speaker reemphasized, the primary characteristic of the British is their deepseated fear of another war.

An appeal, whether or not accompanied by a formal summary, is itself a strong restatement of the speaker's expectations of the listeners. Speaking to an audience of young Americans of Mexican descent, Armando M. Rodriguez of the Department of Health, Education and Welfare said:

> I urge that you exhaust every avenue to secure the maximum education possible. Every *Chicano* is needed. We must become experts in the guerilla warfare of attitude and behavior change. We must become experts in the psychology and sociology of human relations. . . . We must become experts in the politics of human rights and equal educational opportunities. I can't think of a tougher, but more rewarding role. And your preparation and training for these tasks must begin with your presence and participation in the educational opportunities available right now. . . .
>
> All institutions of higher learning must play a more active and aggressive role in seeking out, assisting in college decisions, and financially supporting the Mexican-American student. . . . The *Chicano* is coming out of Tortilla Flat—*now*—you here today represent that movement.[4]

The French Minister of Culture did honor to the United States and to his American listeners when he phrased this beautifully worded tribute:

> The only nation that has waged war but not worshipped it, that has won the greatest power in the world but not sought it, that has wrought the greatest weapon of death but has not wished to wield it, . . . may it inspire men with dreams worthy of its action.[5]

Application   At times the speaker can lift a thought to a higher plane by giving it a special application at the end.

A student whose home was in the eastern mountains, and whose family had for generations amplified its income by merchandising a

---

[4]Lester Thonssen, ed., *Representative American Speeches, 1968–1969* (New York: The H. W. Wilson Co., 1969), pp. 139–142.

On the importance of speech making today, Mr. Rodriguez wrote: "I took public speaking for the first time in college, and I have made use of that experience probably more than any other college course.

"As an educator, I am constantly asked to speak to audiences related to educational problems especially those of the Spanish speaking. I certainly feel that if I had not had the public speaking course in college, I would have been very disadvantaged in attempting to respond to the various requests which I receive."

[5]André Malraux in *Vital Speeches of the Day,* 33 (September 15, 1966): 13–14. Quoted by General Bruce K. Holloway in the conclusion of his speech, "The Atlantic Alliance: Southeast Asia."

superior brand of moonshine, once entertained a class by describing in detail methods used in selecting the grain, preparing the mash, distilling the liquor, and aging the final product. His listeners were amused as he told about skirmishes with revenue agents, and as he described how he personally had made deliveries to well-known families in the big cities. As he approached the end of his talk, he said that the war had interrupted his moonshining career; during his years in the service, he learned a different set of values; when he was discharged, he found himself with a GI income that encouraged him to get an education. "I want you to know," he concluded, "that although I honor my folks, I have received an opportunity they never had. I will be the first of my family ever to get a university education. I am going to get a B.A. degree, and then enter law school; and when I leave this campus with my LL.B., I will be the first member of my family to be on the side of the law instead of opposed to it." This comment made a deep impression. What achieved this result was the good-humored discussion of the steps involved in making moonshine, followed by the contrast of his announcement that he was dedicating himself to the life of a law-abiding citizen.

This principle is exemplified in sermons, when the pastor talks twenty minutes on a modest plane, and then, at the end, applies his thought to a present-day problem in a way that grips interest. Motion pictures or plays sometimes, after a slow opening, move to a striking climax. If a speech, a sermon, or a drama has a powerful conclusion, we are impressed even though the beginning and the middle are only average.

Occasionally in the conclusion you may find a way to look back at the beginning of the message. An incident or turn of phrase you used in the opening may be referred to again in the closing. The application is a subtle and artistic way of relating the ending to the beginning, although other types of conclusions mentioned may also achieve this effect.

Quotation At times a conclusion may be further strengthened with a quotation. Often an appropriate one may be found in books of quotations, which invariably have their selections classified under headings such as *courage, education, fidelity, democracy, lawyer, gentleman,* and the like.

Herman Kenin, president of the American Federation of Musicians, concluded his address to the International Association of Concert Managers as follows:

> As we work, we will meet with many obstacles and numerous frustrations. But the rewards will be well worth it. In this regard, the thoughtful words of actor Robert Morley come to my mind:

" . . . What does the public really know of the despair of those who try to paint its pictures, or compose its music, or write its books and plays. It seldom hangs the picture or listens to the music or reads the books; it walks out on the plays. . . .

"It tells itself that it is mystified, or bored, or affronted; it drags along like a child who has been taken for a walk and cries to turn back.

"And then, suddenly, it catches up and takes the hand of the one who has gone on ahead and these two stand together to glimpse a view or pick a flower or drink at a fountain which one of them knew was there all the time."[6]

Illustration Mark Twain used an illustration to close a famous after-dinner speech:

There was a presumptuous little self-important skipper in a coasting sloop . . . always hailing every ship that came in sight. He did it just to hear himself talk and to air his small grandeur. One day a majestic Indiaman came ploughing by with course on course of canvas towering into the sky. . . . It was a noble spectacle, a sublime spectacle! Of course, the little skipper popped into the shrouds and squeaked out a hail, "Ship ahoy! What ship is that? And whence and whither?" In a deep and thunderous bass the answer came back through the speaking trumpet, "The *Begum,* of Bengal, one hundred and forty-two days out from Canton, homeward bound! What ship is that?" Well, it just crushed the poor little creature's vanity flat! and he squeaked back most humbly, "Only the *Mary Ann*—fourteen hours out from Boston . . . !"

That is just my case. During just one hour in the twenty-four—not more—I pause and reflect in the stillness of the night with the echoes of your English welcome still lingering in my ears, and then I am humble. Then I am properly meek, and for that little while I am only the *Mary Ann,* fourteen hours out, cargoed with vegetables and tinware; but during all the twenty-three hours my vain self-complacency rides high on the white crest of your approval, and then I am a stately Indiaman, ploughing the great seas under a cloud of canvas and laden with the kindest words that have ever been vouchsafed to any wandering alien in this world, I think; then my twenty-six fortunate days on this old mother soil seem to be multiplied by six, and *I* am the *Begum* of Bengal, one hundred and forty-two days out from Canton, homeward bound![7]

Importance of the Conclusion An audience is usually aware that the end of a speech is at hand, and hates to hear a speaker go past a natural, forceful ending.

When you have completed your last point, summon your energies for an appropriate ending: summary, summary plus appeal, illustration, application, or quotation; then stop.

---

[6]*Congressional Record,* 115, 111 (June 4, 1969): 14768.
[7]*Mark Twain's Speeches* (New York: Harper and Brothers, 1923), p. 374.

Speakers are more likely to neglect the preparation of their conclusions than they are any other part of the speech. Often when they finish the presentation of their last supporting idea, they apparently suddenly realize that they have devised no good way of ending the speech. Knowing they must have some kind of ending, they close with a lamely worded sentence. The remedy is to work out in advance the best conclusion you can prepare.

Undoubtedly this best conclusion is one that will remind your audience again of the meaning and purpose of your talk. The more specific and pointed your appeals and recommendations, the more likely the listeners will respond as you wish.

Joseph T. Klapper reports an experiment in which 700 U.S. Air Force recruits listened to tape recordings designed to convince hearers that the United States was right to participate in the Korean war. In two versions of the recording, *well-stated conclusions* were drawn and in two versions they were not. Clear organization was used in certain versions, not in others. The versions with well-stated conclusions and clearly defined organization were better comprehended, particularly among the less intelligent. Quite obviously a well-organized talk with a specific conclusion will reach more people than an unorganized talk with a vague ending; although the more intelligent listeners can perform the necessary operations of mentally rearranging and interpreting the speaker's materials, other listeners may find these materials "actually inaccessible" to them.[8]

Although a speaker may prepare an implicit conclusion, stating evidence without making specific application, the preponderance of theory and practice favors the explicit conclusion, in which listeners are told what the speaker wants them to believe or to do. Exceptions may arise, but in general listeners like to know what the speaker personally recommends. A recommendation is a commitment by the speaker; it shows candidly what he favors and where he stands; it shows his willingness to risk dissent and disagreement; and it represents an opening up of his personality to his listeners.[9]

ICATIONS TO ERPERSONAL MUNICATION The ritualistic significance of first impressions and last impressions is deeply imbedded in our culture. We honor the beginning of an association, personal or public, and mark its anniversaries. We observe the terminal point with appropriate ceremony and invariably with mingled feelings. We recall the first time we met someone who is now a good friend; we note the first medal, the first sale, the first

[8]Joseph T. Klapper, *The Effects of Mass Communication* (Glencoe, Ill.: The Free Press, 1960), pp. 87–88.

[9]Stewart L. Tubbs, "Explicit versus Implicit Conclusions and Audience Commitment," *Speech Monographs*, 35 (March 1968): 14–19.

day on the first job. The last day of school receives more than usual attention. Anyone in the armed services knows to the day when, duty fulfilled, he or she can be discharged.

In situations that are purely or mainly communicative in nature, first impressions and last impressions are important. What has been said about beginning and ending a speech, the introduction and the conclusion, is relevant to other kinds of messages.

In merchandising operations, the approach is all important. You cannot sell the customer unless you get her into the store. The front door is broad, readily identified, easy to find and to open. The area is well lighted. Attractive merchandise is displayed in the windows. Smaller establishments along the highways have bright lights, arrows, broad driveways, and large signs reading "Open." If the merchandise is sold door-to-door, the problem is to get past the front door of the resident. Insurance companies tempt prospects with "We would like to give you this handsome leather wallet." It will of course be delivered by a representative of the firm. One finds it embarrassing to refuse to listen to a message from a man who gives him a handsome leather wallet. The gift becomes the introductory part of the selling message.

Magazine salesmen are notorious for using elaborate opening approaches. "I am working for a scholarship, and I would like to have you vote for me," the handsome young man says. You will, of course, vote for the handsome young man so he can get a scholarship. Turns out that with a $5 subscription he gets 500 votes, etc. The wary householder is not deceived by that approach more than once.

Both parties to a first date take pains to make a good first impression. If the first impression is not favorable, the opportunity may never arise for a second impression. In many situations there is no second prize. One might not, on a date, begin with a striking statement, but he might begin with an illustration. "A funny thing happened to me on the way over here." Certainly there will be an attempt to explore common ground: for example, mutual acquaintances. Each individual will make himself or herself more receiver-oriented than source-oriented. After listening to your personal experience, I will likely ask you questions about it before plunging into my personal experience. This attitude rewards your self-disclosure and in turn encourages mine.

Most interview situations begin with both prospective employer and prospective employee attempting to make a good first impression; the employer becomes especially cordial in a seller's market. As a college student operating in a buyer's market I quickly learned that I had to make a good case for myself in the *opening sentences*. Later as a teacher I have sometimes found myself in a seller's market. The employer might have three or four prospects, but I also had three or four opportunities. Here both parties show interest in parlaying the opening interview into a permanent connection. The interviewee's opening sentences indicate that he is well informed about the institution; the interviewer in turn is informed about the interviewee's qualifications. A good first impression leads to further consideration.

After a sales person has aroused the prospect's interest in the magazine subscription, insurance policy, or encyclopedia, the time comes when he or she must close the sale. Sales people are fully briefed on methods of closing. They are well aware of the different kinds of human needs. They may summarize or end with an appeal—not an appeal like "please buy," but an arousal of feelings like pride or self-esteem. The magazine solicitor tells you the product keeps people well informed, up-to-date on what is happening. Probably every insurance sale ever concluded had "fear" wrapped in the package somewhere: fear of lawsuits, hospital bills, or children left without funds for an education. In turn the appeal is followed by a suggestion to act now.

The evening with your date is spent in an interchange of messages. The good-night message may be anticipated more than even the good-night kiss. The final message (the conclusion) says something about how much the evening was enjoyed, perhaps also about another engagement in the future. Interesting moments may be recalled *(summary)*, future events suggested *(application)*, and evocative statements uttered *(appeal:* pride, self-esteem, affection).

Our culture has also established formulas of *leave-taking* at parties or other social events. Small children have it beat into them by their parents that they must not leave a friend's birthday party without telling the hostess they had a nice time. As a child it was sufficient simply to babble, "had a nice time," but in later years socially wise adults have their own individual and distinctive ways of expressing, to the hostess and the host, their appreciation of the high points of the evening: the dinner, the companionship, the entertainment. If the party is not too large, the leave-taking courtesies are extended to the other guests as well as to the host couple. In your own mind you may review different ways of leave-taking as applied to a wide range of communication situations.

You are the chairperson of a committee or the president of an organization. You are at a meeting at which detailed plans are discussed and at which agreements are reached. The *conclusion* is important (Bill and Sue will hire the orchestra, Dick and Elaine will supervise the decorations) so that each person knows what needs to be done. As a good chairperson you summarize the agreement, watching for feedback (you make sure that Bill and Sue and the other members assent to your summary). You set up deadlines at which each one is to report.

A broker and his client spend a quarter hour discussing investments. Many stocks are discussed and certain decisions are reached along the way. At the end of the interview the broker says: "Now let's see. You want to sell 100 Standard—I am to try to get 52— and buy 200 Harris at the market price" *(summary)*. And so on. The broker makes notes and the client agrees to each item. There can be no chance for misunderstanding. The broker might add, "I believe that's a good move. With your Harris you are buying not only into a good stock but into a good industry. On the other hand your Standard has about made its run. It may go up some more, but your Harris ought to go up as rapidly." Good salespersons often say, "You just bought a fine suit. You will get a lot of satisfaction from it" *(appeal)*. They don't just grab your money and abruptly turn to the next customer. The physician, after the examination, says, "Okay. Take two of the green pills every morning—I've written it down—and three of the red pills every evening. You should get quick relief. If you should get worse, though, be sure to call me" *(summary* and *appeal)*. These "conclusions" added little that had not already been said, but much to the general effectiveness of the communication as a whole. This process shows not only communicative *artistry* but an understanding of basic communication *theory* as applied to message and receiver. Similarly in everyday interpersonal situations the *conclusion* usually enhances human efficiency greatly, and human satisfactions as well.

**ASSIGN-
MENTS AND
EXERCISES**

1 After a round of classroom speeches, discuss the *introductions* and *conclusions*. Which were outstanding? Which can be strengthened, and how?

2 If you were to give an entertaining speech, and wanted to begin with one funny story and end with another, in which spot— beginning or ending—would you put the *funnier* of the two stories? If you were to give a sermon and had an extremely impressive story that summed up the central point of your speech, would you *begin* with it, *close* with it, or put it in the *middle?*

3 You are to give a pep talk before the student body on the evening before the homecoming game with an extremely formidable opponent. In your talk you want to include a story that describes how an inspired team that refused to give up came from far behind to defeat what ordinarily was a superior team. Would you open with this story, put it in the middle of your speech, or close with it?

4 Comment on beginnings and endings as you have observed them in interpersonal situations: conversations, interviews, committee sessions, group meetings, academic or religious situations, and the like.

5 Inspect speeches in the annual volumes of *Representative American Speeches* and in the semimonthly issues of *Vital Speeches* for examples of introductions and conclusions that catch your attention.

6 Prepare an introduction of . . . minutes for a twenty-minute talk. The chairperson will present you, announcing the title of the talk, but you are to give the introduction only, followed by a sentence or two to suggest the direction the main part of your talk would take if you gave it. Your introduction should show how you would arouse interest in your topic, or remove any prejudice or misunderstanding that might exist about it.

7 Prepare a conclusion of . . . minutes for a twenty-minute talk. The chairperson will present you, announcing the title of your talk. Open with a sentence or two summarizing what you would have said in the body of the talk; then deliver an appropriate conclusion for it. Select an effective type of conclusion: *summary, summary plus appeal, application, quotation,* or *illustration.*
("Incident in Nepal," pages 148–149, could serve as the introduction or conclusion for a longer talk.)

PART THREE
NONVERBAL FEATURES OF COMMUNICATION

This section discusses nonverbal features of communication, one chapter focussing on body action and the use of space, and the other on voice and pronunciation. Most people readily accept the basic premise that others react not only to the words that are uttered, but also to the tone of voice and facial expression or other body activity that accompanies them; these chapters suggest specific ways of self-improvement.

12 Use of Space; Bodily Action

Use of space □ The usefulness of action □ Basic principles
□ The desire to communicate □ Assignments and exercises

During the last twenty years, interest in nonverbal aspects of communication has vastly increased. Research in both the theoretical and empirical levels has poured from a wide variety of disciplines: psychiatry, speech communication, social psychology, general psychology, linguistics, and anthropology. Each year sees major works, articles in journals, and chapters in books of readings.[1]

Nonverbal communication is seen to be relevant to the expression of ideas and feelings, the perception that one person has of others, good mental health and the treatment of poor mental health (psychotherapy), and other interpersonal and small group relationships. Parent and child, teacher and student, physician and patient, and professional person and client, suggest areas in which nonverbal communication is important, to say nothing of areas in which persons communicate as peers.

Actually the idea that nonverbal symbols are highly effective in communication has been kicking around for some time—say 2,500 years. The older term was *delivery*—applied to formal speaking, reading aloud, storytelling, and drama—and embraced voice and body. As used in this book, *delivery* refers to these physical aspects of voice projection, gesture and other body action, and facial expression. The term *nonverbal* includes these aspects, but also others, such as the use of space and distance (the simple act of moving closer to a person itself transmits a meaning). A century ago (1872) Charles Darwin in his *Expression of Emotions in Man and Animals* argued that nonverbal behavior had survival value, and would be continued, modified, or dropped accordingly. People then, however, were more interested in other aspects of his theory of evolution.

Concepts of nonverbal behavior represent an idea whose time has been born anew; partly because of the steady growth of the disciplines mentioned above; partly because the increasing density of populations requires more kinds of communicative contact; partly because we now are more interested in other cultures, and in cultural differences, than we were formerly; partly because we are more aware of the forces operating in our own American culture. And partly because, to use an overworked word, the concept is *heuristic,* a Greek-based word meaning *to discover;* once an idea about nonverbal communication is stated, researchers find it interesting to apply it to still different areas, and thus one study generates others.

In 1927, Edward Sapir wrote: "We respond to gestures with an extreme alertness, and, one might almost say, in accordance with an elaborate and secret code that is written nowhere, known by none,

---

[1]M. Davis, *Understanding Body Movement: An Annotated Bibliography* (New York: Arno, 1972), contains references to nearly a thousand books and articles.

and understood by all.''[2] Now we are beginning to set down the code, and are finding it both interesting and serviceable. It tells us: the difference between glancing and staring; the difference between dwelling on fondly and looking impatiently; when to stand close and when to stand apart; when to talk and when to keep silent; when to make the opening moves toward ending the party and starting home; when to use a full voice and when to use a gentle voice or a whisper; when or whether the moment is opportune to ask a favor; when to move in front of somebody and when to step back; when to touch or embrace and when to refrain from touching or embracing; when and how to talk to strangers; when to begin to close the sale; whether the summer romance will carry over into the autumn; whether the speech is less successful than expected and also whether to try to pump new life into it or bring it to a conclusion.

In the 1930s and 1940s, Hitler, who had notions about art and architecture as well as about rhetoric, combined his passionate appeals to the German people with nonverbal devices such as banners, standards, uniforms, music, torches, elaborate staging, salutes, and insignia. After the huge crowd had assembled and the stage was set, he made his slow, deliberate entrance.

USE OF SPACE Edward T. Hall, Northwestern University anthropologist, whose books have had wide readership, described vividly this everyday incident:

> When a husband comes home from the office, takes off his hat, hangs up his coat, and says "Hi" to his wife, the way in which he says "Hi," reinforced by the manner in which he sheds his overcoat, summarizes his feelings about the way things went at the office. If his wife wants the details she may have to listen for a while, yet she grasps in an instant the significant message for her; namely, what kind of evening they are going to spend and how she is going to have to cope with it.[3]

Hall's observations have focused the attention of practitioners in other learned disciplines upon the kinds of meanings that can be attached to space and the movements that individuals make in order to adjust to space. Distances at which people sit or stand from one another, for example, are rooted in cultural preferences and are observed by sensitive communicators.

The point is sharply made by a study of cultural preferences. Japanese and Arabs, Hall reports, have a higher tolerance for

---

[2]E. S. Drummer, ed., *The Unconscious: A Symposium* (New York: Knopf, 1927), p. 137.
[3]*The Silent Language* (Greenwich, Conn.: Fawcett, 1969), p. 94. Copyright 1959 by Doubleday & Co., New York.

crowding in public spaces and in conveyances than do Americans. Arabs use space differently from us; in some situations they prefer to stand closer than we do, when they communicate, and in others they operate at a greater distance. They look each other in the eye when talking, "with an intensity that makes most Americans highly uncomfortable." In conversation, Americans maintain a certain distance between one another; if someone stands too close, the other is likely to edge away. These are factors that we quickly learn to keep in mind if we find ourselves in discussions with people of other cultures.

We have other understandings about space usage. An important personage will arrange his office with different space areas: with one interviewer he will remain at his desk, so that the desk is between the two; another will be seated at a comfortable chair in a different part of the office, he himself taking a chair nearby. He also gives attention to his conference table. One that is too long and narrow puts conferees at a disadvantage. One that is oval, round, or diamond-shaped makes conferees more visible to one another. Dean C. Barnlund, in a helpful survey of a number of instances of furniture arrangement and placement, cites the observation of a physician who noted that cardiac patients were sometimes at ease and sometimes ill at ease:

> He decided to test whether or not the desk between doctor and patient was a barrier to communication. Removing the desk on alternate days showed that when it did not intervene 55 per cent of his patients seemed at ease in contrast to approximately 11 per cent when the desk was present.[4]

In Hall's language, everyone maintains an invisible bubble of space surrounding him that he protects in his relationship with other individuals. The size of the bubble varies with individuals and with cultures, but Americans begin to feel uncomfortable if other persons move closer than 30 to 36 inches, except for intimate situations. At home, a woman answering the doorbell might keep the caller on the outside; she might step outside to converse with the caller; she might invite him just inside the door; or she might escort him to the living room and seat him. The housewife arranges her furniture with regard for conversational areas and distances. She does not want her guests to have to talk across wide spaces. So important is the concept of space that Hall found that 5,000 words, or one-fifth of a

---

[4]*Interpersonal Communication: Survey and Studies* (Boston: Houghton Mifflin, 1968), p. 517. For summary and discussion of the use of space, see Mark L. Knapp, *Nonverbal Communication in Human Interaction* (New York: Holt, 1972), Chap. 2, "The Effects of Environment and Space on Human Communication."

pocket dictionary, were concerned with space: *under, over, next to, above, level,* and others.[5]

Formal communication also has its customs in the use of space. In selecting an auditorium, the speaker seeks one that matches the size of the probable audience. Communication is more effective if the room is comfortably filled. If the auditorium is much too large for the audience, the chairperson usually invites those present to take the seats down front. We do not like to talk across rows of empty chairs. Excessively high platforms also add to a feeling of remoteness between source and receivers. The auditorium can be too wide for its length, or vice versa; in the former instance communication is relatively more difficult to those at the sides of the room, and in the latter the speaker has the feeling of talking in a tunnel.

Some details are beyond the control of the speaker, but others are manageable: whether to leave the lectern where it is or move it; whether to stand behind it or at one side; whether to stand on the platform or at floor level. John Bright, English liberal, thought a speaker could not be fully effective unless listeners could see his boots; there is a tiny element of truth buried in this statement if it is not taken too literally. Certainly a speaker who is nearly engulfed by a massive lectern is likely to feel at a disadvantage.

THE USEFULNESS OF ACTION

Certain kinds of meanings, therefore, are communicated between sender and receiver, and between receiver and sender, by the spatial adjustments described above. Degrees of friendliness, intimacy, warmth, and concern may be suggested. One's position in the assigned space, through movement, posture, gesture, and muscle tension, communicates meanings before a single word is spoken.

People who sense that they are too reserved and that they do not have enough enthusiasm in their voices may improve the situation. Say "This is very important" with your hands hanging quietly at your side; then repeat the words, clenching your fist and shaking it as you utter *very;* quite likely your gesture will encourage you to speak that word with more vigor and meaning. In this way *action* can add to variety of voice.

Nothing stated here should be taken to imply that action can communicate an attitude that one does *not* experience; listeners are probably able to detect strained enthusiasm or forced concern. The real loss to an individual comes when restraint and inhibition prevent the communication of a deeply felt attitude.

---

[5]*The Hidden Dimension* (New York: Doubleday, 1966), pp. x and 58. See also Chapter 4, "The Perception of Space: Distance Receptors—Eyes, Ears, and Nose," and *The Silent Language,* previously cited.

One who can put the whole body to work when speaking is likely to feel more at ease. Moreover, facial expression, posture, and gesture communicate feeling as well as meaning. When a public figure gives an important address at a time of crisis, newspaper reports often include a statement about delivery as well as an analysis of ideas. At a time of crisis, President Kennedy's delivery was particularly noted, including such details as his being in complete command of the situation, his sober bearing, his restrained voice, the quiet smile that dimly but gently lit up his features—all these characteristics contributed to the listener's feeling of confidence and respect. Many newspapers reported that President Ford not only wrote and rewrote the speech accepting his party's nomination but rehearsed his delivery as well.

Gestures and facial expression can say "yes" or "no" with differing degrees of positiveness. Pictorial gestures can convey accurate impressions of size, shape, slope, direction, and the like. When the actor George Arliss first read the play, *Disraeli,* he advised the author to delete two pages. "I can say all that with a look," he said. "What look?" asked the author. Arliss demonstrated, and the pages came out. Speaking and gesturing accompany each other continually. A certain amount of animation needs to accompany speaking if ideas are to be fully communicated.

Experimental studies in listening show that members of an audience may develop an initial prejudice against a speaker who has a mannerism or who in some way does not measure up to their ideal of what a speaker should *look like* while speaking. Some listeners who criticize speeches seem overly concerned with gesture and other aspects of action. If they mean what they say, you should capitalize upon their general interest in action by improving your own.

Effective speaking is lively and animated. Although listeners are willing to listen to one who is restrained, they are more responsive, other things being equal, to speakers who radiate vitality and who are stirred up about what they are saying. This quality, not to be mistaken for restlessness, grows out of a strong impulse to communicate an idea or a feeling to someone else.

Using the Hands

Often a message opens with a smile and a handshake. An American handshake is firm and consists of several up-and-down pumping motions. Men offer, but women respond. A continental handshake consists of many more pumping motions, and women are as likely to offer to shake hands as men. A continental observer once introduced to Lincoln said that the American president did not take his hand and ring it like a bell or wave it like a flag; he merely took it and "quietly and silently squeezed it into dough."[6] This description is obviously pure hyperbole, designed to dramatize the difference between differing cultures. Certainly many people react unfavorably to a flabby handshake. Probably many a young man or young woman has made a poor impression because the interviewer felt an overly firm handshake was too presumptious or aggressive or a soft, droopy handshake bespoke a soft, droopy personality.[7]

What to do with the hands is a problem of many a beginning speaker. Clutching the lectern or toying with articles on it, holding hands behind back or putting hands in pockets, adjusting clothing or hairdo, reflect a lack of ease. For random movement of these sorts, substitute positive, purposive movement that helps you with the job of communicating. Primarily the hands can be used in two kinds of gesture, described below.

A type of action with which to begin is the simple descriptive gesture employing one or both hands. If you want to describe shape, size, or length, use the hands to demonstrate what shape, size, or length. If a hara-kiri dagger is eight inches long, or a jet plane has a swept-back wing of so many degrees, make these facts vivid by picturing them with simple hand gestures. *Show* an audience, just as you would show a friend, the length of a cricket bat as compared with a baseball bat. Simple gestures help the listener contrast, for example, Gothic lines as compared with Greek lines.

Visualize an appropriate gesture for the following assertions:[8]

Our ignorance is like a vast jungle.
What causes this inner cohesion of our society?
Hang this picture in the corner of your room.
I do not see our country huddled in a paralysis of fear.

Although a few people may use their hands too much in conversing, giving the impression of nervousness, most people add liveliness to their conversing by a few gestures; and this kind of descriptive action can well be carried over into speaking. You may seem too restrained if your *words* call for illustrative gesture but your *hands* hang motionless at your side. Descriptive gestures are so natural that almost any speaker can use them in moderation.

The hands may also be used to *emphasize* ideas. A simple

---

[6]*Manchester Guardian,* February 27, 1864.

[7]Richard Haas describes differing styles of political handshakes in his article, "The Political Handshake: Non-verbal Persuasion in Image Construction," *Quarterly Journal of Speech,* 58 (October 1972): 340–343.

[8]The illustrative sentences in this chapter are taken from speeches. In a few instances, slight changes in wording have been made.

pointing gesture may accompany ideas like "This fact is the key to the problem," or "Here is the idea I want you to grasp," or "The one most important export is cotton." The gesture clearly says that *one idea* is singled out for emphasis. Saying "Remember this one thought as you leave," and accompanying the words *one thought* with a vigorous index-finger gesture, gives the sentence an emphasis that the speaker could not make with his or her hands held, for example, behind the back.

Practice an appropriate pointing gesture for each of the following:

Let us first briefly glance at our military power.

He argued for freedom of speech in his very first law lecture.

I will start predicting from the housetops that hard times are on their way.

Let me make this point perfectly clear.

The very charge of hypocrisy, I would remind you, is a dangerous one.

This nation is the world's foremost manufacturer, farmer, banker, consumer, and exporter.

There is another side of the picture.

The flow of news, accurately reported, influences the public. And I stress *accurately.*

Since the end of World War II, we have given away nearly $80 billion to the people of other countries.

The United States, with less than 6 percent of the people of the world, eats 35 percent of the world's food.

It's not a recession. Any time you get 16 million people out of work, it's a depression.

Government employment the last twenty-two years has doubled.

Forty percent of all black teenagers are out of work.

Real black power is the use of green power to support black colleges and black community organizations.

Probably the greatest untapped wealth in the world is the potential consuming power of the $2^{1}/_{2}$ billion people of the Third World who are now trying to exist on annual incomes of $60 or $75.

As with all gestures, the movement accompanies the word or phrase emphasized by the voice: "Let us *first* briefly glance at our military power" or "Let us first briefly glance at our *military* power."

Just as we emphasize an idea by using one finger to show its singleness, we can emphasize groups of ideas by simple counting gestures. Thus you may hold up two fingers when you say, "Only *two* objections to the sales tax really concern us." You have seen speakers make an imposing gesture out of this, letting the audience see that one finger stands for one objection and the other represents the second objection. This gesture naturally fits certain groups of ideas and helps to single them out for special attention by the listener.

Another kind of gesture may be used with thoughts like "We want to do everything we can to reduce the smoke menace" or "I appeal to you to join me in the campaign to put an end to the pollution of our streams." Simply extend a hand toward the listener, much as if you were offering to shake hands with him. This is one of the most gracious and most effective of the emphatic gestures. Women may use it as freely as men. You may use either or both hands. It suggests emphasis, reconsideration, or appeal. Here are other sentences which conceivably this gesture could accompany:

Five precious weeks have already been lost.
I know your hearts are troubled.
A belief in liberty was his greatest contribution to the American people.
We need a new law—a wholly new approach—a bold new instrument of American trade policy.
We are living in the most fateful period of world history.
Why should we be saved?
We will never know unless we try.
We must make the effort to put our policies into perspective.
I ask you to share with me today the majesty of this moment.

The gesture should accompany the word or phrase that is also emphasized by the voice: "*Five precious weeks* have already been lost." "I know *your hearts are troubled*" (or "*I know* your hearts are troubled").

Essentially the opposite in effect and meaning of the conciliating gesture, the rejecting gesture is a sideward or downward thrust of the hand, as if the speaker is rejecting or disapproving an idea. "We should *abandon* the idea of economy in time of war," he declares, the vigorous down-thrust palm accompanying *abandon;* or "We have *too many* required courses." In each of the following sentences also is a suggestion of viewing with disfavor:

His advice about early rising was especially objectionable.
Communism is repugnant to the people.
It is important to see that nothing is wasted on nonessentials.
This most respected historian says the West is not worth saving.
This republic was not established by cowards; and cowards will not preserve it.
Let me say that I am no economist.
I do not think I will ever understand what kind of values can be

THE "DOCTOR FOX EFFECT"

One who has good delivery, other things being equal, has a decided advantage over one who does not have. But can good delivery seduce the listener into believing that poor content is better than it actually is?

Two hundred and eighty undergraduate and graduate students in general studies at Southern Illinois University, listened to videotaped lectures on "The Biochemistry of Memory." The lecturer, not formally introduced, later known as "Doctor Fox," was a Hollywood actor. He had been coached by the experimenters, John E. Ware, Jr. and Reed G. Williams, about what to say and how to say it. What material there was came largely from *Science* and *Saturday Review* articles.

Six different lectures were prepared to be delivered to six different groups of students. Three lectures were delivered in dramatic fashion, with gesture, vocal variety, humor, friendliness, and general charisma; they were characterized as "high seduction" lectures. Of these three, one possessed a high degree of factual information (twenty-six substantive teaching points, one a medium degree (fourteen points), and one a low degree (only four points). To lower the content, the experimenters removed substantive teaching points and substituted unrelated examples, mention of experimental details without results, mention of what was going to be covered, and circular discussions of meaningless ideas. These three lectures were also presented in a restrained, "low-seduction" style.

Each of the six groups took an objective test over the material. Each group also rated the lecturer on a standard eighteen-item questionnaire of the sort used for evaluating teachers. (Afterwards the students were informed about the hoax and given opportunity to discuss the results.)

Here are some of the findings based on *test scores:*

1   Students who heard the high-seduction lecture scored significantly higher than those who heard the low-seduction lecture.

involved in spending 9 billion on elaborate and unnecessary weapons.

The demands of students are simply not going to await the traditional amiable pace of academic debate.

The myth of the "Eurodollar" or "petrodollar" should be eliminated.

2 Among all students, those who heard the high-content version scored significantly higher than those who heard the average-content version.

Here are findings based on an analysis of the *teacher-rating blanks:*

1 Students give significantly more favorable ratings under conditions of high seduction regardless of the level of content. "Ratings of students who viewed a lecture covering 26 substantive points did not differ from the ratings of students who saw a lecture covering only 4 substantive points."
2 "It appears that student ratings of faculty may, under all conditions, reflect the influence of seduction, i.e., the 'Doctor Fox effect.'"[9]

The "Doctor Fox effect" seemed to work as well with experts as with students. On a previous occasion a group of 55 psychiatrists, psychologists, medical educators, and educational administrators had heard Doctor Fox and had filled out an evaluation blank afterwards. Overall the group gave favorable response to the lecture. His charismatic style seemed to have created an illusion of being learned. (*New York Times,* May 19, 1974, p. 9; *Chronicle of Higher Education,* October 15, 1973, p. 1.) The study has been translated and reprinted in twenty different languages, published in forty different countries, and has provoked numerous editorials, articles, and professional discussions.

Questions for discussion appear in Assignment 5 at the end of this chapter.

[9](Source: Ware and Williams, "The Doctor Fox Effect: A Study of Lecture Effectiveness and Ratings of Instruction," *Journal of Medical Education,* 50 (February 1975): 149–156, based on Ware, "The Doctor Fox Effect: an experimental study of the effectiveness of lecture presentations and the validity of student ratings," unpublished doctoral dissertation, Southern Illinois University, 1974.)

A motion picture film taken of Sir Winston Churchill addressing the Canadian parliament shows him speaking these words:

These gangs of bandits . . . shall themselves be cast into the pit of death and shame, and only when the earth has been *cleansed and purged* of their crimes and their villainy shall we turn from the task which they have forced upon us.

When he uttered the words in italics not only did his voice reflect his grim determination but he used a sweeping, downward gesture to reenforce his meaning.·

Clenching the fist shows that you are ready to do battle for your belief. It has the utmost emphasis. "We *cannot trifle* with this scheme any longer," you say, shaking your fist vigorously on the phrase in italics. "We must put our plans into *immediate effect.*"

Read these sentences, using a clenched fist gesture to accompany what seems to you to be the emphatic phrase:

Our party's fortunes must suddenly improve.

He waged an unrelenting war on all forms of tyranny over the minds of men.

We have proved the dynamic character of the principle of competition.

I believe profoundly that this country needs more of what your organization stands for.

Liberty—not Communism—is the most contagious force in the world.

You must give us at home what we fought for abroad.

We are determined to live no longer with the threat of fear and war.

The suitability of this or any gesture is determined in part by temper, mood, and size of the group. Women sometimes feel that strong gestures are not for them, but determined, embattled women use these kinds of gestures as freely as men.

Other Types of Action
Effective action also involves the use of other parts of the body. Head, face, eyes, may be employed; one may move around on the platform as occasion warrants.

A shrug of the shoulders, a twinkle of the eye, a lift of the eyebrow, or a toss of the head may suggest attitudes like indifference, contempt, hopelessness, or resignation. A slight gesture of the hands may or may not accompany the other movements. Consider these statements:

I shall not attempt here to catalog all of the many broken promises of the Communists.

A typical student agony is, "What shall I do? Where am I headed?"

Let us stop this senseless exchange of abuse.

My captain continually gave the impression of being an exceedingly pious and sanctimonious person.

So far as posture is concerned, the ideal toward which to work is a physical bearing that suggests ease, self-assurance, and competence. Stand with your feet far enough apart so that you do not sway, but not so far apart that you are too immovable.

You may use your hands to describe simple concepts of size or shape. You may employ your whole body if the description becomes complicated. In explaining the semaphore alphabet, a golf stance or grip, a football referee's signals, or other complicated procedures or processes, you may use your body to make the exposition clear. Other relationships can also be demonstrated to the listener: over on this side of the room (walking and pointing) is Longstreet Hill, over on the other side is Cemetery Ridge, and here is Little Round Top; thus the stage is set for a retelling of Pickett's famous charge at Gettysburg.

You may effectively punctuate your remarks with vigorous noddings or shakings of the head. President Roosevelt, being crippled, needed to support himself while speaking by holding the lectern; since his hands were therefore not free to gesture, his emphatic nodding of the head became a trademark.

Facial expression is probably the most effective single agent of nonverbal communication. No part of you is so expressive as your face. You must know a person well to be able to identify him or her by the back of the head. Professional dancers are taught not to look at their feet, but to look forward and let the viewers see by the performer's facial expression, as well as by body posture, what is being communicated. Full face is more expressive than profile; when you look at someone in profile you gain an ear but lose most of the rest. We want to *see* the face.

Consider the amazing facial versatility of Ingrid Bergman, Flip Wilson, Albert Finney, Wendy Hiller, Helen Hayes, and Jimmy Durante. Photographs of Eisenhower, Truman, Kennedy, and others show a variety of facial expressions: serious, thoughtful, determined, friendly, playful. John Gunther wrote this about President Roosevelt:

> FDR could refresh the whole nation by the atmosphere he gave out at a press conference. The first one he ever held as President came on March 8, 1933, when most of the banks were still closed and the entire nation was prostrate and quivering with panic. Within two minutes the newspapermen, whose words would reach the ends of the earth in an hour, were rocking with healthy, hearty laughter. A photograph taken of FDR on this occasion tells much about his character; he was the very epitome of robust vitality, cheerful assurance, and solid optimism.[10]

---

[10]*Roosevelt in Retrospect* (New York, Harper, 1950), p. 136.

Individuals of your acquaintance add to their richness as personalities by facial expression—their quizzical, astonished, reflective, anguished, surprised, warning, or playful glances add to your delight in their conversation.

The eyes are the focal point of an expression of the face. Contrast, for example, the downcast glance at the floor with the clear, direct, level gaze of the speaker who looks each member of the classroom audience in the eyes. Contrast the sparkle and brilliance of the eyes of a speaker who feels on sure ground with the tense stare of one who is trying to explain too complicated a topic. But no extended argument for facial expression is necessary to readers today who have watched successful actors in closeups on cinema and TV screens. Occasionally a speaker needs to be advised not to overwork the facial muscles—to much hamming can get in the way of an idea—but many need to put themselves more into the speech by using a variety of motivated, purposeful expressions of the face.

We now realize that the familiar notion of eye contact must be interpreted in terms of one's own culture. Black Americans may regard the matter differently from white Americans, and may feel more comfortable using less direct eye contact than white Americans. Within either culture, individual differences exist as to the amount of direct eye contact that is comfortable during casual conversation. Norms of facial expression may also differ. An American of Indian ancestry may use less expression, an American of Spanish ancestry may use more, than Americans of other racial or national origins. Again, however, there are many individual differences. One who wishes to communicate with large groups of people of differing American cultures should become aware of the different norms. One of my students was the son of a New York alderman who spoke Yiddish, Spanish, or English, depending upon the particular group of voters among whom he was campaigning. The student said he could tell by looking at his father's facial expression which language was being used, not only because of the different lip movement but also because of other aspects of the father's features.

Physiologists have estimated that the facial musculature is such that more than 20,000 different facial expressions are possible. Ray L. Birdwhistell, whose studies over the last two decades have pioneered in the field, has identified 32 *kinemes* (i.e., basic groups of expression) in the face and head area: for example, kinemes in the mouth area include protruded lips, retracted lips, snarl, and perhaps four others.[11] In a class critique, one perceptive student made this comment about one of his classmates: "He has a speaker's face." This sentence caught the fancy of the class: it was decided that a speaker's face was mobile, sincere, earnest—in short, *communicative.*

Random pacing is distracting, but one may move from one area to another to emphasize ideas or to indicate major divisions. Stepping forward tends to emphasize an idea; stepping backward suggests review or reconsideration. If you are standing behind a lectern during the first supporting idea of your speech, you may step to one side as you begin the second and cross to the opposite side for the third. If you move while you are speaking your transition sentence, your movement may seem less mechanical. If, however, you are speaking over a fixed microphone, you may not be able to move around at all. In classroom speeches it may help to shift your position a bit between main points. This advice is offered gingerly as area movement often seems artificial unless well motivated.

---

[11]*Kinesics and Context* (Philadelphia: University of Pennsylvania Press, 1970), pp. 99–110.

BASIC PRINCIPLES   Although the chapter has spoken of gestures of different parts of the body, actually the whole body is employed to some extent in all gesturing. A simple gesture involves not only the hand but the forearm, upper arm, shoulders, and back. Even slight shifts of weight give movement added vigor. If a gesture seems awkward, a reason may be that part of the body is working, part is holding back.

The essence of good action lies in its timing. Consider for example a pointing gesture. The stroke of the gesture—the actual pointing movement itself—should accompany or precede the key word or phrase that carries most of the meaning. Suppose that in saying, "I do not know what course others may take," you choose to emphasize *others*. Some may want to do one thing, you are saying in effect, some may prefer another: "I do not know what course *others* may take." The stroke of your gesture firmly accompanies *others*.

A gesture may *precede* the key phrase, and this principle you should practice for yourself: "I do not know what course (short pause, during which you make two or three emphatic, vigorous strokes of your clenched fist) *others* may take." Or the fist-shaking may accompany *others*. But if the gesture is delayed until *after* you have uttered that word, it may have a distracting or even ludicrous effect.

Timing of other action, such as facial expression, is not so crucial. A broad smile may accompany several sentences if it is appropriate to the passage. Even so, the smiling should be suited to the words being uttered; if your language suddenly becomes somber, your smile must be replaced by a serious gaze. This "rapid play of expression," to quote an old phrase, is highly communicative.

Another aspect of timing is that the gesture should be truly vigorous, forceful, expressive. A weak, flabby hand gesture is worth little. A feeble smile or a timid scowl is not impressive. Think of the enigmatic Bob Hope smile that says so much. The smile of three-time presidential candidate William Jennings Bryan was so broad, his fans alleged, he could whisper in his own ear.

Good speakers use a variety of gestures: sometimes one kind, sometimes another. They are skillful with either hand; they use head, eyes, and face; they move around the platform; they employ informal or unconventional types of gestures.

Repetition of a single gesture, even a good one, becomes monotonous. A conciliating gesture is wonderfully effective, but you would be unwise to repeat it constantly. Some sentences may call for different kinds of gestures. Combinations seem natural with longer statements, like "America was built by men of *courage and daring* who had confidence in themselves, and who were willing to risk their fortunes and their lives for *what they wanted.*" Try this and similar sentences with different kinds of gestures, letting one flow into the other. Think also of what facial expression would be appropriate.

THE DESIRE TO COMMU- NICATE   You must have confidence in your message; you must have a strong feeling that what you have planned to say *will be* interesting, and *will be* effective. You therefore should do enough preparation, and over long enough time, so that you have located the materials you need and have them well in mind.

You may not be able to say to yourself, "Today I am really going to shake the world," but perhaps you can reassure yourself with the thought, "This subject is worthwhile; this information should be shared; what I have to say may prove someday to be important to my listeners." The nonverbal modes as well as the words you use may reveal your eagerness to share your personal thoughts and feelings with listeners and to risk their approval of both ideas and attitudes. You may be approved by some, disapproved by others. Even so, you have made the basic decision *not* to be neutral, level, noncommittal; you have decided to express your commitment to the fullest degree your listeners can be persuaded to accept. Hence, start with the thought in the back of your mind, "I want to get this idea across *to these people*"; "I want to explain this concept *to these listeners in front of me*"; "I want to talk *to you*"; "I want *you* to understand and believe me." Some of this resolution and determination will make it seem *more natural* for you to gesture, and to gesture *forcefully* and *convincingly*.

The philosopher-humorist Abe Martin once said, "There's more difference between a professional and an amateur than between anything else on earth." Posture, bearing, eye contact, facial expression, gesture, movement, truly help distinguish the professional—a *person with a strong desire to communicate*—from the amateur— one who is simply *saying words*. Start with this strong desire to communicate, and let it flow to your listeners with your resources of language, voice, and action.

ASSIGN- MENTS AND EXERCISES   1 Plan a speech of . . . minutes in which you present an idea about which you are concerned. Make a special effort to use a number and a variety of gestures. You may use more than you ordinarily would, largely for the purpose of trying various kinds of gestures. In rehearsing this speech, give attention not only to the idea but also to the *voice* and the accompanying *action*.

2 Study each of the following sentences for meaning: note emphatic words, words or phrases that are echoed, repeated, or contrasted. Say each sentence aloud, giving the words suitable vocal emphasis, accompanied by appropriate nonverbal communication.

A variety of good interpretations is possible; seek one that best represents you as a *concerned, energetic, forceful,* and *thoughtful* person.

Here is exposed the naked, calculated cruelty of official policy.

I have not been asked to speak about political matters but rather about trade and economics.

If two diplomats have the same amount of native ability, the one who has the most facts about a given situation is likely to prove the better officer.

It is not our objective to sell America, or American policy, or even the American way of life.

We are here today to examine the role that education has played in world progress.

Make no mistake about it—the diesel engine brought about the biggest single advance in railroad economics in this country.

A driver who is in a drunken condition when he operates a motor vehicle is in possession of a deadly weapon.

Last year for the first time in fifteen years oil men failed to discover as much new oil as the nation used.

I need not stress that these are days of hard decisions.

It is time to penetrate deeper and to see what goes on in the very soul of the mathematician.

The first pictures taken of Mars showed a world of magnificent dilapidation.

To say that Omaha has the same rules as Rome or Florence does not mean that it is like Rome or Florence.

America was the first country to teach nearly everybody to read.

Is this simply a way of saying that man will always be eager to investigate anything that appears new?

The one all-important law of human conduct—the deepest principle in human nature—the standard guiding all behavior—is the need to feel appreciated.

Take my advice, young man: choose your pleasures for yourself, and do not let them be chosen for you.

Is a week too much to spend in the search of a brand new method?

Academic freedom may be defined as a threefold right or privilege.

There is no fundamental cure except better teaching of English by all teachers, in all classes, and in all schools.

3 Comment on this statement by William Norwood Brigance, distinguished editor, writer, and speaker: "Action tells the listeners the real meaning: the false smile, the evasive glance, the grimaces of confusion, the wandering hands. There is the real speech and the listeners know it" [*Speech: Its Techniques and Disciplines in a Free Society* (New York: Appleton-Century-Crofts, 1961), p. 322]. Are you more persuaded by the speaker's words (verbal) or by his earnestness (voice, facial expression)? Comment on both short-term and long-term influence.

4 Probing question: What is the relation between gesture and facial expression and self-concept? and self-disclosure?

5 Questions on the "Doctor Fox effect":

a. If Doctor Fox had given several low-content, high-seduction lectures, not merely a single lecture, to the same group, would listeners have continued to rate him favorably?

b. Doctor Fox was introduced as an expert (with phony degrees, etc.) to the second group of fifty-five; would this introduction help to explain his favorable reception?

c. Does your own observation support the statement that students can be taken in by high-seduction lectures? Does your own observation support the statement that good delivery adds notably to effectiveness?

d. What are the implications for critical listening?

e. Compare and contrast, in your judgment, the relative usefulness of your rating of your teachers now, with your rating of these teachers five years from now. Looking back over junior high and senior high school days, have you altered your judgment of the effectiveness of any of your teachers?

 Voice
and Pronunciation

Can voice be improved? ☐ Observations about the voice ☐
Studying one's own voice ☐ Articulation and pronunciation ☐
Assignments and exercises

In interpersonal situations we often interpret more from vocal tones than from the words themselves. When we are extended congratulations, or condolences, we readily detect varying degrees of warmth, friendliness, and personal concern, regardless of the choice of words making up the message. In formal situations also we can tell from the speaker's voice something about excitement, depression, enthusiasm, sincerity, anger, wonder, surprise, confidence, and other moods that add to or detract from the total impact of the communication. If these situations involve dialects or languages that we do not understand, or understand imperfectly, we interpret as much as we can from the vocal tones of those trying to communicate to us.

One study involving doctors and patients pointed to the conclusion that the doctor's speech and tone of voice were related to his success in referring his alcoholic patients for additional treatment. Admittedly the study involved a small number of people (twenty patients, nine doctors), but it appeared that if the doctor's tone reflected sympathy or kindness as opposed to anger or irritation, the alcoholics were more likely to follow his suggestions about seeking treatment. A pilot study of another group suggested that a mother's voice produces reactions in her baby early in life and may have important effects.[1]

Radio and TV commentators have shared a variety of experiences with the American people and with people all over the world. We look to them for messages about national elections, the disasters associated with floods and tornadoes, and lesser happenings in the news. Now: speculate upon the importance of the voice of your favorite news reporter in the total effect that he or she is able to achieve. But for his or her remarkable voice, and general manner and bearing, your favorite would be less effective.

Within your circle of acquaintances are some voices that elicit your comment as having present effectiveness and others as having future potential. Actually a teacher of speech communication would ponder a while before ruling out any student as *not* having potential for voice improvement. Two aspects of the problem are to explain the importance of voice and to alert you to possibilities that exist for you personally.

CAN VOICE BE IMPROVED? Let us answer this question first, in the event you have misgivings about the feasibility of developing your own voice.

---

[1]Susan Milmoe, Robert Rosenthal, Howard T. Blane, Morris E. Chafetz, and Irving Wolf, "The Doctor's Voice: Postdictor of Successful Referral of Alcoholic Patients," and Susan Milmoe, Michael S. Novey, Jerome Kagan, and Robert Rosenthal, "The Mother's Voice: Postdictor of Aspects of Her Baby's Behavior," both cited in Shirley Weitz, ed., *Nonverbal Communication: Readings with Commentary* (London: Oxford University Press, 1974), pp. 112–126.

An old story is that of Demosthenes, who went to the seashore and practiced reading in a voice that could be heard above the beating and splashing of the waves. By this procedure, according to tradition, he developed a strong voice. By arduous preparation of content as well as careful attention to delivery, he became Greece's greatest orator, able to hold the attention of large outdoor audiences on Mars Hill and in other places. One student decided that if practice would work for Demosthenes, it would work for him. He did not have a surf handy, but as he spent his evenings feeding noisy newspaper presses, he practiced his speeches in a voice that could be heard above the clatter of the machinery. A few weeks of this vocal exercise convinced him that both he and Demosthenes were on the right track.

Winston Churchill in his early days practiced speech making in his bedroom; members of the family had to accustom themselves to hearing his baritone sounds reverberating through the walls. Once when his valet knocked on the door and said, "Did you call me, sir?" he gravely replied, "I was just addressing the House of Commons." These men developed voices of flexibility and power while young. Student debaters have such an opportunity today; after practice sessions and tournament debates they find their voices have become more vigorous. As voice is produced by the operation of vocal muscles, they, like all muscles, are strengthened by proper exercise.

The good voices among your acquaintances probably belong to students who have done considerable speaking or singing. Much of this activity may have been informal: reciting in class, taking a lively interest in conversation, appearing on church, club, or assembly programs. Weak voices among your acquaintances belong to students who have done little of this, just as frail bodies belong to people who have had a lifelong disinterest in participating in sports, games, exercises, or physical labor. Still, a fragile body or a delicate voice can be made stronger once the owner's concern is aroused.

By the thousands, students in speech classes have observed the kind and the degree of the improvement of their voices. Tape recordings made of speeches both at the beginning and at the end of the course show that the student is rare who demonstrates no improvement at all.

OBSERVATIONS ABOUT THE VOICE

A beginning may be made by gaining more insight into the problem. For example:

Energy

Listen to recordings of Roosevelt, Churchill, Truman, or Edward R. Murrow, and you will note that they spend a good deal of *energy*. The amazing variety of these and other voices recorded on the *I Can*

Hear It Now series reflects vitality. Contemporary personalities like Barbara Walters, Walter Cronkite, and Joe Garagiola have energetic voices. The simple fact is that more energy is required to talk to a group or a room full of people than to one lone individual.

At times you may not speak loudly enough, whether to one listener or several, because you believe you are exerting more vocal energy than you actually are. What you believe your voice to be is something different from what it actually is. A Washington observer noted that a certain Cabinet member found it difficult to convince the President because although the Cabinet member was not a soft man, he spoke with a soft voice. Eventually the President came to realize that the Cabinet member earnestly meant what he said, despite the mildness. In some situations you may have enough vocal energy but do not use it. In others you may simply lack disposable energy.

Responsiveness A good voice responds to the varying emotions of the speaker. *Enthusiasm,* for instance, is one of the priceless virtues—not the enthusiasm of the shallow, easily-put-on-and-quickly-taken-off variety, but the sustained enthusiasm that grows out of an honest conviction, a keen appreciation, a fine sensitivity. Emerson says in a famous quotation: "Nothing great is ever achieved without enthusiasm." *Earnestness, warmth,* and *spiritedness* are other associated qualities. The voice should react to these inner states. When a woman talks about the profession of law, for example, and has a profound belief in the social importance of law, some of that belief should show in her *voice,* over and above what her words express; and thus a part of her interest in her profession will rub off on her listeners.

One way to make voice convey attitudes, feelings, and convictions is to use care in the selection of material. You have a growing belief that the *new drugs are wonderful.* You have read this, you have heard others say so, and you recently made a speedy recovery from a once-baffling type of pneumonia. This experience is certainly enough to start you out making a speech on the subject. Get facts: for example, the fearful diseases of childhood—scarlet fever, diphtheria, whooping cough, and measles—have dropped 90 percent. An imposing, armor-plated fact like *90 percent* should have effect upon your voice if you utter it with the importance it deserves. Somehow manage to say it more forcefully: perhaps louder, perhaps slower, perhaps both. Thus your realization of the significance of your statistic can put more vitality in your speaking voice. You explain that twenty years ago, an average pneumonia case like the one from which you just recovered cost $300 to $400 for hospital-type care, and if the victim didn't die, he lost five weeks from work or school. This fact should bring a little joy into your voice as you contrast this experience with your own two-day stay in the student clinic. Perhaps you can work in a little of the dialog between you and the physician when he broke the news to you that your ailment was pneumonia. You might also want to mention the dramatic, almost-complete disappearance of polio from the contemporary scene. Perhaps one day rabies will be as treatable as typhoid now is.

Thus the use of specific example and other forms of narrative can intensify your own belief and conviction, and lead you to voice your ideas with more assurance than if you gave a vague, somewhat generalized, talk that *new drugs are wonderful. Wonderful* doesn't begin to say it; the new drugs are *miraculous;* the treatment of disease in our own decade has, to use the words of your source, undergone a *revolution.*

As the saying goes, ten thousand dollars is a lot of money even if you say it rapidly, but the way you say it shows how you feel about it.

STUDYING ONE'S OWN VOICE

One may improve voice in four different ways: (1) pitch, (2) loudness, (3) duration, and (4) quality—the *four attributes of sound.*

Improving Pitch

Pitch is the highness or lowness of the voice. If you can recall how a piano works, you know the keys at one end produce high-pitched notes, and the keys at the other bring forth low-pitched sounds. If you are an average male, you will find the average pitch of your voice in the neighborhood of C below middle C on the keyboard. If you are an average female, your average pitch will be about G sharp below middle C. Individuals vary, however, and if your average pitch is within two or three tones, either higher or lower, of the foregoing, you are within normal limits. One researcher suggests that if you read something rapidly, to the point of using a monotone, you may then assume that monotone to be your habitual pitch.[2]

As voices rise in pitch, they tend to carry better, other things being equal, than voices pitched too low; these latter voices some-times become muffled, throaty, or breathy, and consequently more difficult to hear. Voices that get too high, however, become unpleasant. Between the limits of high and low is a broad, comfortable region of vocal pitch acceptable to everybody.

You will find it difficult to judge your own voice, since it sounds different to you from the way it sounds to other listeners. The reason is that when you speak the sound you hear is accompanied by vibrations that travel from your vocal folds to your ears by way of

---

[2]J. Richard Franks, "Determining Habitual Pitch by Means of Increased Reading Rate," *Western Speech,* 31 (Fall 1967): 281-287.

bones, cartilage, and tissue. To the listener, your voice is entirely airborne. It is a little like listening to the piano, first with your ear pressed against the sounding board, and then standing a few feet away. You may have already discovered that, when you first heard your recorded voice played back to you, you were surprised that you could not recognize it. On the same occasion you also noted that your friends could not recognize themselves, either.

So far as pitch is concerned, you may note two kinds of suggestions. First, is the pitch of your voice about right? Is it within normal limits—not too close to the high or to the low end of the scale? And second, does your pitch have enough flexibility and variety? Poor control of pitch leads to monotonous or chantlike effects, which make it difficult for the listener to hear you with pleasure. We rely largely on pitch changes to make thoughts emphatic and also to suggest emotional attitudes. A difference between the mild "this is very important" and the emphatic "this is *very* important" is the difference in pitch with which the word *very* is uttered in the two statements. It would, moreover, be difficult to express one's earnestness, conviction, sympathy, kindliness, approval, or anger, without appropriate pitch changes.

These pitch changes, or *inflections,* may be classified as *rising, falling,* or *circumflex.* Rising inflections may be used to express questioning, surprise: You *are?* She *did?* In this *way?* Falling inflections express certainty, approval, finality, and the like: It can't be *done.* I'm *sure.* Come this *way.* Circumflex inflections may rise, fall, and rise—or fall, rise, and fall—as in expressions of unusual hesitation, reflection, or doubt: *Ye-e-es. No-o-o.* English inflection, however, is too complicated a subject to dispose of in a single paragraph; one can take a single word, like *oh, yes, no, hello, goodbye, forever, always, never,* or your own first name, and say it with different kinds of inflections to suggest different meanings.

Read the following, using such pitch changes as are appropriate:

An automobile manufacturer has to plan not one, not two, not three, but ten and fifteen years ahead.

Ninety percent of the drugs prescribed today were not even known to your physician fifteen years ago.

You ask me what my program for the company is? I say it is to make the Acme Box Corporation known all over the country, from the Atlantic to the Pacific.

You cannot call yourself a good citizen unless you cast an intelligent ballot in every election.

Even if the plan will save only one life—one single life—I would say it will be worth all the trouble it takes.

What the world needs today, even more than a giant leap into outer space, is a giant leap toward peace.

Loudness Possibly you have a better insight into the *loudness* or *softness* of your voice than you have into its pitch. Your friends may have complimented you on your vigorous voice and have called upon you when announcements were to be made to large assemblies. Or perhaps they have said, "Speak up. Back here we can't hear you." Another possibility, however, exists: perhaps you speak just barely loud enough so that people hear you if they make an effort; they may miss a few words, but not many; and thus it has happened that you have developed a level of loudness adequate only for small conversational situations. You now need information about whether your voice is loud enough for making talks, because speech making calls for more energy than does carrying on a conversation. You can be guided by seeing whether listeners in the back row are hearing you comfortably, and by asking them, later, if you made yourself heard—not just barely heard, but easily heard. You may be advised to talk louder—so much louder that what is right for them seems like shouting to you. In this circumstance you need to be guided by the listener, because you can be as deceived about the loudness of your own voice as you can about its pitch.

Once you learn to use a good loudness level, you need also to consider using *variety* of loudness. Although most monotones and singsongs are caused by sameness of pitch, or sameness of inflections, loudness may contribute to the fault. Some ideas need to be expressed with more vigor than others. To emphasize the word *very* in "This is *very* important," you raise the pitch of the voice as stated above; you also need to say *very* a little louder. Speakers of unusual force and power achieve striking effects by using different degrees of loudness: one idea may be expressed with great energy, and a contrasting idea may be spoken somewhat softly. When you feel determined and positive, when you have a conviction that much is at stake, when you are sure your course is right, when you know your facts are correct, you may communicate your sincerity, your conviction, and your high purpose by suiting the energy in your voice to the importance of the idea. "If the trumpet give an uncertain sound, who shall prepare himself for the battle?" If, similarly, the speaker's voice seems uncertain, his listeners will not leap into action.

Emphasize the important words in the following passages by changes in loudness. You may, of course, hear yourself making some pitch changes also. In studying these sentences, first decide which words should be spoken more loudly.

Each night one-third of the world's population goes to bed hungry.

I did not say simply that freedom was valuable—I said it was the most priceless gift we had in our possession.

Of all the nations of recorded history, the United States has proved itself to be the most generous, the most selfless, the most willing to share its vast wealth to alleviate human suffering.

I remember how the excitement in his voice increased as he started the countdown: Five—four—three—two—one—*Fire!*

I say this in all honesty—and I mean every word of it—we are doomed if we do not act now.

In a famous debate, Senator Daniel Webster was once vexed by an accusing remark by Senator Andrew Butler. In his reply, Webster looked his opponent straight in the eye:

> If the honorable member shall . . . inform the Senate . . . on what occasion . . . Massachusetts . . . has broken the compromise of the Constitution, he will find in me a *combatant* on that question.

Webster uttered the word *combatant*, an observer declared, as if it weighed ten tons. Webster had at his command a tremendous amount of disposable energy. When he needed a ten-ton voice, he could summon it. At Bunker Hill, for example, on the occasion of the laying of the cornerstone of the monument, a section of temporary bleachers collapsed and threw the crowd into such confusion that some feared order could not be restored. Webster stepped to the edge of the platform and called for quiet in commanding tones. As injuries were not serious, people quickly sorted themselves out and the proceedings were able to continue.[3]

Duration *Duration* is a third term used to describe the voice. It refers to the length of time a sound is prolonged. One can say "Vote *n-o-w,*" the prolonging of the second word serving to make it more urgent. So also a person could say "This is *v-e-r-y* important," not changing the pitch or loudness of the key word much, but so prolonging it that its effectiveness is increased. "Time marches rapidly past us; tomorrows become todays, and then yesterdays; before we realize it, a *w-h-o-l-e* semester is *g-o-n-e.*"

Nearly everyone has heard a classmate reproved for speaking too rapidly. The universal admonition of parents and teachers is *slow down; make the sounds distinct; don't run words together.* What the elders are saying, assuming for the moment that their impressions are well founded, is that students should improve their duration by stretching out the main words. Whereas the average *rate* of

---

[3]Margaret L. Coit, *John C. Calhoun: American Portrait* (Boston: Houghton Mifflin, 1950), p. 471.

experienced speakers is 100 to 150 words a minute, many beginners try for 175 or 200. Ultimately your rate of speaking depends upon the way you are built, and the kind of nervous and muscular systems you have; 100 words a minute may be all right for a deliberate speaker, but too slow for you.

A point which students may consider is the use of *pause*. As previously stated, observers have reported that British speakers use pauses effectively; it is with them a compelling and dramatic device. Utter an idea and then pause; let the idea soak in. The sign in the boiler factory is reputed to say, "In case of emergency, there will be a five-second blast of silence, followed by two thunderous intervals of quiet." You, too, can punctuate your flow of words with blasts of silence now and then.

The pause helps combat the tendency to talk too hurriedly; it also gives the listener opportunity to reflect upon what the speaker has uttered. "Does anyone in this audience really think that our school spirit is as good this year as it was last? (PAUSE) Has anyone here been impressed by the attendance at our home games? (PAUSE) Has anyone recently heard praise for the present student government administration? (PAUSE)" Obviously these questions are less forceful when read *without* the pauses than when read *with* them. Pauses therefore not only slow the speaker's rate of utterance but also add emphasis to the ideas they follow. Vary your rate to suit the idea. At times a speaker may speak deliberately, at other times rapidly. Whether your rate is fast or slow, however, you should not forget the value of the pause.

Walt Whitman praised Ralph Waldo Emerson's ease, naturalness, deliberateness—he said: "His don't-care-a-damnativeness was sublime." Emerson would mount the platform, arrange his papers deliberately, look over his audience, then proceed. After a bit, a point would come; he would strike a deliberate pause, perhaps half a minute, which is a long time to make an audience wait, yet he would do it as if it were the most natural thing in the world. Emerson, a truly brilliant lecturer, must be particularly praised for the depth and the originality of his thinking—but his delivery added to his impact on listeners.

No stretch of the imagination is needed to visualize even a beginning speaker, sure of his facts and personally deeply concerned, uttering something like the following:

> What has been the record for traffic safety in Collegetown the last six months? (PAUSE) I asked the chief of police that question yesterday. (LONGER PAUSE) This is what I discovered. (PAUSE) There are eight new graves in the city cemetery (SHORT PAUSE) five of them from a single accident. (LONG PAUSE) The number of accidents requiring hospitalization increased from thirty-four to forty-seven. (PAUSE)

In the following sentences, seek opportunities to vary the rate by prolonging a key word, or by pausing.[4] (You will also note opportunities for varying *pitch* and *loudness.*)

Labor racketeering—no matter how limited—smears all labor with the taint of corruption.

I am not here to justify the past, to gloss over the problems of the present, or to propose any easy solutions for the future.

It is not enough to prove that despotism is bad. It is equally necessary to go on—and on—proving that freedom is good.

We hope to show the entire world the value of the philosophy that has led to our prosperity. I do not have a name which adequately describes it. It has been called the new capitalism; the people's capitalism, or consumer capitalism. . . . Whatever it is, it is something new and far better than anything the world has ever seen before.

Quality   That pitch, loudness, and duration are three separate aspects of voice may be shown when speech is recorded visually, by mechanical or electronic devices, as a graph. On such a graph sounds appear as a series of waves of varying shapes and patterns. *Pitch* is shown by the *number* of waves per second—the faster the waves are created, the higher the pitch. *Loudness* is shown by the *size* of the waves—the higher or taller they appear, the greater the loudness. *Duration* is shown by the *number* of waves required to make one sound: more sound waves go into *n-o-o-o* than into *no*.

The fourth aspect of voice is *quality,* a characteristic of vocal sound more difficult to describe than the others. On the recorded sound wave described in the foregoing paragraph, quality is indicated by the *complexity* of the wave pattern. Quality refers not to pitch, loudness, or duration, but to the basic tone itself. Whereas pitch can be described by *high* or *low,* loudness by *loud* or *soft,* and duration by *short* or *prolonged,* quality is described by words like *hoarse, harsh, shrill, muffled, nasal, breathy, infantile, dull, rasping,* or by *resonant, melodious, brilliant, musical,* and the like. Tom, Dick, and Harry can say "Oh, no, sir," almost identically so far as pitch, loudness, and duration are concerned—but something basic in their tones will enable you to tell, without looking, which was Tom, which Dick, and which Harry. These are differences in *quality:* Tom may have a voice that is fuller and richer (quality); Dick is shrill and nasal (quality); Harry's voice was breathy and muffled (again, quality). Yet the three may have used identical inflections, made the tones

---

[4]For an impressive demonstration of the use of pause, listen to the Hal Holbrook recording, "Mark Twain Tonight."

equally loud, and required the same length of time to utter the phrase.

You may use changes in quality when you make your voice more breathy (as in excitement), more tense (when suspense or expectation is involved), more harsh, hoarse, or nasal (as when depicting different characters in a dialog), more full or resonant (as when quoting the Bible or when using solemn language). Changes in quality represent a sophisticated use of the voice. Try the following (attempt to get a little extra seriousness or solemnity into the quality of your voice):

> For the complete dimension of the Christian faith is contained, on the one hand, in the petition, "Give us this day our daily bread," and on the other, in the observance, "man does not live by bread alone."
>
> And perhaps if we ask what is the innermost nature of solitude, we should answer: It is the presence of the eternal upon the crowded roads of the temporal. It is the experience of being alone but not lonely, in view of the eternal presence which shines through the face of the Christ and which includes everybody and everything from which we are separated. Let us dare to have solitude: to face the eternal, to find others, to see ourselves.

Vocal Variety   As would be expected, people can use their voices to express their feelings with wide variations in effectiveness. In a Teachers College, Columbia, experiment, in which individuals tape-recorded the alphabet in such a way as to express feelings like anger, happiness, sadness, and seven other emotions, followed by listening sessions in which selected listeners noted the emotion they thought each speaker was attempting to convey, the most effective speaker communicated his feelings accurately a total of 161 times—the least effective 70 times.[5] Although you can choose words, or use facial expression, to communicate to listeners how earnest, or sincere, or determined you are, in the last analysis much of this earnestness, sincerity, or determination must be communicated by the voice. A good voice has a *communicative* quality as opposed to one that sounds *dull, feeble, withdrawn, monotonous.*

Choose materials that you strongly wish to communicate about. You may find it easier if you include in your speech sentences that show you are thinking about the listener. You have heard examples like these: *"This point is especially important . . . Here's the root of the whole difficulty . . . I hope you agree with what I've said thus far . . . You may want to question me on this later . . . These were his*

---

[5]See the study by Joel R. Davitz and Lois Jean Davitz in *The Journal of Communication,* 9 (March 1959): 6-13.

RADIO CAN DO IT BETTER

Satirist ad-writer Stan Freberg was arguing with a guy about radio versus TV, and the other guy said, "All right, tell me what radio can do that television can't do better." Freberg says, "O.K., here's what I'm gonna do. First, I'm gonna drain all the water out of Lake Erie." And then are these gurgling, down-the-drain sounds—*burble, burble, glug, glug,* you know. Then Freberg says, "And I'm gonna fill Lake Erie with whipped cream."

The sound goes *splllllssssshhhhshsh.* Now Freberg says, "And I got this 40,000-ton cherry sitting on a field in Ohio and I'm gonna call out the whole Air Force to fly up there and get it." So you hear *zzzzzzzzzzzzzzz,* the roar of a million airplanes. Freberg says, "O.K., they got that big cherry up in the air now, and they're carrying it toward the whipped cream in Lake Erie." *zzzzzzzzzzzzzzzzzzzz.* The planes are working hard now, and Freberg says, "They're over the lake, and now I'm gonna order 'em to drop that 40,000-ton cherry into that whipped cream. Okay, boys, let 'er GOOO-O-O-O-O-O!!!"

Then you hear a gigantic *spppplllllssssshhhh-llllooooopppp!!!* The cherry has fallen square into the whipped cream in Lake Erie—you've seen it in your mind's eye, and Freberg says, "Now, lemme see TV do *that.*"

(Adapted and reprinted by permission from *Sports Illustrated,* 29 [September 16, 1968], "And In This Corner . . . NCR 315," by William Johnson [quoting Murry Woroner]. © 1968, Time, Inc.)

exact words . . . You remember that Helen made this argument last Monday . . . What follows is complex but let me see if I can make it clear. . . ." The use of *you* helps to bring the listener into your speech and into your thinking, and may perhaps help you project more of your meaning.

At times you may use a striking variation in quality, loudness, pitch, or duration to enhance your communicativeness.

This book has mentioned that using dialog to suggest the vocal manner of another person adds variety and interest. One speaker imitated the demonstrators in Africa chanting "free-dom, free-dom, free-dom." Perhaps your narrative calls for a slow count: *one—two—three—four,* or a countdown: *seven—six—five.* Maybe you would like to suggest the chant of the spectators at the Madrid bullfight:

olé—olé—olé. Or use a special sound (these come from student speeches): "As the Arab leaped into the air his cape made a big *whoosh.*" "We made a sudden stop and *smack!* the car behind plowed into us." A student explaining the procedures used by the National Rifle Association in pistol competition called off the commands heard on the firing range: "Ready on the right (PAUSE) ready on the left (PAUSE) ready on the firing line (PAUSE) FIRE!" These commands, spoken in an authoritative tone, spaced with the long, ten-second pauses used in competition, made the description highly realistic.

The sketch, "Radio Can Do It Better," on the preceding page, amusingly illustrates a wide variety of vocal effects—and makes the useful point that radio can stimulate the listener's imagination.

An example of the effective use of all attributes of voice is a sentence from a speech of William Jennings Bryan, heard in Des Moines, Iowa, one hot summer afternoon. During the speech he quoted what is everywhere known as the great commandment, "Thou shalt love the Lord thy God with all thy heart, and with all thy soul, and with all thy mind." The speaker continued:

> Jesus did not say, Thou shalt love the Lord thy God with a *part* of thy heart, and a *part* of thy soul, and a *part* of thy mind: what he did say, thou shalt love the Lord thy God with *all* thy heart, and with *all* thy soul, and with *all* thy mind.

An obvious scorn was revealed in the pitch and quality of the speaker's voice as he repeated each *part;* and when he came to each *all,* he uttered these words with notable increase of loudness and duration: *a-l-l.* This example is cited from the memory of an incident that happened some sixty years ago; and that it is remembered is explained in part by the simple and vivid choice of words and in part by the tremendous force and power of the speaker's voice.

The message is carried not only by words but by tones and actions—even silences. Anthropologist Edward T. Hall's deservedly popular *The Silent Language* is eloquent on this point. He writes:

> Take the example of a salesman who has been trying to sell something to an important client for a number of months. The client . . . promises to let the salesman know the verdict in a week. The first half second of the interview that follows usually tells the salesman . . . whether he has been successful or not.
>
> A political figure makes a speech which is supposed to be reassuring. It has the opposite effect. When the words are read *they* are reassuring. Yet the total message as delivered is not. Why . . . Sen-

tences can be meaningless by themselves. Other signs may be much more eloquent.[6]

One may give this excerpt an intercultural application by adding that in conversation with people of other cultures who speak English imperfectly, we react to their tones and actions as well as to their words. When we find ourselves in situations in other lands and are addressed by people who speak a language that is foreign to us, again we rely on vocal tones, facial expressions, and gestures—and if we cannot communicate through these, we communicate imperfectly or perhaps not at all.

ARTICULA-TION AND PRONUNCIATION

Closely related to voice production is the shaping of vocal sounds into words, phrases, and sentences.

By *articulation* is meant the *precision* and *clarity* with which sounds of speech are uttered. A synonym is *enunciation*. Mumbling and indistinctness are forms of faulty articulation.

By *pronunciation* is meant the traditional or customary utterance of words. *Nuclear* pronounced as "nucular," *perspiration* pronounced as "prespiration," are examples of mispronunciation.

Experience has shown that one can modify habits of articulation and pronunciation, though the magic cannot be worked overnight. Good habits of articulation and pronunciation may be considered as technical achievements, like refinements of grammar, but they may also be viewed in a larger framework. Although the reception of a message may be garbled because of indistinct utterance, the flow of words may carry a burden of incidental messages to the receiver that the sender did not intend: messages with social overtones that comment on the sender's background, education, sophistication or lack of sophistication, forthrightness or lack of forthrightness.

If you have serious faults of voice or articulation, you may want to take a special course or to consult a speech and hearing clinic. The discussion that follows offers practical advice with respect to situations in which students with average or even good speech habits may need to take special care.

First Impressions

Good first impressions are important. Clear articulation suggests poise and self-assurance. If you stop a stranger to ask directions, you may need to take extra care with your first words, to be sure you have his attention and to make it easier for him to adjust to you as a

---

[6]Edward T. Hall, *The Silent Language* (Greenwich, Conn.: Fawcett, 1969), p. 94. Copyright 1959 by Doubleday & Co., New York.

person and to your habits of utterance. You do not want to begin to broadcast until he is ready to receive. Talking to an audience presents a similar problem. "Friends" or "Ladies and gentlemen" (not "la'ies and gennulmun") can be spoken with clarity (and with cordiality). Extra care with the opening sentences may help add to your feeling of assurance.

Ends of Sentences English sentences have a pitch or melody pattern that ordinarily calls for a falling inflection at the end of a sentence; in this way the sender shows a full stop. Loudness and clarity of articulation are needed for those last words so that the listener will hear them. If your sentence is, "I want to pay a special tribute to the three best students in our class this year," do not let the final words sound like "inner class susseer."

Proper Nouns We cannot tell whether Johnson or Jensen is said by the context of the sentence—our sole clue is the way the first vowel in the name is pronounced. Other examples: *Bunsen* burner, *Stokely Carmichael's* speech, *Doppler* effect, *Grimm's* law, *Broca's* area, *Bill Vaughan's* article, *Lewis and Clark* expedition, *Monroe's* administration, a new play by *Gristlethwaite* and *Oppensteiner,* the trial was held at *Ipswich.* If the name is unusual, you will confer a favor on your listeners by repeating it, spelling it, or even writing it on the board.

Unusual or Technical Words *Gaiter, retrorocket, laparotomy, monitor, turbine, vault, launching pad, cornering, tight end, trajectory, placket, placebo,* may not be as familiar to your listeners as to you.

Other Important Words Some words carry a special burden of meaning. Any teacher of experience would quickly see why a group of children showed up at the Smithsonian Institution asking to see *Dinah Shore's bones,* or why *Dentist the Menace* appeared in a composition written during class. The punch line of a narrative must be articulated with clarity, or listeners will miss the point of the humor. Imagine a three-minute story ending with the line "Oh, you've shot him!" The total effect of the story, the fate of the joke, hinges on the single word "shot"; any faltering here, and the effect is destroyed. A half-shod tramp is different from a half-shot tramp.

If *foreign policy* sounds like *farm policy,* the listener may be confused for the dozen following sentences. *Visibility unlimited* may be heard as *visibility limited* if *"un"* is not spoken with precision. Perhaps you have said, "This isn't difficult," and your listener has said, "Did you say *is* or *isn't?*"

Quotations "The chief thing in art" (this is you, quoting Cicero) "is that what you do shall be fitting." Nearly all these words are important to understanding: *chief thing, art, what you do,* and *fitting.* What meaning can the listener wring from "The chief glub in art is that whaddado shall be fliffglmp," originally uttered, you go on to say, by Sestero. ("What did she say?" mumble the listeners.)

Ending of the Speech Don't weaken the important last impression. "We should all get behind the drive to raise funds for the student union." Make the words distinct. This is the give-me-liberty-or-give-me-death part of your message, the appeal to give us the tools and we will finish the job.

Names What standard of pronunciation governs names in the news, or, for that matter, any proper name? The first president Roosevelt reputedly preferred his last name pronounced in two syllables, *Rose*-velt; the second president Roosevelt preferred three, *Rose*-uh-velt. To pronounce "Roose" to rhyme with *moose,* in either instance, is not acceptable. We try to pronounce a person's name as he or she pronounces it. If the name is that of a community, we accept the prevailing usage of the citizens of the community wherever it is made clear. The city of *Cairo,* in Illinois, rhymes with *Karo;* it is not pronounced like the Egyptian city. Good usage may be divided, as in *Missouri, Los Angeles, Louisiana;* here we may side with either camp.

Words of Foreign Origin Words of foreign origin are quickly given an American equivalent that gains currency in American speech. Radio and TV announcers set the pattern; their decisions are followed without much question. When the Korean city of Seoul made the news, broadcasters at first differed among themselves, then settled upon *"sole",* this pronunciation became standard. *Volkswagen* is pronounced much as spelled, disregarding German practice in which letter *v* is pronounced *f* and letter *w* pronounced *v* ("folksvagen"). Air Force personnel stationed in *Wiesbaden* pronounce the first syllable "weese." Yet we respect the German pronunciations of *Wagner, Beethoven,* and *Bach,* since these pronunciations are in the custody of cultured classes; to Americanize them as "wagner, bee-thoven, and batch" stamps one as intellectually beyond repair. (The *ch* in *Bach* calls for a German sound that does not exist in English; professional musicians at times employ that sound, though others pronounce *Bach* like *bock* with no ill effects.)

Unless, therefore, the foreign pronunciation, or one close to it, seems to prevail, you will be in good standing if you adopt any widely used Americanized form (our pronunciation of *pizza* is close enough to the Italian to satisfy us, but would not fool a native).

1   What demands do radio and TV make upon the speaker?

2   Distinguish between *voice* and *voice control*.

3   Read the illustrative sentences included in the foregoing chapter for drill purposes. After each sentence, ask yourself this question: Exactly what is communicated by the *words* in the sentence, and exactly what is communicated by the *voice?* Demonstrate to the satisfaction of the class that you can, through changes of *voice*, make the message more forceful, convincing, and emphatic.

4   Make a "Voices of the Campus" survey. Collect examples of interesting voice uses gleaned from conversations, lectures, movies, broadcast programs, or other sources or activities available to the campus. Your examples collectively may illustrate pitch, quality, pause, rate, and other aspects of voice.

5   Make a speech of . . . minutes in which you attempt to demonstrate something different in the way of vocal variety.

Treat this assignment in the spirit of trial, experiment, venture. No attempt is being made to introduce unnatural inflections in your voice—yet everyone needs to try to extend the range, the flexibility, and the power of his or her speaking voice—along lines that are natural to him or her. To achieve this result, you may go through an awkward stage.

For example: in your talk, introduce a bit of dialog, which will give you an opportunity to *suggest* different characterizations. Or you may make a talk giving some of your favorite passages from poetry—and in reading these short passages, try to bring out the deeper meanings. The reading of poetry has always been considered an extremely useful way of developing vocal variety, just as the writing of poetry is one of the best ways of increasing your vocabulary and general sensitivity to language. Or you may describe two or three professors, or ministers, or salespeople (with characterizations). Or make a talk on a subject close to your heart, and try to show us something arresting in *force*. Or describe a battle between you and your conscience (perhaps on the order of Eugene O'Neill), with you speaking in one voice and your conscience in a slightly different one. Or talk about some business or profession that requires a good voice; demonstrate the voice of command of an officer; the volume and endurance needed by a tour conductor, an executive, an auctioneer.

6   If you have difficulty pronouncing words, study this list of words most commonly mispronounced:

address	column	homage
alias	comparable	humor
ally	dour	impotent
because	electoral	secretive
clique	exquisite	superfluous
larynx	research	statistics
library	respite	status
maintenance	genuine	toward
mischievous	gesture	tremendous
often	height	vehement
orgy	heinous	victuals

7 If you feel insecure about your ability to manage long words, read the following aloud, giving each syllable its proper value. Consult a good college-level dictionary, to learn acceptable pronunciations; the syllables written in italics will give you a clue. Although in several instances other pronunciations are acceptable, if you find yourself accenting a word differently from the pronunciation given below, check your pronunciation in a dictionary for acceptability. Repeat combinations that are bothersome, and group several words in drill sentences: "The repercussions of those formidable archaeological findings are peculiarly lamentable."

ab*dom*inal	dis*in*terestedly	persev*er*ance
ac*com*paniment	*for*midable	pronuncia*tion*
*ad*mirable	*hos*pitable	reper*cus*sion
*ap*plicable	imme*diately	sacri*le*gious
ap*prox*imately	*in*quiry	scien*tif*ically
archaeo*log*ical	incom*parable	simul*tane*ity
argu*men*tative	indis*put*able	subsi*di*zation
aristo*crat*ic	inex*plicable	suc*cinct*
ar*tic*ulatory	intel*lec*tualize	superin*ten*dent
*ar*tis*tically	*in*tricacy	sur*pris*ing
as*pir*ant	ir*rep*arable	*sus*tenance
authori*ta*tively	*lam*entable	un*que*stionably
*bar*barous	manu*fac*turer	*veg*etable
characte*ris*tic	oleo*mar*garine	vehemence
civiliza*tion*	paren*thet*ically	*ver*batim
con*tem*plative	par*tic*ularly	*vet*erinary
deter*i*orate	pe*cul*iarly	zo*ol*ogy

PART FOUR

GROUP COMMUNICATION

The purpose of studying group discussion is to consider
not only efficient ways of solving a problem, but also
ways of encouraging each member to participate to the
fullest. The chapter on leadership describes the
functions that help a group achieve its purpose; most of
these are performed by the designated leader, but may
be initiated by other members. You may want to use a
topic discussed by the group as a springboard for a
speech of your own later on.

 Communicating
in Small Groups:
Basic Concepts

Nature of discussion ☐ Task orientation and social orientation
☐ Characteristics of discussion ☐ Values of discussion ☐
Disadvantages of discussion ☐ Discussion procedures ☐
Types of discussion ☐ To become a better participant ☐
Assignments and exercises

The problem of communicating in small groups touches a basic and elemental need in all of us. George Herbert Mead, philosopher and social psychologist, long ago wrote that a human being is dependent upon society for his major qualities as a human being. Charles Horton Cooley, founder of sociology, also emphasized the social nature of the individual. Americans belong to all sorts of business, professional, religious, and social groups. The current issue of the *World Almanac* lists fifteen pages of societies and associations, from the Association for the Study of Abortion to the American Society of Zoologists. In addition to these formally organized groups, Americans also find themselves in numerous informal committees and groups, assembled, perhaps temporarily, for a specific purpose.

NATURE OF DISCUSSION

Small-group discussion involves:

1 **Small membership** The size of the group varies, but is perhaps closer to five than to fifteen. The group has an identity or boundary.
2 **Symbolic activity** Free use of verbal and nonverbal symbols is evident: words, voice, facial expression, gesture. Somewhat arbitrarily this chapter considers only face-to-face situations, although conferences may be carried on among several individuals by a special telephone or television hookup, even though the participants are miles apart.
3 **Purpose** The group has a common problem or goal. Six persons traveling together by chance on a small, feeder-line aircraft would not be considered a "group" under this definition. If, however, the six were told that their flight was cancelled, and they entered into a discussion to find other means of transportation, they would constitute a group, facing a common problem and pooling their resources to solve it.

TASK ORIENTATION AND SOCIAL ORIENTATION

Discussion groups are usually thought of as being (a) *task-oriented,* as when they meet to solve a problem, or (b) *socially oriented,* as when they meet for mutual encouragement or support. A task-oriented group usually works toward a formal or informal statement of a solution or policy. A socially oriented group usually aims at individual satisfaction. The classification is not mutually exclusive. A task-oriented group should produce a certain amount of individual satisfaction if members are pleased with their decision and with their separate contributions to it. In fact it is difficult to think of a task-oriented group which does not have a social dimension; the climate of such a discussion would be grim and mechanical. A socially oriented group exists to exchange insights and experiences. It ordinarily does not attempt to "settle" a specific problem, though here and there individual members will pick up notions that help them to manage their personal problems.

CHARACTER-ISTICS OF DISCUSSION

It will be helpful to look at certain characteristics of discussants and of the discussion process.

Participation

Decisions arrived at are more likely to be carried out when members of a group make them, than when orders are handed down by superiors.

In a classic study, Coch and French described an experiment in which changes were to be made in the method of making garments. In the experimental groups, workers were told about the proposed changes, and invited to offer suggestions. General agreement was reached through discussion about the new changes and the new piece rates. In fact, the workers would make references to "our job" and "our rate." A control group was simply called together and "told" about the new routine and the new rate. After the change went into effect, workers in the experimental groups produced about ten more units per hour than before, and workers in the control group, who had had no say in the plan, produced about ten units less. On a subsequent experiment, the control group was included in the discussion, and produced as high as the experimental groups had. The obvious conclusion was that the fact of holding a discussion with those concerned, soliciting their opinions, and gaining their interest, gave them a stake in the successful operation of the new plan and a commitment to make it work.[1]

This process is generally referred to as *participatory decision making*. Maier gives an example of a group that had only a fleeting existence but in other aspects illustrates the functioning of a small group. A supervisor with three women in his office needed two of them to work on Sunday. He asked them individually, and each said she had made a date she could not break. Double pay for Sunday work was no inducement. Maier continues:

> He asked the girls to meet in his office on Friday morning and told them about the emergency job. Since he needed the help of two of them, he wondered what would be the fairest way to handle it. The girls readily entered into the discussion. It turned out that all had dates, but one had a date with some other girls, and all three girls agreed that a date with

---

[1]Lester Coch and J. R. P. French, Jr., "Overcoming Resistance to Change," *Human Relations,* 1 (1948): 512–522.

other girls was not a "real" date. Thus this girl agreed that it was only fair that she should work. . . .

Further discussion revealed that one girl had a date with the man to whom she was engaged, and the third had a date with a new boyfriend. All girls agreed that a date with a fiance was a real date, but it was not a "heavy" date. It was decided that the third girl, who had the date with a new conquest, should be excused.[2]

Whereas the supervisor might have been overly concerned with problems of seniority or previous overtime assignments, the women discussing the matter among themselves, found an issue meaningful to them and decided the problem on that issue. They were happier with a decision that they had arrived at themselves than they would have been with one made for them.

This group existed as a task-oriented group, and evolved a solution because of their agreed-upon habits of dating behavior. The influence of American culture is also interesting to note. A group of French, German, or Japanese women may have arrived at a different solution because of their different attitudes toward working and dating. Perhaps they would rather have been told what to do; perhaps they could not have arrived at a solution at all.

Consensus   The basic purpose of any group that faces a problem is to arrive at a *consensus*. Some members will, of course, be happier with the consensus than others, but each will have decided that desirable features outweigh doubts and objections, and probably also that, as Benjamin Franklin said after the deliberations on the Constitution (see the Appendix), no other convention would have been able to make a better Constitution.

Because of the importance of consensus, researchers have taken a special look at the characteristics of discussants that are likely to bring about consensus. One of these characteristics is *orientation*. A statement has orientation if its maker is trying to assist the discussion process itself: by trying to resolve a conflict, by proposing a compromise, by making a helpful suggestion, or in other similar ways. The concept of consensus, and the part that orientation and some other variables play in arriving at consensus, is currently undergoing considerable investigation. It is helpful to the discussion to have someone in the group take an interest in reconciling differing views—this individual may or may not be the chairperson.[3] Words that signal the presence of orientation in a discussion

---

[2]*Problem-solving Discussions and Conferences* (New York: McGraw-Hill, 1963), pp. 12–13.
[3]Interested students may want to read the research papers. See Dennis S. Gouran's pioneering study, "Variables Related to Consensus in Group Discussion of Questions of Policy," *Speech Monographs,* 36 (August 1969): 388, 391; Thomas J. Knutson's "Experimental Study of the Effects of Orientation Behavior on Small Group Consensus," *Speech Monographs,* 39 (August 1972): 159–165. Knutson's and William E. Holdridge's recent study, "Orientation Behavior,

are *you, your,* and *yours* as opposed to *I, me,* and *mine.*[4] Words such as *agree, disagree, decide, adopt, propose,* and *vote* automatically suggest that someone in the group is thinking about the discussion as a discussion and is seeking areas in which a decision can be reached.

Obviously the time at which to begin to work for consensus is after the important facts, opinions, and judgments have been presented to the group. Perhaps by calling upon the group's imagination, ingenuity, and resourcefulness, someone can lead the discussion to a consensus that respects the best of those facts, opinions, and judgments.

Cohesiveness
Cohesiveness is the characteristic of a group in which members have the feeling of belonging to it and liking it. The group works well together. Members feel they know each other, respect each other, can depend on each other. A sense of solidarity is in the air. Individuals can state their positions candidly. If a disagreement arises, it is frankly discussed without fear that the group will be shattered. Assignments or duties are willingly accepted without a feeling of being imposed on, or that someone else is not doing a fair share. Morale is good. By contrast, a group with poor cohesiveness is marked with reluctance, unwillingness, and generally neutral attitudes. Often as members communicate more freely with each other, their liking for one another increases, as does the cohesiveness of the group.

Power
Power is the personal influence one member has over other members of the group because of:

1 **Knowledge** You have expert knowledge; you have information that is desired or needed; you know the road and the others don't; you know how to fix the machine; you have faced a situation more often than others have.
2 **Social graces** You are poised, cordial, friendly. You are perceived as showing respect for the sensitivities of others. You are also perceived as having inner strength, not weakness.
3 **Fear** You may have the ability to punish others by words or actions. This kind of power may be better for the short term than for the long term, but it nevertheless exists.
4 **Reward** You may be able to reward others by prizes, votes, grades, salary increases, promotions, or other preferment.

Leadership and Consensus: A Possible Functional Relationship," *Speech Monographs,* 42 (January 1975): 107-114, raises further questions about orientation, but notes that individuals engaging in orientation behavior will be perceived as leaders (p. 110). John A. Kline's "Indices of Orienting and Opinionated Statements in Problem-Solving Discussion," *Speech Monographs,* 37 (November 1970): 282–286.
    [4]Kline, "Indices of Orienting . . . ," 282–286.

5 **Communicative ability** You may be more persuasive than others because you are more logical, more analytical, better attuned to the needs or wishes of others.

6 **Acquaintance** In nearly every organization is an institution known as the grapevine. The grapevine exists because of the need of individuals for information that may affect their future. You may be one of those in a key position to attract information and disseminate it through useful channels.

7 **Position** You hold a superior title; you are the boss, the chair-person, the president, the colonel. Those who put you in office gave you the power to perform its duties. Or: you may be able to exert influence because you are a *peer*—you can talk as an equal; you have no more either to gain or to lose than they do.[5]

Occasionally the person who holds the *title* is only a figurehead or stand-in for someone in the background who is the real source of power. We use the expression "the power behind the throne." To get something accomplished in the Acme Box Corporation you may go not to the president or to the chairman of the board but to the major stockholder.

Power obviously works both ways; the designated leader can exert strong influence because of the resources he controls (rewards that only he can bestow or withhold), but the other members also have resources of their own (they can revolt, rebel, protest, and issue minority reports) with which they can influence the leader. Both leader and followers have a *power reservoir,* as pointed out by R. Victor Harnack, Thorrel B. Fest, and others. The leader occasionally has to dip into his power reservoir to remind the others that he is aware of his resources (this action does not quite have to be like the whiff of grapeshot that Napoleon recommended). Followers likewise are aware of their own potential.[6]

Role is the part played, or the function assumed, by a member of the group. Role depends partly on the status of the individual, partly on a way of behaving, partly on the expectations of others. In one situation, Ms. A is quiet and reserved; in another situation, she is relaxed and outgoing. Mr. B, stopping to help a stranded motorist, takes command of the difficulty; finding himself in a social situation, he lets others do the introducing or suggest the entertainment. Each student plays a complex role: when reciting in class, when discuss-

---

[5]For a comprehensive review of these and other kinds of power, see Gardner Lindzey and Elliot Aronson, eds., *The Handbook of Social Psychology*, 2d ed., vol. 4 (Reading, Mass.: Addison-Wesley, 1969), pp. 166–184.

[6]*Group Discussion: Theory and Technique* (New York: Appleton-Century-Crofts, 1964), pp. 203–207. George C. Homans, "Fundamental Social Processes," in Neil J. Smelser, ed., *Sociology: An Introduction* (New York: Wiley, 1967), p. 54.

ing the course with other students, when conversing with the instructor.

In discussion, one student may play the role of a tension-reliever. His sense of humor bubbles out at critical moments, cools the rhetoric of more tense participants, and thus makes a special contribution to the group. The group has steadily given him its approval in this role, so he is happy in it. Another student plays the role of information seeker. She spots the places at which hard facts are needed and sees to it that they are introduced. Someone else is a harmonizer of conflicting positions. Some students block, antagonize, or plead special interests. Behind these labels is the kind of content found in discussions: supplying information, asking questions, lending encouragement, recalling related decisions or procedures, getting the discussion on the track, dissolving tension, evolving a compromise—and the opposites. These roles emerge in different degrees depending on whether the group is task-oriented or otherwise. Role refers not to the complete person but to selected facets of his behavior.

A fertile example of categories of roles is that of Kenneth D. Benne and Paul Sheats. They speak of (1) *group task roles,* which may be identified by such key words as *initiator, information seeker, information giver, opinion seeker, opinion giver, clarifier, coordinator,* and *orienter;* (2) *group building and maintenance roles,* identified by such key words as *supporter, harmonizer,* and *tension reliever;* and (3) *self-centered roles,* most of which are harmful to the discussion process: *blocker, aggressor, recognition seeker, playboy,* and *special-interest pleader.*[7]

Standards Groups tend to agree upon *standards* of behavior. One such standard may be a willingness to do one's full share; to volunteer for routine or other tasks or assignments. In a committee of five planning a dance, for example, with four of the members willingly undertaking assignments relating to hiring the band, planning the decorations, etc., a member who seemed to avoid his share of the work would fail to meet the expectations of the others. A standard of productivity is being set to which it is hoped everyone will agree. Or the standard may relate to dress, promptness, language, and the like. It may be announced by a formal rule, "Absentees will be fined 25¢." Announced or unannounced, it is operative just the same, and the group member who is insensitive to it will discover he or she is missing one of the satisfactions of group membership.

---

[7]"Functional Roles of Group Members," *Journal of Social Issues,* 4 (1948): 41–49.

VALUES OF DISCUSSION

Values of discussion include:

1   **Discussion evolves a better solution**   The group will nearly always foresee more difficulties, explore more facets, visualize more outcomes, than can a single individual.

2   **Discussion improves group spirit**   People like to be consulted. They like to be in on prospective developments. They cherish a feeling of being a member of the group. Points of friction between faculty and students, between labor and management, and between other groups—even between nations—can be resolved through discussion.

3   **Discussion improves individual morale**   If individuals have had a reasonable opportunity to participate and have got a grievance stated, an idea accepted, a point of view maintained, or an attitude supported, they are particularly likely to have a favorable attitude toward the discussion activity.

4   **The agreed-upon solution is more likely to work**   Some bugs will have been removed by process of discussion itself. The individuals participating, moreover, will exert extra effort to make the solution a success. We have already commented on the evidence that decisions are more effectively carried out when they have been made by the group concerned. Those present see that others also are willing to accept the decision of the group (pay the fee, change working hours, close the branch office, join the community committee) and understand the reasons for it.

5   **Discussion is vital to the survival of democracy**   When issues of massive concern sweep a country, the forums, panels, symposiums, debates, hearings, buzz sessions, and discussions of all kinds, formal and informal, organized and spontaneous, legislative and nonlegislative, help a free people to analyze the problem, ascertain the facts, weigh the possible outcomes, and take the necessary steps.

DISADVANTAGES OF DISCUSSION

1   **Discussion is time-consuming**   A certain amount of time is lost in digressing, repeating, soothing ruffled egos, listening to uninformed viewpoints. One who believes in the discussion process has to be patient with it.

2   **Discussion spreads and divides responsibility**   Group members may be less careful of statements made and positions taken.

3   **The decision made by a group is not always superior**   Some one member of the group may have been overly influential. Members may protect one another's vested interests. Often committee reports, prepared after lengthy discussion, are completely rejected by the larger group that created the committee.

Knowing these and other disadvantages of group discussion may enable you to participate more effectively as a discussant. From the long-term point of view, the values of discussion far outweigh the disadvantages. The most likely alternative, decision making by a single leader, has even graver disadvantages.

DISCUSSION PROCEDURES

Discussion is often described in language that originated with philosopher-educator John Dewey. Its procedure begins with (1) a *question* or *problem.* Your group asks itself, "How can we lessen the number of traffic accidents in this community?" or puts before itself some other topic. Next (2) comes a *definition* and *analysis* of the problem. If the group wants to make constructive suggestions for reducing traffic fatalities, it should know such facts as these: 43 percent of deaths on the highway come from exceeding speed limits, 18 percent of fatal accidents occur between 1 a.m. and 6 a.m., and 36 percent of pedestrians who are killed meet their deaths while trying to cross a street between intersections. If a board of directors is trying to discover why the company lost money, it needs to know whether the difficulty is low income or high expenses or both, and it will want to look at a breakdown of figures to determine the low-income projects and the high-cost areas.

The group next considers (3) *possible solutions.* Several solutions may be presented to the group, bearing on everything from new statutes or ordinances to changing requirements for drivers' licenses. Possible solutions are then combined or narrowed to (4) the *most feasible* solution. This solution is finally (5) *formally stated* and presented to the group as its consensus, or phrased as a recommendation for consideration by another group or agency.

Various modifications have been proposed to the Dewey model by careful observers who have seen that discussion does not follow a straight line from statement of the problem to a good solution of it, but rather leaps ahead or doubles back, or moves in a circular or spiral fashion. B. Aubrey Fisher has offered a good description of the process by which decisions are arrived at in small groups. He observed that group members introduced a proposal, discussed it for a length of time, dropped it in favor of another proposal, and then reintroduced it. Groups arrive at consensus, he concluded, not in a gradual evolutionary pattern but in spurts of energy. He noted four phases:

Phase 1: Orientation Getting acquainted, clarifying, and tentatively expressing attitudes.
Phase 2: Conflict Disputing, dissenting, controversy, conflict. Members leave the tentative stage and begin to make up their minds.

Phase 3: Emergence Dispute, dissent, conflict begin to dissipate. Members whose point of view is beginning to lose out retreat from their firm positions by making ambiguous statements. The eventual outcome of the discussion is beginning to emerge.

Phase 4: Reinforcement Argument no longer seems important. Comments favoring the emerging outcome are reinforced.[8]

The Dewey model of group discussion is ordered and methodical; the later models, based on more detailed observation, are closer to what actually goes on. All are useful though no model can state the final word. The creative process is not invariably channeled into set grooves but instead expresses itself in irregular, unsummoned, and unannounced hunches and flashes of insight. Ordinarily the leader of a discussion group will suggest a plan or agenda for the approval of members and they will agree to follow it step by step; situations may arise, however, when the group discusses some item at greater length or in a different order from what it had planned. The leader, sometimes assisted by members, sometimes not, usually follows the agreed plan but may see good reasons for modifying it.

TYPES OF DISCUSSION

A description of conventional types, and others not so conventional, follows.

Group Discussion with a Leader

Discussion with a leader consists of a group of individuals—for example a speech communication class and a member of the group chosen as leader, chairperson, or moderator. The discussion may open with a statement by the leader explaining the question to be discussed: "In what ways can the American college be improved?" "How may each of us enhance the ability to communicate with other human beings?" The leader may then do one or more of the following:

Comment briefly about the importance or the timeliness of the question.

Suggest a procedure to be followed.

Encourage the group to define and expand the statement of the question, offer possible solutions, and collectively arrive at the preferred solution.

Make the necessary transitions as the group is led from one phase of the discussion to another: sometimes helping the group to

---

[8]"Decision Emergence: Phases in Group Decision-Making," *Speech Monographs,* 37 (March 1970): 53–66. These categories are fully explained in his *Small Group Decision Making: Communication and the Group Process* (New York: McGraw-Hill, 1974), chap. 7, "The Decision-Making Process."

pursue an idea, sometimes being guided by the mood of the participants.

Point out relationships between statements uttered later in the discussion with those uttered earlier.

Summarize progress from time to time; close with a summary.

These items are task-oriented. The leader may also encourage, support, relieve tension—often by a phrase: "Good point," "As Mary was saying . . ."—invite contributions from the reticent, and so on; these items are *supportive,* or socially oriented.

Panel Discussion

A panel discussion may be described as a conversation in front of an audience. It is characterized by informal interchange of opinion, as contrasted with the series of short, previously prepared speeches that describe the *symposium* (see below). It requires a leader and a panel of discussion participants; three is a good number, as this small size means that everyone will have a chance to contribute.

A panel on the topic "Should the Schools Educate for Marriage?" could proceed as follows:

The chairperson may comment on the importance of the subject: couples marry at younger ages now than fifteen years ago.

The chairperson and the panel speakers may first explore the topic, "What is the present situation?" Are families doing acceptably the job of educating their children for marriage? Is there evidence that young people are marrying without proper knowledge of their new responsibilities? What conclusions can be reached from the fact that the divorce rate is increasing? That family patterns are changing?

The second phase of the discussion may approach the question, "What can we do to meet the problem?" Should a special course be offered, a series of lectures? What are other institutions doing? What topics should be included in such a course? Should the course be coeducational? Various solutions may be suggested.

The third part of the discussion may follow: "What appears to be the best solution of the problem?" Here members of the panel may begin to take sides, in favor of one solution as against another. Again, sometimes aided by members of the panel, the leader will at times clarify, at times urge, at times harmonize, at times encourage digressions, at other times pull back to the main track. After some give and take, a member of the panel may offer a resolution: "It is the opinion of this group that a series of lectures on the problem of education for marriage would be helpful, and we recommend that a faculty-student committee be appointed to study the matter further." When the panel has finished its discussion, the leader invites questions from the audience and may also summarize if the panel itself did not arrive at a formal resolution or specific proposal.

This example follows the Dewey model. The chairperson could depart from this formal plan if the group seemed to be arriving at useful solutions by other routes.

Before the panel meets, the chairperson may assemble the members and talk about matters to come up for discussion. Each member may be detailed to investigate certain aspects: one may look into the divorce question, another into the kinds of marriage courses taught at other institutions, another may interview students or young married couples. This kind of preparation should give substance to the discussion.

Symposium The symposium is more formal in its operation than is the panel. It consists of a leader and a selected group of participants. The discussion begins with an opening statement from the leader. Participant 1 is then introduced and makes a short speech on some aspect of the question. Participant 2 follows with another short speech, and thus the symposium continues until all participants have spoken. The discussion then becomes more informal, as the leader invites members of the symposium to ask questions of one another. After this interlude, listeners may ask questions of participants.

Assume that the symposium is concerned with the question, "What Should Be Done to Promote Greater Safety on the Highway?"

In an opening talk the chairperson describes the gravity of the present situation, saying that in one year 50,000 Americans lost their lives in motor vehicle accidents, including X deaths in the state of Y (approximate figures range from 120 in Rhode Island to 5,000 in California—consult the current issue of the *World Almanac* for figures for your own state). Speaker *A,* who has consulted magazines and has corresponded with state highway commissions, talks about what is now being done: education, highway patrol, and legislation. Speaker *B,* a student majoring in civil engineering, talks about good and bad types of highway design and construction, the importance of a highway engineer to a safety program, and lessons learned from the construction of freeways and throughways. Speaker *C* talks about drivers: she has investigated men versus women drivers, young versus old drivers, and accident-prone drivers; she also has recent evidence demonstrating the decrease in fatalities following the nationwide reduction of the speed limit. When Speaker *C* resumes her seat, the leader may invite members of the symposium to interrogate one another; after a few minutes' exchange of ideas, the leader then invites members of the audience to ask questions or offer brief comment, summarizing the discussion at the end.

Forum: Other Conventional Types

The *forum* period is a term describing the time spent in questioning the leader, lecturer, panel, or symposium speakers. Listeners appreciate the opportunity of having a say, and the popularity of the practice gives rise to self-explanatory terms like *panel-forum, symposium-forum, debate-forum, lecture-forum,* when a panel, symposium, debate, or lecture, respectively, is followed by a question period.

Round table, staff conference, committee meeting, meeting of governing board or board of directors, colloquy, bargaining session, public hearing are forms of discussion that do not call for special treatment here. With the exception of the last-named, the *public hearing,* discussions are carried on by small groups, usually with no audience present. These groups explore questions, the chairperson following a discussion outline or agenda. Presentations may be made, as by a budget officer or supply officer at a staff conference, or by the representative of an organization, institution, or individual at a public hearing or bargaining session; but these formal interludes will be followed by informal discussion. The *round table* is so called because the participants sit around a large table, in a fashion that suggests each is on an equal footing with everyone else; the discussion that follows is likely to be exploratory or informative rather than policy-making. A *colloquy* resembles a panel except that the term *colloquy* suggests the presence of highly qualified experts (although the distinction is not hard and fast; panel experts may be as authoritative as colloquy experts). Meetings of *committees, governing boards, boards of directors,* may or may not be open to the public, and may or may not hear expert opinion or testimony. They bring in reports, recommendations, fact-finding studies, and even resolutions or decisions.

Other Types of Discussion   Discussion is often stimulated by devices other than the conventional approach. It may be initiated by an impromptu dramatization in which individuals may assume roles similar to or different from the ones they normally play. For example, instead of the leader opening the discussion with a formal statement, a small group may enact an improvised play showing poor sportsmanship, customer complaints, good versus bad on-the-job instruction, good versus bad handling of a worker's grievance. For additional effect, one of the employees present may be asked to play the part of the foreman, and a foreman may be invited to assume the role of a new man just starting work. The play may consist of the new man (actually the foreman) asking questions of the sort that a beginner would likely ask, and the foreman (actually an employee) giving curt, gruff, and overly technical replies. This play could be followed by another version in which the foreman demonstrated a more helpful attitude. Afterwards members of the group are invited to comment and question; the role playing has reminded them of other situations arising in employer-employee relations that may not have been effectively handled. Or suppose store policy in dealing with customer complaints is involved. After briefly outlining the circumstances of a typical complaint, the leader selects someone to role-play the clerk and another to role-play the customer. The two then dramatize the situation, inventing dialog to bring out the nature of the complaint and a way of handling it. Afterwards the group comments on the outcome. Was the customer pleased with the adjustment? Did the clerk retain the customer's good will? Was a satisfactory precedent set by the clerk for handling this type of complaint in the future? Was company policy followed? If not, should it have been? Should company policy be modifed? The *role-playing* approach to discussion is frequently used at training sessions or short courses conducted by corporations or management-training counselors to develop managerial talent, improve employer-employee relations, build good will for the institution, etc. It is also used by religious and educational organizations at retreats, special seminars, or short courses to study human relations.

Games are often used in groups meeting together for the first time (termed *zero-history*), usually with two purposes: to help members become acquainted, and to demonstrate an aspect of group theory.

The Prisoner's Dilemma, one of the oldest, described in Chapter 3, has been often used both as a classroom exercise and as a field of research. Another is Jay Hall's *Lost on the Moon.*[9] Astronauts have crash-landed on the moon; they need to hike to the mother ship 200 miles away, on the lighted surface. They salvage fifteen items, as indicated in the following box.

		Your ranking	Group ranking
1	Box of matches		
2	Food concentrate		
3	Fifty feet of nylon rope		
4	Parachute silk		
5	Solar-powered portable heating unit		
6	Two 45-caliber pistols		
7	One case dehydrated Pet milk		
8	Two 100-pound tanks of oxygen		
9	Stellar map (of the moon's constellation)		
10	Semi-inflating life raft		
11	Magnetic compass		
12	Five gallons of water		
13	Signal flares		
14	First-aid kit containing injection needles		
15	Solar-powered FM receiver-transmitter		

For key and method of scoring, see the Appendix

[9]"Decisions, Decisions, Decisions," *Psychology Today,* 4 (February 1971): 88. Special permission for the reproduction of above material is granted by the author, Jay Hall, Ph.D., and publisher, Teleometrics International. All rights reserved.

The problem is to rank these items in terms of usefulness for making the hike to the mother ship and thus to survival. Obviously air, food, and signal flares have differing degrees of usefulness. If you first make your own rankings, and then if you join a small group and compare and discuss your various rankings, you will collectively discover some facts which individually you may have overlooked. "Lost on the Moon" demonstrates that a group decision is usually better than an individual decision. Hall reported that 75 percent of the groups he tested did better than their best individuals. The decision of NASA experts, and the method of scoring, may be found in the Appendix.

Games are used by a wide variety of experts: not only teachers of speech communication, but also psychologists, psychiatrists, sociologists, management consultants, and many others.

If a problem has several parts, it is often feasible to assign one part to one group, other parts to other groups. A group may attain the efficiency of its most expert member; she may have good ideas and also the ability to persuade others. Complex problems, i.e., solving codes during wartime, often need the cooperative help of several experts.[10]

TO BECOME A BETTER PARTICIPANT

The following suggestions should be helpful:

1 Avoid arguing for your own position. Present your position as lucidly and logically as possible, but listen to the other members' reactions and consider them before you press your point.
2 Do not assume that someone must win and someone must lose when discussion reaches a stalemate. Instead, look for the next most acceptable alternative for all parties.
3 Do not change your mind simply to avoid conflict and reach agreement and harmony. When agreement seems to come too quickly and easily, be suspicious. Explore the reasons.
4 Delay conflict-reducing techniques such as majority vote, averages, coin-flips, and bargaining. If a dissenting member finally agrees, don't feel that he or she must be rewarded by having his or her own way on some later point.
5 Differences of opinion are natural and expected. Seek them out and try to involve everyone in the decision process. Disagreements can help the group's decision because with a wide range

---

[10]See Harold H. Kelley and John W. Thibaut, "Group Problem-Solving," in Lindzey and Elliot's *Handbook of Social Psychology*, vol. 4, pp. 1–101.

of information and opinions there is a greater chance that the group will hit upon more adequate solutions.

6 Use group words such as *we, us,* and *our* rather than self-referent words such as *I, me,* and *my.* Use of group words tends to reinforce the identity of the group.

7 Use statements that give facts and interpretations of facts about the discussion itself. Statements such as "I believe we're getting off the track" or "Let's hear what Beth has to say" help keep the discussion going and provide discussion about the discussion.

8 Although each member should be free to present an opinion, avoid an excessive number of opinionated statements that illustrate a narrow or limited approach.

9 Be willing to admit you were wrong.[11]

Margaret Mead writes about still other dimensions of those who participate effectively in discussion, mentioning nonverbal as well as verbal aspects:

> The good conference participant must ... enjoy multi-sensory cues. . . . He should enjoy attending to several levels at once, what is being said, what is not being said that one might expect to have been said, what other meanings are being carried by cadence and pace, what types of images underlie an utterance, how an utterance parallels in some way a previous utterance, how tone of voice reinforces the manifest content or negates it. . . .
>
> The conference style of discourse has to be attended to as if it were simultaneously exposition and poetry, denotative and evocative, and such multiple attention must be sufficiently congenial so that the participants feel enhanced by participation, rather than diminished and fatigued.[12]

Americans will find themselves increasingly involved in group process, involving participants of different backgrounds and cultures, each individual bearing his own sensibilities and sensitivities. Together we can best talk out the complexities of our ancient problems: our relation to God, to the universe, to other human beings, to the other creatures that inhabit the earth, to the ground we walk on, the air we breathe, and the water we drink. Singly, by twos and threes, by dozens and scores, by communities, and by states and nations, we will certainly arrive at solutions that we can live with.

---

[11]The first five suggestions are based on Hall, "Decisions, Decisions, Decisions," p. 86. The remaining items were suggested in a note to the author by John A. Kline, and are based on his research and observation.

[12]Margaret Mead and Paul Byers, *The Small Conference: An Innovation in Communication* (Paris: Mouton & Co., 1968), p. 19.

1 Plan a discussion involving three or more persons. The following checklist may serve as a guide:

   a Select a discussion leader.

   b Determine the type of discussion: panel (an informal discussion in front of the class), symposium (set reports by each discussant), role playing (dramatizing a situation, followed by comment), other.

   c Select a topic to be discussed. See the lists on pages 330–331 and 367–369 for suggestions; add others. Consider also timely campus, community, or national issues.

   d Partition the topic into subtopics; assign one or more to each discussant for further research.

   e Consider charts, graphs, other visual aids.

   f Determine purpose: to disseminate information, to get listeners to sign a petition or take other action.

   g Determine date of next meeting for further preparation.

2 Comment on the "multisensory cues," the problem of "attending to several levels at once," described by Margaret Mead on the preceding page, applied to participants and the group leader.

3 With a small group, role-play an incident growing out of the work of a religious or educational institution. Suggestions: An incident involving the pledge, the new member, or the new student; the rebel or nonconformist; the search for spiritual or intellectual insights; the every-member campaign for funds; counseling and guidance; the problem of stimulating or maintaining interest (in many organizations the burden of the work falls on a few individuals). Follow the role play by class discussion.

4 With a small group, role-play a case study. Suggestions: A case involving a communication barrier (parent and child, supervisor and worker, professor and lab assistant, airline and flight attendant, editor and reporter, president and vice-president, coach and member of the team, etc.). A case involving a dismissal (employee, member of the team, member of the play cast or debate squad, sorority or fraternity pledge). Perhaps the case involved a rule infraction (was the rule actually broken, is the proposed punishment fair, are there extenuating circumstances?).

5 Divide the class into small groups. Each group will discuss the following situation:

Crisis in the Forest

Bob Cains and Roger Holden, 20 and 24 years old, were hiking in the Sierra Nevada mountains. They had driven as far up as the side road would take them and after packing their food and camping equipment into knapsacks, headed for the top of

Donner Pass. They reached their objective the morning of the second day of the hike. They decided to return by another trail in order to enjoy a variety of scenery, and they thought it would be worthwhile to take their time and explore interesting side trails. However, they took the wrong turn and became hopelessly lost. They had wandered for three days without food and had hiked about 35 miles when they accidentally stumbled upon a good trail. They followed it downhill for about seven miles, and came to a fork which was clearly marked. The sign pointing to the right said, "Kyber Creek—5 miles" and a sign to the left said "Camino Ranger Station—4 miles." (A ranger station is a place where U.S. Forest Rangers or Forest Guards live the year around.)

"We've gone around in a circle!" Bob observed. "Our car would be about one mile upstream from where this trail hits Kyber Creek, or about three miles by the highway downstream from the Ranger station which is also on Kyber Creek."

"That's right," said Roger, scratching his head. "That means it is about six miles to our car if we take the trail to the right and about seven miles if we go by way of the Ranger Station. It's cold now but it won't be dark for three more hours."

"Okay, Roger," Bob replied. "Since it is downhill either way and the trails are both good, we had better head for. . . ."

Assuming that Bob and Roger's assessment of the situation making the decision is correct, which way would they go?[13]

---

[13](From Raymond L. Gorden, *Interviewing: Strategy, Techniques and Tactics* [Homewood, Ill.: Dorsey, 1969], pp. 26–27. Author's discussion will be found at the end of the Appendix.)

 Communicating
in Small Groups:
Leadership

Characteristics of leadership □ Functions of leadership □
Planning a meeting □ Procedures during a meeting □
Assignments and exercises

This chapter is concerned with characteristics of leadership and functions performed by the leader, particularly as they are displayed in committees and other small groups, and in public discussions.

In this bicentennial decade commemorating the years between the signing of the Declaration of Independence and the adoption of the Constitution, we are continually being reminded of the part played by discussion in the colonies and in the newly formed states.

An important aspect of our culture, then as now, is the impulse to get together, to select a leader, and to discuss our problems. This practice goes back to the English Parliament, which, seven centuries ago, experimented with different styles of leading and discussing. At the outset it seemed only fair to rotate leaders frequently—thus giving many people the opportunity of leading—but that plan was abandoned in favor of having a single leader, keeping him in authority for a substantial period of time, and giving him wide powers. Parliament also evolved the practice of allowing everyone to have a say and a vote, and to abide by the decision of the majority.

Today a group even of school children would follow these principles almost intuitively. Such a group would choose a single leader and would practice a kind of government by consent. If the chosen leader were inept, the members would displace him, but otherwise would accept his leadership. Even members who originally supported other candidates would nonetheless give the selected leader their support. All would feel free to criticize his or her policies.

The major parties in British politics are characterized as "Her (or His) Majesty's loyal government" and "Her (or His) Majesty's loyal opposition." Both sides are seen equally as being loyal. Any group will make occasional "partisan" decisions, but it cannot survive unless all segments are "loyal" to the major concerns of the group.

These observations are basically true whether the leader emerges informally, is appointed, or is elected. In some other culture the prevailing mode may be to yell and shout instead of discuss, or to claim power by force instead of the ballot box. Violent and revolutionary movements are known to our culture, but they tend either to disappear from the scene or, after an initial show of power, to depose their violent leaders and select those who can work through other channels.

CHARACTER-ISTICS OF LEADERSHIP   Leadership, according to Ralph M. Stogdill in his recent and highly authoritative review and interpretation of some 3,500 research studies, may be thought of as:

> an aspect of personality and character
> a form of persuasion

a special kind of role, or
a result of time and place.[1]

The characteristics of the leader, moreover, should be studied in connection with the *group*. People tend to choose leaders whose values and traits are similar to their own. (In the ancient fable, the frogs were unwise to choose to be governed by a stork.)

Interpersonal factors enter into the selection of a leader. One who talks and participates actively in the discussion is the one most likely to emerge as a leader; or one who possesses information enabling him or her to contribute more than other members; or one who encourages the participation of others, and accepts a wide range of personalities.[2] In the preceding chapter we saw also that one who facilitates the discussion process itself also is likely to emerge as a leader. A leader who works with different groups quickly realizes that he or she acts differently in each group, and gets different kinds of results. From our point of view, moreover, we note that a leader uses the principles of exposition and persuasion discussed in this text, in connection with evolving solutions, in achieving the group's goals, and in increasing each individual's satisfaction with the group.

Stogdill notes that the following characteristics are associated with leadership:

1 *Capacity*   Intelligence, alertness, verbal facility, originality, judgment
2 *Achievement*   Scholarship, knowledge, athletic accomplishments
3 *Responsibility*   Dependability, initiative, persistence
4 *Participation*   Activity, sociability, cooperation, adaptability, humor
5 *Status*   Social or economic position, popularity
6 *Situation*   Mental level, status, skills, needs and interests of followers, objectives to be achieved, etc.[3]

Looking at this list from the point of view of speech communication, you can see that your own facility for both talking and listening is related to each of these factors. Some of them are task-oriented characteristics (originality, initiative, responsibility), and some are socially-oriented (sociability, cooperation, adaptability).[4]

---

[1]*Handbook of Leadership* (New York: Free Press, 1974), pp. 11–15; 18.

[2]Ibid., pp. 230–231. (See also the discussion of "Leadership Emergence" in B. Aubrey Fisher, *Small Group Decision Making: Communication and the Group Process* (New York: McGraw-Hill, 1974), pp. 85–98.)

[3]Ibid., p. 63. For further discussion of task functions and maintenance functions, see William R. Lassey, ed., *Leadership and Social Change* (Iowa City: University Associates, 1971), pp. 5–6.

[4]See A. W. Halpin and B. J. Winer, *The Leadership Behavior of the Airplane Commander* (Columbus: Ohio State University Research Foundation, 1952), cited in Gardner Lindzey and Elliot Aronson, eds., *The Handbook of Social Psychology*, 2d ed. (Reading, Mass.: Addison-Wesley, 1969), vol. 4, p. 231; Joe Kelly, *Organizational Behaviour: An Existential-Systems Approach*, rev.

Many of the topics discussed in the preceding chapter apply to leadership. *Cohesiveness, productivity,* and *orientation,* for example, are desirable ends to which a member can contribute, whether he or she has the official title of leader or not.

FUNCTIONS OF LEADERSHIP   The leader carries out certain functions related to improving the *structure* of the group. If a secretary, treasurer, or other official is not provided for, the leader will arrange to have those posts filled as needed. This step provides involved helpers. Special talents of members should be utilized in committees or other assignments. Time and place of meetings need to be determined, and a format of meetings evolved if one is not already established. A constitution, bylaws, or simple set of rules may be necessary; if these exist, they may have to be amended from time to time. The leader keeps in touch with these assigned operations partly so that a committee or an individual will complete the task on schedule, and partly because the personal interest of the leader is a strongly motivating factor. Once a task is assigned, however, the leader gives the individual or committee a large measure of responsibility for discharging it. A commonly observed fault of leaders is the attempt to try to manage too much detail instead of letting others share the burden.

The leader *explains, persuades, exhorts.* Members are kept informed; different points of view are consulted. If the group contains liberal-conservative, male-female, Greek-independent, management-labor, Democrat-Republican points of view, each segment should feel that it is not being overlooked. The leader must be continually persuasive. Good reasons must be given. The leader must also from time to time exhort others to do their best, to make a second effort, to surpass the competition, to fulfill the group's program.

The leader is a *spokesman* for the group. Others may want to know about the group's program; newspaper reporters want information about special meetings; other groups may seek an alliance. More "open meetings" are held now than formerly. At times the leader is spokesman for the group to a superior authority such as employer, city council, planning and zoning commission, park board, board of directors. This type of responsibility can seldom be completely delegated, though the leader may be accompanied by knowledgeable and persuasive members.

The leader has qualities of patience and tolerance. Members

ed. (Homewood, Ill.: Richard D. Irwin, Inc., 1974), pp. 366–367; David G. Bowers and Stanley E. Seashore, "Predicting Organizational Effectiveness with a Four-Factor Theory of Leadership," cited in Joseph L. Massie and John Douglas, *Managing: A Contemporary Introduction* (Englewood Cliffs, N.J.: Prentice-Hall, 1973), p. 306.

feel free to express their ideas and find themselves treated with consideration and respect. At the same time the leader may need to restrain unruly discussion or behavior, simply for the good of the whole. A word like *intimidate,* fashionable though it currently is, is not likely to appear in a leader's vocabulary.

Many of these functions are the normal accompaniments of good discussion, and have been commented on previously.

It is my judgment, moreover, based on the observation of many leadership situations, that leadership functions can be related to two overall points of view:

The "caretaker" leader   Many leaders carry on the activities of the group in the tradition already established by the group. They do the things that the group has always done, in the way the group has always done them. Or, if the group is a new one, they do the kinds of things that one would expect that kind of group to do.

The "innovative" leader   The innovative leader reflects, "How can this activity be done better?" "Is this group achieving its purpose?" "Would the group be better if we undertook new activities?" Members are challenged to review purposes and to redefine policies.

Since the leader must work with the group, he or she may need to delay innovative policies until the time is feasible. Changes may need to be introduced gradually. The new minister does not alter the service the first Sunday. Once the climate becomes favorable to vigorous thinking, the group is likely to lend its enthusiasm to new procedures or activities.

The same leader may be a caretaker leader in one situation and innovative in another. In one situation policies may be so ingrained that only slight change can be made. In another the situation may invite new policies if the leader is imaginative enough to envision them. As chairperson of one committee, you may be able to plan an entertainment that is novel and unusual. As chairperson of another committee, you may not be able to persuade members to undertake changes. Each type of leadership serves a useful purpose. After a period of high activity, a group may need to devote its energies to consolidating its gains. After a period of inactivity, the group may become stagnant and need vigorous direction.

PLANNING A MEETING   We now consider the leader as a presiding officer, either in a small, continuing group, such as a committee, or in a one-time, zero-history, situation. A discussion, with its leader and other participants, may take place in a closed room or before an audience, either as a single situation or as one discussion in a series. An example of the latter is illustrated by the ten-year effort to build the New Orleans Superdome, which involved lawsuits, planning and design, strikes by a dozen unions, and even legislative enactments and a constitutional amendment. Many of these discussions were routine; many were certainly innovative; but each addressed itself to a problem-question or a series of problem-questions.

We start with a relatively typical discussion-type meeting, preparation for which begins with the formulation of the problem or question, such as: "How can we prevent juvenile delinquency in Middletown?" "Should we approve the construction of a nuclear power plant at the edge of the county?" "To what use should the recently abandoned airport be put?" "Should parking be banned in the downtown area?" A mayor and council also have formally worded questions: "Should we annex Sunnyvale?" "Shall we fire the city manager?"

Questions for discussion may be loosely cataloged as *questions of fact, questions of value,* or *questions of policy.*

1 **Questions of fact** propose an inquiry. They may or may not be good subjects for discussion. A question like "What league has the best hitters this season?" would not make a good subject, since the answers can be found simply by consulting printed batting averages. A question like "Is there a widespread taxpayers' revolt?" could be usefully discussed, as the facts must be sought in a variety of places, as needed facts will inevitably be missing, as facts that are located will require interpretation. A question like "Do students approve proposal X for modifying the calendar of vacations?" could better be answered by a survey than by a discussion (though discussion might be helpful to bring out pros and cons).

2 **Questions of value** ask for judgments: Are television programs of satisfactory quality? Should capital punishment be abolished? Is euthanasia justified? What moral standards should be followed in organ transplants? What is man's obligation to the environment? Questions like these bring up matters of ethics, morals, and standards. Discussions entered into by instructional, therapeutic, or other types of socially oriented groups are likely to focus on value-type questions: how can we, as individuals, or as a group, improve—in our techniques of discussion, on one hand, or in the quality of our individual lives, on the other.

3 **Questions of policy** discuss what people should do. Most discussion questions probably fall into this category. "How can the United States best meet the challenge of communism?" "Should we change to a policy of less free trade, more protection?" "How can we get better campus speakers?" "How can the large college or university improve its image?" "Should Zenith attract more small industry?"

The leader does not have the sole responsibility of making sure that a given question or issue is precisely stated, but he or she does have the ultimate responsibility in the matter. The leader may, as the discussion progresses, see ways of limiting, extending, or clarifying the question. Regardless of the kind of discussion, however, a central, directing purpose, focused on a problem, should be made apparent to all: what Margaret Mead perceptively calls "the invisible idea in the middle of the table" may need to be brought to the group's attention.

Advance Arrangements

For many discussions, plans need to be made in advance. This checklist is suggested:

1 **How is the question to be worded?** It should not be too broad or too narrow. It should have focus. The question form is used: "Should students finish college before doing military service?" "How can we increase interest in campus cultural activities?"

2 **Who is to participate?** Unless the membership of the group is fixed, the presiding officer needs to invite the participants. Different points of view should be represented: in a discussion, "The Tensions of Big-City Living," the discussants included a corporation executive, the president of a labor union, a physician, a judge. Each saw the problem differently, and the group as a whole was able to cover a variety of aspects. Moreover the participants were well informed and articulate. If you were planning a discussion of the forthcoming city election, you would certainly want students representing both "Reform" and "Liberal" tickets.

3 **What kind of discussion plan should be worked out?** For a policymaking group, the agenda may look like this:

Agenda for a Conference
1 Minutes of last meeting
2 Consideration of next year's calendar
  a Report of committee A
  b Report of committee B
  c Report of committee C
  d Report of committee D
3 Summary by chairperson of recommendations

The discussion plan may include such questions as, "What is the nature of the problem?" "What are possible solutions?" and "What is the best solution?"

Preparing an agenda is an important phase of leadership. Members may be invited to contribute to it in advance, so that everyone will have a sense of participating. Putting an item on an agenda, moreover, is a commitment to seeking differing points of view about it.

4   Is a preliminary meeting necessary?   In some instances a discussion is improved if participants meet in advance and agree upon a discussion outline and the points of view that each is to express. This procedure is generally used if the discussion is to be held in public. The need of an additional expert may be suggested. In formal committee sessions it may be helpful to send an agenda to participants before the meeting, or to notify key people ahead of time to be prepared to discuss certain aspects. At the meeting itself the chairperson distributes copies of the agenda, and invites additions.

5   What publicity should be given the discussion?   If the public is to be invited, possible news channels should be explored. If the discussion is closed, the chairperson will want to make sure that all concerned parties are to be represented.

6   What equipment is needed?   Here the leader needs to concern himself or herself with graphs, charts, slides, films, and exhibits.

7   What other arrangements need to be made?   Here the checklist consists of items concerned with reserving the room, notifying or reminding the participants, procuring and preparing copies of the outline or agenda, and the like.

In all this planning you have in mind both your role as a task specialist—what do you want to get done—and as a human relations specialist (who needs to be consulted?). Looking at the planning another way, you perceive that some of these items are routine or caretaking in nature—designed to encourage a smooth-running operation—and others open possibilities for innovation.

PROCEDURES DURING A MEETING   The preceding chapter discussed overall procedures, including the Dewey model (statement of problem, analysis of problem, possible solutions, most feasible solution) and the Fisher model (orientation, conflict, emergence, reinforcement). Having a model in mind may help the leader to recognize different aspects of the discussion as it develops and to guide it from one phase to the next. The following may help with some of the details:

1   Preliminary remarks   The leader may introduce the participants, state the topic, and open with a brief comment. Good judgment must be used as to the extent of these preliminary remarks; in general it is desirable to get the discussion under way quickly. If, however, the meeting is highly controversial and feeling is high, the opening remarks have a special significance for getting the issue in proportion, indicating the importance of arriving at a consensus, and assuring all of a desire to be fair. You may have attended a meeting expecting to participate in a heated discussion, but the preliminary statement of the leader served to calm the group and thus enable it to arrive at a more rational solution than it might have otherwise.

2 **Intermediate summaries** During the discussion itself the leader may make occasional brief statements about the progress of the discussion that tie it into the agenda or program outline. The preceding chapter spoke of this procedure as *orientation* of members to the discussion itself. The members themselves often make comments that summarize, refocus, or redirect the discussion.

3 **Questions** A good leader uses a variety of types of questions:
   a *Indirect question* (aimed at no one in particular). "How prevalent is unemployment?" or "In what fields is unemployment the most severe?"
   b *Direct question* (aimed at a specific individual). "Dean Thompson, how many company representatives have visited your college this year as compared with last year?"
   c *Relay question* Someone asks a question of the chairperson who relays it to the group. Member: "How extensive is unemployment among individuals who hold a Ph.D. in physics or chemistry?" Chairperson: "You've heard the question; Dean Williams, can you answer it?"
   d *Reverse question* Someone asks a question of the chairperson who reverses it to the questioner. Dean Harrison: "How extensive is unemployment among individuals who hold the Ph.D.?" Chairperson: "Well, to start with, Dean Harrison, how many Ph.D.'s in your field have been unable to find situations?"

Discussion leaders raise the question, "How much guidance should the discussion have?" On this point the chairperson must exercise judgment. Out of what appears to be wandering, digressing, or reminiscing may develop the idea that best solves the problem. A discussion may be slowed down simply to give everyone a say; but what is lost in minutes may be gained in morale. Experienced presiders combine careful guidance with flexible management so as to achieve the greatest amount of creativity. They have enough command of the situation so that they can either follow the agenda rigidly or allow digressions that may develop a long-term value. Presiding officers tend to fall into one of three categories; *authoritarian, democratic,* or *laissez faire,* most of the time. One who is, however, democratic in most situations, may, at times, move into another category.

Research studies agree that the overall approach taken by the leader can affect the productivity of the group. Members exposed to the autocratic style of leadership show more direct and indirect discontent than those working under democratic-type leaders. Members of autocratic groups are also more likely not to work when the leader is absent, and often show the most absenteeism. Members of democratically led groups tend to continue their work whether the leader is present or not. They also display greater cohesiveness than do members of either the autocratic or laissez faire groups.[5]

Another view of leadership is whether it is supportive or nonsupportive. Likert argues that widespread participation is one of the principal approaches distinguishing managers who get high production from those who get mediocre or low results. The better managers are supportive, as perceived by the subordinate, rather than autocratic or hostile. Likert comments:

> [The leader] is kind but firm, never threatening, genuinely interested in the well-being of subordinates . . . shows confidence . . . rather than suspicion and distrust. . . .
>
> His confidence in subordinates leads him to have high expectations as to their level of performance.[6]

High expectation is fundamentally a supportive relationship.

FURTHER COMMENT
In recent years, researchers and research teams have reached a reasonable amount of agreement on the following:

1   Leaders at an intermediate level have a dual role. Their superiors must be able to perceive these intermediate-level leaders as effectively administering overall policies. But subordinates must perceive these same intermediate-level leaders as human and friendly, and as willing to represent the subordinate in his struggle against the topmost level. The chairperson of an academic department, the captain of a company, or the foreman of a shop are instances of intermediate-level leaders.
2   Leaders who are excellent in taking charge of demonstrations, mass meetings, or other "rebellious" type activity, are often supplanted when specific, long-term solutions must be patiently hammered out.

---

[5]Lassey, *Leadership and Social Change*, pp. 262ff.
[6]Rensis Likert, *New Patterns of Management* (New York: McGraw-Hill, 1961), pp. 101–102.

3 As a group becomes large, say more than thirty, members are more willing for the leader to exert control over the activities of the group.

4 Cohesiveness or morale is generally higher when the leader is democratic rather than authoritarian. Moreover, a group that participates actively in working out a solution has a better understanding of it.

5 The leader is often not the best-liked person but the person with the best ideas.

6 If a group evolves two or more possible solutions to a problem, a condition of uncertainty develops, which makes it more difficult to arrive at a single solution.

7 When a group is presented with a problem involving a degree of risk, the group usually agrees to take more risk than any individual would have recommended (the "risky shift").[7]

ASSIGN-MENTS AND EXERCISES

1 Prepare a list of the kinds of discussion situations encountered by students, both on campus and off campus.

2 Consider the advantages of a tightly reined, closely scheduled discussion; of a loosely run, permissive, flexible discussion. What are the advantages and disadvantages of each type? What has been your observation of the effectiveness of discussion in groups in which you have found yourself?

(See also the suggestions at the end of the preceding chapter.)

---

[7]See Chapter 29, Harold H. Kelley and John W. Thibault, "Group Problem Solving;" Chapter 30, Barry E. Collins and Bertram H. Raven, "Group Structure: Attraction, Coalitions, Communication, and Power," Chapter 31, Cecil A. Gibb, "Leadership," in *The Handbook of Social Psychology*, 2d ed., vol. 4, previously cited.

PART FIVE

INTERESTING AND INFORMING

This section is designed to help you improve further your competence in communication. It assumes you are making progress with the basic concepts discussed in earlier sections and are ready to move ahead. Narrative speaking, discussed in the chapter that follows, applies to a wide variety of situations: a well-told narrative may be useful for its own sake, or as part of a speech to inform or persuade. Most students not only appreciate humor and other forms of entertainment, but find they can develop this talent in their communication to others. Expository strategy is applicable to the great majority of communication situations. Being clear is not only a matter of finding the right words but putting them into some kind of plan. The chapter on visual aids describes so many different possibilities that you may find yourself using charts, maps, or actual objects in a variety of situations.

 Narrative Strategies

Planning a narrative ☐ Heightening the narrative effect ☐ Uses of narrative ☐ Assignments and exercises

Using a narrative to begin, develop, or close a message is helpful in a wide variety of communication situations. The strategy of the narrative may be to reduce tension, to clarify a point, to make an idea more dramatic or vivid, or simply to entertain. Many a social hour is spent in the exchanging of narrative experiences. Narrative materials find a place both in small group discussions and in public speeches. Like many speakers, President Kennedy collected narratives that he might use later on in his public appearances, jotting them down in a little book that he kept at hand for ready reference.

This chapter explains principles of planning and presenting narrative materials.

PLANNING A NARRATIVE

In informal situations the usefulness of a narrative grows immediately out of the situation. One may be in the position of wanting to tell a story, but not recall any; or in the position of knowing a story, but not being able to use this kind of material effectively. Or one's self-concept may be: I know a good story that fits this situation, and I have had good luck in telling stories.

Most people can profit by the suggestion to begin a collection of narratives. Good places to begin are with current issues of the *Reader's Digest* or the "They Said It" section of *Sports Illustrated.* Making notes of these and other stories aids the memory (a story that is not a part of your own experience is almost as readily forgotten as the name of a stranger whom you met so casually that you had little opportunity to fix face and name in your mind). Preparing a narrative may follow the steps mentioned below.

The Opening

Usually the narrative is developed chronologically; your task is to tell the story as it happened. The opening should move briskly, with enough details to allow the listener to see the situation you are about to describe.

A speech entitled "A Concerned Citizen Speaks About America's Turmoil" was made in Omaha by the vice-chairman of the Board of Governors of the Federal Reserve System, James L. Robertson. It has been printed in various places, including the *Congressional Record.* The excerpt below includes not only the narrative introduction, but also the speaker's transition to the central idea:

> A truck driver was sitting all by himself at the counter of the Neverclose Restaurant down by the depot in my hometown, Broken Bow, Nebraska. The waitress had just served him when three swaggering, leather-jacketed motorcyclists—of the Hell's Angels type—rushed in, apparently spoiling for a fight. One grabbed the hamburger off his plate; another took a handful of his French fries; and the third picked up his coffee and began to drink it.

The trucker did not respond as one might expect of a Nebraskan. Instead, he calmly rose, picked up his check, walked to the front of the room, put the check and his dollar on the cash register, and went out the door. The waitress followed him to put the money in the till and stood watching out the window as he drove off. When she returned, one of the cyclists said to her: "Well, he's not much of a man, is he?" She replied: "Nope. He's not much of a truck driver either—he just ran over three motorcycles."

Like the trucker's response, mine will be different, too—hopefully though without running over any motorcycles. As a central banker, I might be expected to talk about the awesome domestic and international financial problems which are the subject of my official concern. . . .

I will be glad to discuss those matters later, in response to questions, if first you will let me speak briefly—not as a central banker, but as a concerned citizen—about a matter which is or should be of deep concern to each and every citizen of this great land. I refer to the crisis that is manifest in the chaotic conditions that have developed in many of our institutions of higher learning, and even in some of our high schools.[1]

No time is wasted in preliminaries; the truck driver, the waitress, and the three cyclists are promptly introduced. The scene is set in Nebraska, entirely appropriate since the speaker is a Nebraskan and the story is being told in Omaha. The story is used mainly for its interest value, but the transition is quickly made to the central theme.

The Complications A good narrative has a *complication* in the plot. If the story progresses so matter-of-factly that participants face no difficulties or complexities, if there are no conflicts, it may not arouse the interest of listeners.

The complication in Mr. Robertson's narrative appears with the entry of the three cyclists. Each makes his own move: one with the hamburger, one with the french fries, and one with the coffee. The affront is obvious; something has to happen. From here you can supply your own analysis.

It would not be easy to create a rousing speech about the average first ride in an aircraft. The personal excitement of the takeoff, the thrill of rising into the air the first time, the pleasure of

---

[1]Text from the *Congressional Record,* 115, 11 (June 3, 1969): 14610. It also appears in J. L. Robertson, *What Generation Gap* (Washington: Acropolis, 1970).

Mr. Robertson, an undergraduate at Grinnell College and George Washington University (A.B., 1931), also has a law degree from Harvard and an honorary degree from Grinnell. As to his belief in the importance of speaking well, he wrote the author as follows: "For any man or woman who would improve the public service by his own efforts, the ability to speak is an absolute 'must.' The sooner it is mastered, the better." Mr. Robertson is vice-chairman of the Board of Governors of the Federal Reserve.

recognizing familiar sights from high above them, are by now commonplace. In short, there seem to be no complications.

One student, however, speaking about an airplane ride, said that when his plane started to land, a mechanic ran out and waved the aircraft back up into the sky. This detail introduced a complication; this plane ride was no routine trip. The pilot circled, leaned out of the window to inspect his landing gear, and saw that the wheels had dropped off. Meanwhile he received confirming word over the plane's radio. He explained the predicament to the passenger, offering a choice between bailing out and riding the plane down for a belly landing. The aircraft continued to circle while the passenger deliberated these two unpleasant choices. This situation the speaker dwelled on for a sentence or two; then he asked the pilot, yelling to make himself heard: "What do you think we'd better do?" The pilot shouted back, "I think we'd better try to land." By now the complication was developed, and the interest of listeners aroused. From then on the narrative progressed swiftly: after a few sharply worded instructions about how to brace for a crash, the pilot started his final approach to the landing strip. The student described the landing itself, with its grinding and bouncing, but the plane was finally brought to a stop, and pilot and passenger emerged, badly shaken but not injured.

When Henry Ford decided to put a V-8 motor in his popular-priced car, he wanted to cast the engine block in a single piece in order to gain the advantages of economy and efficiency. His experts assured him that this was impossible. Not discouraged, he proceeded anyway; his engineers made drawing after drawing, and finally evolved a solution. Since then, more than 30,000,000 one-piece castings have been made.[2]

This short narrative is a satisfying one, and could be used to illustrate a variety of situations. But imagine a narrative about an automobile magnate who wanted to design an engine block cast in a single piece; the engineers declared this could not be done; the magnate said, "By George, you're right!" and abandoned his project! Now that the complication is gone, this narrative loses its interest.

The Development

Sometimes the development is simple and straightforward. The pilot learns that he has lost an essential part of his landing gear but swiftly reviews the choices that remain and takes the most favorable one.

---

[2]Details supplied by Henry E. Edmunds, Manager, Research and Information Department, Ford Motor Company.

Sometimes, however, the development builds in steps or stages. We are familiar with the series of threes that is a feature of most humorous stories: Catholic, Protestant, and Jew; Englishman, Frenchman, and American; young man, middle-aged man, and old man—the punch line being given to the third of the trio. An example, based on the thoroughly human situation of the teacher asking a question that no one seems to be able to answer, illustrates a series of four:

> First the teacher called on a freshman, who said: "I'm sorry, I can't answer the question." Next he called on a sophomore, who ventured, "Would you mind repeating the question?" He then turned to a junior, who replied: "Sir, I studied the wrong assignment." Finally he directed the question toward a senior: "I do not believe I can add anything to what has already been said."

Obviously the series design heightens the development.

A narrative may be entertaining through its sheer absurdity; as the listener hears it, he is able to call up images that are grotesque and ludicrous. Lincoln was a man of towering strength, whose long legs, long arms, and muscular shoulders are often associated with rail-splitting. Once he was challenged to a duel by a lesser man, and not wanting to fight, declined the challenge. His tormentor was so persistent, however, that Lincoln finally said: "As the challenged party I assume I have the choice of weapons?" "You have, sir." "Very well," said Lincoln, "I choose broad-axes, at three paces." Anyone who can visualize a double-bitted axe at the end of Lincoln's long, powerful right arm can understand why his challenger lost all appetite for a duel.

Sometimes the development involves not activity, but a state of mind: helplessness, desperation, or other emotion. Narratives like these follow in the wake of a hurricane or earthquake, for example, when those involved are completely at the mercy of immense, unleashed forces.

The Conclusion

The conclusion of a narrative is ordinarily brief; the narrator gathers up the loose ends and rounds the story out. Although in a speaking situation the speaker may tell a story just for the fun or excitement of it, often he or she wants to apply it to the theme at hand. The lecturer who mentioned Lincoln's duel continued by demonstrating Lincoln's effective gesturing, his raising his long right arm high above his head, clenching his fist, shaking it in the air, and then bringing it down: "It made the hair on a man's head stand up, and the breath stop in his throat."

**HEIGHTENING
THE NARRATIVE
EFFECT**

Suspense Consider the airplane passenger who had to face the risks of a crash landing. What will be the outcome? Don't reveal the answer until you have developed the suspense in the situation. Recall Oscar Wilde: "The suspense is terrible. I hope it will last."

The woman who said, "I want to tell you about the time I won first prize in a beauty contest" stripped her possibilities for suspense to one: the story of *how* she did it. Ordinarily it is preferable to unfold the story as it happened: "I was a little surprised to find a note on my typewriter, 'See Mr. Phelps at once' and, like any employee, I wondered if I was in for a bawling out. Even when I was in his office, he must have talked a full two minutes before I realized that instead of scolding me he was nominating me as the firm's entry in the citywide 'Miss Greater Chattanooga' beauty contest." This narrative was developed so that listeners did not know until the finish whether she eventually won first, or was disqualified, or announced as second but through a mistake in the adding was later declared first.

Point of View If you are an upperclassman telling about your bewildering first days on a big campus, relate the long lines, the delays, and the frustrations as you experienced them as a freshman. You may not have been able to identify "Franklin Hall" or the women's gym because you did not know at the time what building you were in. Your point of view may be that of a practice teacher facing her first class or of a tourist in Mexico puzzling over the strange currency—but whatever it is maintain it consistently. In other words, you are assuming a role for the occasion and should faithfully act it out.

Humor Although a narrative may owe its effectiveness to its action, suspense, excitement, or other qualities, a usual ingredient is humor and one may possibly enhance his use of humor if he appreciates its basic characteristics.

A source of humor is incongruity: something out of place. When a fine young male tells about enrolling in Girl's Cooking I and later in Girl's Cooking II, the listeners enjoy the incongruity of the situation. In a national pie-baking contest he found himself as state winner competing with women and pondering situations such as the rule that required each contestant to wear a simple white dress, white apron, and white cap. He was able to surmount one obstacle after another, and eventually won one of the awards.

A Moslem student from India entertained a class of American

students by talking about some observations made in this country. "At first I had a bitter prejudice against Christians," he said. This would seem incongruous to all who feel that true Christians should be loved by everyone. He went on to say he had thought their habits of eating and drinking objectionable, and many of their religious beliefs untenable. "But," he continued with a twinkle, "as I got to know a few Christians well, I decided they were a high-type, entirely moral lot."

Another source of humor is spontaneity. The colorful phrase or the vivid detail that grows naturally out of the situation has special appeal. When Lady Astor said to Winston Churchill, "Winston, if I were your wife I'd put poison in your tea," and Churchill at once retorted, "Madame, if I were your husband I'd drink it," the amusement grows not only out of the turning of the tables but out of the promptness and spontaneity with which they are turned. Puns and plays on words are amusing, like the athlete's comment: "I'm on a seafood diet. I eat everything I see."

Humor is also heightened by *overstatement* and *understatement.* The narrative about a day in the life of a student at a university that was building fifty million dollars' worth of new buildings employed overstatement as he told in exaggerated fashion of the dangers of overhead cranes, unexpected tunnels, blocked streets, holes in the ground where parking lots formerly stood, and professors' lectures punctuated by riveting machines. A computer salesman likes to tell about what happens when communication breaks down between sales and engineering; the engineers did not understand what the sales department wanted, and designed a machine, as he put it, that took three hands and two heads to operate and two people on their knees to load. A student, narrating a strafing attack, included the detail of a 300-pound sergeant hiding under a Volkswagen. Another described a man who had become so thin by dieting that it took two of him to make a shadow. Bob Hope described Los Angeles county floods as being so severe that a house, cantilevered on a hillside, was floated so far down the valley that it changed zip codes three times. *Understatement* appeared in the speech of a young man who described himself and his friends in a gang fight with another group; when the police suddenly appeared, the student said he decided to stroll home. *Stroll* is an understatement for the word the audience might have expected: *ran, dashed, scurried,* or *rushed.* "What did you do when Camille struck?" a survivor was asked. "Oh, I more or less went to the basement" is another example of understatement.

Another characteristic of humor is that *source and receiver share a bit of information well known to both.* We are aware that it is useless to tell certain stories to certain people because they would not get the point. If you tell such a story, and the listener says, "I don't get it," you realize that you misjudged the extent of his information. Bob Hope opened one of his famous Christmas shows to the troops in Vietnam by saying, "Well, here we are again, back at Saigon. Those hijackers are never around when you need them." The troops roared their appreciation, but a listener who had to be filled in about hijacking and unscheduled foreign landings would miss the fun, and, even when every detail was explained, would not be particularly amused. On the visit of a President to Chicago, the introducer said to the large crowd, "Ladies and gentlemen (PAUSE) the President of the United States of America (IMPRESSIVE PAUSE), the honorable Hoobert Heever." Any American would sense the fun immediately. But what about this comment from Mark Twain: "When I was a boy of 14, my father was so ignorant I could hardly stand to have the old man around. But when I had got to be 21, I was astonished at how much he had learned in 7 years." Possibly fathers would see more humor here than would sons. When a pro basketball team won an unexpected victory, an opponent exclaimed: "Those fellows rose like Lazarus from the ashes." The speaker that used this quotation was interested, however, mainly in this naive mix of Egyptian mythology with a Biblical incident.

A new member of a residence hall will not at once be able to share all the fun of the established residents, but with time he will absorb the information that becomes common to all. Out of the mutual experiences of a teacher and the students in his class come possibilities for humor that they enjoy but would not be understood by a class meeting in another room down the hall. As you find yourself enjoying humor you will realize that in addition to spontaneity, understatement, overstatement, incongruity, and the like, is a thread of information shared by narrator and listener. Without this sharing, the humor simply ceases to exist.

Charles R. Gruner made a study to determine the effect of humor in a speech primarily designed to inform. Two versions of a similar speech, both designed to be interesting, but one with apt humorous materials added, were delivered to four groups of upperclassmen. His conclusions supported the assumption that a speaker who used apt humor in informative discourse is more likely to be perceived by his audience as higher in attributes of "character" than he would be if he does not.[3]

---

[3]"Effect of Humor on Speaker Ethos and Audience Information Gain," *Journal of Communication,* 17 (September 1967): 228–233. In a follow-up study, Gruner confirmed that humor in informative speaking enhanced the character rating of the speaker; so also do an interesting verbal style and vocal delivery ("The Effect of Humor in Dull and Interesting Informative Speeches," *Central States Speech Journal,* 21 [Fall 1970]: 166).

The usual caution should be noted: you can use humor so much that listeners will expect you to be humorous, and will be disappointed if you do not live up to this expectation. A recent experimental study notes also that the use of humor should not cause the listener to lose sight of the communicator's real purpose—in this event the humor might have a boomerang effect.[4]

Other researchers have reported findings, at least tentatively, as follows: humor may be used to control the behavior of a group (jokes about tardiness tend to establish a standard of punctuality); humor tends to solidify a group and make it more cohesive (jocular griping of hospital patients about the service offered by the staff helps patients to establish a group identity).[5] On a more philosophical level: humor deflates the pompous, shows us things in a new light, relieves daily tensions, and is a victory of the human spirit over the world. In these respects humor is a way that human beings have of adjusting themselves to the cares of life. The fact that human beings are the only creatures that both laugh and cry has helped immensely our survival as a species.

Dialog Interest in a narrative is heightened by the use of dialog. Instead of saying, "The pilot told us to bail out!" say, "I heard the order from the pilot, 'Pilot to crew! Pilot to crew! Prepare to bail out!'" A moment later this speaker described the descent:

> I saw six other members of my crew floating in the dark sky. Over to my left I saw a large form that had to be our co-pilot, a man six feet three inches tall who weighed more than 200 pounds. As we hung there in the sky he yelled over to me, "Who are you?" I identified myself and he yelled back, "Let's stick together!"

The dialog helps the listeners to recreate the scene and relive it with the speaker.

Dialog enhances the following narrative:

> "Mother," he said, "I'm not going to school today. The bus drivers have it in for me, the kids don't like me, the superintendent wants to transfer me."
>
> "Son," the mother replied, "You've just got to go to school. You're a bright person. You have many fine qualities. You are a leader. Besides, you're forty-nine and the principal."

---

[4]Pat M. Taylor, "An Experimental Study of Humor and Ethos," *Southern Speech Communication Journal,* 39 (Summer 1974): 365–366.

[5]William H. Martineau, "A Model of the Social Functions of Humor," in Jeffrey H. Goldstein and Paul E. McGhee, eds., *The Psychology of Humor* (New York: Academic, 1972), pp. 100–125.

In this familiar narrative, dialog is prominent:

> Keep awake, then; for you do not know on what day your Lord is to come. . . . [On that day] the kingdom of Heaven will be like this. There were ten girls, who took their lamps and went out to meet the bridegroom. Five of them were foolish, and five prudent; when the foolish ones took their lamps, they took no oil with them, but the others took flasks of oil with their lamps. As the bridegroom was late in coming they all dozed off to sleep. But at midnight a cry was heard: "Here is the bridegroom! Come to meet him." With that the girls all got up and trimmed their lamps. The foolish said to the prudent, "Our lamps are going out; give us some of your oil." "No," they said, "there will never be enough for us both. You had better go to the shop and buy some for yourselves." While they were away the bridegroom arrived; those who were ready went in with him to the wedding; and the door was shut. And then the other five came back. "Sir, sir," they cried, "open the door for us." But he answered, "I declare, I do not know you." Keep awake then; for you never know the day or the hour.[6]

Dialect The skillful use of dialect is entrancing to an audience; a few people make it a point to develop a German accent, a Swedish accent, a Southern accent, or some other—preferably one that they grew up with. A former New York alderman in his campaign talks told Polish stories in the Polish sector, Yiddish stories in the Jewish sector, and Spanish stories in the Puerto Rican sector—to the delight of his constituents. Even a novice using dialect can gain effectiveness by *suggesting* a dialect. He does not need to use it exactly. Today, of course, speakers use dialect in a way that does not offend the sensibilities of listeners. The best examples come from speakers who are poking fun at themselves or at others of their own ethnic background.

Names If the narrative is short, "old Swedish prospector" is identification enough. If the narrative is longer, identify characters by name. Otherwise you will hear yourself awkwardly saying "the first girl," "the second girl," etc. The usual names like *John* and *Mary* may not be as colorful as others, and identifications like *Mr. X* and *Mr. Y* are generally improvable.

USES OF NARRATIVE In this chapter, narrative strategies are conceived of as ways of enhancing the communicator's ability to inform, persuade, or impress—or as an end in themselves. The narrative bit adds variety to a message; it may make a point in and of itself; it may add to the

---

[6]Matthew 25: 1-13. The translation is that of *The New English Bible*.

humanness of the communicator, helping him or her to identify with listeners; it may clarify, or it may relieve tension or lessen antagonism. In one or more of these ways a mastery of the narrative method heightens the communicator's effectiveness.

ASSIGN-
MENTS AND
EXERCISES

1   Make a week's collection of narrative materials.
2   Discuss: In what situations is narrative appropriate?
3   What suggestions can you give about the use of humor?
4   Formulate simple rules to help build suspense.
5   What talents of the actor are helpful to a speaker who plans to give a narrative speech? How can a speaker without special dramatic ability nevertheless improve his skill in the use of the narrative method?
6   What is the place of the narrative in interpersonal situations?
7   Survey recent issues of *Vital Speeches,* the *Congressional Record, National Observer, Wall Street Journal, Saturday Review, The Listener, Congressional Digest, U.S. News and World Report, The New York Times,* or current volumes of *Representative American Speeches,* and decide for yourself what use speakers make of examples, illustration, anecdote, dialog, complication, climax, specific details, and other narrative techniques.
8   Make a narrative speech (your instructor will suggest time limit). Review your experiences or adventures, and select one that you think your audience will enjoy. Choose a point of view, and follow it consistently; let your narrative unfold as it actually happened, in order to generate suspense; conflict and complications heighten interest.

A LIST OF ENTERTAINING TOPICS

Survival on the Freeway
How to Drive in Rome
The Hand is Quicker Than the IQ
Prospecting for Future Wives
How to Meet and Marry a Millionaire (or a Doctor)
Lost on a Used-car Lot
A New Code for Pedestrians
How to Fail in Business
Shortcuts to Success in Society
I Was an Investigator for the FBI
An Egghead on Diamond Head
How I Got into the Computer Business
A Strange Experience at Camp

Learning to Sell the Hard Way
Working in a Factory in Illinois
How a New Lake Changed Our Town
My German Wife in America
The Championship Finals
An Adventure in Rock
Advantages of Being a Minister's Son
Passing the Finals
The Strange Case of the Lost Passport
Experiences in Selling Bibles
Five Sisters Are Too Many
A Trip to Disneyland
I Am Not Superstitious, But—
The Fable of the Wise Fox
Prisoner of War for a Day
Why I Collect Autographs
The Incident that Sent Me Back to School
How to Stop Drinking
Computerized Dating Bureaus
New Rules for Rushing
If I Were President (or the Boss)
My Favorite Comic and How I Met Him
Some of the Splendors of Love
My Tastes, Alas, Are Expensive
How to Cash a Check in a Strange Place
Kid Brothers Should Be Leashed
Noise Pollution in Dorms
Life in the Fast-foods Business
Twelve Countries in Twelve Days

 Expository
Strategies

Kinds of exposition ☐ Expository strategies ☐ A sample
expository outline ☐ Presenting expository materials ☐ Barriers
to effective informing ☐ Assignments and exercises

You use expository strategies when the goal is to *explain* or *inform*. Of the available strategies you determine what will best simplify the complex, make clear what is obscure, or remove a false concept. When you explain the role of VISTA or the Peace Corps, when you demonstrate a method of defense against an attacker, when you outline the history of the women's rights movement, you are in the realm of exposition.

Exposition is, basically, the communication of *information*. For all practical purposes, information is a message that is in some respect *new* to the receiver: a statistic, an example, an interpretation. To be effective in a communicative situation, the sender must transmit symbols that the receiver chooses to receive. The receiver will give but slight attention to well-known materials; at best he or she will keep listening mainly with the expectation that genuine "information" will come along. This information, moreover, must arouse a certain degree of interest by being related to a past experience of the receiver, a present or future need or concern.

Principles of exposition may also be employed when the real purpose is to *persuade.* Thus you may explain ghetto unrest simply to give information about it or in order to persuade listeners to be concerned about it and seek a way to alleviate it; in the latter instance you may follow the information with a suitable appeal. Again, you may explain the duties of the highway commission to inform listeners about this important state agency or to persuade them to use their influence to get increased appropriations for it.

No intention exists here to draw a clean, hard line between exposition and persuasion. The sender of a message has little control over what the receiver will do about it, so that what the sender intended simply to be an explanation may lead the receiver not only to think but also to act. Or the receiver may elect to ignore the message altogether, especially if it is his or her first exposure to the idea. In that event, the next sender of a similar message may have better luck. If the receiver has received previous messages on the subject, something in the sender's earnestness or fund of information and experience may be the stimulus that triggers the receiver to take action.

In dealing with expository themes, one likes to operate at as high a level as the situation warrants. In the interpersonal situation of two men discussing sports, neither is likely to spend much time making obvious, simplistic statements. If the two men have not had previous conversations on this topic, they will quickly sense the level of information that is satisfying to both. In speaking to a class or some other group, you will draw upon your previous knowledge of the group to make decisions about topic complexity or language difficulty. If you have no specific information about the group, you will make an educated guess about what that general type of person is likely to be interested in. If after you start your talk you suspect your explanation, or the vocabulary you are using, is either too simple or too detailed, you can, after experience, read the signals, indicating understanding or bewilderment, that your listeners are broadcasting and modify your message accordingly.

KINDS OF EXPOSITION

You use principles of exposition when you attempt one or more of the following:

What something is What is communism, the honor system, the Monroe Doctrine, Europeanism, fundamentalism, or a tax shelter? Sensing that your listeners have imperfect information about your topic, or no information at all, you inform them what it is.

Why something is what it is Why is juvenile delinquency on the increase? Why are people marrying earlier? What are the reasons for the strong interest in modern art forms? Why is the current business situation stagnant? Why did the modern university develop as it did? Sensing that your listeners are interested in a current issue, and will be responsive to an explanation of the reasons behind it, you inform them *why* something is what it is. Sometimes your notions are chronological or historical, and you find yourself talking about an early phase, a middle phase, and a later phase.

How something works How do missiles, or antimissiles, work? How do counter-radar detection devices work? How is atmospheric pollution decreased? How are metals, detergents, pesticides, etc., recycled? How does the Mafia operate? How is a prime minister selected? How does marijuana, or heroin, affect the body? Having a special interest in the operation of a device, a principle, or a system, you inform your listeners how it works.

EXPOSITORY STRATEGIES

Chapter 10 discussed *time order, space order,* and *comparison and contrast,* perhaps the most commonly used types of expository strategies. In this section we will discuss other strategies: *classification and division, definition, analysis,* and *example,* both positive and negative. Although all of these strategies are usually associated with expository messages, they may be used at times with other kinds of messages. Right now, of course, we are interested in *informing*—and the word *inform* itself suggests that the message should be put in a "form," revealing its shape, dimension, and boundary in a way that makes it clear.

Classification and Division

The ability to classify and divide is an intrinsic measure of one's facility to think and speak logically. Classification involves the perception to see a basic and fundamental similarity in a group of items that in other ways are dissimilar to one another. Human beings were not able to come out of the trees and meet the world on their own terms until they could make the kind of distinction inherent in classification: what was friend and what was foe, what was edible and what was not, what had sharp claws and would attack, what had sharp claws but would run away. Aldous Huxley once stated: "The first and indispensable condition of systematic thought is classification." William James observed that even a polyp would be a conceptual thinker if a feeling of "Hollo! thingumbob again!" ever flitted through its mind. We are dealing here not with a nicety or a gimmick but with an essence of meaningful communication.

When you prepare a message of any length you invariably seek a way to break it up into manageable and logical chunks, partly so you can understand it yourself, partly so the receiver can comprehend it at a single hearing, and remember it. Often one can make use of classification. We may think that classification is the exclusive method of the scientist, but it is in fact the common property of all disciplines. Hence we classify items as various and assorted as time *zones;* blood *types;* bird or animal *species;* course *grades;* college *classes; kinds* of movies; *varieties* of roommates, personalities, students, professors, and others around us. The classification we adopt helps us sort out and mobilize our data. Moreover, it gives us opportunity to share insights that others might have missed.

Classification, moreover, may become not only a means of sharpening an idea that we have, but it may also lead to a new idea: out of random reflections about motives that lead people to seek a college education, we may suddenly reflect that students might be classified according to their motives; thus reflections and observations begin to order themselves and fall into a pattern that had not previously occurred to us.

To use classification effectively, you should consider these principles:

1 **The extensiveness of the classification should be indicated.** If you are discussing (a) persuasive and (b) expository speeches, you may advise listeners that you are limiting the discussion to these two types; otherwise the listeners may wonder why you are omitting other types, such as (c) entertaining speeches. You may say, simply, that your intent is to talk about "main" or "principal" types: "I would like to describe the three principal varieties of oaks that one can see on a tour of this campus." (A sentence like this says several things about the communicator's adeptness in

classifying, skill in sorting, omitting, and arranging, and analysis of possible interests of listeners.)

2   **The classification should be useful.**   Does it clarify and illuminate the subject; does it help make the point? Little virtue would be revealed by a classification of orators as to height or facial adornment unless one were trying to spoof either the art of oratory or the art of classification. A message, however, that discussed *types* of traffic violations or felonies, and punishments therefor, would be useful because, among other reasons, the punishments differ according to types. A driver might be more careful to avoid committing a *moving* violation after being made fully aware of the gravity of this *type* of offense.

3   **The classification should be based on a single principle.**   Here is where intelligence tests claim many victims, with items like: "Look at these four words: *dog, cat, river, horse.* Underline the one thing that is different from all the others." From this simple example the intelligence test proceeds to exceedingly complex series. Suppose you heard a speech on *drugs* with these three types: *stimulants, depressants,* and *habit-forming.* Here the speaker started to use the principle of *immediate effects on the user* but the item "habit-forming" departed from the single-principle requirement. Alcohol, a depressant, and benzedrine, a stimulant, are both habit-forming.

Students may be classified in many ways for many purposes: (1) freshman, sophomore, etc., (2) male, female, (3) in-state, out-of-state, or (4) good standing, on probation. Each of these classifications follows a single principle. Put another way, each member of the classification shares a characteristic or characteristics in common. ("Freshmen" differ enormously among themselves, but in category 1 they share the fact of being in their first year in school.) For category 1, the principle of classification is year in school; for category 2, sex; for category 3, residence; and for category 4, scholastic standing.

The items in each category are mutually exclusive: one cannot be a freshman and a sophomore at the same time (in the faulty categories described above, a drug could be both a depressant and habit-forming). As a further example, "mammals" is a major classification within the animal kingdom. "Mammals" includes individual species as different as *dog, cat,* and *horse,* but all share the common characteristic of having mammary glands, a brain with four lobes, and a diaphragm separating chest from abdomen.

Common sense dictates that classification, viewed rhetorically, need be no more exhaustive or exact than is necessary for the purpose of the message. To the classification *freshman, sophomore, junior, senior* it may or may not be communicatively wise to add *special* or *unclassified.* If the message is too complicated, the receiver bogs down; the Greeks were aware of this interesting phenomenon, but each of us at one time or another has to learn it anew. It may or may not be necessary to append precise definitions to each category (a freshman is one who has completed X hours in residence on this campus or in residence elsewhere but accepted for credit on this campus). For most discussions *male* and *female* are entirely clear and separate concepts though in the world of competitive sport, *female* has to be genetically defined.

The division of a message into smaller parts may illustrate the principle of *division* rather than classification. Instead of ending with *kinds, types,* or *varieties,* the subdivisions are more properly *aspects, phases,* or *steps.* The people who populate a campus may be *classified* as administrators, faculty, students, and nonacademic employees. An explanation of the educational process might be *divided* into (a) the assignment, (b) the recitation, (c) the homework, and (d) the appraisal. A message about *drugs* could be based upon a *classification* of kinds or types, or on a *division:* why people experiment with drugs, what are the immediate effects, what are the dangers. *Communication* was *divided,* in an earlier discussion, into *source, message, channel,* etc. Division, like classification, is a way of giving a message form and structure to help clarify its content for the listener.

As you prepare your message you should assure yourself that you have covered the types that the listeners might reasonably expect, although you do not need to make an exhaustive presentation. Actually it is often wiser to limit your subject. You may say:

> As you realize, a good automobile designer must take into consideration not only his own artistic preferences; he must also consider the requirements of the factory engineers and cost accountants, of the dealer and service mechanics, and of the ultimate purchaser, the driver. Today I would simply like to report ways in which driver preferences influence automobile design.

Definition To engage in definition is to participate in another basic form of reasoning: a definition is an attempt to capture and set down the ultimate essence of the concept being defined. A definition sets out something fundamental in the term under discussion, and usually in a straightforward and disarming way, so that most or all those who hear it will be willing to start their reasoning at that point. It suggests intellectual competence plus a wish to be fair, and a hope that misunderstanding might be avoided.

Civil rights, one of the controversial terms of this decade, was once defined as follows:

1 Equal opportunity to be educated to the full extent of their human talents;

2 Equal opportunity to work to the fullness of their potential contribution to our society;

3 Equal opportunity at least to live in decent housing and in wholesome neighborhoods consonant with their basic human dignity as befits their means and social development; and

4 Equal opportunity to participate in the body politic through free and universal exercise of the voting franchise.[1]

With such a definition before them, speaker and listeners could proceed to discuss the problem further and to explore possible solutions. A definition may take a humorous turn, as when Vince Lombardi objected to the definition of football as a contact sport. Dancing is a contact sport, he declared; football is a collision sport.

John Henry, Cardinal Newman often lectured about the significance of *speech* in intellectual life. In a famous lecture on "Literature" he argued that literature itself was addressed to the ear, not the eye. "We call it the power of speech, we call it language, that is, the use of the tongue; and, even when we write, we still keep in mind what was its original instrument, for we use freely such terms in our books as 'saying,' 'speaking,' 'telling,' 'talking,' 'calling' . . . as if we were still addressing ourselves to the ear." In his discourse, he often defines *literature* as "the expression of thought in language, where by 'thought' I mean the ideas, feelings, views, reasonings, and other operations of the human mind." This definition, he explained, was particularly offered to refute those who thought that literature is mainly a matter of "conceits, fancies, and prettinesses, decked out in choice words."[2]

In a host of informal discussions, people say, "What do you mean by X?" leading to the reply, "What I mean by X is . . ." More than likely this kind of question and answer comes about because of the training that results from good classroom discussion. Both the question and the answer clarify the issue so that the discussion can proceed on a more useful basis.

Analysis   A complex idea may be explained by subjecting it to an analysis that reveals different aspects of the idea. Abraham Lincoln was often called upon to explain his position on the Union and on the institution of slavery. Many thought he could not at the same time be *for* the Union and *against* slavery. He therefore found it necessary to explain *what* he was for and *what* he was against, and at the same

---

[1]Lester Thonssen, ed., *Representative American Speeches: 1965–1966,* (New York: H. W. Wilson, 1966), p. 95. The speaker was John A. Hannah, Michigan State University, quoting the Reverend Theodore M. Hesburgh, president, University of Notre Dame.
[2]From *The Idea of a University* (Garden City: Image Books, 1959), pp. 263–283.

time to distinguish between his official duty and his personal belief.
Here is his analysis:

> My paramount object in this struggle *is* to save the Union, and it is *not*
> either to save or to destroy slavery.
>
> If I could save the Union without freeing *any* slave, I would do it,
> and if I could save it by freeing *all* the slaves, I would do it; and if I
> could save it by freeing some and leaving others alone I would also do
> that.
>
> What I do about slavery, and the colored race, I do because I
> believe it helps to save the Union; and what I forbear, I forbear because
> I do *not* believe it would help to save the Union.
>
> I shall do *less* whenever I shall believe that what I am doing hurts
> the cause, and I shall do *more* whenever I shall believe doing more will
> help the cause.
>
> I shall try to correct errors when shown to be errors; and I shall
> adopt new views as fast as they shall appear to be true views.
>
> I have here stated my purpose according to my view of *official*
> duty; and I intend no modification of my oft-expressed *personal* wish
> that all men every where could be free.[3]

What Lincoln has done here is to state clearly not only what he would
do but what he would not do; and to restate the basic issue, with
variations, about six different times. He also distinguishes between
his *official* duty and his *personal* duty. People often have to clarify
what they can do in one role, and what they cannot do in another. In
his campaign for office, John F. Kennedy often explained that so far
as the Catholic religion was concerned, he would distinguish
between personal beliefs and presidential duties.

You may take a difficult concept and put it in your own words;
you may explain not only what it is, but what it is not; you may point
out situations when your concept is applicable and when it is not;
you may restate your concept from different points of view. If you
wanted to explain *biodegradable, euthanasia, business ethics, seg-
regation* or *desegregation, the right to strike, libel, oil depletion
allowances, eutrophication, immigration quotas,* or any other complex, easily misunderstood social, political, or economic problem,
you could employ methods of analysis to make the concept
understandable.

---

[3]These thoughts were expressed in a letter to Horace Greeley, August 22, 1862. The italics
are Lincoln's, and reinforce his desire to be clear. *Collected Works of Abraham Lincoln*, vol. 5, pp.
388–389.

As to his ability as a speaker, Lincoln is said to have delivered the greatest five-minute
speech ever made, the Gettysburg address; the greatest twenty-minute speech, the Second
Inaugural; and the greatest hour lecture, the Cooper Union address.

FOUR CHARACTERISTICS OF GOOD TEACHING

Two researchers[4] asked the question "What qualities characterize teachers whose students make the most achievement?" They were not interested in qualities that make teachers popular but those that resulted in a high degree of learning by students.

The results of the study are helpful because all of us, at one time or another, are teachers. Four characteristics emerged:

1 **Clarity**

Less time required to answer questions about what the teacher said.

The questions asked could be answered without the necessity of rephrasing or of supplying additional data.

Fewer vague words such as *some, many, a little* were used.

Material was coherent and had structure.

2 **Variety**

Different kinds of materials were used such as displays or other instructional aids; teacher showed adaptability, flexibility.

3 **Enthusiasm**

Instruction had vigor, excitement; stimulating as opposed to dull; original as opposed to stereotyped.

4 **Businesslike behavior (task-oriented)**

Responsible as opposed to evasive; steady as opposed to erratic; systematic as opposed to disorganized.

All in all, eleven qualities emerged, including criticism, use of summaries, overviews, or other structuring devices, and level of difficulty of the instruction. The close relationship between classroom instruction and the preparation of expository messages in interpersonal communication, group discussion, and speech making is obvious. *Clarity, variety, enthusiasm,* and *businesslike behavior* are well worth striving for.

[4]Barak Rosenshine and Norma Furst, "Research on Teacher Performance Criteria," in B. Othanel Smith, ed., *Research in Teacher Education: A Symposium* (Englewood Cliffs, N.J.: Prentice-Hall, 1971), pp. 37–72. The authors based their findings on a survey of fifty research studies. The four variables mentioned above were those that had the strongest support.

Example This strategy allows you to draw richly from your own reading and your own experience. If you sought to explain the "battered baby" syndrome, or professionalism in athletics, or collecting art or books as an investment, you could develop your point through a series of examples. This text has used *example* more than any other device as a means of illustrating procedures and concepts.

Negative Example We are now beginning to believe that *negative* example has a powerful effect in explaining an idea by showing what it is *not*. We have already seen that *negative analysis,* by reasoning what something is not, is also effective. Lincoln analyzed not only what his purpose *was* but what it *was not.* You may offer examples to show both what something is and what it is not.

To illustrate: Those who travel have learned the complexities of going from one country to another. You are in France, going east; you come to signs or horizontal bars across the highway indicating that you have reached the German border. Now you must go through a series of interesting maneuvers. You park your car and carry your passport and other papers to French immigration officials who examine your documents. French customs officials may also want to see your luggage. You have a few francs left and decide to spend them at the small shops nearby; their value will be discounted if you try to exchange them in Germany for Deutschmarks. These matters attended to, you return to your car and drive a hundred yards or so where German officials are waiting to greet you.

Here you repeat the process; your passport is stamped; your insurance certificate is scanned to make sure you can meet claims growing out of an accident; your luggage may be inspected. As you will need Deutschmarks, you pause at a money-changing window and present a traveller's check. When these transactions are completed, you return to your car and proceed. Next day you may find yourself repeating these steps at the Italian border.

In the United States, however, you can drive three or four thousand miles and stop only when you want to. That is a tangible benefit of the union under which we have operated for two centuries. If the concept of *union* had not prevailed, the United States as we know it would have been not one nation but several. When we come to a state line, we see a sign such as "Leaving Ohio. Hurry back." Soon we see a sign such as "Welcome to Indiana," with the name of its governor. There may be another sign, "Please obey our speed laws." But you do not need to halt, display a passport or a certificate of insurance, or open your luggage. Coins or bills acquired in Ohio will be gratefully accepted in Indiana.

The use of a negative example—what an American in his homeland does not need to do—makes doubly clear one of the solid advantages of living in a *United* States. The outline that follows ("The Modern University—Theirs and Ours") could also be developed with negative examples. Our educational policies can be made more understandable if we show what they are *not*.

A SAMPLE
EXPOSITORY
OUTLINE

The Modern University: Ours and Theirs

Introduction
Opening statement: In these days when students and professors alike are studying the nature and the quality of higher education, I believe a useful perspective will be gained by examining higher education in other lands.
Central idea: My purpose is to contrast basic differences between higher education in this country and higher education overseas by examining the numbers taught, the range of course offerings, and the relationship between students and professors. My analysis, if correct, will supply a background to the kinds of questions that are being raised in connection with proposed reforms.

Body
I   Wide variations exist in the numbers of young people for whom higher education is provided.
   A   The United States enrolls 8,390,000 students, about one out of every twenty-four of the total population. (*Britannica Book of the Year*, 1973, p. 714.)
   B   Other countries enroll a much smaller proportion of their populations.
      1   Japan enrolls 1,631,000, about one out of sixty-five. (Ibid., p. 391.)
      2   France enrolls 616,000, about one out of eighty-three. (Ibid., p. 312.)
      3   Italy enrolls 678,000, about one out of eighty. (Ibid., p. 388.)
      4   The United Kingdom enrolls 227,000, about one out of one hundred ninety. (Ibid., p. 705.)
      5   The U.S.S.R. enrolls 4,549,000, about one out of fifty-four. (Ibid., p. 702.)
II   Wide variations exist in the range of course offerings and kinds of degrees available to students.
   A   United States institutions are designed to meet a wide variety of student interests and national needs.

1 The 110-year-old Morrill Land Grant Act provided for a large number of institutions across the land for the education of farmers and engineers.

2 Most colleges and universities have from twenty to forty different departments, or more, from which the student may select fields of study.

3 Advising and counseling facilities on every campus give the student opportunity to explore different options.

4 Course offerings are organized in quarter or semester units so that the student is given a sense of progress as he completes one unit after another.

5 Various kinds of bachelor's, master's, and doctor's degrees are available, the requirements for each known to and respected by professors and students.

B Other countries offer a narrower range of fields of study.

   1 Soviet education is at least 25 percent behind that of the United States, particularly in preparation of elementary school teachers, instructional resources and equipment, and guidance and counseling procedures. [*School and Society,* 95 (November 25, 1967): 458–461.]

   2 The British school system is poorly designed to provide the numbers of managers and engineers needed to operate modern industry. [*U.S. News and World Report,* 64 (February 12, 1968): 65.]

   3 Japanese students make the opposite complaint: that their universities stress science and technology at the expense of humanities and social studies. [*Comparative Education Review,* 13 (October 1969): 336.]

   4 French students complain that the doors are so tightly barred even to what education is available, because of harsh examinations, that "the prizes of the school system are nothing but a mockery or a disappointment to 90 percent of the population." [Edmund J. King, *Other Schools and Ours* (New York: Holt, 1962), p. 67.]

   5 Numbers and kinds of degrees are limited, with requirements not precisely stated.

      a For most French students the only available degree is the six-year doctorate. [*Comparative Education Review,* 12 (February 1968): 32–33.]

      b German students may spend an unlimited number of years working for a degree, the requirements being in the hands of the professor. [*Times Educational Supplement,* 58 (May 10, 1968): 1559.]

      c In general, examinations are so infrequent and so

exacting that the European student is uncertain about the outcome of his studies.

III Variations exist in the quality of the relation between students and professors, though in this area the contrast may be less marked.

   A The American professoriat is characterized by several distinct features.

      1 As a profession, professors belong to a mobile group, seeking new contacts and experiences.

         a Many foreign-born students who enjoyed their experiences as students in American universities stay on as professors. [*Comparative Education Review,* 12 (February 1968): 35.]

         b The yearly exchange of professors among United States universities is so extensive as to "amount to 100,000 new contacts a year." (Ibid.)

         c The staff of almost any American department consists of professors educated on a variety of other campuses.

         d Presumably the mobile professor will have more on-campus interests and commitments than would one who had long been rooted in off-campus social, business, or professional activities.

      2 By long tradition, many American professors participate extensively in student life.

         a They participate in campus discussion groups and informal programs.

         b They participate in advising and registration procedures.

         c They participate in various student-faculty social and recreational activities.

      3 They utilize a variety of audio-visual instructional aids.

      4 Increasingly they meet with students on officially constituted academic committees.

   B In other countries professors tend to be more aloof.

      1 In Germany the powers and privileges of the aristocratic Herr Doktor Professor and the rigid, formal educational system generally are resistant to change. [*Times Educational Supplement,* 58 (April 19, 1968): 1286; (May 10, 1968): 1559; (May 24, 1968): 1763.]

      2 In France "the professor leaves his practice or other job for an hour to lecture in the university, and hurries back." [*Comparative Education Review,* 12 (February 1968): 30.]

3   In many continental universities, counseling and tutorial advice are unknown; every student must fend for himself. (King, *Other Schools. . . .*, p. 53.)

4   In Italy, France, Japan, and Germany student-professor participation in running the universities and determining the direction of their curricula is minimal or nonexistent.

5   In most countries the relationship between student and professor is hindered by serious overcrowding.

   a   In Italy enrollment has doubled in the last decade, resulting in inadequate physical facilities. [*Collier's Yearbook,* 1968, p. 312, and *U.S. News and World Report,* 64 (February 12, 1968): 90.]

   b   In France the overcrowding in lecture halls is so severe that even institutions like the Sorbonne can provide only 4,000 library seats for 40,000 students. [*Time,* 91 (May 31, 1968): 23.]

   c   In Germany the teacher-student ratio, once 600 to 1, is now still 300 to 1. [*Times Educational Supplement,* 58 (May 10, 1968): 1559.]

   d   In the United States enrollment has doubled in the last decade, and while physical plants are reasonably adequate, large lecture classes have made it increasingly difficult for professors and students to know one another.

Conclusion

I   We have established a tradition of educating a large percentage of our people.

II   We have provided a wide variety of courses, organized into manageable quarter and semester units, and offering several degree options.

III   We are not so vulnerable to the charge of professorial aloofness as some countries, although increasing enrollments are hindering this facet of campus life.

IV   A knowledge of these and related characteristics of the American university will guide us as we study problems of policy relating to curricula, degrees, administrative structure, utilization of resources, financial aids, and the like.

Comment: The symbols, indentation, and spacing illustrated above have become a standard feature of the American collegiate outline. The style is one that students and instructors have become accustomed to, so that anyone reading the outline can sort out the major and the supporting ideas. Slight variations from the foregoing are also commonplace.

To adapt the outline to a specific audience, a speaker could pursue these lines of thought:

1 Can the introduction, or other parts of the outline, be slanted toward a recent happening? Has the prospective audience heard a recent talk on the subject by a well-known authority? Has it been the subject of classroom discussion?

2 Can the speaker introduce materials into the outline based on personal experience? Can a special reason be established for discussing this topic? Can reference be made to specific beliefs or experiences of the listeners—perhaps comments they had made in previous speeches or class discussions?

3 Can the speaker use *negative* as well as *positive* examples, instances, steps in analysis?

4 Can the speech be given a different emphasis by omitting parts of the outline and strengthening other parts by additional research?

In illustration of this last question, consider main idea II. As you move through college you take courses that have specific beginning and ending points. During each course you may take two or three exams, or more, so that you have an opportunity to learn whether your work is of passing quality. If you meet the requirements of the course, you are credited with so many hours on the college records. If you fail one course, your standing is not jeopardized in other courses. Suppose, on the other hand, you attended class all year long and took no examinations until June; you might, without having had much warning, fail a year's work. Research of this sort would help you make interesting comparisons between American universities and others.

Other points in the outline can also be amplified. Professors in French or German universities have privileges and prerogatives that American students would find it difficult to adjust to. Physical facilities overseas are inclined to be meager. The Sorbonne reputedly has 4,000 library seats for 40,000 students (says the outline). The American Library Association recommends that (ideally) a library should have a seat for every four students. Professional schools set even higher standards; the American Association of Law Schools recommends a seat for every two law students. This statistic is just the beginning. How many hours a day is the library open? Do students have stack privileges? Are quick-copying facilities available? Can books be checked out?

Still other nations are left altogether out of the outline—nations that would be brought to light by investigation. Great Britain's Open University is open to everyone, regardless of previous education; it utilizes television lectures, correspondence courses, and short intensive summer workshops. American universities are also experimenting with open-admission policies. Other questions arise: Is it true that the English student, the French student, and the German student acquire an intellectuality superior to that of the American student? Is it true that the graduate of an English secondary school knows as much French (for example) as an American college French major? Is it likely that a French degree holder knows as much as three American graduates? Would Americans support a system of higher education in which the entrance examinations were so high as to flunk 50 percent of the selected high school graduates who took them? Before we become too chauvinistic, we should know something about the breadth and depth of the problem of higher education overseas.

PRESENTING EXPOSITORY MATERIALS

Although any expository speech is factual, the presentation need not be matter of fact. Information can be of the highest importance. Someone's life may depend upon it. It may guide an individual, shape a career. It may save time or money. It may open up an intellectual adventure, a new line of thought. It may touch on community welfare or national security. It may add to enjoyment, improve leisure time. If you feel your information is important and worthwhile, let your voice, your facial expression, your choice of words, reflect that feeling. "Note this step especially" . . . "This discovery was the key to the whole situation" . . . "This is of the highest importance" . . . "I want to emphasize the idea that . . ." and so on are typical of the kind of comment reflecting your conviction that what you are explaining is meaningful, authoritative, dependable, *worth remembering.*

BARRIERS TO EFFECTIVE INFORMING

Even a promising strategy may succeed only partly because of barriers between sender and receiver. For example:

1 **Misarranging** The sender violates a logical sequence of messages. "Turn right at the next corner; go straight ahead for three traffic lights; then take a left. . . . Oh, I forgot to tell you: after you leave the driveway, turn left, *then* turn right at the first corner, then. . . ."
2 **Distortion** Words may carry different meanings to different people. A headline may give the wrong emphasis. The title of the talk may be inexactly worded so that impressions are created which are not fulfilled. A statement may be quoted out of context. ("Did the President really say that the nation would use armed force to protect its supply of oil?") The words themselves may say one thing but the tone of voice may unwittingly say something else.

3 Overloading The sender talks so rapidly that the channel is jammed. Or the sender talks so much of the time that the receiver cannot transmit helpful feedback. Or the sender gives a second set of instructions before the first is comprehended.

4 Selection A message may be a half-truth because relevant parts are omitted. "How's business?" "Fine; I wrote half a million dollars worth of life insurance this year." (Omitted: "In each of the preceding five years I wrote more than a million.")

ASSIGN-
MENTS AND
EXERCISES

1 After reading the list of barriers just above, you may think of others. Sometimes we cannot inform our listeners because:

a We cannot catch the interest of the listener.
b The listener does not *need* the information.
c The listener feels that the speaker does not *understand*.
d The speaker uses unfamiliar or technical words.
e The speaker has no plan: backtracks, omits essential details, rambles or repeats unnecessarily.

Discuss each of these, showing how the speaker can make the right sort of preparation to avoid each fault.

2 General Electric reported the results of a communications program: Average output per employee more than doubled; labor required per unit was cut in half; waste was reduced two-thirds; spoilage was reduced two-thirds; absenteeism fell from nearly 10 percent to slightly more than 2 percent. Explain how such a program (conference, discussion, clear exposition, freedom to offer suggestions) could account for this result. See the charts in David C. Phillips, *Oral Communication in Business* (New York: McGraw-Hill, 1955), pp. 4–5.

3 In how many ways can you classify these fictitious animals?[5]

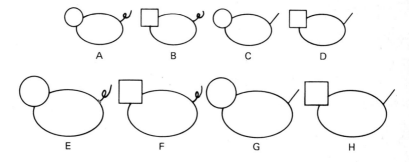

A   B   C   D

E   F   G   H

---

[5]From S. I. Hayakawa, *Language in Action* (New York: Harcourt, Brace, 1941), p. 149.

4 Plan a small-group discussion on an expository topic.

5 Make a speech of . . . minutes, the purpose of which is to *inform*. Your intent will therefore be to make an idea, concept, principle, or method *clear;* you are not trying to persuade us, or sell us, but you do wish to have us *understand*.

Choose a topic about which you have firsthand information. You may not need to go beyond your own experience; or you may find it advisable to do observing, interviewing, or reading to secure needed details.

a You may explain a process, a procedure, a method, a device, a technique, an art, a craft, a skill, a game, or a sport.

b You may explain a theory, a principle, an invention, or a discovery.

c You may explain a historical, economic, social, literary, or artistic movement, period, or custom.

d You may interpret a personality, a group, an organization. (Avoid a purely *descriptive* character sketch; *explain* the greatness or the significance of this person or group.)

Limit your subject; you will probably not be able to tell everything you know.

One of the suggested plans may help you select, arrange, and order your materials. Consider the possibilities of time order, space order, comparison and contrast, definition, analysis, example.

A LIST OF EXPOSITORY TOPICS
Opinion Polls
Trends in (Fashion, Art, Literature)
Guidelines for Better Grades
Recruitment on Campus
Computer-assisted Career Exploration
Optical Illusions
National (World) Population Trends
Birth Control
Pragmatism
How Bigotry Is Born
Preschool Education
Race Relations
Social Class and Educational Achievement
Sensitivity Training (Esalen)
Charisma (of great leaders, etc.)
Federal and State Support to Schools
Developments in Hydraulic (energy-absorbing) Bumpers
Recycling Petrodollars

Recycling Paper, Glass, etc.
Amending the Constitution
How to Buy a Share of Common Stock in the Stock Market
The Importance of Ghana in African Politics
The Greatest Blunder of (Civil War, World War I, Korean War, etc.)
How to Succeed in Business
Air (or Water) Pollution
A discovery or invention (DDD, transistorized ignition, lasers)
Molecular Biology
Analyzing the Outcome of the Election
How to Hedge against Inflation
Safeguards for Color TV
Detergents (Fertilizers, Pesticides) that Recycle
Rackets and Pools
Our Investment in Panama (Libya, Venezuela)
Safety Engineering in the Automotive Industry
When Disaster Strikes
Diversification in Stock Buying
Catastrophe Insurance
New Methods of Weather Forecasting
New Ideas on Prison Reform
Courtesy on the Freeway
Winning an Argument without Too Much Arguing
Legalized Gambling
Good Teachers I Have Known
How Benzedrine (or some other drug) Acts
How a Satellite is Launched (or operates)
Building the Pipeline
The Hunger Crisis
Causes of Inflation (Unemployment, Recession)
Some Aspect of Modern Art (Music, Poetry)
How something works (electronic brain, offset printing, transistors, radar, photoelectric cell; investigation of credit, insurance applications, or automobile accidents)
The Chemical Revolution on the Farm
New Trends in (Church, Hospital, Home, Office) Building Architecture
Danger of High Altitude Explosions
Peacetime Uses of the Atom
New Discoveries about Diet
Fighting Forest Fires
Proper Gear for Mountain Climbing
Increasing Traffic on the Lakes
New Developments in Instrument Flying

Mach 3 (or other advanced aircraft)
Keeping Up with New Books
Financing State Government (sales tax, income tax)
What the Egyptians (Russians, Israelis) Want
Malpractice Insurance
Figure Skating (or some other major or minor sport)
Fraudulent Advertising
New Nations of Africa (or some one of the new nations)
DNA: What We Have Learned about Heredity
Why Traffic Fatalities Are Decreasing
Alaska's Future
Decreasing Fuel Consumption
Aviation Safety
Standards of Judging Textbooks
Refugees
Improving the Postal Service
Boating
Drugs
Sexual Behavior and Ethics
Population Explosion
Poverty, Slums
Rights of Smokers (or Nonsmokers)
Inflation
Crime and Criminals
Terrorism
Option Trading: Chicago Board of Exchange and others
Solar Energy
The Gold (or Silver) Coin Boom
Citizen-Band Radios

 Visual
Aids

Kinds of visual aids □ Basic principles □ Use suitable aids
□ Assignments and Exercises

The use of visual aids has previously been mentioned (Chapter 5) as a way of adding to poise and self-confidence. A chart, map, or blackboard sketch, for example, helps you with problems such as where to stand or what to do with your hands. A visual aid may even help to structure the message; for example, it may suggest a space-order strategy that encourages you to begin at one end of the sketch or chart and work systematically to the other. A further, more important, use is that some receivers learn more through the eye channel than through the ear channel. We speak of them as being eye-minded as well as ear-minded. Other receivers are more comfortable with figures than with words, or the other way around; the visual aid may help you clarify either or both.

We are a generation of people that has been exposed to television and motion pictures at a time when these arts are engaged in the most imaginative experiments in their history. We have seen various programs designed for children that visualize all kinds of concepts about arithmetic, foreign language, grammar, and so on. When you are helping a friend with a problem, you are likely to reach for a pencil—or you may sketch a map so your friend will be able to find your home.

KINDS OF VISUAL AIDS

Visual aids have become so sophisticated in recent years that all kinds have made their way into classrooms to help with discussions, reports, and speeches. The imaginative use of color, arrangement, and animation add to the originality of the presentation and at the same time simplify the message.

The following kinds of aids are widely used:

Chalkboard Diagrams and Sketches

This type of visual aid is the most frequently used in classroom communications both by teachers and students. A good diagram or sketch may rescue a talk from mediocrity and give it a clarity that will make it more easily remembered.

An obvious advantage of the chalkboard is its readiness and convenience. It becomes the most natural thing in the world for you to walk to the board and draw as you talk, thus adding a visual stimulus to an oral one and, in general, allowing you to become a more animated message-transmitter. If you had previously allowed yourself to use a restrained style of delivery, using the board allows you to vary it: you draw a sketch, turn to the listeners to comment on it, pause to see if the feedback indicates comprehension or doubt, point at the sketch as you talk, walk past it to get to the other side, back away from it to answer a question or add more explanation, then return to it to continue the sketching. You have moved around a bit, varied your voice, used a change of rate, and in general have presented yourself as a livelier personality. These suggestions call for making a large, not a tiny, sketch, and discussing it in an animated, dynamic fashion.

Unless the diagrams and sketches are simple, you may make a preliminary drawing as a part of your preparation, to reassure yourself that you can handle the chalk effectively in front of listeners. You may, moreover, experiment with different designs, arrangements, shadings, and the like, in order to make the result as striking as possible; the method otherwise is open to the charge of being commonplace. Imaginative or not, you should at least be accurate. During a war large-scale models of beaches to be assaulted or targets to be bombed are prepared by intelligence officers. The men preparing for these missions study the models, retire to another room, *draw a diagram of what they have seen,* and then compare their diagram with the original to see if their learning is accurate.

A second advantage of the method is that it makes possible a step-by-step animated presentation of the drawing. If this inherent advantage is to be exploited, you should develop your sketch or diagram in *the presence of the listeners.* When explaining, for example, the method of interpreting a weather map, you may draw a large outline map of the United States on the board, locate H's and L's, indicate cold fronts, identify regions having precipitation, and jot down other meaningful features—gesturing as necessary to indicate the direction that various meteorological phenomena will take. If the topic is new ideas in women's styles, you may sketch a new dress on the board, commenting on each style feature as you draw it in.

You may be able to devise an original way of varying or supplementing the sketch. Colored chalks are striking. Colored tapes are easily stuck into place, and do not leave adhesive on the board. Your sketch may be used with cutouts on colored paper; or you may use two boards, one sliding in front of the other. A board that can be reversed, bringing the other side into view, may make it possible for you to achieve a bold effect.

Charts and Maps   Charts and maps, less frequently used than chalkboard sketches, are consequently more novel. You may mount your chart or map on an easel and refer to it with a pointer. You may have a series of charts, turning the sheets from time to time.

If the chart is a large one and you wish to explain it in parts, you may have each part covered with a strip of paper, held in place with a piece of tape so it can easily be detached. Thus you may detach one strip, explain the part of the chart that is revealed, detach a second strip, explain that part of the chart, and so on.

Sometimes a chart consists of a series of catchy words or phrases. A talk on counterfeiting, given by a speaker who wanted to point out why counterfeit money was inferior in appearance to good money, could be based on these points:

1 Counterfeit money is made from defective plates.
2 Counterfeit money is printed with cheap ink.
3 Counterfeit money is printed on cheap paper.
4 Counterfeit money shows poor workmanship.

The chart might contain these phrases:

```
DEFECTIVE PLATES
    CHEAP INK
   CHEAP PAPER
POOR WORKMANSHIP
```

To expose this chart to the audience all at once would blunt the effectiveness of the speech, as some listeners would look at one line while hearing about another. To avoid this eye-wandering, the speaker covers each line with a horizontal slip of paper. During the opening comments, the entire chart is covered. As the speaker begins the first point, one of the slips is pulled off and the audience sees the phrase:

```
DEFECTIVE PLATES
```

When the speaker begins the second point and removes the second slip, the listeners than see:

```
DEFECTIVE PLATES
    CHEAP INK
```

and so the speech unfolds before them visually.

This method is used so frequently by military instructors in their lectures that it has acquired a name: *the strip tease*. The method may also be used with maps. If you wanted to show an audience how the United States grew across the continent, you could prepare a large map showing the successive additions to U.S. territory—the Louisiana Purchase, the purchase of Florida from Spain, the annexation of Texas, the acquisition of the Oregon country, the Mexican cession, the Gadsden Purchase. Each of these *areas* would be hidden by a paper cutout the size and shape of the area it covered.

As you progressed you would detach the cutouts in chronological order, thus demonstrating the dramatic story of America's territorial growth.

One student, who wanted to explain the growing use of modern conveniences in rural homes, used colored pictures cut out of magazines. Colored tapes can be used to fashion letters, or as edgings and borders for maps. If, for example, you wanted to show on a map a plan of intercity railroad passenger service, you could use strips of black tape. If you need areas of solid color, use crayons, or cut out pieces of colored paper and paste them in place. For novel effects, such as "before and after," prepare a part of your chart in layers; as you peel off one layer you reveal another.

Overlays, made of cellophane or other transparent material, may be used with forceful effect. Suppose, displaying a map of your state, you wish to discuss the future highway construction program. After identifying principal cities, you may attach to the map the cellophane overlay on which you have previously traced, with a marking pencil, the route of the proposed throughways. You may also have second or third overlays on which are traced routes of new secondary or farm-to-market roads. An electrical engineer, interested in a specialty described as bioelectric medical technology, explained various types of pacemaker that have been designed to regulate the heart action of patients with heart disorders. He drew on a sheet of white cardboard an outline of the chest with a large red heart in the appropriate place. On a sheet of Saranwrap he drew a schematic diagram of one type of pacemaker; this sheet he wrapped around a cardboard mailing tube. At the proper point in his speech he rolled the mailing tube over the white cardboard and the Saranwrap overlay stuck in place without need for further attachment.

You may use *cutouts:* arrows, squares, stars, etc., in bright colors, to be stuck on a map or chart during a demonstration, to identify special features or locations. For a simple adhesive, fashion a small loop of masking tape with adhesive on the outside; attach this loop to the back of the cutout, leaving an exposed section of sticky loop, so that the cutout remains in place when it is pressed against the map or chart. Charts may be constructed with windows or flaps that can be opened, circular discs that can be revolved, sections that can be adjusted or removed. If you keep reminding yourself that your purpose is to be clear, you may devise other special means to help your explanation.

If your talk contains figures, construct a *bar graph* or *pie graph.* Suppose you want to explain to college students the high cost of owning and operating a car. Your research reveals that a low-priced automobile with a six-cylinder engine and a manual gearshift costs $1,679 a year. This figure is divided into: depreciation, $715; insurance, $336; gas and oil, $318; and other expenses, $310. These last four figures could be represented by four tall bars of proportionate lengths, or the total sum could be represented by a circle, the wedges, like pieces of pie, being of proportionate sizes. You could go on to explain that these estimates are based on 8,000 miles of driving per year.

You should not attempt to make the chart too detailed; it is a means to an end, not an end in itself. Make letters and figures large so that listeners in the rear row can see. Use plenty of white space, and a variety of bold and striking colors: pale pinks, light yellows, and feeble greens do not have much impact at the back of the room.

Suppose you have drawn on a piece of cardboard and have exhausted your fund of imagination and ingenuity so far as colors, overlays, and pull-strips are concerned. As a further way of making the aid effective, you may be able to *animate* part of it. If part of it should move, like a piston in a cylinder, you might prepare a cardboard cutout of a piston and attach it to the chart so that its motion up and down in the cylinder can be demonstrated. If you have a pie graph and want to show the percentage of crops annually eaten by insects, you can devise a piece of pie that slowly increases in size to represent hordes of locusts chomping away at the total wheat crop. (Ditto for the increasing costs of higher education biting away at the family budget.) Let your imagination ponder interesting ways of representing the green revolution in Asia, the congestion of national parks, the pollution of streams and waterways, the world-wide discovery of oil in offshore areas, the population explosion, the shortage of physicians, the war against malaria and other diseases, or the increasing extent of education.

Listeners often realize and often appreciate the special pains that a speaker takes to prepare material for them. This preparation may take the form of locating or constructing visual aids—or any other kind of helpful investigation and research.

Actual Objects

Actual objects or replicas may be demonstrated with compelling effect. Don't be content to *talk* about the slide trombone—bring it to class. Manipulate it in the presence of the audience, so your listeners can see how it works; give them a sample of your sweet tones. Everyone has seen a slide trombone, but in your hands it may be an exciting and imposing instrument. If you collect native beetles, as one student did, bring a few cards of them to class and display them—pick out the large ones with shiny wing-cases and big pincers. If you want to explain the operation of a transit, use an actual transit to help you. A photographer brought to class twenty cut-film holders and twenty sets of negatives in order to teach his listeners how to load a cut-film holder of the type used in press cameras. With the actual materials in front of him, each member of the audience learned to perform the operation by watching the speaker and going

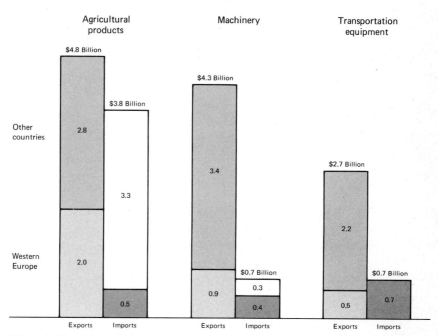

EXPORTS FAR EXCEED IMPORTS FOR MAJOR COMMODITY GROUPS

This variation of the usual bar graph combines two indicators in the same upright bar. The left-hand bar under "agricultural products" divides the figure of $4.8 billion into $2.0 billion to "Western Europe" and $2.8 billion to "other countries." These charts, 4 × 6 feet in size, were used in a presidential broadcast. Similarly, if you wished to use a bar graph to show changes in enrollment at your school, you could subdivide each bar into "male, female," "underclass, upperclass," or other categories.

through the procedure step by step as he explained and demonstrated. A policeman used toy buses, cars, and traffic lights to demonstrate an automobile accident. The Secretary of Agriculture brought a loaf of sliced bread to the news conference; he successively removed slices of bread to show the farmer's profit, the commercial baker's profit, and the retailer's profit.

An electrical engineer mounted on a large board a distributor, coil, and spark plug, all properly connected to a storage battery, to demonstrate an ignition system. Many groups have probably not yet heard about new kinds of typewriters, copying machines, portable computers, gas turbines, teaching machines—all new products in the field of industrial research.

If the actual mechanism is too small to demonstrate—for example, the valve of an aerosol container—you may need to make a large model of it, or use a picture or diagram. If the object is well known, the small size may not be so objectionable. In a talk on how to use a first-aid kit, a surgeon held up a safety pin and talked about it so impressively that listeners quickly felt that, small and common-place though it was, it had an important role in first-aid treatment.

Industrial concerns sometimes prepare special *mock-ups* for demonstration or instructional purposes, made of plywood or other materials. Often the mock-up is prepared so that a side or top can be removed, exposing what is within with startling effect. These are often displayed at industrial fairs. Sometimes they are modified versions of the real thing itself—as, for example, a demonstration version of a new type motor, with the outer wall cut away and the inner mechanism exposed, to show the operation of valves, gears, and cams.

At times you may use a helper from the audience in order to demonstrate a point: you may need a victim for a demonstration of artificial respiration or a "thug" on whom to practice the art of self-defense. The police officer who demonstrated ways of breaking a choke hold used a listener to show exact holds and best defenses. One student used his audience as a kind of visual aid. The cost of production, he said, takes 35 percent of the consumer's dollar: here he indicated with his outstretched hands a 35 percent segment of his audience; distribution takes 55 percent; here he moved his hands to take in 55 percent more of the group; profit is only 10 percent: here he indicated with his hands the thin slice of the audience that remained.

An old campaign trick—and a novel use of a visual aid—is for a candidate, when the opponent has refused to debate the issues, to stage debates with an empty chair.

Slides, Film Strips, Moving Pictures
Slides, film strips, tapes, cassettes, and moving pictures are also used in present-day messages. They may not be suitable for a short talk as they themselves may consume so many minutes that not much opportunity is left for the talk; if time permits, however, they have much to recommend them. A physician, after preparing an elaborate set of charts for a medical convention, realized his charts would be too small for the expected audience of a thousand people; so he had slides made from the charts, and thus his pictures could be projected on a large screen. If you plan to use mechanical gadgets of this sort, do not overlook pointers, extension cords, alternating and direct current, ways of darkening the room, the advisability of using an assistant, getting your slides turned the proper way, and the like. In fact any sort of visual presentation needs attention to details like easels, colored chalk, thumb tacks, and tape. Like Bob Hope's hijackers, these items are seldom around when you need them.

Special projectors are made today in a variety of designs; new models are coming out all the time. The opaque projector allows you to stand behind the machine, either at the back or the front of the room, and show pictures, newspaper clippings, music scores, and similar materials. Or you may insert a sheet of blank paper into the proper receptacle, and as you speak draw a chart, sketch, or diagram, which is simultaneously projected on the screen.

Auditory aids may be helpful. One can use a tape recorder to play snatches from tunes to illustrate various musical idioms.

Imaginary Visual Aids Occasionally you can *imagine* the presence of a visual aid. "If we had a chalkboard," you will say, "we would write over here a list of all the members of the class who cannot swim." This statement is accompanied by an appropriate gesture to help the listener visualize the imaginary chalkboard. "Over here," you would continue, indicating, "we would write a list of those who can swim." You might then go on to explain what the people on the first list need to do in order to have their names written on the second list. Or you might say, "I want you to imagine four statues, one in each corner of this room, representing four great virtues. Over here in this corner is a statue representing *sincerity*." You continue by describing and exemplifying sincerity. Another corner represents another virtue; for example, *integrity*. Strictly speaking, the examples illustrate visual *imagery,* but you can lead the audience to imagine that the actual *object* is in the room.

BASIC PRINCIPLES The following suggestions will help you use visual aids effectively.

If you are using a chart, tell what it is: "This is a cross section of the human heart, viewed from the front—here is the right side, here is the left." If it is a map, identify it: "This is a map of Memphis and its suburbs—this is north, this is the Mississippi River, here is Arkansas, etc." Some orientation is necessary unless the diagram or chart is immediately self-explanatory.

Make your talk to the audience, not to the visual aid If you are explaining a drawing, look at your audience as much as you can. If you are exhibiting a magazine, hold it boldly out to them, saying "This is a copy of the November *Harper's*"—don't hold it at your side, saying "This is a copy of the—" (quick peek) "—November—" (another quick peek) "—*Harper's*." Perhaps you have had teachers who wrote on the board, sometimes mumbling so you could not hear what they said; sometimes standing so you could not see what they were writing; sometimes hiding completely what they were writing, which they would quickly erase before turning around to face the class. Honor them for other virtues, but do not imitate their method of using visual aids. Charts are often too tiny. Exhibits are set up in positions impossible for some listeners to view. So, think of the listener in the back row or at the extreme side of the room.

Use the visual aid in a lively, animated fashion   If you are demonstrating a steering wheel incorporating a new safety principle, hold it up so all can see it; demonstrate this feature and that; ask your audience questions like, "Can you see?" "See how this works?" "Isn't that ingenious?" and the like. You may even walk across the front of the room, to make sure everyone gets a clear view. Good communication requires a concern that everyone present has a fair opportunity to understand. If you put the steering wheel down to demonstrate a chart or make a sketch, you may want to pick it up again when you review or summarize. You may need to invite people sitting in the back of the room to come closer; or you may have the whole class gather around you, if the group is not too large or the situation too formal. Or you may need to stand on the platform, or on a bench.

Do not pass around a photograph, folder, book, wire puzzle, or other articles   for listeners to examine during the course of a speech. If you are describing your trip West and pass around a photograph of your camping outfit, the attention of each listener will be momentarily distracted from what you are saying as the photograph reaches him.

If all need to see the photograph, it may be better for you to walk around the room and display it to everybody and then return to the front of the room and resume your speech. This solution is awkward, but possible if the group is not too large.

Students planning careers in business and industry will be interested in a study by Thomas L. Dahle. Experts in management know that a paramount problem is to transmit information from manager to employee. An employee who is kept fully informed, who is given a chance to express his opinion, not only has better morale but will produce more and spoil less. (See the quotation from Phillips on page 329.) Dahle asked the question, "What is the best way to transmit information?" Should one let it travel by the grapevine; post it on the bulletin board; put the information in writing and hand it out; or call the group together, explain the information, and at the same time distribute material containing the information? A thousand and thirty Purdue students, 84 employees of a nearby industrial plant, and 528 employees of a Chicago department store participated in the experiments, which clearly showed the superiority of the oral explanation plus handout method.[1]

Use different kinds of visual aids, whenever practicable, in order to make a point vivid. Use charts, maps, graphs, blackboard diagrams, models, and actual objects—in any combination that is feasible. A student explaining the refining of crude oil used charts, chalkboard sketches, and actual samples of the material in various stages of the process. A student explaining methods of straightening teeth used drawings, a skull, and plaster casts of teeth before and after. A girl who wanted to teach her classmates to make a good chocolate fudge began by handing them a mimeographed copy of the recipe; mixing the ingredients before their eyes, showing how the recipe was followed step by step; and then passing around samples.

USE
SUITABLE
AIDS

Not every speech requires visual devices. No record exists that Jesus on the Mount used charts reading "Blessed are the meek" and the like. Daniel Webster argued that the Union could not be divided into North and South as long as the great Mississippi separated it into East and West, but he conveyed that idea by words and gesture, not by a board and chalk or a projected slide. Undoubtedly the greatest speeches ever made employed no visual devices whatever.

On the other hand, visual devices are centuries old. Mark Anthony's funeral oration with Caesar's torn and rent gown,

---

[1]Thomas L. Dahle, " . . .Five Methods of Transmitting Information to Business and Industrial Employees," *Speech Monographs,* 21 (March 1954): 21–28.

Chatham's crutch, Burke's dagger, and lawyers who have used an "exhibit" to further the case for prosecution or defense, all swell the long list of speeches that have employed visuals. A visual aid in a speech is as helpful as an illustration in a book. When the purpose is not so much *to impress* as it is *to inform* or *to persuade,* when the subject is complex, when exact comprehension and complete grasp are sought, wisely selected and competently employed visual aids have wide usefulness.

Simple materials may be used with satisfactory results. To make a pie graph, use a string-and-pencil compass or a large dinner plate to draw the circle, and a ruler to draw the wedges. Ordinary colored crayons may be used to shade the various areas. To construct a bar graph, use colored tape; contrasting colors may be employed for striking effects. To letter, make lightly penciled parallel lines, and draw the letters between the lines; for bold letters, use a colored crayon, india ink with a special wide pen point, or the special drawing pens on sale at any bookstore. Special alphabets or lettering devices are available. It is not necessary to apologize for the lack of quality of a visual aid. At times a homemade effort, showing that the speaker has given personal thought to the problem, is effective. At other times high quality, professionally built visuals seem advisable.

ASSIGN-MENTS AND EXERCISES

1   Under what conditions will a visual or auditory aid make a speech *worse* instead of *better?*

2   Recall speeches where the novelty of the visual aid or the *variety of kinds of visual aids employed* added to the effectiveness of the speech.

3   What advice would you give someone who was going to give a travelog illustrated with color slides? Consider possibilities for novelty and variety. List some dos and don'ts.

4   An animated drawing of a split-level head, used as a TV commercial for a painkiller, is said to have cost $20,000 and to have increased sales $35 million. Formulate a statement, "The Ethics of Visual Aids."

5   Make a speech to inform of . . . . minutes in which you employ visual or auditory aids.

You may:

Demonstrate an object: musical instrument, chain saw, sporting goods item—new versus old type of helmet, etc.—mechanical device, chemistry experiment, or magic trick.

Use a map—actual map, or one drawn on the blackboard to explain a part of the world that is in the news or a sketch of a military or naval battle.

Use statistics: employ a line graph, bar graph, pie graph.
Demonstrate a process: how to make homemade ice cream, how to string a racket, or how to fence.
Use your body to demonstrate a skill: how to model a dress, how to jump the low hurdles, how to tap or rhumba, or how to improve posture. Variation: ask a classmate to assist you in demonstrating a dance step, a wrestling hold, or a football play.
Use a diagram or chart—either previously prepared, or drawn on the blackboard to explain: air conditioning, the Van Allen radiation zone, or problems in orbiting a satellite or space station.

PART SIX
PERSUADING

In a sense the best is saved until the last. We are continually involved in persuading others. The first chapter of this section considers the rational, logical aspects of persuasion. It discusses deductive, inductive, causal, and other types of reasoning. The next chapter considers aspects just as vital: motives, needs, emotional appeals, and the personal credibility of the speaker as a persuasive force. Once you have studied the available means of persuasion, you are prepared to adapt them to your own persuasive message. Persuading others carries an ethical responsibility, which is increasingly becoming a factor not only in politics and government but in other aspects of human affairs.

19 Persuading: Reasoning

Importance of logical argument □ Start with a specific question
□ Supporting your reasons □ Basic assumptions □
Developing your speech: overall strategy □ Two-step and
multistep flow □ Common faults □ Refutation □ Nonverbal
aspects □ Good evidence, good reasoning □ A suggested list
of topics □ Assignments and exercises

The term *persuasion* has very nearly come to mean a word designating the outcome of all communication. We cannot be positive even when "entertaining" or "informing" that we may not also change somebody's belief or arouse him or her to some action.

As used here, persuasion is a form of communication in which one individual, through audible and visible symbols, seeks to influence the belief or the conduct of one or more other individuals. This definition ignores, for instructional reasons, the notion that an individual can be "persuaded" by weapons, muscular force, or seductive perfumes.

Persuasion may be attempted through a single message or a series of messages. The message may go from *A* to *B* and then from *B* to *C*. *B* may be an influential person who can add the weight of his own credibility to *A*'s message to persuade *C*. The persuader must further accept the fact that the message will be interpreted in terms of the receiver's own previous experiences, and thus it may be received differently from what was intended.

In persuasive, as in other communicative situations, sender and receiver are operating in a culture—a field of customs and beliefs that touches us all. One who wanted to persuade us to abandon expensive funerals, for example, would have to take into consideration deeply-seated beliefs about the traditional ways in which we show our respect for the dead.

Persuasion may be effected through reasoning: assumptions, instances, statistics, authority. These materials will be discussed in this chapter. Persuasion may also be effected because the sender is perceived as competent and trustworthy. Further, persuasion may be effected through emotional appeals: fears, hopes, loyalties, sense of responsibility. These materials will be discussed in the following chapter.

These concepts are not mutually exclusive, but support and reinforce each other.

A single example will illustrate several persuasive methods. The Communication Arts Center of the University of Denver undertook a campaign to persuade drivers to improve driving habits. The center secured data from traffic safety experts, and constructed a "National Drivers' Test," broadcast by CBS television. The program dramatized traffic situations, each followed by multiple-choice questions asking viewers to indicate the best action for drivers to take in those circumstances. The Center also made a film showing the relation between alcohol and traffic safety. Here they used emotional appeals—not a high-fear, "blood-and-warped-steel-on-the-pavement" approach, but a low-fear appeal, with humorous sequences as well as factual data.

The first film was viewed by an estimated 30 million Americans. Later, 35,000 drivers enrolled in driver improvement programs, a three-fold increase in previous total annual voluntary registrations. The second film generated audience response that indicated that 43 percent became concerned about the problem, and 48 percent indicated that it had increased interest in traffic safety.[1] The films suggest the ready inference that one considering a persuasive effort should consider all possible resources: facts and reasons, emotional appeals, credibility of the source, charts and other pictorial or dramatic materials, ways of getting the listener to make a specific response.

IMPORTANCE OF LOGICAL ARGUMENT

Although the behavior of human beings is often influenced by non-logical communications, we nevertheless can be reached through logical demonstration. The failure to face realities, to interpret evidence correctly, to assess alternatives judiciously, and even to ignore percentages, brings its own penalties. A persuasive speech should be supported by facts, reasons, logic. Even though the persistent issues that human beings discuss cannot be decided on the basis of facts alone since most vital decisions are in the realm of probability, you as a persuader are in a better situation if the weight of both fact and probability is on your side.

The impelling value of logical argument is that when its method is calm, deliberate, and objective, the listener is given a chance to *reason for himself.* This statement is not designed to minimize, however, the well-founded observation that what appears calm, deliberate, and objective to most of the group may seem slanted or biased to others. Yet everyone should learn to speak as objectively as possible. Your responsibility is to present the evidence fairly; your listeners' responsibility is to weigh this evidence. Hence good persuasive speaking allows the listener to persuade himself or herself. "A fool convinces me with his reasons, a wise man convinces me with my reasons."

Sometimes a listener has not given a proposal much thought and is not in a good position to appraise evidence. If you can present your case in steps the listener can follow—and if, moreover, you can establish your credibility—favorable and neutral listeners may lean toward your viewpoint, and even opposing listeners may become less confident of their own position.

---

[1]Harold Mendelssohn, "Some Reasons Why Information Campaigns Can Succeed," *Public Opinion Quarterly,* 37 (Spring 1973): 50–61.

On each subject your listeners probably align themselves differently. Some subjects involve more deep-seated prejudice or preference than others. You may plan to vote a straight Republican ticket the rest of your days, and your neighbor may be an equally loyal Democrat. But perhaps neither of you has had to give thought to the advantages or disadvantages of having a nuclear power plant in the neighboring county. On this issue neither of you has taken a public position or made a personal commitment. Neither of you is ego-involved. Hence if both of you listened to an argument that although the hazards of nuclear power were formidable, the plant could be built with adequate safeguards, you and your neighbor might find yourselves in agreement. You might set aside your fears if the facts were convincing.

START WITH A SPECIFIC QUESTION   In preparing a persuasive message, your first step is to start with a specific question. Should welfare benefits be more strictly regulated? Should capital punishment be abolished?

After your study of the question, you decide what your own position is to be. You may emerge with a statement like this:

Welfare benefits should be more strictly regulated.

Or:

Capital punishment should be abolished in this state.

Such a central idea helps define the specific task you wish to accomplish. Later you might qualify it: Welfare benefits should be made available only to those who can meet specific standards of eligibility. Or: Capital punishment should be abolished in this state except in crimes involving the killing of a police officer.

The supporting statements in the body of your speech should help establish the central idea. You will use statistics, examples, instances, testimony of authority, and similar materials. You will use a strategy of development, such as those described later in this chapter.

SUPPORTING YOUR REASONS   Among the kinds of support available for establishing a central idea are the following:

Example   Examples are as useful in persuasive speaking as in expository speaking. If you sought to persuade listeners to participate in gymnastics. you could use as an example what gymnastic training had done for you. Or use as an example Olga Korbut, the 4'11", 84-pound Olympic champion, who was always embarrassed by being the shortest in her class, and tried to compensate by learning to run faster than anyone else. Her determination attracted the attention of a teacher, who urged her to enter a class in gymnastics. Another fascinating story may be found in the career of Nadia Comaneci. Although you cannot prove a point by a single example, you can use it to gain and hold attention, following it with statistics that cover more cases, or other evidence.

Instances An instance is a shortened example—often as short as a single sentence. Speakers often present them in clusters of five or six or more. Henry B. du Pont, vice president of E. I. du Pont de Nemours and Company, delivering the annual Budd lecture at the Franklin Institute in Philadelphia, wanted to convince his listeners that communication was important to science: that "poor communication led to frequent duplication of effort, with the result that many things were invented several times by different people who were ignorant of each other's work." Mr. du Pont clinched his point with a series of instances:

> When Eli Whitney set up his factory to make guns with interchangeable parts, he spent a large amount of time working out machine tools which already had been developed, or at least anticipated, in other countries. He had no way of knowing that they even existed. Fitch worked for years on a double-acting steam engine, apparently ignorant of the fact that James Watt and Matthew Boulton had already solved many of the problems he faced. Oliver Evans started from scratch, and had no access to technical books, although many had been written in the fields in which he worked. Henry worked for six years on magnetism and electric currents before discovering that Faraday, an ocean away, was doing the same research.[2]

Here four instances are presented in one sentence each.

Arthur E. Teale wanted to persuade his listeners that the black colleges of America were producing distinguished graduates. He supported this point with a number of instances, among which were:

1   Four of the seven most recent black ambassadors graduated from black colleges.
2   Seven of the ten black federal judges graduated from black colleges, including Supreme Court Justice Thurgood Marshall.
3   At least seventy-five percent of all black army officers commissioned each year come from black colleges.
4   Sixty-four percent of black representatives and senators who attended college went to black colleges.[3]

---

[2]From a copy of a speech supplied by Mr. du Pont.
[3]*Vital Speeches of the Day*, 40 (April 1, 1974): 361.

The use of instances is more sophisticated than one might suspect at first glance. It makes a heavy demand upon the speaker to have a wide fund of information, and at the same time allows the presentation of much information in an understated style. The listener may not remember the individual details but cannot miss the main point that they support.

Imagine yourself using instances to support your argument that students should take a greater part in the intellectual life of the campus. "Only two hundred students attended the Hungarian Quartet last week," you may say. You continue, with instance after instance:

> But the Ringling Trio filled the auditorium twice—1800 each time. Seventy-two students—I counted them—attended the debate with Wesleyan. But the gymnasium was full when the basketball team met Tech in the conference playoff. At the library last night I counted 161 students: 8 in the reference room, 32 in the reserved book room, 14 in the stacks and around the card catalog, and 107 chatting in the halls and on the steps. We started a literary magazine last semester, but the first issue did not pay off and we had to abandon the project. We wanted to invite James Michener to give a public lecture, but couldn't raise the guarantee.

Each of these items could be expanded into an *example*. The method of specific instances, however, is an excellent way to present much evidence in brief compass.

Gordon Sinclair's "America"—which has been heard by millions of Americans—is composed almost altogether of one- and two-sentence instances. Read it in the Appendix.

Authority Sometimes listeners become more willing to accept your belief if you can support your position with the testimony of an authority well known to them. The student who presented a carefully reasoned speech to show that women drivers, contrary to popular belief, had good traffic records, secured a statement from the city's chief of police supporting her position.

Ask yourself, as you prepare your persuasive speech, whether a quotation from a recognized authority will strengthen your argument. If your authority is not known to your listeners, identify him for them. Make your identification convincing; a perfunctory statement is not helpful.

Statistics As noted, a series of instances can be enhanced by a statistic which in itself sums up a large number of similar items. In the following excerpt, James M. Roche, former General Motors executive, made an interesting use of statistical information:

Today you can predict fairly accurately just how many alcoholics there are in any company. If there are 100 employees, there are five to ten alcoholics. If there are 100,000 employees, you will find five to ten thousand . . . alcoholics. At General Motors we have more than 500,000 employees, so you will find 25,000 to 50,000 who are involved in an alcoholic problem.[4]

Donald S. Macleod, an executive of the North American Rockwell Corporation, used statistical data in novel fashion in the excerpt below. During the year that had just passed, he observed, 96,459,-483 men did *not* commit a criminal offense; 201,489,710 citizens did *not* use illegal drugs; and so on. He added:

Those are majority groups. Those are some of the people who have been almost forgotten and now are being ignored. Why? Because their minority counterparts—those who *did* commit a crime—got all the attention.[5]

This approach—to look at the opposite side of the picture—can be used in a variety of situations.

BASIC ASSUMPTIONS A special note should be made of basic assumptions. Your assumptions, which may or may not be formally stated, govern your choice and your interpretation of instances, statistics, and other materials. One who argued for a readjustment of postal rates might assume that each class of mail should pay its own way, or, conversely, that certain classes of mail, such as educational materials, should be given a favored rate. The differing assumptions would lead to different arguments and certainly to different schedules of rates.

Najeeb E. Halaby, president of Pan-American World Airways, speaking to the Greater Miami Chamber of Commerce, discussed the future of air traffic in Miami, starting with these assumptions:

Let's make two assumptions about Miami, 1985. The first assumption is that Miami will continue its population growth of the last two decades. . . . The second assumption is that tourism will continue to be one of the area's principal industries.[6]

If either of these assumptions proved to be unfounded, then the future of air traffic in Miami would not follow the speaker's predic-

---

[4]*Vital Speeches of the Day,* 39 (December 1, 1972): 120.
[5]Ibid., 36 (October 15, 1969): 17. For further suggestions about the interpretation of statistics, see pages 140–143.
[6]*Congressional Record,* 115, 13 (June 26, 1969), 17550.

tions. In communicative situations involving major issues, especially those looking into the future, you should be aware of what basic assumptions are being made.

DEVELOPING YOUR SPEECH; OVERALL STRATEGY

Once you have your collection of materials, you may consider what kind of overall strategy to use.

Deductive

The basis of deductive argument is the *syllogism,* which starts with a general statement and then applies it to a specific situation. The most famous syllogism is: "All men are mortal; Socrates is a man; therefore Socrates is mortal." The general statement is "All men are mortal," and the application is to Socrates, a specific man.

Deductive argument may also be used when the general statement is not a certainty, such as "All men are mortal," but a *probability:* "All citizens should vote." Starting with such a probability, deductive reasoning may proceed as follows: "All good citizens should vote for the hospital bonds. You are a good citizen. You should vote for the hospital bonds." Obviously you are more likely to use deductive reasoning in the realm of probability than in certainty, since most persuasion concerns social, economic, political, or religious issues that have room for valid differences of opinion or judgment.

In most speech making, the deductive approach is simplified still further, involving first the statement of the position you wish to establish, followed by your reasons. Hence, after your preliminary opening remarks, you specifically state the central idea: "Capital punishment should be abolished in this state," and then proceed with your specific reasons.

Reasoning from a general statement—either a certainty such as "All men are mortal" or a probability such as "All who want to protect themselves against industrial accidents should wear the prescribed safety gear"—to a specific conclusion, illustrates deductive strategy.

Although the deductive approach is not particularly novel, it has the advantage of being clear and straightforward. The listener knows at the outset what the speaker's position is going to be. It may be too formal for some situations; you might not want to say to a prospective interviewer, "I am going to set forth three reasons why you should employ me." However, considering the many vague messages to which we are exposed daily (vague because we do not know what the sender is driving at) we can conclude that much communication would be improved—and much misunderstanding avoided—if the persuader used even this simple strategy.

Inductive   Instance 1: A Buick overturned at Mill Road corner last week.

Instance 2: An oil truck hit a Chevrolet convertible at Mill Road corner Monday.

Instance 3: Two out-of-town drivers had a bad side-swiping accident at Mill Road corner yesterday.

General conclusion: *Mill Road is dangerous.* The conclusion would be even stronger if the speaker added a statistic: "Last year, according to police records, twenty-two accidents occurred at Mill Road corner." Statistics are compilations of *specific instances.*

This kind of argument is persuasive, provided you have *enough* instances, that your instances are *typical,* and that no important evidence conflicts (negative instances). Similarly, you may collect specific instances to show that *tax loopholes are being plugged,* that *alumni are increasing their financial support to colleges,* that *the scholarship of athletes is improving,* or that *unmarried male drivers under twenty-five are a traffic hazard.* In dealing with topics of this kind, you need to take into account exceptions and contrary evidence; you can then argue the high probability that your position is tenable.

Inductive strategy makes possible an element of surprise or suspense. The listener is not told outright the precise direction of the speaker's argument, but is allowed to share in its development and mentally anticipate the conclusion. Inductive strategy is more of an entering-wedge procedure than is deductive strategy, since its persuasive force develops gradually.

At times the dividing line between induction and deduction is difficult to determine. In your preparation you may read two or three examples, leap to a tentative conclusion, then look for further evidence to support it. You have gone from specific instance to general statement and then on to specific instance. Or you may begin your preparation with a general statement in mind, locate instances that support it, and use them to reaffirm or restate the general statement you started with. If you establish inductively by instances that "Mill Road corner is dangerous," then, using that conclusion as a general principle, you can argue that accidents will continue to happen at Mill Road corner and also at corners like it.

Causal   Causal reasoning, although related to other forms of reasoning, is here considered separately. One type of causal reasoning is *cause to effect;* a better way of describing it is to call it *known*-cause to *probable*-effect. In its January meeting, the National Collegiate Athletic Association (NCAA) introduces changes in the football rules. You reason that these changes (*known*-cause) will produce a faster game (*probable*-effect).

Another type of causal reasoning is *effect to cause;* in other language, *known*-effect to *probable*-cause. "The federal budget is not balanced," you say. This is a *known*-effect that can be demonstrated. What caused this effect? Here the causes are probable or speculative, but you reason about them and then propose a remedy. Again: "Zenith has a higher tax structure than Afton," you say; this is a *known*-effect that can be demonstrated by comparing the tax rates. "Why should this be? The two cities are of equal size, and have comparable resources, yet Afton has better streets, more parking, better lighting, a better municipal library. Afton citizens are therefore getting more for their tax dollar than are Zenith citizens. Now the *(probable)* cause is, Zenith has an unwieldy, mayor-and-council system and Afton has a city manager." So you reason in favor of the city manager system.

The use of causal strategy often creates a mood of intellectual excitement between you and your listener if the reasoning is clear to both. "What will happen if we make this change?" you ask, and then, step by step, present the events. Or: "What got us into this deplorable situation?" you ask, and then, step by step, offer your analysis. In the first instance, the listener is given an opportunity to look into the future with you; and in the second, the listener can review with you the past events that led to the current problem.

Analogy   An analogy is a comparison. You may well reason that an honor system which worked at Liberal Arts College A and Liberal Arts College B will work at Liberal Arts College C. Or you may reason that because the welfare state faces serious difficulties in Great Britain, it is likely to run into similar problems here. Your analogy is valid to the extent that conditions in liberal arts colleges A, B, and C, or in Great Britain and the United States, are comparable. When the items being compared are similar in kind—two colleges, two social systems—the analogy is termed *literal*. In the speech below Henry B. du Pont uses a literal analogy to compare two kinds of problems—those of management and those of the scientist:

> . . . Few ventures of lasting significance are totally free from risk, and where there are risks there will always be some failures. On this score, I think that the attitude of the scientists could well be applied to our problem [the problem of management]. The scientists discovered long ago that man learns most rapidly by pushing his way into unexplored territory, even though he may stumble and lose his way from time to time. . . .[7]

---

[7]Delivered to the Midwest Management Faculty Conference, Bowling Green State University, Bowling Green, Ohio. Used by permission.

At times a speaker achieves an almost unexplainable effectiveness through *figurative analogy*. Here the objects being compared bear a resemblance only in an imaginative way. Jesus used *figurative* analogies when he preached about the sower of the seed (some of which fell on rocky ground), the house built on the sand, the feast prepared at the return of the prodigal son.

Counter-suggestion   Countersuggestion may be used as a persuasive strategy. Basically it consists of telling someone to do or not to do something, hoping and expecting that he or she will do the opposite. Often the strategy is used for its novel effect; speaker and listener alike realize that no one is being fooled, but the mood and tone nevertheless make the method an effective one.

A young woman gave countersuggestion an interesting variation when she discussed food poisoning. She was eager to impress upon food-handlers the proper way of preparing and storing food. Instead she reversed the procedure; she began by asking the question, "Suppose you deliberately tried to cause food poisoning. What would you do?" The way in which she described wrong practices led her audience to see that she was in reality advocating good practice.

Consider the strategy underlying the sermon entitled "Six Reasons for Drinking More Liquor":

> Many people of our day have accepted the practice of drinking liquor, and in many areas of our society one is suspected of being strange if he does not drink. Sometimes it has seemed that the only dissenting group has been the Protestant clergy, and many times some church people are almost embarrassed by the unrelenting stand of their ministers.
>
> But living in a college community, we are trained in the ways of free and honest thought. We can find facts and deal with them logically, and with our contemporary viewpoint. This we must do, regardless of how we may differ with voices around us.
>
> Thus we can find factual and logical reasons for drinking more liquor.

The foregoing statement, coming from a Methodist pulpit, aroused tremendous interest in the large congregation. The minister continued:

> The first of these reasons is that this is the best method we have for keeping the population explosion from making the earth too crowded.

By this time the audience was showing a high degree of alertness, as the minister went on to develop the idea that drinking while driving helps to reduce the population:

We are able to eliminate more people by highway slaughter than by any other way. War is pretty good, but we kill more people month by month on our highways than any month of fatalities of American lives in either World War I or II.

Other "reasons" were "to continue to drink and get more people to drink to keep unchallenged our world supremacy in crime," and "to keep way out front with the highest divorce rate in history." The special twist given the wording of the reasons, combined with the factual evidence presented, made the sermon impressive.[8]

Change of Position   A young male voter opened his speech with this statement:

I am a registered member of the Democratic Party. Already I have voted in two national and two congressional elections, and each time I have voted for the complete Democratic slate. My parents have been lifelong Democrats; in fact my father for six years held a political office in the Truman administration.

Such an opening naturally leads listeners to feel that the speaker is establishing his authority to speak as a Democrat. But let him continue:

When this year opened, I looked with favor upon the candidacies of the various Democratic aspirants to the presidential nomination. As the months have gone by, however, I have been forced to conclude that this November I should support the Republican candidate.

Now the speech has fallen into the change-of-position strategy; the speaker opened with a statement of his former position; his central idea is a strong statement of his changed position; the supporting ideas will present reasons for his change.

Here is another illustration:

When I was a high school senior and first began to think seriously about my future, I resolved that I would not get married until I had a good job and a thousand dollars in the bank.

Then I came to college and took part in lots of bull sessions, but whenever the question of marriage was discussed, I insisted that no one should get married until he had a good job and a thousand dollars in the bank. My senior year I started dating a charming woman, and inevitably we found ourselves one evening talking about marriage; she

---

[8]Delivered by the Reverend Mr. Monk Bryan, minister of the Methodist Church, Columbia, Missouri, *Missouri Methodist Messenger,* 19 (March 6, 1959): 2.

agreed with me when I expressed my view that we should not get married until I had a good job and a thousand dollars in the bank.

This opening sets the stage for the change-of-position plan:

Well, I was finally graduated, worked a while, and went off to graduate school; but I got more and more lonesome, and one day I hunted up the lady and told her I wanted to get married soon. "Do you have a good job?" she asked, and I had to say "No, I don't have any job at all; and I've got two more years of graduate school." She reflected on that a second, and continued: "Do you have a thousand dollars in the bank?" I had to confess that all I had was two hundred dollars and forty cents. "That's close enough," she said, and soon we were married.

Then comes the central idea:

I've decided since then that it is just as foolish to be too cautious about marriage as it is to be too reckless about marriage. It is just as bad to underestimate what two people can do in order to establish a home as to overestimate what they can do. And here's why.

The speaker states reasons, offers examples, and so proceeds to the conclusion.

One who shifts position excessively, like the notorious vicar of Bray, who managed to hold his title regardless of who was archbishop, can of course be flagged with the label *opportunist*. Sir Winston Churchill opened his political career as a Conservative, crossed the floor of the House to become a Liberal, then returned to the Conservative side. To head off the criticism he blandly said, "Any politician can rat. It takes a certain amount of ingenuity to re-rat." Mainly he trusted that his strength of conviction would thunder louder than the whisper of inconsistency. A convert can be forgiven for the zeal with which he takes his new stance—the isolationist who becomes internationalist or the militant who offers a constructive solution and finds himself entirely convincing when he says, "Although I formerly believed in X and was opposed to Z, I am now convinced that we on both sides should adopt Y, the compromise proposal now before us" (or even, "we should adopt Z").

In general we expect people to be consistent. We feel that if they change their position on one issue, they might be equally wrong on other issues. On the other hand it takes courage to admit having been wrong. History is filled with famous converts: Saul of Tarsus for one, St. Augustine for another.

The change of position does not need to be a complete turnaround. You may abandon a position you had strongly supported in order to meet the other side halfway. You may accept a plan explaining that you dislike some features but do like others. You may say, "This is the best plan we can evolve," or, "I do not believe another group could evolve a better plan," or "I'm unhappy with this plan but am willing to give it a trial," and then try to persuade others of your revised position.

Defensive Strategies Rhetorical theory provides several strategies in situations in which the individual is attacked or accused and needs to persuade others that the accusation is unwarranted or unjustified:

Denial If the charge is untrue, the best defense is outright denial. *A* did not kill *B*. *A* did not drive in excess of fifty-five miles an hour. *A* did not accept a $5,000 bribe. The denial is supported by witnesses or other proof.

Redefinition The individual admits doing what is alleged, but argues that this deed is mislabelled. *A* killed *B,* but instead of the deed being first degree murder, as charged, it is in fact homicide. *A* drove in excess of fifty-five miles an hour, but *A* is in fact a plain-clothes officer in pursuit of a suspect. *A* did accept the $5,000, but it was payment for legitimate services, not a bribe.

Higher law or nobler sentiment The individual admits breaking a local regulation, but argues that the local law is contrary to the Constitution. Martin Luther King argued that although the nonviolent demonstrations of the 1960s broke local laws, those laws were contrary to Supreme Court decisions.[9]

TWO-STEP AND MULTISTEP FLOW In making basic decisions about content and overall strategy, you may consider the notion of *two-step* or *multistep flow.* This concept has practical application for those planning persuasive campaigns.

Much persuasion takes place through a two-step flow: messages go from a speaker, broadcaster, or editorial writer to (1) opinion leaders, and (2) from them to less active segments of the population. Many who learn about new ideas are not likely to take action until their own beliefs are reinforced by an intermediate opinion leader.

The phenomenon has been observed in many areas. If a new drug is put on the market, for example, and information about it made

[9]For further discussion, see B. L. Ware and Wil A Linkugel, "They Spoke in Defense of Themselves: On the Generic Criticism of Apologia," *Quarterly Journal of Speech,* 59 (October 1973): 273–283.

generally available, the drug will first be tried by a select segment of the medical profession, and from this segment passed on to the rank and file. A publisher who brings out a new book tries to get favorable reviews by critics. The inventor of a novelty can not have much luck with his product until he can persuade well-known people to talk about it. Opinion leaders are seen to be more innovative than others. This theory, originated by Paul F. Lazarsfeld and his colleagues who studied the 1940 presidential elections, has attracted much attention.

The two-step flow theory, modified by later research, is now conceived of as a *multistep flow,* the new idea moving through relays of opinion leaders. The process is further seen to involve not only persuasion but also information giving and seeking. Interpersonal communication, as well as mass communication, is given an increasing role; for example, one study concluded that 57 percent of the general public learned of the assassination of President Kennedy through interpersonal sources.[10]

If you were interested in promoting a community project, for instance, you would first meet individual civic leaders or groups of civic leaders before moving to large-group meetings. Candidates for office regularly contact small groups of influential people as well as participate in debates or other public appearances.

COMMON FAULTS

What are trouble spots to avoid in planning the content or strategy of a persuasive message?

Exaggeration

At times one is tempted to say *all* when *most* is more accurate; or *nearly all* when *a good majority* is better; or *never* when almost anyone can think of a real or supposed exception. One needs to distinguish among *many, several, a few,* and *often* and *occasionally.* Listeners may not challenge the statement publicly but they may privately. Statements such as "I believe I have shown that," or "It seems more likely that," may be more favorably received by many listeners.

If you quote a fact that is incorrect or out of date, any expert in the audience will find it easy to correct you. Letters to the editors of national magazines frequently point out that the experts have slipped. Many years of reading, learning, and observing experience are found in any audience. As Lincoln said, "You can fool part of the

---

people all of the time, and all of the people part of the time, but you can not fool all the people all of the time."

Hasty Generalizing

This is a fault in inductive reasoning. If Team A in the Southwestern Conference is strong and Team B is strong, it does not follow that all teams in this conference are strong, or that it is a strong conference. A listener may have observations to offer about mediocre Team C. If Law School Graduate A gets his first position at $600 a month and Law School Graduate B gets $700 whereas Engineer A commands $650 and Engineer B $750, it does not follow that law school graduates start at lower salaries than engineers. Note that a listener does not have to be informed about starting salaries to see that the reasoning here is faulty; all that is necessary is to reflect, "You can't prove anything with two examples."

If you have time for only two examples, perhaps you can comment that these are typical of additional evidence that you can produce on request.

Inefficiencies in the postal system have fueled considerable seasoned criticism by public officials and others. The Congressman, however, who described in detail the slow progress of a registered, air mail special letter, posted in Washington on a Tuesday and not delivered in Connecticut until Thursday, and who declared he was "tempted" to vote against the Post Office Department's entire $7 billion appropriation, uttered one of the hastiest generalizations ever recorded.

Faulty Causal Relation

Much speaking attempts to show that a certain effect was produced by a given cause: the Democrats lost the election because too many Democrats stayed home. If this reasoning is to be valid, the speaker will need to show that the *alleged* reason (too many Democrats stayed home) is the *actual* reason. Much speaking also attempts to show that, if certain steps are taken, certain other steps will follow. If we regulate labor unions, the speakers argue, certain irresponsible practices will stop. If we build a throughway north of town, the town will grow. The evidence should show that the alleged causes were actually the real causes of the effect, or that if the proposed steps are taken, the predicted result will follow. If it can be demonstrated that certain factors were not considered that should have been, the causal relationship no longer holds.

Faulty Analogy

This suggestion grows out of the sentence just above. If Coach Throckmorton previously had good seasons at Desert State College and at Mountain State College, a speaker can state that *there is every likelihood* that he will have a good season this year at Valley State. If conditions in the three schools are similar, the speaker can strengthen his reasoning by pointing this out. If Valley State has different conditions—poorer material, more difficult schedule, shattered morale, and the like—the speaker will be wise to admit this. Someone in the audience is *likely to spot this flaw in the reasoning* if the speaker does not.

One reason for studying communication is to learn to amass facts so that the speaker can make decisions that look to the future. If you assert that because something happened in the past, a certain other thing is going to happen in the future, or when you argue that because something worked out one way one time it will work out the same way next time, you are taking a leap beyond the facts into the realm of conjecture. Since you need to take this leap if you are to make long-range plans, listeners will be more certain to accept your conclusions about what will likely happen next year if they are convinced you have the available evidence about what has happened in the past and what is happening now.

REFUTATION When speeches are made on persuasive topics, opportunities for disagreement arise. Here are suggestions for expressing a different opinion.

1 **Begin by stating, fairly, the opposing argument** State this argument clearly, accurately, courteously. Avoid misquoting another speaker—someone in your audience may recognize that you are inaccurate. State the argument so clearly that the other speaker can admit, "Yes, that is exactly what I said."

2 **Show the importance of this opposing argument** Don't minimize or belittle it; if the speaker's conclusion largely hangs on this argument, say so: "This is probably the strongest argument in Mr. Goodson's speech."

3 **Keep language fair and objective** Probably you should not use language like "I disagree with you," "This is inaccurate," or "This is stupid." The trouble with "I disagree with you" is that it draws the lines hard and fast; you then make it difficult to convert the other person to your way of thinking. Statements like "This is inaccurate" or "This is stupid" refer to conclusions which the listener should draw. Show by careful reasoning or evidence that an argument is inaccurate, outdated, or fallacious, without these labels.

Often, instead of saying "I disagree," a more persuasive tactic is not to refute the other person's argument, but to reemphasize your own. Suppose the speaker says, "I am opposed to the new city library tax; taxes are too high already." Instead of saying, "I disagree that taxes are too high already," keep the argument on your ground: "Ten years ago the population of the city was 30,000"; "now," you say, "it is 45,000. Ten years ago total bank deposits were $22,000,-000; now the total is $37,000,000. Ten years ago the library circulated 141,000 pieces of material a year; now the circulation is 274,000. The children's department alone needs many more titles; if the young people of the community are to have a chance to develop the habit of reading good literature, we must strengthen the juvenile collection." And so on. Let her argue *cost;* you argue *need.*

Refute evidence with evidence: "Mr. Hammell gave strong reasons why we should continue capital punishment. He pointed out that capital crimes increased in this state from 77 last year to 93 this year. This increase is of course alarming, and it worries me, as it does Mr. Hammell. His argument is that we should continue capital punishment, or crime will increase even more rapidly. Now you will have to judge for yourself whether this will happen. Let us look at five states that have abolished capital punishment. In these states the number of capital crimes has steadily decreased (quote figures). I have also studied the opinions of three criminologists on this matter. Professor Young states that capital punishment is no deterrent (quote him)."

And so on. If you handle evidence skillfully, you may lead your listeners to persuade themselves that capital punishment should be abolished, and without using discourteous language ("This is stupid") or gratuitous labeling ("This is inaccurate"). These statements must, of course, be interpreted in terms of listener attitude, bias, possible dissonance, open- or closed-mindedness.

In refutation, as in other aspects of communication, one needs to consider the long-term as well as the short-term effects. Occasionally you may want to counter with an aggressive or even intimidating stance. Life has its share of bullies or pompous little tyrants who mistake civility for weakness. For the long term, however, fairness and candor in your statement of arguments, and respect for the opinions and judgments of your adversary, are more effective.

NONVERBAL ASPECTS

The opening of this chapter indicated that nonverbal aspects of persuasion can be highly useful. Your sincerity and strength of conviction can be shown by voice and body as well as by words. An experiment reported by Erwin P. Bettinghaus emphasizes this point as well as any. He chose four speakers to prepare speeches on persuasive subjects: "Drinking Regulations," "Grading Curves," "Parking Regulations," and "The Eighteen Year Old Vote," each speaker being assigned one subject. After practice, each speaker was able to present his speech (a) with good delivery and (b) with bad delivery, to different, although matched, audiences. The general conclusion, says Bettinghaus, "confirms what rhetorical theorists have said for centuries . . . the speaker with better delivery is more persuasive than the speaker with poorer delivery."[11]

GOOD EVIDENCE, GOOD REASONING

The basis of most exposition and persuasion is a knowledge of the facts. We need to have the evidence; we need to warrant our statements. We listen to someone who knows half of the facts only until someone else comes along who knows more.

We also need to interpret the facts, to reason about them. We need to be able to read from an experience in the past to one in the future, and from an experience in one situation to the possibility of the same result in a similar or even slightly different situation. Educators who argue the importance of being able to think and analyze have in mind the principles and procedures that you have studied in this chapter.

A SUGGESTED LIST OF TOPICS

Occasions arise when it is helpful to start a communication project by reviewing a list of topics. You may be asked to give a speech, in or out of class; a list such as the following may uncover your own latent thoughts or resources. You, with two or three others, may be asked to present a discussion; again, this list may help you locate topics of mutual interest.

Should students have greater voice in decisions that regulate their behavior in dormitories, fraternities, and sororities?

Should welfare benefits be decreased?

Should the consumer pay for industrial pollution?

Should student health services dispense birth control pills?

Should the laws against use and sale of marijuana be abolished?

Should state educational institutions be governed by trustees, regents, or curators?

Should defense spending be reduced?

Should suburbs be integrated?

---

[11]Erwin P. Bettinghaus, "The Operation of Congruity in an Oral Communication Situation," *Speech Monographs,* 28 (August 1961): 131–142. This finding should alert the student to listen critically to what the speaker says. Moreover it should be clear that if content and delivery are both good, the effect of the message will be more durable.

James C. McCroskey, who surveyed a score of research studies, his own and others, interrelating evidence, attitude change, source credibility, and delivery, concluded that even the use of good evidence "has little, if any impact on immediate audience attitude change if the message is delivered poorly." "A Summary of Experimental Research on the Effects of Evidence in Communication," *Quarterly Journal of Speech,* 55 (April 1969): 169–176.

Should students be bused to schools to achieve school integration?

Should every American be guaranteed a minimum wage?

Should we recognize the government of. . . . ?

Should federal aid scholarships be based entirely on need?

Should more strict gun control legislation be enacted?

Should this state adopt (increase) (repeal) the sales tax?

Should the foreign aid program as presently operated be continued?

Should colleges adopt a learn-now, pay-later tuition and fees plan?

Should early marriages be encouraged?

Should teachers have scheduled salary increases plus merit increases?

How can juvenile delinquency be lessened?

Should parents be allowed income tax deductions for college expenses?

Should we raise standards of admission to this institution?

Should popular election of the President be substituted for the present electoral-college system?

Should the Catholic clergy be allowed to marry?

Should X be the next candidate for president on the Y ticket?

Should unconditional amnesty be granted?

Should prayer be restored to the public schools?

Should capital punishment be abolished?

Should science education be improved?

Are the humanities sufficiently emphasized?

Should the sales tax be extended to include services?

Should students buy insurance while they are in college?

Should athletics be deemphasized?

Should we amend the state liquor laws?

Should the college course be shortened to 3 or 3½ years?

Should the GI bill of rights be extended?

Should you invest in common stocks, bonds, or mutual funds?

Should Public Speaking be a required course?

Should we have more superhighways and toll roads?

Should Puerto Rico be admitted as the fifty-first state?

Should the rating system (industrial, military) be modified?

Should students grade their professors?

Should we change the state divorce laws?

Should universal fingerprinting be required?

Should industry hire the handicapped?

Should punitive antipollution legislation be enacted?

Should pleasure-boat drivers be licensed?

Should you join the Rod and Gun Club (or Toastmaster's Club or Le Cercle Français)?

Will communism expand in Latin America (or Africa)?

Should you read the works of (your favorite author), or become familiar with the architecture of (your favorite architect) or with the music of (your favorite composer)?

Should all instructors be required to take a course in speech communication?

Should less emphasis be placed on final examinations?

Should the wage scale for student employees be increased?

Should students be more widely represented on college committees?

Should regulations against wiretapping be further modified?

What should be governmental policy about informing the public on matters of national security?

Should access to higher education be available to all?

Is functionalism commendable in architecture?

Should women be admitted to the priesthood?

Should we boycott the products of countries that fail to join in fishing and whaling conservation practices?

Does Congress have the right to investigate individuals?

Should high schools prepare their graduates for college entrance examinations?

Is the criticism of modern art justified?

Should we approve of Europeanism?

Should capital punishment be mandatory for hijackers and other terrorists?

Should sororities and fraternities be forbidden on college campuses?

Are term papers an effective way of learning?

Should divorces be made easier to acquire?

Should the history of minority groups be taught?

Should students be more involved in formulating campus regulations?

Is due process too slow?

Should there be laws restricting cruel parents?

Should interest rates be reduced?

ASSIGN-MENTS AND EXERCISES

1 When would you suggest the use of instances and when the use of illustrations?

2 What are common ways in which statistics are misused?

3 What are common ways in which quotations from authority are misused? From the point of view of delivery, how can the presentation of quoted material be improved?

4 How can visual aids be used in the persuasive speech?

5 What basic assumptions underlie the arguments that college authorities can regulate the use of automobiles by students, that the American system of education is preferable to the British, that smoking should be forbidden in public places, that persons who work in the city but live elsewhere should pay an earnings tax, that standards of censorship can be imposed, that the "right to live" is justifiable, that the government should bear the cost of improving the environment, that out-of-state students should be charged a higher tuition rate by state-supported universities.

6 Examine reference works like *World Almanac, Britannica Book of the Year, Statesman's Yearbook,* and *U.S. Census Reports* and magazines like *U.S. News and World Report* as sources of factual materials.

7 Examine the library collection of special periodical indexes (*Education Index, Art Index, Public Affairs Information Service, New York Times Index,* etc.) as sources of factual material for speakers.

8 Secure a recent issue of *Vital Speeches.* Study speeches in this issue that best illustrate logical argument: statistics, causal relationship, example, and illustration.

9 Make a speech of . . . minutes in which your purpose is to change or modify a belief of your listeners.

Choose a topic for which immediate action on the part of the listener is not required. This topic may deal with a campus, social, political, religious, or educational problem. Consult the list of topics on the preceding pages.

This speech should be fortified with logical proofs. Instead of unsupported assertion or opinion, use statistics, examples, instances, quotations from well-informed authorities. Consult reference sources such as *Readers' Guide to Periodical Literature* or *The New York Times Index.* For some topics you may wish to interview authorities on your campus or in your community.

10 Make a speech of . . . minutes in which your persuasive material is organized according to one of the less commonly used strategies discussed in this chapter. Consider, for example:

a Analogy
b Countersuggestion
c Change of position
d Redefinition
e Higher law or nobler sentiment

20 Persuading: Other Aspects

Needs, values, emotional aspects □ Credibility □
Suggestion □ Ethical responsibilities of the communicator □
The persuasive imperative □ Assignments and exercises

Human beings would need unusual persistence to believe something or do something that their wisest friends thought was contrary to reason or logic. Justice Oliver Wendell Holmes once said that a sensible man would recognize that if he were in a minority of one he was likely to get locked up.[1] At the same time we like to *feel* that our beliefs or actions are suitable to our own sentiments and emotions. We think, we feel, we strive. Almost anything we do is a mixture of reasons, attitudes, and strivings.

The preceding chapter discussed the *logical* basis of persuasion. Supreme court justices seek a logical basis for deciding as they do. Space experts, facing one of the great scientific problems of the century, made hundreds of major and minor decisions on the basis of hard fact. The venture to put a man on the moon and return him safely was not like the voyage of Columbus who did not know where he was going, how long it would take, nor when he would return. At the same time the space exploit had *emotional* aspects: *patriotism, curiosity.* There was also *fear* that the astronauts might be killed, and *fear* that if we did not do the job the Soviet Union would. In daily life, too, we persuade ourselves and our associates to do many things on the basis of logic. If other things are equal, we persuade ourselves to buy at the lowest available price. If an expert in whom we have confidence recommends A instead of B, we choose A. Or we may persuade ourselves to do something for reasons of pure sentiment: *duty, loyalty, patriotism, prestige, pride.*

Imagine a young man in your class who has established an image of good scholarship. Not only his strong interest but his achievements as a scholar give him competence to discuss this topic. He may have received tangible marks of his scholarly ability: dean's list, junior Phi Beta Kappa, scholarship or fellowship awards. Imagine that he plans a talk on the central idea, "You should improve your scholarship." In preparing his message he could well consider not only logical materials but emotional materials. Logical support might include data about study methods, daily schedules, a good environment for study. The mere presentation of information, however, might not change the behavior of any of his classmates. He has not motivated them to become good scholars, nor sparked any inner drive that might get them to alter their study habits. To motivate them he needs to use emotional materials, and here he has a choice of both negative and positive approaches. Although he could take a negative view and describe the social disapproval, the personal disappointment, the financial burden that may accompany failing

---

[1]Dorothy I. Anderson, "The Public Speeches of Justice Oliver Wendell Holmes," in *American Public Address: Studies in Honor of Albert Craig Baird* (Columbia: University of Missouri Press, 1961), p. 9.

grades or even low grades, he will be wiser to take the positive side: the pride of doing well, the satisfaction that comes from exploring a scholarly field, the hope of success in one's career, the greater opportunity to serve humanity.

The persuader, to reemphasize, offers good reasons but does not overlook other aspects of persuasion. This chapter considers needs, values, and emotional aspects; credibility; suggestion; and the ethical responsibilities of the persuader.

NEEDS, VALUES, EMOTIONAL ASPECTS

Abraham H. Maslow has formulated a theory of human motivation that has been well received by speech communication teachers. He conceives the basic needs of human beings as falling into these categories:[2]

1 **Physiological needs:** hunger, thirst, sex.
2 **Safety needs:** protection from threat or danger; preference for the familiar rather than the unfamiliar.
3 **Belongingness and love needs:** affection, warmth, a place in the group.
4 **Esteem needs:** (a) strength, achievement, mastery and competence, independence, and freedom, and (b) reputation, prestige, status, recognition, attention, and appreciation. Self-esteem should be based on real capacity and competence, not on unwarranted celebrity or adulation.
5 **Self-actualization needs:** the individual's doing what he is fitted for. "In one individual it may take the form of the desire to be an ideal mother, in another it may be expressed athletically, and in still another it may be expressed in painting pictures or in inventions."

Maslow arranges these needs in a hierarchy: physiological needs, at the one end of the scale, being those which must be satisfied before others emerge; self-actualization, at the other end, emerging after other needs are satisfied. Appeals for contributions to the Red Cross would mainly be related to the first three categories: feed the hungry, prevent disease, rebuild disaster areas, and especially, show that you care.

The persuader attempts to ascertain not only what *needs* but what *values* are involved. These certainly overlap. Milton Rokeach described a value as being

---

[2]"A Theory of Human Motivation," in *Motivation and Personality* (New York: Harper & Row, 1954), chap. 5.

a type of belief, centrally located within one's total belief system, about how one ought or ought not to behave, or about some end-state of existence worth or not worth attaining. Values are thus abstract ideals, positive or negative . . . representing a person's beliefs about ideal modes of conduct and ideal terminal goals. . . . A person's values . . . must be inferred from what a person says or does.[3]

Rokeach described the following as *terminal* values: a comfortable life, equality, an exciting life, family security, freedom, happiness, inner harmony, mature love, national security, pleasure, salvation, self-respect, a sense of accomplishment, social recognition, true friendship, wisdom, a world of beauty, a world at peace. He also listed adjectives that were *instrumental* in attaining one's values: ambitious, broadminded, capable, cheerful, clean, courageous, forgiving, helpful, honest, imaginative, independent, intellectual, logical, loving, obedient, polite, responsible, self-controlled, and others.

Appeals to human needs and values challenge the idea that we as individuals are primarily governed by economic motivations. Some choices of appeals, however, are better than others. The Red Cross discovered that an appeal to patriotism was not effective in getting people to give blood. Nor did it help much to stress the importance of a blood bank in times of national emergency. What did help was an appeal to pride, by giving the donor a pin in the shape of a drop of blood, roughly equivalent to a purple heart. These changes in tactics resulted in "a sudden, dramatic increase in blood donations." Airlines that used the appeal of going by jet, thus letting a business man get quickly to City X, noted that sales declined. Apparently this appeal made a husband and father feel guilty about getting away from his family. "On the basis of depth interviews the appeal was changed to 'In only . . . hours you can *return* from your business trip to City X to your family.' Sales rose sharply."[4]

It is beyond the scope of this book to discuss all of the sentiments and emotional appeals that are touched upon by human beings as they strive to persuade one another. The short list that follows can be supplemented from your own experience and reading.

Fear   The notion of persuading by fear appeals is deeply rooted in American culture. From childhood we are exposed to threats of consequences to keep us well behaved. We hear messages warning us to eat properly, to drive safely, to avoid drugs, tobacco, and alcohol.

---

[3]*Beliefs, Attitudes, and Values* (San Francisco: Jossey-Bass, Inc., 1969), p. 124.
[4]Philip Zimbardo and Ebbe B. Ebbesen, *Influencing Attitudes and Changing Behavior* (Reading, Mass.: Addison-Wesley, 1969), p. 110.

These warnings point out such serious consequences as injury, illness, and even death. A poor diet leads to malnutrition; excessive smoking causes lung cancer ("it's a matter of life and breath"); driving while drunk leads to fatal collisions ("the life you save may be your own").

We also hear messages about the deteriorating quality of the environment. Problems involving oil spills, methyl mercury, thermal and other industrial wastes, lead poisoning, radiation, population density, automobile and jet plane emissions, overcrowding in national parks and elsewhere, must be faced and studied. Along with the technical data, cost estimates, and predictions come statements that arouse not only feelings of indignation and neighborhood pride, but also fear.[5]

Fear appeals may also be used when the message relates to financial security. We are urged to carry fire or burglary insurance, and on trips to carry travellers' checks. We hear a narrative about a young couple who had long saved for a vacation but lost the accumulated cash and had to cancel the trip. Fear appeals may also be introduced into a message involving the disapproval of others. One could show that littering, for example, not only wastes resources that should be recycled but subjects the litterer to criticism by peers or neighbors.[6]

Fear appeals may be described as high, low, or moderate. High-fear appeals (as in discussions of alcoholism, cancer, etc.) may include vivid clinical descriptions; references to pain, suffering, or other consequences of neglecting health recommendations; colorful charts or displays; emotion-charged words such as *kill, dismember, tragic, devastating, incurable, ruined careers, wrecked family life;* personal references that indicate "this can happen to you." Low-fear appeals are factual; threats, if any, are low-key; language is neutral and objective; setting is impersonal rather than personal; bad consequences are minimized. Moderate-fear appeals are, obviously, in between. Listen to the messages broadcast by the American Cancer Society, American Heart Association, and various insurance companies, study the fear appeals, and ask yourself how

---

[5]The material in this section is based on several sources. A helpful, readable article is Howard Leventhal, "Fear—For Your Health," *Psychology Today,* 1 (September 1967): 55–58. The article by Kenneth L. Higbee, "Fifteen Years of Fear Arousal: Research on Threat Appeals: 1953–68," *Psychological Bulletin,* 72 (December 1969): 426–444, helpfully analyzes the research of that period. See also Irving L. Janis and Seymour Feshbach's pioneering study, "Effects of Fear-Arousing Communications," *Journal of Abnormal and Social Psychology,* 48 (January 1953): 78–92; Frederick A. Powell and Gerald R. Miller's "Social Approval and Disapproval Cues in Anxiety-Arousing Situations," *Speech Monographs,* 34 (June 1967): 152–159; Leonard Berkowitz and Donald R. Cottingham's "Interest Value and Relevance of Fear-Arousing Communications," *Journal of Abnormal and Social Psychology,* 60 (January 1960): 37–43.

[6]Powell and Miller, "Social Approval and Disapproval Cues . . .," Social disapproval cues, to be effective, should come from high-credibility sources.

these appeals could be classified, and whether they would be more effective if either stronger or more moderate.

In making a decision about whether to use high-fear, moderate-fear, or low-fear appeals, we can get guidance from research studies such as those cited in the footnotes to this section. You should first of all consider your own credibility. High-fear arousal is more effective than low-fear arousal when the message source is perceived as highly credible. The spokesman for the firemen putting on a demonstration to a public audience is perceived as highly credible when he talks about the insidious danger of smoking in bed or of overloading an outlet. We are familiar with the persuasiveness of the former alcoholic or drug user who, after personal tragedy, finally kicked the habit. If you drove an ambulance, worked as a lifeguard, were a doctor's or dentist's receptionist, or did a tour of duty as a ranger, you can talk about the dangers you saw with special credibility.

Still another consideration is that people react differently to the same fear appeal. If your self-esteem is high, you are more likely to be persuaded by threatening messages than if your self-esteem is low. "Copers" seem to receive strong fear appeals better than "avoiders."[7] Those who are vulnerable, such as heavy smokers, may resist fear appeals, but their behavior is complex; they tend to avoid the advice to take x-rays, but also tend to reduce their smoking; a few, however, thought they would get lung cancer even if they stopped smoking.[8] Or you may be less persuaded by fear appeals because you feel confident you can handle the problem; you are an experienced driver, trained to react to highway situations, or you are a karate expert and can repel the advances of a rapist. Lacking these relevant qualifications, you may be more readily persuadable.[9]

If you are exposed to a particular danger, you will be more readily persuaded by fear appeals than if you are not exposed. You are not likely to take flu or typhoid shots unless an epidemic is looming. But if you were talking to a group preparing for a junior year abroad, you could warn that typhoid epidemics break out sporadically even in Europe. You may discuss the statistics showing that teenage marriages often break up. A listener might think, however, that he or she is so certain of his or her own maturity that marriage would endure regardless of age. This same listener, however, might be impressed by statements describing the problems confronting an early marriage; in other words, by a low-fear rather than a high-fear appeal.[10]

---

[7]Higbee, "Fifteen years . . . ," 430; Leventhal, "Fear . . . ," 56.
[8]Leventhal, 57–58.
[9]Berkowitz and Cottingham, "Interest Value and Relevance . . . ," 42.
[10]This strategy is suggested by the research of Ruth Anne Clark and Geraldine Hines reported in *Speech Monographs*, 37 (August 1970): 206.

Researchers agree that fear appeals should also (a) suggest positive courses of action, and, even better, (b) show that these courses of action are immediately available.[11] An example of (a): "To get a typhoid shot, go to the student clinic. You do not need an appointment." An example of (b): "A mobile x-ray unit is set up just outside the building. You can get a picture taken in minutes and learn for sure whether you have spots on your lungs." After hearing message (a) the listener has the information he needs, and can take action whenever he feels like it without making further inquiry. After hearing (b), however, he has every reason to take action at once. This finding is entirely in accord with the general principle of persuasion that a persuasive message is more effective if the listener is given a specific suggestion for action.

Responsibility   Speakers, ministers, editorial writers, and others often try to persuade by insisting that the listener or reader is responsible for acting in a certain way. In a celebrated murder trial, Daniel Webster, after reviewing the evidence, closed with an appeal to the jurors not to shrink from rendering a verdict, even though it involved capital punishment. "You are the judges of the whole case," he said. "You owe a duty to the public, as well as to the prisoner at the bar. You cannot presume to be wiser than the law." Human beings cannot neglect their obligations: "We cannot escape their power nor fly from their presence. They are with us in this life, will be with us at its close." Clarence Darrow made an equally emotional appeal to a jury *not* to hang his client: "You are trying the jury system. . . . No power on earth can relieve you of your obligation. This jury alone stands between this boy and the gallows. Bill Haywood can't die unless you kill him. You must tie the rope."[12]

Certainly nearly everyone can recall thinking, "This is my job—my responsibility," or "If I don't do this, no one will." We strive to meet our expectations, as we perceive them, even when they are arduous and exacting. By the same token we can attempt to persuade others to meet their responsibilities.

The notion of responsibility will be expressed with increasing frequency in the years ahead. No doubt many speakers will dwell upon new rights and enhanced freedom that are being extended to women, young voters, and other groups, but other speakers will certainly discuss the accompanying responsibilities. Other people, for example those discussing environmental problems, will emphasize our responsibility to the future. We owe, they will say, an unavoidable and inescapable debt to the generations that follow us.

---

[11]Leventhal, "Fear . . .," 55–58; Higbee, "Fifteen Years . . .," 430.
[12]Horace G. Rahskopf, "The Speaking of Clarence Darrow," in *American Public Address: Studies in Honor of Albert Craig Baird* (Columbia: University of Missouri Press, 1961), pp. 41–42.

Still others, discussing even broader themes, will urge us to develop responsibility as a cornerstone of our personality.

You cannot very well persuade people to show their responsibility by taking up a collection for you personally, but you can often persuade them to accept responsibility for sustaining something greater than themselves: the church, the community, the company, the school, the organization, the nation, the human race.

Confrontation, Defiance Speakers sometimes challenge the attitudes of listeners by admitting that the speaker's view may be an unpopular one. A suggestion of this appears in Patrick Henry's defiant phrase, "I know not what course others may take." John Bright, one of the exceptionally eloquent orators in nineteenth-century England, often used a thought like this: *"I am but one in this audience,"* continuing, "and but one in the citizenship of this country; but if all other tongues are silent, mine shall speak." At times, in fact, a speaker may challenge the assumptions and beliefs of an entire audience. The message may be uttered in defiance of everything the listeners are believed to stand for. The language may be offensive. Instead of trying to identify with his listeners, the speaker obviously wishes to nonidentify with them. Instances that come to mind are black speakers before white audiences or Catholic speakers before Protestant audiences: spokesmen for one group attempting to challenge or shock listeners belonging to another group. This procedure has met with varied success. Bernadette Devlin was elected at the age of 22 to represent a Catholic constituency in Northern Ireland in the House of Commons. Although in her maiden speech she bitterly denounced the Labor government for what it had done and for what it had failed to do with respect to Northern Ireland's underprivileged Catholic minority, members of the House stood and applauded. Malcolm X, in his speech, "The Ballot or the Bullet," used instances of direct confrontation. He began by addressing his listeners, "Mr. Moderator, . . . brothers and sisters, friends and enemies." As he said, "I just can't believe everyone in here is a friend and I don't want to leave anybody out." Later he declared: "I'm not an American. I'm one of the 22 million black people who are the victims of Americanism."[13]

Confrontational persuasion is increasingly being called to our attention. Its ancestry is ancient. In another day Frederick Douglass insisted: "For revolting barbarity and shameless hypocrisy, America reigns without an equal." Wendell Phillips and other abolitionist speakers denounced Congress and called the compact that existed between the North and the South, in language borrowed from Isaiah,

---

[13]The speech may be read in *Malcolm X Speaks* (New York: Merit Publishers, 1965).

"a covenant with death and an agreement with hell." Many members of Congress and of Parliament are famous for severe, continued criticism of the government.

It may be speculated that the nonidentification technique—not merely "I differ with you," but "I denounce you and all your works"—may have powerful short-term shock effect, but may lose that novelty and efficacy after a time. Examples could be cited to support this generalization, including some from the speaking careers of the individuals noted above.

Hope In our personal lives as well as in our public appearances we often express our hope that events will turn out well. Hope for recovery from illness. Hope for admission to graduate or professional school. Hope that a marriage will work out. Hope that a business venture will succeed. Hope that victory will come to the nation.

A physician is talking to a victim of cancer. "You not only have cancer of the kidneys but it has spread through your system. However, such great progress has been made with chemotherapy that we will do everything we can." The patient grasps at the hope of recovery. Chemotherapy *has been* successful, and the patient *may* recover.

Sometimes we can express only a bare, unadorned hope. Sometimes, however, we can support it with a reason. "You are sure to get a job. The unemployment figure has gone down a full percent. Tom and Harry, whose qualifications are no better than yours, got jobs last week, after a good many interviews." "Yes, you're flunking organic chemistry, but the semester is only half over, and we'll get Dick to tutor you. If he's tied up, we'll get Joe." ("Hope is a chain with many links.")

Hope not only helps us face disaster, but encourages us to strive for something better. Martin Luther said, "Everything that is done in the world is done by hope." Samuel Johnson declared, "Where there is no hope there can be no endeavor."

In time of national emergency, great leaders proclaim hope even when the ammunition is low. "We shall nobly save, or meanly lose, the last best hope of earth," said Lincoln, and also: "Fondly do we hope, fervently do we pray, that this mighty scourge of war may speedily pass away." Churchill roared, "You ask, What is our aim? I can answer in one word: Victory—victory at all costs . . . I take up my task with buoyancy and hope." Roosevelt gravely but courageously affirmed, the day after Pearl Harbor, "With confidence in our armed forces, with the unbounding determination of our people, we will gain the inevitable triumph. So help us God." Listeners agreed, and grimly set to it.

Hope is an appeal of great strength, and fits a wide variety of human situations. "Hope is the mother of faith," wrote Walter Savage Landor. Human beings can take a variety of attitudes towards the future. At one end of the scale is resignation; at the other, defiance. Hope implies a quiet but firm confidence that what we desire can be achieved. When the other person loses hope, we need to share ours.

Courage Times arise when an individual must take a position on a public issue; must say yes or no; must stand up and be counted. Simply to cast a silent vote, even a judicious one, may not be enough. Your office, your role in the group, or your sense of responsibility, compels you to tell others why you believe as you do. You may think of yourself primarily as a follower, but in a real sense you are also an opinion leader. The circle of people who look to you may not be immense, but it exists. Other people might be able to make a better presentation, but they are not on the spot. Accordingly, it is up to you.

John F. Kennedy's prize-winning *Profiles in Courage* is a series of narratives about United States senators who spoke on heated issues, taking a side that was currently unpopular: Senator Sam Houston arguing against the secession of Texas from the Union, Senator Edmund G. Ross standing up against the impeachment of Andrew Johnson, other senators taking a position that represented a political sacrifice. At times society denies its immediate prize but later pays tribute of a substantial sort. In the long run the battles one loses are often regarded more highly than those one wins.

When an American president takes a highly controversial stand, and is criticized in newspapers and on TV from Hawaii to the Virgin Islands, citizens should recall a statement made by President Lincoln more than a century ago: "If the end brings me out all right, what is said against me won't amount to anything. If the end brings me out wrong, ten angels swearing I was right would make no difference."

CREDIBILITY All of us have to make so many decisions in fields where we cannot make firsthand observations and in situations where we cannot understand the technical data involved, that we have to rely on each other for advice and counsel. Listeners feel that some speakers are more credible and believable than others. The following characteristics are of prime importance.

Similarity Researchers in the field of persuasion have strongly affirmed the proposition that communicators who are perceived to be similar to their listeners are more likely to be persuasive than are communicators who are perceived as dissimilar. The similarities or dissimilarities must be related to the message. If the message involves physical fitness, a communicator whom I perceive to be, with respect to physical fitness, somewhat similar to me and my problems, will be more likely to persuade me than one whom I perceive as dissimilar (i.e., Mr. Bookworm, pale, stoop-shouldered, and fragile). Researchers like the concept that the message sender should be superrepresentative of the group—i.e., show more competence, more information, or access to wider sources of information.[14]

Competence Much experimental research has focused on an attempt to identify the factors of speaker credibility that operate most efficiently; the notion of *competence* looms large repeatedly. Another important characteristic is *trustworthiness*. After these two factors, the rank order as reported by listeners is less certain: terms suggested include *safety* (friendly-unfriendly, honest-dishonest), *dynamism* (bold, emphatic, or the opposite), *open-mindedness* (objectivity and impartiality), and perhaps even *style* (command of English, wording, and grammar).[15]

Listeners like to be assured that the speaker knows the subject. As modestly and as unassumingly as you can, you should let your hearers know about your special competence, whether you are talking to one person or many. If you spent a summer reading Kurt Vonnegut and heard him lecture, tell us; that leads us to listen more carefully to your opinions of his novels. With certain topics you can do this easily and indirectly; with others you have to make something of an announcement.

How do speakers reveal their competence to speak on a given subject? Listen to the senior senator from Illinois, reporting to his constituents on the crisis in Berlin: "The day Congress adjourned I left for Western Europe where I spent the bulk of my time in Germany and Berlin." Listen to a West Coast newspaper publisher: "I speak to you as a newspaperman and as a newspaper reader who has been watching world developments for many years." Listen to a university administrator speaking about trends on campuses: "I visited nine universities in England, Germany, and France. On every campus I felt the winds of great change blowing." Pope Paul VI, addressing the United Nations, described his position and gave his message in these words:

> [Y]ou know well who we are. Whatever may be the opinion you have of the Pontiff of Rome, you know our mission. We are the bearer of a message for all mankind. . . . we are very ancient; we here represent a

---

[14]Herbert W. Simons, Nancy A. Berkowitz, and R. John Moyer, "Similarity, Credibility, and Attitude Change," *Psychological Bulletin,* 73 (January 1970): 1.

[15]David K. Berlo, James B. Lemert, and Robert J. Mertz, "Dimensions for Evaluating the Acceptablility of Message Sources," *Public Opinion Quarterly,* 33 (Winter 1969–70); Jack L. Whitehead, Jr., "Factors of Source Credibility," *Quarterly Journal of Speech,* 54 (February 1968): 59–63 and Don A. Schweitzer, "The Effect of Presentation on Source Evaluation," *Quarterly Journal of Speech,* 56 (February 1970): 33–39.

long history; we here celebrate the epilogue of a wearying pilgrimage in search of a conversation with the entire world, ever since the command was given to us: go and bring the good news to all peoples. Now, you here represent all peoples.[16]

If the Pontiff of Rome and other speakers of high credibility and established standing find statements like these useful, one of more modest attainment can show listeners that he or she has a reason for discussing the subject chosen. The point is not to boast but simply to offer one's credentials.

The principle has been restated in these words:

> We know an individual's acceptance of information and ideas is based in part on "who said it." This variable, the source's role in communication effectiveness, has been given many names: *ethos, prestige, charisma,* or, most frequently, *source credibility.* Whichever label is used, research consistently has indicated that the more of "it" the communicator is perceived to have, the more likely the receiver is to accept the transmitted information.[17]

Trustworthiness   The importance of trust has been discussed earlier, in Chapter 3. Through language one can show honesty, sincerity, and trustworthiness. One ingredient of trust is accuracy; if listeners sense that the speaker is inaccurate in discussing the things they know about, they may be less likely to accept his or her judgment in matters that they do not know about. If you can convince your listeners that you will keep your promises in every detail, and if your past record shows that you are indeed that sort of person, you should be perceived as a credible individual. Harry Emerson Fosdick, who for more than two decades was "the most important popular figure in the Protestant pulpit," said: "There is no process by which wise and useful discourses can be distilled from unwise and useless personalities. . . . The ultimate necessity . . . is sound and intelligent character."[18]

Any social, economic, or political issue about which we try to persuade others calls for shades of judgment and discernment. The more we study such a problem, the more of its complexities we appreciate. All the truth is not on one side. You will likely be more persuasive about the advantages of a large institution (or a small college) if you are equally ready to admit its faults. "The large university (or the small college) is not perfect, but here are two of its

---

[16]*Vital Speeches of the Day,* 32 (October 15, 1965): 2–3.
[17]Berlo, Lemert, and Mertz, "Dimensions for Evaluating the Acceptability of Message Sources," 563.
[18]Quoted by Roy C. McCall, "Harry Emerson Fosdick: A Study in Sources of Effectiveness," in *American Public Address: Studies in Honor of Albert Craig Baird* (Columbia: University of Missouri Press, 1961), p. 61.

outstanding merits." Or: "At times I have been embarrassed by the behavior of certain Americans overseas, but on these two matters we compare favorably with nationals of other countries." Again: "The stock market can go down as well as up, but a prudent investor should realize substantial gains from his purchases." In everyday life we sometimes reflect: "Was she really sincere in paying me that compliment?" "Was he really too busy to go to the movie with me?"

Candor Candor is a trait resembling fairness, but also carries the suggestion that the speaker wishes to state the issue frankly and honestly, even to his or her disadvantage. A candid mood reveals that one does not hesitate to utter a challenging responsibility nor to bring sober news. "I have nothing to offer but blood, toil, tears, and sweat" is more than being frank; it reflects great candor. One may confess, "We have had our worst season in years." Or: "The remedy I propose is not an easy one." Or: "I wish I could report that our book pool showed a profit, but actually the figures show it has operated at a heavy loss." A good teacher can use candor to advantage: "The assignment for next week is one of the most difficult of the course." Statements like these will likely put listeners in a more receptive frame of mind than will soft-pedaling unpleasant news or overstating good features.

The address of Elmer Ellis, then president of the University of Missouri, to the graduates of the Granite City, Illinois, high school, candidly presents the challenge of the future to citizens, to faculties, and especially to the students themselves:

> It is not only *more* education for *more* people that is being demanded, it is *better* education also. The years ahead will present to the colleges and universities both the opportunity and the challenge to improve their staffs, their practices, and the effectiveness of their educational programs. . . . There will be no place in next year's college for the idle student. Teachers and facilities are too scarce, and society's needs are too great, to waste time and effort on the indolent.[19]

Presumably a university president in days of uncertain enrollments would want to polish the image of a university campus as being a good place for a graduating high school senior to go, but this speaker candidly suggested that professors and students alike must face up to the challenges that lie ahead.

Advertising firms often exploit the virtues of candor in their campaigns. One automobile makes a virtue of not changing its basic design; another confesses that one model was a disaster but the current model has eliminated the bugs. When General Telephone

---

[19]Text furnished through the courtesy of Dr. Elmer Ellis.

over a period of years had accumulated stupendous public ill will for mediocre service, the admen designed a campaign in which the company's poor image was frankly admitted. *Time* described one commercial in the series:

> The neat middle-aged executive peers out from the television screen. "Hello," he says, his face crinkling into a sheepish grin. "I'm from General Telephone." Boos and hisses explode off-camera. "Now, I'm aware that General Telephone provides less than adequate service." Plop. A rotten tomato slides down his chin. "But we're spending $200 million in California this year on improving our service." He is hit with an egg. "Cables, switches, personnel, everything." A cream pie splatters over his face. "Thank you for your patience," he mumbles through the goo.[20]

The admen hope that the campaign will win sympathy for the company, while incidentally inserting the thought that money is being spent to improve service.

Students have learned that a frank confession of reasons for turning in a paper late is not a bad ploy; professors detachedly reveal difficulties that keep a lecture from being up to snuff. The mood is not apology or self-abnegation, which hardly anyone approves, but rather one of leveling. The physician candidly says, "At present we really do not know much about shingles;" the mechanic says, "Your water pump will probably hold out until you get home, though it could go out in the next ten miles." The communicator who refuses to downgrade problems and difficulties may run the risk of dissuading some listeners, but the long-term advantages should be favorable.

Good Will   Speakers show good will for listeners when they promise to be brief, and are brief; when they are aware that the hour is late or that conditions do not favor comfortable listening; when they are considerate of the views of others, and when in general they have the interest of listeners at heart.

A persuasive speech in the United States Senate—one that is reputed to have changed votes—was made by Arthur H. Vandenberg endorsing the appointment of David E. Lilienthal as chairman of the Atomic Energy Commission. Note these short excerpts:

> I wish briefly to make a matter of record my reasons for believing that under all existing circumstances Mr. David Lilienthal should be confirmed as Chairman of the Atomic Energy Commission without further delay.

---

[20] *Time* (July 27, 1970): 67. Reprinted by permission from *Time: The Weekly Newsmagazine;* © Time Inc.

> I do so with no illusions that any Senator, at this late hour, after weeks and months of bitter controversy, is still open to persuasion. I do so with complete respect for the good conscience with which every Senator will take his position. I quarrel with none.
>
> I have heard or read every word of the testimony. As a result, I have been driven away from the adverse prejudice with which I started. I have been driven to the belief that logic, equity, fair play, and a just regard to urgent public welfare combine to recommend Mr. Lilienthal's confirmation in the light of today's realities.
>
> I say this with full appreciation of the earnest zeal with which others hold a contrary view, including many of my warmest friends. . . . [21]

This opening part of the speech shows the speaker's resolution to take a firm position against many of his hearers, yet he was considerate of their views. To speak "with complete respect for the good conscience with which every Senator will take his position" invites a friendlier hearing than to say, in blunt language, "I flatly disagree . . . my friend is misinformed . . . he talked ten minutes and said nothing worth refuting . . . on my part I have absolutely proved. . . ." This highly persuasive speech is worth reading and rereading.

Reputation Often we make an effort to hear a public address or lecture because of the speaker's reputation. When she discusses topics in the field of her special competence, we are inclined to give favorable attention.

A student in a speech communication class may establish a reputation with his classmates that adds to his effectiveness. It may be for competence in a special field, like sports, livestock judging, home economics education, or politics. It may be for fairness, a sense of humor, an appreciation of the good efforts of others. Even if his early speeches are poor, he will gain respect when he begins to solve his difficulties and demonstrate new abilities to stimulate interest and hold attention. When he graduates and enters civic, business, and professional worlds, his early efforts will help him build a reputation. Achievements in nonspeaking fields may add to his prestige as an individual and, consequently, as a speaker. You cannot make every speech better than the one preceding—no one can accomplish such an impossibility—but through the weeks, in school, and over the years, after school, your reputation should be enhanced slowly even though irregularly.

SUGGESTION Suggestion is a form of persuasion in which messages are presented in such a way as to make it unlikely that the listener will listen critically or logically. In front of the hat check attendant is a saucer

---

[21]From the *Congressional Record* for April 3, 1947. Quoted in A. Craig Baird, ed., *Representative American Speeches, 1946–1947* (New York: The H. W. Wilson Co., 1947), pp. 122–123.

with quarters or dollar bills; this exhibit suggests that to offer smaller tips is inappropriate. At the soft-drink counter the student says, "Coke"; the well-trained soda-dispenser says "Large one?" and the customer replies without reflecting, "Yes."

Suggestion may be *direct* as when the speaker says, "Sign here," "Line up over here." It may be *indirect,* when the speaker wishes the real purpose to be concealed, like Iago's sly insinuations to Othello that his wife was unfaithful. Suggestion may be phrased in *positive* language when the speaker says "Vote for Hawkins" or in *negative* language: "Don't buy common stocks." A speaker using *countersuggestion* says one thing, hoping the listener will do the opposite. Thus: "Miss Oliver is a demanding, exacting English teacher," hoping that the words, though discouraging, will challenge the listener to make a maximum effort. Countersuggestion, however, may boomerang; the listener may panic and drop the course altogether. In fact many kinds of suggestion may boomerang; not being founded on logical reasoning, they may not be substantial enough for the long pull.

Many of the principles described under "Credibility" in this chapter are often referred to under the heading *prestige suggestion*. A speaker who enjoys the high confidence of the listeners is in a position to use direct suggestion effectively. Lacking this high confidence, he or she would depend more on evidence and less on suggestion. One with whom you have long transacted business might persuade you simply by suggesting, "This is a fine bargain; if I were you I'd take it." You might act upon the suggestion without reasoning the matter out for yourself.

Throughout this chapter principles are described which rely more on suggestion for their effect than upon reason. The speaker's personality, use of emotional appeal, telling a story rather than stating an argument, or asking a question rather than making a direct statement, may be received favorably by the listener without too much exercise of critical faculties. Persuasion is more effective when it has a basis in logic and reason as well as in suggestion, emotional appeal, and other nonlogical methods. Otherwise the listener may, after reflection, decide not to do what was suggested, or to do it just this once, but to be more critical in the future.

ETHICAL RESPONSI-BILITIES OF THE COMMU-NICATOR Every day we are exposed to emotional appeals that threaten our good sense and good judgment. Advertisers employ attractive, talented people to flatter us, alarm us, cajole us. Often their claims are so unwarranted that they are compelled by governmental agencies to revise their advertising. We therefore need to set such standards of ethics in communication situations as the following:

1 **Information** As human beings we must depend upon one another for information on a wide variety of subjects. "How do I get from here to there?" "Exactly what is wrong with my motor?" "Is this the latest model?"

We feel a deep cordiality toward people who give us exact answers, in a friendly manner. As a society we could not exist if people took pride in giving us misinformation. If the one who is asked is not certain, he can say "I think" or "I believe," so that we may be guided accordingly. To tell falsehoods is reprehensible both in interpersonal and in public speaking.

2 **Judgment** As human beings, we also rely on the judgment of one another. In many instances exact information is not available. Do I need new tires now, or can I wait another season? Can I postpone this operation until the Christmas holidays? If I major in X, will I be able to get a job two years from now? Is A better than B? To each of these questions an informed answer, an educated guess, is possible. We can do better than flip a coin. The person answering the question should give as well-reasoned a response as if he or she were asking the question. A part of the response may be to indicate the degree of confidence one has in it. A listener deserves the speaker's best, not second-best or third-best, judgment.

3 **Personal interests and loyalties** One may speak as a citizen, as a member of a political party, as a spokesman for a religious faith, as the manager or owner of a business firm, as a member or officer of an organization. If, however, I appear to speak as a public official, whereas secretly I am working for a commercial firm, my ethical responsibilities are badly warped. As a speaker once declared, I cannot morally lead you to believe that I am speaking for the Sons and Daughters of William Tell whereas, in fact, I am secretly representing the Swiss Armament Works.

4 **Originality** If a speaker uses ideas that clearly belong to someone else, he or she should say so. One should not use someone else's outline or repeat someone else's speech; he should not use a striking phrase or title that someone else has created— without giving credit to that other person. Often, in fact, it is better to identify the sources: that statistic comes from the Bureau of the Census, this quotation comes from *The Handbook of Social Psychology.* The speech can still reflect one's own original interpreting and thinking: sometimes by arrangement, sometimes by phrasing an idea, sometimes by showing new insights or relationships, and sometimes by making application to the specific audience.

Occasions arise when, for a special purpose, a speaker will deviate from these standards. For example, one is allowed to

THE INCREASING INTEREST IN ETHICS

In an editorial entitled "Newcomer on Campus," Howard Flieger, editor of *U.S. News and World Report,* comments that instruction in morals and ethics is becoming more popular on the campuses, and makes these further observations:

If moral education is about to make a comeback, there are those who are convinced it is just in the nick of time. They trace rising crime, political chicanery, even inflation, the federal deficit and setbacks in foreign policy to a nationwide decline in moral and ethical values that have been eroding at an accelerated pace for years.

The Thomas Jefferson Research Center is a nonprofit institution founded in 1963 by a group of businessmen to make continuing studies of America's social problems. Says its president, Frank Goble:

"It is our opinion, based upon hundreds of thousands of hours of research, that a basic cause of our society's exploding problems is personal and organizational irresponsibility. Irresponsibility is a social disease that, if left untreated, destroys individuals, families, communities and nations. The world is littered with the ruins of societies destroyed by irresponsibility. We cannot succeed by trying to treat the symptoms—crime, anger, hostility, poverty and war. We must seek the root causes and deal with them.

"What causes irresponsible human behavior? Moral ignorance! Why is moral ignorance increasing in a society which is spending more for education each year and more on education as a percentage of its total production than any other society in history?"

The Center reports abundant evidence that for years the American system of education has put less and less emphasis on morals and ethics. It cites a study of old textbooks made by John Nietz, who found:

Before 1775, religion and morals accounted for more than 90 percent of the content of school readers. By 1926, the figure was only 6 percent, and it has since dropped to where it is almost immeasurable. . . .

History makes a truism of Mr. Goble's statement that a society cannot survive without a workable system of values.

Yet, how does one educate people to be moral, ethical and responsible? There's the rub. Many scholars insist there is no way to teach morals; you can only teach *about* them. That is a way of saying humans can be taught *how* and *why* to follow a certain code of conduct, but nothing can make them do the right thing if they don't care to.

> Any signal of increasing interest in the study of morals and ethics can be taken as an indicator that today's young people do, indeed, care about such things.[22]
>
> Mr. Flieger's comments are pertinent to any discussion of the responsibilities of communication. Our utterances, private and public, nearly always have an ethical underpinning. In entertaining, we hold in mind the moral sensitivities of the community. In sharing information, we face the double problem of making a selection of available facts and of being accurate. In persuading, we need to consider the listener's welfare as much as our own.
>
> [22]*U.S. News and World Report,* 81 (September 29, 1975), 92. (Copyright 1975, *U.S. News and World Report, Inc.*)

deceive the enemy when national security is at stake. The deviations, however, can be clearly labeled as exceptions, and cannot be labeled as generally sound practice.

In business, professional, and public life, men and women often rely on others to gather speech materials for them. This situation brings up the term *ghost-written speech.* Often these are incredibly dull and routine. When, however, the speaker refers to *personal* experiences, or when he draws the kinds of inferences that can be drawn only by one in his position, the speech grows in liveliness and impact. A business or public official must often use facts supplied by the lower echelons of his organization; the final wording, however, should be original.

5 **Emotional appeals** Ethical standards require that we be particularly sensitive to the use of emotional appeals. Often it is in our power to make people angry, indignant, frightened; or calm, poised, forgiving. We can make them proud or ashamed, generous or grasping. We are most likely to approve of emotional appeal when used in the best interests of the individual, the family, society in general. We are also likely to approve if the long-term, as opposed to the short-term, point of view prevails. And, as stated above, we are most critical when we perceive the operation of a self-serving motive.[23]

---

[23]For further reading, see Winston L. Brembeck and William S. Howell, *Persuasion: a Means of Social Influence and Control* (Englewood Cliffs, N.J.: Prentice-Hall, 1976), chap. 10, "The Ethical Basis of Persuasion"; Richard L. Johannesen, *Ethics in Human Communication* (Columbus: Merrill, 1975); and the references in these recent texts.

When all is said and done, when your persuasive message with its mix of logical and emotional, verbal and nonverbal, personal and impersonal components has been delivered, you should be able to *go back* to the listener with the steady assurance that you will be heard again.

Going back means that you can face the teacher or student, the buyer or seller, the professional person or client, the child or adult—whomever you were trying to persuade—and persuade him or her once again. *Going back* means that you had facts, evidence, quality control, honest motives, good will, and understanding of needs and wants. It means that you are interested in the future, not merely the moment; the long-term, not merely the short-term.

If you cannot *go back,* you lose your credibility with one listener after another. You may be able to fool a new face at least once, but you will seldom be able to persuade those whose trust in your information, your motives, or your credibility has been shaken.

**ASSIGN-
MENTS AND
EXERCISES**

1 Considering that the art of persuasion gives great advantage to teacher, minister, salesman, statesman, and military leader, discuss: What are the ethical responsibilities of those who use the spoken word?

    a Does a speaker have an ethical responsibility in selecting examples, instances, other facts—for what he *chooses* and what he *omits?*

    b Does a speaker have an ethical responsibility in his *interpretation* of the facts—upon the emphasis, or importance, that he assigns to them?

2 Patrick Henry said, "I have but one lamp by which my feet are guided, and that is the lamp of experience." As Patrick Henry looked over that past experience with the British ministry, he thought the solution was *independence:* "Give me liberty, or give me death." Yet others, with that same experience, were recommending *conciliation.* How do you explain this type of conflict among speakers?

3 Are you justified in declaring, "We will never surrender," when, actually, you cannot know for sure? May you say, "This nation will endure forever" when, actually, you may not be around to verify it? May you say, "This is history's proudest hour" or "These are the most critical times in the history of the race" considering that history has had many proud hours, and the race has experienced many critical times? May you say "Prices will go up," or "Shortages will not develop," or "The market will suffer a severe reversal during the six months just ahead" when everyone's view of the future is inevitably uncertain?

4 Could an argument be successfully based on the notion of *compulsion,* or is this a four-letter word stretched to ten letters? Could you be persuaded to put yourself into a situation where you would be compelled to do something that would be good for you? For example, if you are a smoker, could you be persuaded to sign up for a two-week cruise, during which you would listen to lectures on the evils of smoking and not have access to cigarettes? Again: *Most* correspondence courses are never completed, even though the persons enrolling did so voluntarily and paid substantial fees for the privilege. Is the reason an absence of *compulsion?*

5 Study the advertisements in current magazines and newspapers, looking for examples of persuasion through emotional appeal.

6 Secure a copy of a recent volume of *Representative American Speeches.* Study typical speeches for examples of persuasion through emotional appeal. Look also for sentences that tend to convince listeners of the speaker's honesty, integrity, and fairness.

7 Observe the use of emotional appeals in such informal settings as conversations, interviews, and meetings of your residence hall.

8 Make a speech of . . . minutes in which your purpose is to get your listeners to take some specific action.

The action you seek may be to persuade them to sign a petition, attend a meeting, vote, write their congressman, or buy something you are offering for sale.

Give the strongest arguments you can muster in the time allowed. Feel free to appeal to loyalty, pride, sense of duty and responsibility, or desire to improve our own health or financial position. If you want your listeners to attend a political meeting, be specific about the time and place. If you want them to write a congressman, supply the name and address. If you want them to take the pledge, have it there ready to sign.

For suggestions, consult the list on pages 367–369.

APPENDIX

1. Speeches for Study
2. Suggested Solutions to Assigned Exercises

The speech by Benjamin Franklin is well worth recalling as we approach the bicentennial of the period when we adopted the Constitution. Moreover, its line of argument is one that can be used in many situations when discussion has been resolved by compromise. The speech by John Stuart Mill is a perfectly organized, short speech of praise; and again, it illustrates a strategy that is worth pondering in any situation that calls for honoring an individual. The broadcast speech by Gordon Sinclair was heard by a vast audience, made into a record that topped two million in sales, and was widely reprinted. The speech by Judge Edith S. Sampson deserves its wide reprinting and its popularity with teachers and students of speech communication. The sermon by Dr. Lowell Russell Ditzen, based on a theme that runs through the entire discourse, develops an inspirational theme through, in part, examples. The speech by Professor Leonard R. N. Ashley is a literate and witty plea for the use of clear, vivid English, free of jargon and technicalities that confuse rather than enlighten. Collectively the speeches illustrate different kinds of organization, compelling use of simple language, an abundance of instances and examples, and sincere messages. You will also be able to identify other features.

In the closing pages of the Appendix are answers to the "Lost on the Moon" and the "Crisis in the Forest" exercises.

1 PLEA TO THE CONSTITUTIONAL CONVENTION
Benjamin Franklin

Words make a difference. The scene: final day of the Constitutional Convention. The document had been drawn up, filled with compromises. In its entirety it seemed to please no one. Before the aged Franklin moved that the Constitution be signed by the delegates, his speech, written for this purpose, was read by James Wilson of Pennsylvania:

I confess that there are several parts of this Constitution which I do not at present approve, but I am not sure I shall never approve them; for, having lived long, I have experienced many instances of being obliged by better information or fuller consideration to change opinions, even on important subjects, which I once thought right but found to be otherwise. It is therefore that the older I grow the more apt I am to doubt my own judgment and to pay attention to the judgment of others. Most men, indeed, as well as most sects in religion think themselves in possession of all truth. . . .

In these sentiments, Sir, I agree to this Constitution with all its faults, if they are such; because I think a general government necessary for us, and there is no form of government but what may be a blessing to the people if well administered; and believe farther that this is likely to be well administered for a course of years and can only end in despotism, as other forms have done before it, when the people shall become so corrupt as to need despotic government, being incapable of any other. I doubt too whether any other convention we can obtain may be able to make a better Constitution. For when you assemble a number of men to have the advantage of their joint wisdom, you inevitably assemble with those men all their prejudices, their passions, their errors of opinion, their local interests, and their selfish views. From such an assembly can a perfect production be expected? It therefore astonishes me, Sir, to find this system approaching so near to perfection as it does. . . .

Thus I consent, Sir, to this Constitution because I expect no better, and because I am not sure that it is not the best. The opinions I have had of its errors I sacrifice to the public good. I have never whispered a syllable of them abroad. Within these walls they were born, and here they shall die. . . .

On the whole, Sir, I cannot help expressing a wish that every member of the Convention who may still have objections to it would, with me, on this occasion doubt a little of his infallibility, and, to make manifest our unanimity, put his name to this instrument.[1]

Of sixty-five qualified delegates, only thirty-five signed to express the "unanimous consent of the states present"; on this slender margin, the document went to the several states. Of those who did sign, several had misgivings; perhaps Franklin supplied the reassurance they needed.

Someday you may find yourself a member of a group that has the responsibility of forging a constitution, a charter, or some legislation; you may similarly observe that no member present is entirely happy with the document drawn up by the group. On that occasion perhaps you can recall Franklin's wisdom . . . could any other group we might obtain "be able to make a better Constitution"? . . . and will every member "on this occasion doubt a little of his infallibility"?

[1]From Carl van Doren, *Benjamin Franklin* (New York: Viking, 1938), vol. 3, pp. 753–754.

2 A TRIBUTE TO WILLIAM LLOYD GARRISON
John Stuart Mill

*Shortly after the end of the American Civil War, friends of William
Lloyd Garrison held a public banquet for him in London. Garrison's
long struggle for the abolition of slavery was now at an end. John
Stuart Mill, noted philosopher, who at that time was a member of
Parliament, had long been identified with liberal causes. The advice
he offers in the following speech is as wise today as it was then for
anyone who is about to advocate an unpopular idea or begin a
difficult task.*

The speakers who have preceded me have, with an eloquence
far beyond anything which I can command, laid before our honoured
guest the homage of admiration and gratitude which we all feel is
due to his heroic life. ... I [will] endeavour to recall one or two
lessons applicable to ourselves, which may be drawn from his
career. A noble work nobly done always contains in itself, not one,
but many lessons; and in the case of him whose character and
deeds we are here to commemorate, two may be singled out spe-
cially deserving to be laid to heart by all who would wish to leave the
world better than they found it.

The first lesson is,—Aim at something great; aim at things which
are difficult; and there is no great thing which is not difficult. Do not
pare down your undertaking to what you can hope to see successful
in the next few years, or in the years of your own life. ... After you
have well weighed what you undertake, if you see your way clearly,
and are convinced that you are right, go forward, even though you,
like Mr. Garrison, do it at the risk of being torn to pieces by the very
men through whose changed hearts your purpose will one day be
accomplished. Fight on with all your strength against whatever odds,
and with however small a band of supporters. If you are right, the
time will come when that small band will swell like a multitude; you
will at least lay the foundations of something memorable, and you
may, like Mr. Garrison—though you ought not to need or expect so
great a reward—be spared to see that work completed which, when
you began it, you only hoped it might be given to you to help forward
a few stages on its way.

The other lesson which it appears to me important to enforce,
amongst the many that may be drawn from our friend's life, is this: if
you aim at something noble and succeed in it, you will generally find
that you have succeeded not in that alone. A hundred other good and
noble things which you never dreamed of will have been accomplished by the way, and the more certainly, the sharper and more

agonizing has been the struggle which preceded the victory. The heart and mind of a nation are never stirred from their foundations without manifold good fruits. In the case of the great American contest, these fruits have been already great, and are daily becoming greater. The prejudices which beset every form of society—and of which there was a plentiful crop in America—are rapidly melting away. . . . The mind of America has been emancipated. The whole intellect of the country has been set thinking about the fundamental questions of society and government. . . . This, then, is an additional item of the debt which America and mankind owe to Mr. Garrison and his noble associates; and it is well calculated to deepen our sense of the truth which his whole career most strikingly illustrates— that though our best directed efforts may often seem wasted and lost, nothing coming of them that can be pointed to and distinctly identified as a definite gain to humanity; though this may happen ninety-nine times in every hundred, the hundredth time the result may be so great and dazzling that we had never dared to hope for it. . . . So it has been with Mr. Garrison.[2]

3   THE AMERICANS
Gordon Sinclair

On a glum-news day in June, 1973, when the Watergate scandal, the overseas dollar crisis, and Mississippi River floods were making the headlines, a 73-year-old radio commentator for station CFRB, Toronto, was stirred by a TV interview of American farmers flooded out by the Mississippi. "No one was whining, whimpering, or crying the blues," he said later. "It gave me admiration for those fellows." So he broadcast the following tribute. It was reprinted in American newspapers and in the Congressional Record, *and made into a record that topped 2 million in sales. Royalties went to the American Red Cross.*

This Canadian thinks it's time to speak up for the Americans as the most generous and possibly the least appreciated people in all the world. . . .

Germany, Japan, and, to a lesser extent, Britain and Italy were lifted out of the debris of war by the Americans who poured in billions of dollars and forgave other billions in debts. None of those countries is today paying even the interest on its remaining debts to the United States.

---

[2]Text from *Proceedings at the Public Breakfast Held in Honour of William Lloyd Garrison* (London: Tweedie, 1868), pp. 33–35. John Bright and others spoke on the occasion; for a description, see Loren Reid, "Bright's Tributes to Garrison and Field," *Quarterly Journal of Speech*, 61 (April 1975): 169–177.

When the franc was in danger of collapsing in 1956, it was the Americans who propped it up and their reward was to be insulted and swindled on the streets of Paris. And I was there; I saw that.

When distant cities are hit by earthquake, it's the United States that hurries in to help. . . . So far this spring fifty-nine American communities have been flattened by tornadoes; nobody has helped.

The Marshall Plan, the Truman Policy, all pumped billions upon billions of dollars into discouraged countries. And now newspapers in those countries are writing about the decadent, warmongering Americans.

Now I'd like to see just one of those countries that is gloating over the erosion of the United States dollar build its own airplanes. Come on, now you—let's hear it! Does any country in the world have a plane to equal the Boeing Jumbo Jet, the Lockheed Tristar, or the Douglas 10? If so, why don't they fly them? Why do all international lines except Russia fly American planes?

Why does no other land on earth even *consider* putting a man— or a woman—on the moon? You talk about Japanese technocracy, and you get radios. You talk about German technocracy, and you get automobiles. You talk about American technocracy, and you find men on the moon—not once but several times—and safely home again.

You talk about scandals, and the Americans put theirs right in the store window for everybody to look at. Even the draft-dodgers are not pursued and hounded. They're right here on our streets in Toronto. Most of them, unless they are breaking Canadian laws, are getting American dollars from Ma and Pa at home to spend up here. . . .

When the railways of France, and Germany, and India were breaking down through age, it was the Americans who rebuilt them. When the Pennsylvania Railroad and the New York Central went broke, nobody loaned them an old caboose. Both of them are *still* broke.

I can name to you 5,000 times when the Americans raced to the help of other people in trouble. Can you name to me even *one* time when someone else raced to the Americans in trouble? I don't think there was outside help even during the San Francisco earthquake.

Our neighbors have faced it alone, and I'm one Canadian who is damned tired of hearing them kicked around. They'll come out of this thing with their flag high. And when they do, they're entitled to thumb their noses at the lands that are gloating over their present trouble.

I hope Canada is not one of these.[3]

---

[3]First broadcast on Radio Station CFRB, Toronto, June 5, 1973. © Copyright 1973 by Conestoga Music, 2 St. Clair Ave. W., Toronto, Canada. Used by permission.

4   CHOOSE ONE OF FIVE
Edith S. Sampson

This speech was delivered on the occasion of the 100th annual commencement at North Central College (Illinois) on May 30, 1965. It has been reprinted in various places. Professors Jamye Coleman Williams and McDonald Williams chose it for their anthology, The Negro Speaks: The Rhetoric of Contemporary Black Leaders *(New York: Noble & Noble, 1970).*

Judge Sampson has had an active speaking career. She participated in the world tour for the radio discussion version of America's Town Meeting of the Air. She has served as a member of the United States delegation to the United Nations. In 1962 she was elected to fill a vacancy on the Circuit Court of Cook County, First Municipal District, and has since been overwhelmingly reelected.

This degree that you have bestowed upon me out of your magnificent kindness is not just an honor. It's outright flattery—and I love it. Recognizing that it's impossible adequately to express my gratitude, I shall take the coward's way out and not even try.

Let me, instead, talk briefly to these graduates who have won their degrees the hard way instead of by the simple expedient of traveling from Chicago to Naperville.

You graduates have every right to expect penetrating words of profound wisdom from an LL.D., even when the doctorate is honorary.

You look for too much, of course, if you ask that I settle all affairs, both international and domestic, in anything under an hour. But I surely ought to be able to handle either one or the other of the side-by-side package without imposing too great a strain on your patience and your posteriors.

I should be able to untangle the enigma of Vietnam for you in 10 minutes and solve the Dominican problem in another 5. This would still give me, within a 20-minute limit, ample time to pronounce with authority on the assorted crises in the U.N., NATO, the Organization of American States, the Congo, Laos, Cambodia, Malaysia, Indonesia, India, and Pakistan.

Or, if I were to talk about the domestic scene, I should be able to sum up for you my definitive solutions to the problems of interracial relations, poverty, urban renewal, mass transportation, education—both higher and lower—organized crime, juvenile delinquency, the balance of payments, labor-management controversy, and what's to become of those dreadful people in Peyton Place.

If you wanted an analysis of the current state of art, literature, music, drama, and philosophy, you would naturally have to give me another 10 minutes.

Unfortunately, though, I am going to have to disappoint you, and I can only hope that you survive the sharp shock of disillusion. The degree that I've been given, precious as it is to me, did not endow me with instant wisdom.

As a result, I've been forced to fall back on a substitute for the all-revealing address that is your due today.

It's worse than that, really. Compounding what is already an offense, I'm going to present to you a multiple-choice test—the last of your college career.

The only consolations that I can offer in presenting the test are that it involves no bluebooks, you may consult texts freely, the test is self-scoring, and you have a lifetime at your disposal now to complete it.

This exam will be proctored, though. The proctors will be two—the community in which you live and, hardest taskmaster of all, your inner self.

The question: What do you do with your college education now that you have it—and now that it is beginning to become obsolete even as you sit here?

Choose one of five possible answers.

Choice One:
Put your diploma in a convenient drawer and close the drawer. Put whatever textbooks you've accumulated in a bookcase and close the bookcase. Put your mind to the dailiness of earning a satisfactory livelihood and close your mind.

I should warn you that it will take a bit of doing to follow this course with the rigor that it deserves.

You will have to take care not to read anything except, in the case of men, the sports pages or, in the case of women, columns of household hints.

You'll have to choose your friends with extreme care to make sure that you don't rub up against any stimulating personalities.

You'll have to build your own defenses against a world of complex realities that will insist on trying to intrude on you at the most inconvenient times.

But it can be done. I've known college graduates who have achieved it. They've wrapped themselves in an apathy so thick that they're in position to say in all truth, "No opinion," to any Gallup or Roper pollster who might question them on any subject.

It's a choice that's available to you. *Choice one.*

Choice Two:
Go forth into that waiting world, carefully assess the prevailing opinions, and then conform.

Forget this theoretical nonsense they've been feeding you here at North Central. What do professors and assistants and associates and instructors know about the real world anyway? Academics, all of them.

You'll have your degree. That certifies you're educated. Let it go at that.

This choice gives you more latitude than choice one.

You can scan the whole of the daily newspaper, as long as you make certain it's a newspaper that agrees with you and all other right-thinking citizens on all critical issues.

You can keep *Time* or *Newsweek, Life* or *Look* on the coffee table.

You can subscribe to the *Reader's Digest* and had better read at least some of it for conversational purposes.

You are even permitted, if you take this choice, to buy two books a year as long as you make sure they're best best-sellers. Reading the books is optional.

You don't have to be nearly so selective in making friends if you go this route instead of the first one. Just avoid the kooks—although that's easier said than done when what prevailing opinion recognizes as unmistakable kooks come in bewildering variety. But with a little caution you can easily manage.

After all, about 80, perhaps 85, per cent of the people with whom you'll come in contact fit nicely in this choice-two category. It isn't that they're particularly talented at blending into the background. They are the background.

You, too, can be a pillar-of-society conformist. No strain, no pain.

Well, almost no pain. The anguish of those moments in your middle age when you lie sleepless at 2 a.m. or 3 and wonder whatever happened to all your bright ambitions of college days—that anguish and those moments don't count too much.

Most of the time you can be comfortable with choice two, and who could ask for more than that?

One footnote at this point: Don't worry that your college degree will set you apart and make it impossible for you to be a really thorough-going conformist.

That was a slight danger in my day, but it's none at all now.

Ever since people have come to recognize the dollars-and-cents value of a college diploma as a passport to employment, more and more people have been going to college. Only the bigoted, narrow-minded people hold a degree against a person today, and the ranks of the conformists are filled with those who have had campus and even classroom exposure. B.A.'s, B.S.'s, masters, doctors—they can all live in the ticky-tacky houses.

Choice Three:
Refuse to relax into the commoner forms of conformity. Find yourself, instead, a clique of the elite, an "in" group, and conform yourself to it.

You might imagine, from that bare description of this choice, that this would be a difficult thing to do. It isn't at all.

There are just two requisites.

First, you must have a specialty of your own, some one field—or, better, part of a field—in which you're expert. It might be something in the arts—music before Vivaldi, for instance, or the epic poetry of Afghanistan. On the whole though, it's better if your specialty is a little more practical, intellectual but money-making.

Then to the specialty, whatever it is, you add a dedication to everything that is advance guard and an amused contempt for everything else that isn't.

One thing you can't have if you go the third-choice way—at least not today—and that's a conviction that human beings and the history they have made and are making are important. Nothing is important really—nothing, that is, except your own staked-out small field of specialization.

A James Reeb is beaten to death for daring to assert in action the dignity of man. A Mrs. Liuzzo is shot, killed after the Selma to Montgomery march. Too bad.

But someone suggests that "The Cabinet of Dr. Caligari" isn't really such great shakes as a movie. This is monumental heresy. Tie him to the stake and put a torch to the faggots.

You must preserve the proper hierarchy of values, you see.

If you join the sort of "in" group I have in mind, your reading becomes constricted again, I'm afraid.

You mustn't read the daily papers, or at a minimum you mustn't admit it if you do. The Sunday *New York Times,* on occasion, can be tolerated, but no more than tolerated.

You may not read *Life, Look, Time, Newsweek,* or the *Reader's Digest,* not to mention such unmentionables as *Better Homes and Gardens* or *Family Circle.* Nothing more popular than *Scientific American.*

No best-sellers, of course—that goes without saying. It's much better to criticize Saul Bellow without having read *Herzog* all the way through, although you should read enough to be able to say it nauseated you so much you couldn't finish it.

This constriction of your reading is rather unfortunate in one way, really. You can't read things like the *New Republic* or the *National Review,* or *Commentary,* or *Foreign Affairs* or the *Bulletin of the Atomic Scientists,* or the *Reporter* or anything of the sort. Those all deal with political and social and economic matters, you see, and an "in" conformist who attached importance to such matters would be drummed out of the corps. Serves him right.

Choice Four:
Choice four, though, offers an alternative for those who cannot erase their political-social-economic consciousness.

Join an extremist group.

There is real effort involved in this at the very beginning. You have to study the various groups that present themselves and make your initial commitment.

The beauty of this choice, though, is that once you've made it, you can turn off your thinking and let yourself be carried by the forward surge of what is obviously a significant moment.

Say you link yourself to the far right.

Your enemies are immediately identified for you—Negroes, Jews, and Communists. Communists are easy to recognize—they're all the people who don't agree with you.

You know immediately what to oppose—fluorine in the water supply, income taxes, aid to foreign nations, the Supreme Court, movements for mental health, and any squeamishness about dropping nuclear bombs at will or whim.

You know immediately what to support—anything that the leaders of your group find good and pleasing, although unfortunately they find little that's either.

Say you link yourself to the far left.

Your enemies are immediately identified for you—capitalists, the poor misled sheep of the middle class, and Fascists. Fascists are easy to recognize—they're all the people who don't agree with you.

You know immediately what to oppose—all business corporations, no exceptions; all Trotskyites; all deviationists; all revisionists; all efforts to help established governments resist Communist revolt.

You know immediately what to support—anything that the leaders of your group find good and pleasing, which is whatever the men in Moscow have smiled upon for the day.

What is so attractive about this choice four is that it requires no mental effort of you beyond the initial effort of making your selection. Yet it provides a wide-open emotional release that isn't possible with any of the first three choices.

With choice four you can convince yourself that every action you perform has world-molding significance. In sharp contrast to the choice-three people, choice-four people are convinced that everything is important because everything links somehow to the cause.

Choice Five:

And then, finally, there's CHOICE FIVE. It's hard to state this one. About as close as I can come to it is this: Hang loose, but stay vibrantly alive.

This one's strenuous. This one's demanding.

Choice five would demand of you that you consider today's graduation no more than a pause to catch your breath before continuing the life-long job of education.

It would demand of you that you be your own unique best self. And there is no higher demand than that.

Choice five entails wide-ranging reading and deep-probing thought.

It calls for a contradictory thing—a mind that is constantly open to new facts that dictate change but at the same time is resolutely committed to what seems best at any given point of time.

It calls for human involvement, a compassionate concern for everyone on this fast-shrinking little planet of ours and for the generations to come.

It calls for the resolute rejection of all sterotypes and insists on the thoughtful examination of even the most widely held assumptions that are too easily taken for granted.

If only choice five involved only one thing or the other—thought or action—it would be ever so much easier. It doesn't, though. It involves both.

And as if that weren't bad enough, this choice usually brings with it a certain amount of inner ache, because this way is a lonely way.

Those who make choice four are caught up in a wave of fervent enthusiasm that is all the more compelling because there's so little of the rational in it. They have the company of their Birchite brothers or their Communist comrades.

Those who make choice three clump together with others of their kind to exchange small coins of comment about existentialism and Zen, the hilarious glories of Busby Berkley movies and the charm of Tiffany lamp shades.

Those who make choice two are protected by the great crowd of which they've so willingly, gladly made themselves an anonymous part, no different from every other anonymous part.

Those who make choice one deliberately dull their sensitivities. They are cud-chewing content to join the boys at the bar of a Saturday night or the girls at the bridge table Wednesday afternoon. They vegetate.

But those who make choice five are never fully comfortable.

They are nagged at by their realization that they could be wrong.

They're prodded by their recognition that they've still so much more to learn and even more than that to understand.

They're made restless by their knowledge that no matter how much they do, there's still ever so much more left to be done.

Choice-five people have to live constantly with an acceptance of the fact that there are no simple answers in this world because there are no simple questions.

This makes life exciting for them, challenging, at least intermittently rewarding. But comfortable? No.

I would not urge choice five on any of you graduates. It asks so much of you.

Any of the other four will see you through to age 60 to 65, retirement, and a modest pension. They might easily do better than that and make you rich. In dollars, that is.

Five is there, though, one of the multiple choices on the test.

If any of you in this class of '65 makes that fifth choice, I wish you'd let me know about it. You I'd like to know better than I possibly can just by having made a speech here.

You I would treasure even above the LL.D. with which North Central College has so graciously honored me—and that, you can believe me, is saying a great deal.[4]

5 THE RIGHT TICKET BUT THE WRONG TRAIN
Lowell Russell Ditzen

Dr. Lowell Russell Ditzen, director of the National Presbyterian Center, Washington, D.C., received his first training in public speaking at William Jewell College, where he was active in debating and in speaking contests. In 1932, for example, he won the National Oratorical Contest. He has preached extensively in this country and in Europe and Asia, and his sermons have appeared in dozens of magazines and newspapers and in annual collections of "best sermons." He has lectured at scores of colleges and universities. This sermon was originally preached to a National Presbyterian Church congregation in Washington. One of those who heard it was The Honorable L. H. Fountain, member of Congress from North Carolina, who had it printed, with a tribute to its eloquence, in the Congressional Record.[5]

Text: *"Father, give me the portion of the goods that falleth to me."*—(Luke 15:12.)

Scripture: Luke 16:11–32; II Kings 17:1–12.

If you have talked to a person coming to America to make this land his or her home, you know how keen is the anticipation of that

---

[4]*Vital Speeches of the Day,* 31 (August 15, 1965): 661–663. Reprinted by courtesy of the editor and of Judge Sampson.
[5]*Congressional Record,* 15, 13 (June 24, 1969): 17141–17142.

newcomer. You will be aware, too, of the strange ideas many such pilgrims have about this country and of the odd adventures that befall some. Usually they have a destination in mind, but little knowledge as to how to get there and much misinformation as to what the place is like.

Up in the Mohawk Valley of New York tales are circulated that come from several generations past, when waves of Welshmen migrated to that area. A number settled in and about a little town called Remsen. See it now and it's a couple of stores and a dozen houses. But first comers had written back such glowing accounts of Remsen that some eager settlers landing at New York City and seeing the skyscrapers there, exclaimed, "If this is New York City, what must great Remsen City be!"

A more recent arrival, an emigré from the decimations of Europe before the second World War, arrived destined for Philadelphia. He made his way to the Pennsylvania Station where he bought the right ticket. But through errors unbeknown to him, he got on the wrong train and ended up at Atlantic City. When told he wasn't where he expected to be, he couldn't believe it. Surely he was in Philadelphia! It was stamped right there on his ticket. Hadn't he planned and dreamed for months and miles of being with his relatives to begin a new life in Philadelphia? This must be some strange American joke. You couldn't fool him! But the people at the station refused to be convinced that Atlantic City was Philadelphia. Finally they got the idea across: "Friend, you may have purchased the right ticket, but you've traveled on the wrong train!"

Now are there not those, who in the journey of life, with the best of intentions and the finest of beginnings, get on the wrong train, and when the journey is over, find to their dismay they are where they didn't want to be at all?

I have yet to meet a sensitive and mature couple who come to the time of their wedding without being willing to get the right ticket. There is receptiveness to the counsel that it takes a lot of cooperation and forgiveness and sharing and sacrifice to make a successful marriage and a happy home. That they understand. They have the right ticket. But there are some, who, in the adventure of marriage, end up where they didn't want to be at all: hopes unrealized; sweet anticipations turned rancid; love gone. They had the proper destination in mind at the beginning, but they ended up far from the anticipated goal.

We've known individuals who started out with a strong purpose to make a success in business or some calling. They're going to the top and they have the resources, it would seem, to get there. But while they seem to have their hands on the right ticket, not a few of them find, when the journey is over, that they aren't where they intended to be at all. They got on the wrong train. I've often wished that some Ph.D. student would analyze the "most likely to succeed" individuals in high school annuals. Did they make it? Or did they end up in a far country where no one gave them any attention?

Jesus portrays the thought we're feeling after in an indelible picture of a young man saying, "Father, give me the portion of the goods that is due unto me."

Who will deny that young man in that moment? In the promise of his budding manhood he wants to go away from home to make his own way. He probably is compelled by a vision that sees himself coming back home laden with honors and successes from afar. He had the right ticket. But the way of transport he unwittingly boarded took him to a country way off from the land of which he dreamed. Ask him when he starts off in that moment of high purpose and enthusiasm, if he's intending to end up scrapping with pigs for bits of garbage, and he'd say, "That's ridiculous. Not on your life." But he ended up there just the same. . . .

Certainly, this thought of ours suggests the importance of discipline.

That word comes from the Latin word "discipulus" which has its rootage in the idea "to learn." The word is related to "disciple." A disciplined person is a learning person. He has subjected his life to a purpose, a principle, or a teacher, and so he becomes committed to a definite order and regime. That's necessary, isn't it? Mustn't something comparable to that be given priority in any field of activity if an individual wishes to achieve?

In Machiavelli's classic book, "On the Art of War," he emphasizes the factors that make for success in military struggle. One, he says, is the battle. Then analyzing what makes for success in such engagements, he comes to the determining factor of discipline. "Good order," he writes, "makes men bold. Few men are brave by nature, but discipline makes them so." Isn't that true? Some of you as mothers have had a grand vision of a home of beautiful order and peace, of children going into the world with a mature and high spirit. But what determines whether that dream is to become a reality? Isn't it in the daily battles with the irritations, intrusions, and tasks that drag one down and could make the vision wane? Isn't it "discipline," the fighting for self-control, the learning to grow, to let the heart be enlarged by forgiveness and patience and love?

You men represent many different fields of science, business, and the professions. Don't each of you know no matter what our specialized area, that it's the keeping of appointments, analyzing minute facts, meeting tiny details, that decides whether or not our goal is realized? Who will deny that "discipline" is the sesame to help get through each day and to carry tasks to large fulfillment?

And shouldn't this word of ours give a prod to all of us as

Americans? We have a magnificent ideal in our heritage that comes to the living present saying, "this is to be a nation of free men, who in their freedom will build together for the common good—granting equal and increasing opportunities for all." That is a ticket for corporate living that has been purchased at the price of deep thought and painful effort of generations. But, if, with that ticket we try to ride on the roadbed of individual and group selfishness, God help us, because we'll end up where we didn't want to be at all. No strong nation in the past was destroyed from the outside. There was an inner deterioration which rotted the core of corporate life. When outside pressure came, the structure fell.

The other day I entered a New York taxi to find the driver a lady. Before we reached our destination she had given me her life history, which included a chapter when she returned for a time to her native Puerto Rico. "But I just had to come back to America. This really is the most wonderful country in the world. I want my children to grow up here." How right she is! But we need to remind ourselves of this fact. We need to appreciate and constantly protect what our fathers brought into being.

The time is at hand for us as Americans to say to ourselves and each other, "It's really ourselves that we have to overcome." Our pettiness, our indulgence, our carelessness, our warrings of groups against groups, our lack of responsiveness to public responsibility— these are our real enemies! Let's defeat them! We have the right ticket. Let's be sure we stay on the right train!

There are so many wonderful things about that story of the prodigal son. The picture of that enthusiastic young man, brought up in a fine home, setting out to make his way in the world, how opulent that is in its suggestiveness! But he made mistakes and sank low.

The words, *"he came to himself,"* are suggestive. Though he got into a pathetic state, there was still great good in him. He rediscovered, in his abject state, that self of high potential which he had forgotten. We should remember, that, as we are moved to wipe off the slate some individual who may have deflected from "the accepted way" that there is latent hope and will and goodness in that person. One of the first functions of the Christian is to keep alive in himself and cultivate in others that "good and best self" which is in every man. How sad that no one tried to help the prodigal when he really hit bottom—when he needed help most of all. One of the proofs of our really trying to be Christ's disciples is to give the helping hand and heart to the prodigals of our time.

Then note that the prodigal remembered, when he was really down and out, that he still had a home and a father. Jesus, in telling the parable, was telling more than a story of just one boy and his father. He was trying to tell us that God is like that father, and that we all are like the prodigal son. Being human beings, we at times do foolish things. We end up where we don't want to be. But the love and the compassion of the Father is always concerned for us, reaching out toward us.

As we realize our foolishness, sincerely repent and return to our home, we are forgiven, offered a new start and a fresh opportunity. What an undergirding and comforting assurance that truly is!

There was nothing questionable about the prodigal son's beginning. He had a good ticket, but he got on the wrong train, ending up where he didn't want to be. Yet, coming to himself, seeing his folly and remembering his Father, he went back home where he was received again into the family circle where he belonged.

So it can be with us! We have a Father and an Eternal citizenship! We may wander far. But the Father's love follows us no matter how lost we may seem. That will redeem us as we turn our steps to that home from whence we came.

6   A GUIDED TOUR OF GOBBLEDYGOOK
Leonard R. N. Ashley

Leonard R. N. Ashley (Ph.D. Princeton) teaches at both Brooklyn College and The New School for Social Research. He delivered this address to District II of the American Alumni Council at Pocono Manor Inn, Pennsylvania. It has appeared in Edward Corbett, Classical Rhetoric for the Modern Student *(New York: Oxford University Press, 1965) and in several anthologies.*[6]

Some intelligent person has said—I may have said it myself—that the most important skill a student acquires in college is the ability to express himself in words. Well, perhaps that isn't what he actually acquires, but that's what he pays for. (Education is one of the very few things in this country that people are willing to pay for and not get.)

Seriously, though (as the comedians are beginning to say today) . . . seriously, though, the most fundamental and the most universally applicable skill a student can develop is the ability to communicate: to write and speak, to inform and explain and persuade.

To change tires or to jerk sodas or deliver groceries not much skill in expression is necessary. But at all levels beyond that, in both

---

[6]*American Alumni Council News*, 30 (June 1963): 11–16. Used by permission of the Council for Advancement and Support of Education, successor to the American Alumni Council, and of Professor Ashley.

business and the professions, success, recognition and advancement go to those (and only to those) who can convey their ideas. Men, even in the most technical specialties, must work together. No one makes a product alone any more: it seems that even executives (who manufacture decisions) are being compelled to work in teams. And even those who still enjoy the luxury of thinking for themselves and making their own decisions have to transmit their ideas—straightforwardly, forcefully, accurately, convincingly, even inspiringly. . . .

America's highest-paid and most widely-published authors (I mean the advertising boys) are far more often determined to confuse you rather than tell you something clearly and simply. They bombard you with meaningless statistics, pseudo-scientific jargon, empty phrases studed with vague terms such as "additives" and "conditioners." They're taking the logic out of language. What's the "regular" size of soap? Why the one you don't regularly buy. (It's too small.) What's the "economy" size? The one that costs more.

Advertising ballyhoo has made us all insensitive to superlatives. A Hollywood producer is asked about his latest picture: "How is it?" "It's colossal, magnificent," he replies, "but it's improving." A 21-inch TV screen is described as "huge." If it is, what is a 9' × 12' rug? . . .

The politicians are adding to the confusion. "Nationalization" has become "public ownership." A "bust" has become "deflation," "retrenchment," or "downward readjustment." The word "free" has lost nearly all meaning, now that the "Free World" includes South Africa, Spain, and the vilest governments of South America. "Peace" has become a dirty word. Preparations for war are called "defence programmes." Hydrogen bombs are "thermonuclear deterrents"—which sounds as if they were protections against hydrogen bombs. We even have "clean" bombs. The Ultimate Detergent?

The fact that more than a million young thugs are hauled before the courts every year doesn't sound nearly so bad if you'll call young criminals "juvenile delinquents." A "delinquent," by definition, *hasn't* done something. These kids *have!*. . . .

Even our bright young men and women in the colleges have been infected. Pick up anything they've written: a note, a term paper, an examination. What do you find? Very often you find weak logic, vague language, blatant inaccuracy in more than orthography, and so little imagination that you seldom find an adjective in bed with a noun to which it has not been married for centuries.

Frequently those that are imaginative are deliriously so. Here are some gems of purest ray serene from the dark, unfathomed caves of my student files:

Entrance requirements have gone so high that nobody can get into college, and the reason that nobody can get in is that everybody is going.

Abstinence is a good thing if practised in moderation.

It was the painter Donatello's interest in the female nude that made him The Father of the Renaissance.

(Examination question: Identify "Skylark.") Skylark is the merchant of Shakespeare's play. When we first see him he is on the Rialto, which is the business end of Venus.

(If *pro* is the opposite of *con,* give examples.) Progress and Congress.

In Bernard Shaw's play *Mrs. Warren's Profession* her profession is the Oldest Profession but she is not really a Lost Woman. She is just mislaid.

The food in the cafeteria is absolute poison and they give you such small portions. It's about time the students spoke up about this unspeakable situation. . . .

All these atrocities clearly demonstrate the connection between fuzzy writing and fuzzy thinking and the student's explanation only makes matters worse: "I may be wrong but I'm not far from it." . . . As they say in businesses: "Here is creeping stagnation on a high plateau."

William H. Whyte, Jr. (*Is Anybody Listening,* Simon and Schuster, 1957) tells us about the executives in business who have to speak when they have nothing to say (annual meetings) or don't wish to say anything accurate (retiring employees). He defines their diction on these occasions as *reverse* gobbledygook:

> Where the traditional jargon is multisyllabic, longwinded, and passive, it [reverse gobbledygook] is filled with short, terse words; its sentences are short and the construction of them so much more active than passive that exclamation marks are as frequent as periods. Heavy on personification, homely analogies, and a rigid glossary of hard-hitting words, it lends a powerful straight-from-the-shoulder effect to ambiguity and equivocation.

Whyte and the editors of *Fortune* studied 200 business speeches, identified the 60 most characteristic expressions, and constructed an hilarious composite address. Look it up in Mr. Whyte's book (pages 55–58). You'll vastly enjoy reading it—and, if some day you're stuck for something to say, you can always steal it and deliver it at a board meeting, business convention, Rotary [C]lub gathering, academic convocation, etc. They'll love it. But you must deliver it with a straight face, like the ship captain in the Conrad novel who tended to "enunciate platitudes, not with a desire to dazzle, but from honest conviction."

Some people are deliberately hiding behind words or thinly veiling their meaning. Thus one British parliamentarian says that another "seldom deviates into accuracy," so Churchill describes Attlee as "a sheep in sheep's clothing," so Sam Goldwyn says "The best I can give you is a definite maybe." Subtlety is commendable. But what about other motives for being unclear or devious? What about the undertakers who call themselves "morticians," the carpenters who are "construction consultants" when they are simply driving nails ("interfibrous friction fastener installation")? Aren't things getting confused when a man employed to cut things *out* of TV scripts is called a "continuity *acceptance* man" instead of a "censor"? Why is the garbage man ashamed of his work to the point where he calls himself a "sanitary engineer"? And what happens to people who really are sanitary engineers? Must every man who cleans toilets prettify it into "rest room attendant employment"? Must every Billy Goat Hill become Angora Heights? What's wrong with "rat-catchers" (now "rodent operatives") and "watchmen" ("surveillance personnel")?

This kind of elegant variation can lead to a man whose father was hanged as a horse thief explaining the death by saying that "my father was taking part in a public ceremony when the platform collapsed." (If the father were electrocuted one could make him sound like a deceased professor: "My father occupied the chair of Applied Electricity at a large institution in one of the western states.") . . .

In the soft (or "social") sciences the writers most ridiculed (not always most deservedly) are the sociologists, so I suppose we'd better have a sample of their language. The story of the Good Samaritan. Brace yourselves, for such people are literate only in clichés.

> And behold, a certain Socialite stood up and tempted Him saying, "Master, what shall I do to be socially acceptable?"
>
> And He said unto him, "Thou shalt love thy in-group as thyself."
>
> But he, willing to justify himself, said unto Him, "And who is my in-group?" And He, answering, said:
>
> "A certain fellow travelling down from Aix to Ghent fell among traditionalists, who stripped him of his pretense, offended him, and departed, leaving him half mortified. And by chance there came down a certain realist that way: and, looking upon him as an out-group, he passed him by on the other side. And likewise an idealist, when he was at the place and also looked upon him as an out-group, he passed him

by on the other side. But a certain man with a rounded personality, as he journeyed, came where he was: and when he saw him, he adjusted himself to the social situation. And he went to him and took him to an inn and associated with him. Now which of these three, thinkest thou, was in-grouped with him who fell upon hard times?"

And he said, "He that acted *democratically* towards him."

Then He said unto him: "Go, and adjust thyself."

No wonder there's a rumor going around that sociologists are defining *orgy* as "sexual educational group dynamics."

Our college students see enough bad writing in the newspapers they read (if any) and in the pretentious as well as the shoddier magazines. They shouldn't find it in the textbooks we force them to buy and read in college. There's an ever-present danger that if they don't fall into one trap (impairing their minds by apeing the slangy and inexact dialect of the common man) they may fall into another and plump for padded pedantry.

It's all right to write like Henry James if you're struggling with something subtle and involved, for even Henry James was doing his best to present the complexities lucidly and not consciously attempting to compound the difficulty, but it's pompous foolishness to take a phrase like "there was mob rule at this time" or "you can't concentrate when you are distracted" or "small business is failing in Utica" and make it utterly incomprehensible. There's something radically wrong when a great university cannot turn out a readable catalogue of courses, when students cannot read their psychology textbooks on "the learning process," when professional writers cannot use our language to produce simple income tax instructions. . . .

I invite (exhort) you as executives and administrators and people who deal in communication to speak and write simply yourself. Astound your colleagues! Don't begin letters with "Yours of the 16th *inst.* received and contents duly noted and beg to state. . . ." Get to the point. Resolve that the next dozen letters you write will be only 50 words long each—and watch the results! Build the vocabulary you need—and begin by throwing away all the words you now have that are bent, broken, or worn out. Use what's left (supplemented by new words if necessary) to say honestly and straightforwardly exactly what you mean, to inform rather than to impress or confuse. The ability to handle that vocabulary (and the ideas it represents and contains) is your greatest asset in handling your important jobs, your associates, and your lives.

CRISIS IN THE FOREST
(Comment on Problem on Pages 286–287)

This problem is a clear-cut example of behavior that would be universal to man, primarily because of the simple biological urges of hunger and fatigue. The crux of the problem is to determine which alternative would be chosen by a man who has been without food and has hiked 35 miles in three days. Will he hike four miles to the ranger station where he can obtain food and shelter? Or will he walk six miles to the car which he can drive to get food?

For anyone who has had a similar experience, there is little doubt of what he would do under the circumstances. The basic error made by people who predicted the wrong decision in this case was an overemphasis on the importance of getting to the car rather than to food. They failed to appreciate the significance of two miles under such conditions.

(From Raymond L. Gorden, *Interviewing: Strategy, Techniques and Tactics* [Homewood, Ill.: The Dorsey Press, 1969], pp. 26–27.)

LOST ON THE MOON

ANSWERS TO TEST ON PAGE 283

Item	NASA's Reasoning	NASA's rank	Your rank	Error points	Group rank	Error points
Box of matches	No oxygen on moon to sustain flame; virtually worthless	15				
Food concentrate	Efficient means of supplying energy requirements	4				
Fifty feet of nylon rope	Useful in scaling cliffs, tying injured together	6				
Parachute silk	Protection from sun's rays	8				
Solar powered porta-ble heating unit	Not needed unless on dark side	13				
Two 45-cal. pistols	Possible means of self-propulsion	11				
Case dehydrated milk	Bulkier duplication of food concentrate	12				
Two 100-lb. tanks of oxygen	Most pressing survival need	1				
Stellar map	Primary means of navigation	3				
Self-inflating life raft	CO_2 bottle in military raft may be used for propulsion	9				
Magnetic compass	Magnetic field on moon is not polarized: worthless for navigation	14				

Five gallons of water	Replacement for tremendous liquid loss on lighted side	2
Signal flares	Distress signal when mother ship is sighted	10
First-aid kit, injection needles	Needles for vitamins, medicines, etc. will fit special aperture in NASA space suits	7
Solar-powered FM receiver-transmitter	For communication with mother ship, but FM requires line-of-sight transmission and short ranges	5

Error points are the absolute difference between your ranks and NASA's (disregard plus or minus signs)

Scoring for individuals:

0–25:	Excellent
26–32:	Good
33–45:	Average
46–55:	Fair
56–70:	Poor
71–112:	Very poor (suggests possible faking or use of earth-bound logic)

INDEX